Quantitative Archaeology and Archaeological Modelling

More information about this series at http://www.springer.com/series/14342

Catalin Nicolae Popa

Modelling Identities

A Case Study from the Iron Age of South-East Europe

Springer

Catalin Nicolae Popa
Leiden University, Leiden, Netherlands

ISSN 2366-5998 ISSN 2366-6005 (electronic)
Quantitative Archaeology and Archaeological Modelling
ISBN 978-3-030-09688-5 ISBN 978-3-319-63267-4 (eBook)
https://doi.org/10.1007/978-3-319-63267-4

Printed on acid-free paper

This Springer imprint is published by the registered company Springer Science+Business Media, LLC part of Springer Nature.
The registered company address is: Gewerbestrasse 11, 6330 Cham, Switzerland

Preface

Can we talk of large ethnic groups in South-East Europe during the Late Iron Age? Since ancient authors, such as Strabo, provide us with the names of numerous peoples, archaeologists have made great efforts to link them with particular material culture forms. But are these identity divisions indeed supported by archaeological finds? Did prehistoric people feel that they were part of these large ethnic entities? In this book I address such questions by investigating the funerary practices of Late Iron Age people with the aid of statistical modelling.

This volume comes out of my Ph.D. research, conducted between 2009 and 2014 at the University of Cambridge. I became highly interested in the Late Iron Age of South-East Europe throughout my school years because this period is often regarded as inhabited by the ancestors of many modern European nations: Gauls, Celt-Iberians, Thracians, Illyrians etc. This point is particularly valid for my native country, Romania, a nation that traces its roots back to the Late Iron Age people called Dacians or Geto-Dacians. However, as I delved into the identity literature throughout my university years, I started to question many of the ideas that I had read about "my" Dacian forefathers. What did it mean to be a Dacian? What made someone a Dacian rather than something else? And why were they "my" or anyone else's forefathers in the first place? I was surprised to discover that such question had not been asked before. It became clearer and clearer that much of what we know about the Dacians was born out of the ambition of some Romanian scholars to populate the Late Iron Age past with their nations' ancestors. Yet, if that is indeed the case, can one speak of Dacians, Getae or any other identity group when doing a critical analysis of the archaeological record? With these questions in mind, I embarked on the long and winding road of Ph.D. research.

It may appear unusual that statistical modelling, of all things, was the method of choice for answering questions of group identity. Is it though? There is no doubt that, when looked at in detail, group identity involves a lot of personal, profoundly subjective choices. These choices can be led by the desire for personal gain, by a sense of pre-existing natural order, by previous personal experiences and many other factors. It thus seems logical that gaining a comprehensive understanding of such a complex process requires a highly meticulous, qualitative analysis.

However, with the risk of being reductionist, in my research I was only interested in finding broad manifestations of group identity. When put in very simple terms, much of our current knowledge of group identity points to it being the result of people's identification with or differentiation from the practices carried out by other individuals: identity comes out of some type of practice comparisons. And comparing is one thing that statistics excels at.

Therefore, statistical modelling occupies a central role in this book. Extensive parts are dedicated to illustrating the modelling technique, which is employed to compare archaeological information. The method consists of a highly flexible similarity algorithm combined with clustering procedures. Through its flexibility, the algorithm can be adapted to incorporate and emphasise a large spectrum of elements that researchers may consider to be important. This feature also facilitates the transfer of the method to other contexts with relative ease.

The book also aims to show the compatibility of archaeological theory and statistical modelling. The discussions from archaeological theory rarely find methodological implementations through statistical methods, since the former is seen as relating to qualitative issues, while the latter is perceived as being exclusively quantitative in nature. In this volume theoretical issues form an integrative part of data preparation, method development and results interpretation. The steps of the analysis are grounded in theoretical concepts, which are discussed in varying degrees of detail.

Finally, the volume takes the form of a narrative rather than a manual. The intention is not to teach the workings of particular statistical methods, but rather to answer a complex archaeological question with the aid of statistical modelling. The reader is walked through each stage of the investigation procedure, from data preparation and method adaptation to evaluating and interpreting the results in their broader context. While some parts may be more difficult to comprehend, much of the analysis procedure and general argument should be relatively easy to follow with a minimum of prior knowledge. To facilitate text understanding, when describing data and statistical results, *italics* were used for the names of variables (e.g. *object category 1*) and underlining was employed for the value of variables (e.g. weapon).

I hope that the book will prove useful to both statistics users and readers with an interest in the Late Iron Age of Europe or issues of prehistoric identity.

Leiden, Netherlands
August 2016

Catalin Nicolae Popa

Acknowledgements

This volume would not have been possible without the funding provided by the Arts and Humanities Research Council UK, the Cambridge European Trusts and the Raţiu Family Foundation, which allowed me to complete my Ph.D. research. I am also grateful for the support of my host institutions, the University of Cambridge, the Excellence Cluster Topoi, Freie Universität Berlin and Leiden University.

I would like to express my thanks to the numerous people who have guided me or provided feedback throughout the writing of this volume: Simon Stoddart, Gelu Florea, Aurel Rustoiu, Mariana Egri, Oliver Nakoinz, Kerstin Hofmann, Martin Millet, Stephen Shennan, Kris Lockyear, John Robb and Sheila Kohring.

My deepest gratitude goes to those who have been close to me throughout the years and have endured bravely my incessant ranting about archaeology and statistics: Barbara Hausmair, Maikel Kuijpers, Tiago Hermenegildo, Bela Dimova, Radmila Balaban and Marija Ljustina.

Contents

1 Introduction 1
1.1 General Introduction of Research Area and Topic 1
1.2 State of Research 2
1.3 Justification of Study 6
1.4 Structure of Volume 7
References 9

2 Final Resting Place: The Archaeological Data 15
2.1 Death and Burial 15
2.1.1 Theoretical Concepts About Death: The Potential of Burials in Archaeology 15
2.1.2 Practical Arguments for Using Burials 19
2.2 Data Limits and Overview 19
2.2.1 Spatial Limits 20
2.2.2 Chronological Limits 21
2.2.3 Void of Burials 23
2.2.4 Burials in the Void 23
2.3 Data Organization 24
2.3.1 Data Issues 24
2.3.2 Data Structure 25
2.3.3 Tables Description 27
2.3.4 Queries and Reports 32
2.4 Object Categorization 32
2.4.1 Theoretical Principles 33
2.4.2 Construction of Categories 34
2.4.3 Variables Description: General Information 35
2.4.4 Variables Description: Functional Categories 36
2.4.5 Variables Description: Typological Categories 37
References 44

3 The Working Apparatus: Identity and Statistics ... 51
3.1 The Theoretical Tools: Identity Theory ... 52
3.1.1 Identity Theory Concepts in Archaeology ... 52
3.1.2 Identity: Directly Implementable Ideas ... 55
3.2 The Practical Tools ... 56
3.2.1 Statistical Analysis: Theoretical Considerations ... 57
3.2.2 Statistical Analysis: The Use of R ... 58
3.2.3 Statistical Analysis: The Use of SPSS ... 71
3.2.4 Spatial Analysis: The Use of ArcGIS ... 72
3.3 The Road to the Results ... 73
3.3.1 Weight Calibration Example ... 76
References ... 83

4 A Complex Answer. Results Description ... 87
4.1 General Description and Validation ... 87
4.2 Group 1 ... 90
4.3 Group 2 ... 95
4.4 Group 3 ... 99
4.5 Group 4 ... 101
4.6 Group 5 ... 107
4.7 Group 6 ... 113
4.8 Group 7 ... 115
4.9 Partially Clustered Graves ... 118
4.10 Non-clustered Graves ... 119
References ... 120

5 From Large to Small. Results Discussion ... 123
5.1 Discussion of the Statistically Derived Groups ... 123
5.1.1 General Groups Overview ... 123
5.1.2 Group 1 ... 125
5.1.3 Group 3 ... 131
5.1.4 Group 4 ... 134
5.1.5 Group 5 ... 136
5.1.6 Group 6 ... 139
5.1.7 Group 2 ... 141
5.1.8 Group 7 ... 144
5.1.9 The Clusters and Group Identity ... 146
5.2 The Macro Dimension. The Supra-Groups ... 151
5.3 The Micro Dimension. The Regions ... 159
5.3.1 Moldova ... 159
5.3.2 Muntenia ... 161
5.3.3 Oltenia ... 162
5.3.4 Central Serbia and Vojvodina ... 163
5.3.5 North-West Thrace ... 165
5.3.6 Transylvania ... 167
References ... 171

6 The Overall Picture. Concluding Interpretations 175
6.1 Correspondence to Earlier Statistical Study 175
6.2 Identity and Political Development in the Late Iron Age of the Eastern Carpathian Basin and the Lower Danube 179
6.3 Ethnicity in the Late Iron Age 189
6.3.1 The Issue of Ethnicity in the Iron Age................. 189
6.3.2 The Getae and Dacian Correspondence................ 191
References.. 194

Annex 197

Index.. 269

About the Author

Cătălin Popa is a Postdoctoral Researcher at the University of Leiden. He received his B.A. from the Babeş-Bolyai University and his M.Phil. and Ph.D. (2014) from the University of Cambridge. From 2014 until 2016 he was a Dahlem Research School Postdoctoral Fellow in the Excellence Cluster Topoi, Freie Universität Berlin. Much of his research has been concentrated on the integration of archaeological theory with statistical methods, particularly when applied to issues of identity and landscape. He also has a broad interest in European Prehistory, particularly the Iron Age period. He is additionally working on the relationship between archaeology and nationalism, exploring the instrumentalisation and mythologisation of the past for national purposes or various political aims.

Chapter 1
Introduction

1.1 General Introduction of Research Area and Topic

This volume employs funerary evidence to tackle the issue of large group identity in the Eastern Carpathian basin and the Lower Danube during the final part of the Late Iron Age, the period just prior to the Roman rule. The chosen study area corresponds broadly to today's Romania, North-Western Bulgaria, and Central and Northern Serbia (Fig. 1.1), while the time interval spans from the middle of the second century BC to the end of the first century AD. The main research question is whether there were any large group identities active during this time, as suggested by the traditional interpretation of the many ethnic names supplied by Greek and Latin writers, or whether the community solidarities were more locally based. The solution of this problem is of great interest, since, to this point, much of the information coming from ancient writers was considered to be sufficient evidence for the existence of large, ethnically separated communities. For the study area, the ancient ethnic names that have received most attention are the Getae and Dacians. This is largely a result of the national narrative of the modern Romanian state, which integrated the two populations, considered to be one and the same, as ancestors. Consequently, this research is centred mainly on the regions supposedly inhabited by the two hypothetical populations and their Southern and Western neighbours with whom they were in close contact.

A personalized statistical algorithm was developed by the author to provide an answer to the identity question, by comparing all the funerary finds available in the study area. The algorithm was combined with modelling techniques, mainly cluster analysis, to identify patterns of funerary practice similarities, some of which may be connected to manifestations of group identity. This method, denominated as *comparative contextual modelling* or *contextual statistical analysis*, benefits from its extreme flexibility, showing great potential for its use with other theoretical,

C. N. Popa, *Modelling Identities*, Quantitative Archaeology and Archaeological Modelling, https://doi.org/10.1007/978-3-319-63267-4_1

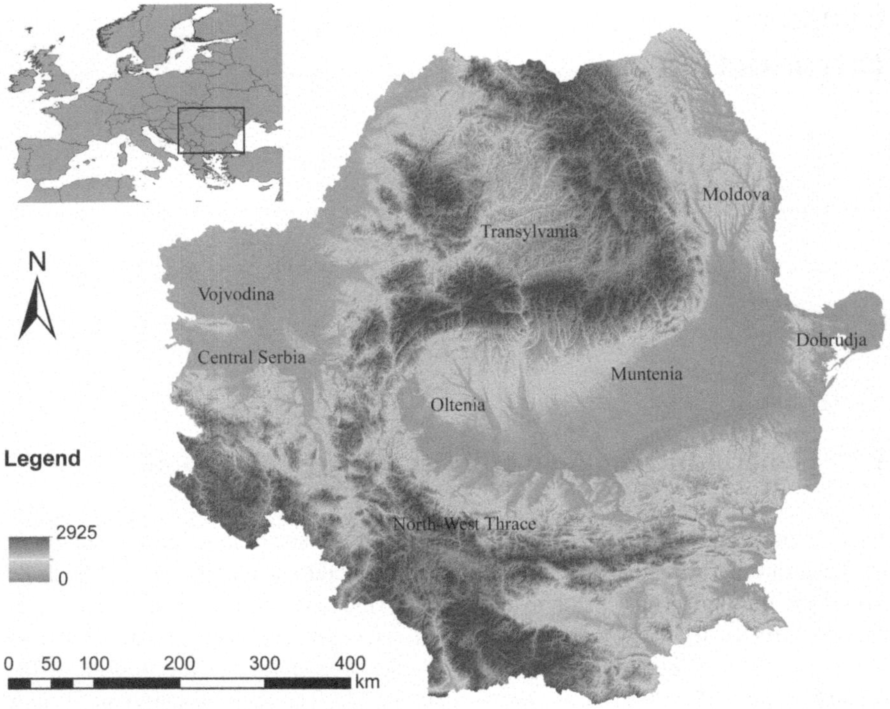

Fig. 1.1 Map of research area with region names

spatial, and temporal parameters.[1] For this reason, a second objective of this research was methodological: to determine a way of comparing large amounts of complex data, coming from similar contexts, to answer questions of identity.

1.2 State of Research

The pre-Roman past of the study area has been the subject of archaeological investigation for nearly two centuries, although, like in much of Europe, most thorough studies are dated after the 1950s. The research themes were and still are varied, covering issues such as military campaigns (Ştefan 2005; Vulpe and Zahariade 1987), social organization (Gostar and Lica 1984), craft production (Glodariu and Iaroslavschi 1979; Rustoiu 1996), and religious life (Crişan 1986; Sanie 1999). Attention has only recently been given to the topics of landscape and environment

[1]The method has already been successfully applied to three Early Medieval cemeteries from Southern Germany (Hausmair 2015).

(Oltean 2007). There are, of course, also a small number of more overarching volumes that have sought to characterize the Iron Age communities from all possible angles, although their usefulness is often limited (e.g., Todorović 1968; Daicoviciu 1972; Tasić 1992; Crişan 1993; Costea 2002). While many features of this particular part of the past were debated over the years, sometimes arguably only in response to radical political shifts at the government level, a constant element remained the professed existence of well-defined ethnic groups that lived in situations of cohabitation or conflict with one another. Only in the last 20 years have there been timid attempts to raise awareness regarding the simplicity of such an ethnic mapping of Late Iron Age people (Babeş 1990; Strobel 1998).

In terms of actual excavations, much attention has been given to the large settlements of this period. In many instances, campaigns stretched over several decades, which is to be expected given the size of some of the sites. The archaeological investigations culminated in a few "lucky" cases with the publication of a monograph, such as at Ocniţa (Berciu 1981), Sprâncenata (Preda 1986), Brad (Ursachi 1995), or Gomolva (Jovanović 1988). Many of these settlements are thought to have reached a proto-urban state, equivalent to the *oppida* of Central and Western Europe (Florea 2011). The Orăştie Mountains region in South-West Transylvania was, and still is, of a special interest. A large number of fortified settlements and military fortification were concentrated in this particular area, which probably functioned as a major political and religious centre during the first century BC and first century AD. Yet, in spite of more than half a century of excavations, most sites remain without even a minimal level of publication (e.g., Glodariu et al. 1988).

A considerable body of literature has been concerned with the burial practices from this period, but only a few have discussed the funerary practice on a wider geographical scale.[2] An older attempt at this can be found in a volume by Protase (1971), in which the author sought to characterize the mortuary rituals of the populations from the territory of modern Romania, which he attributed to the same ethnic group, in the period before and following the Roman conquest. In fact, the large majority of the work is concentrated on the period following the arrival of the Roman administration, mainly because most of the finds are dated to that period. Nonetheless, he produced a list and a short discussion of the Late Iron Age graves, though his definition of burials was much too wide. For this reason, he included in his list finds, like those from Moigrad, which were undoubtedly not the result of mortuary rituals, but rather of other kinds of ritualized activities, such as feasts (Matei and Pop 2001). In addition, Protase also included a number of older chance finds whose integrity cannot be verified. While it seems likely that these findspots were indeed the remains of burials, their dating to the final part of the Late Iron Age is entirely speculative on the basis of the little information available. For all these reasons, the volume of Protase can only be used with extreme caution when approaching the mortuary remains. A more

[2] It should be mentioned here that all such work relating to the Late Iron Age is focused on the territory of Romania and Bulgaria but not Serbia. This is because the large majority of mortuary finds from the latter country was concentrated in a very small number of sites (see Chap. 2), which makes a compendium of such discoveries redundant.

up-to-date and more solid study was produced by Sîrbu (1993). In his volume, Sîrbu attempts to give a list of all the Late Iron Age funerary discoveries, although he uses the same geographical and ethnic principles as Protase to make his selection. The graves were categorized on a series of criteria: the employment of cremation or inhumation, the use of a flat or tumulus burial, whether the finds can be confirmed, or whether they are uncertain. Sîrbu also separates out a series of discoveries which he considers to represent finds of human bones coming from non-funerary contexts, although it is not clear what is meant by non-funerary contexts. The only difference appears to be that the bodies were treated differently from the rest, involving dismemberment or non-anatomical skeletal position. Nonetheless, the volume is overall a good overview of the Iron Age funerary discoveries, and a good starting point for a study of mortuary rituals, particularly since the author provides references for each of the entries that he was able to verify. The most recent and, at the same time, most detailed volume that gives a broad presentation of the Iron Age graves, but also settlements and coin hoards, comes from Theodossiev (2000). In this case, the author focuses on the discoveries from North-Western Bulgaria and his analysis stretches chronologically as far back as the fifth century BC. Although the volume does not concentrate solely on the mortuary finds, most of the Late Iron Age discoveries from this region represent isolated burials or small necropoleis. The inclusion of settlements and coin hoards is actually of great help, since it allows one to note whether the graves were associated with contemporary finds of a different nature. For each findspot, a long list of bibliographical references is given, although in some cases these contained merely a very brief mention of the site name, which is hardly of any help. In any case, Theodossiev's volume is extremely useful in tracking down the Late Iron Age archaeological discoveries from North-Western Bulgaria and is thus an excellent starting point for anyone seeking to gain an insight into the region. A final volume that needs to be mentioned is that compiled by Woźniak (1974), in which the author deals with the La Tène funerary finds from much of South-East Europe, although the main focus was on Southern Romania and North-Western Bulgaria. The scope of the book was to provide a general discussion of the funerary finds and particularly the grave-goods. Therefore, unlike Protase, Sîrbu, and Theodossiev, Woźniak does not stop at each individual findspot to give a short description and interpretation, but rather only briefly lists them in an annex at the end of the volume. The lasting contribution of Woźniak is the identification of particular grave-goods associations in Romania and Bulgaria, which he attributes to a non-homogenous group of warriors that he names the Padea-Panagjurski Kolonii group. While this interpretation has not been accepted fully by all scholars, some researchers, such as Rustoiu (e.g., 2002: 11–23; 2005), have sought to reinforce further the arguments for its existence.[3]

Apart from these four studies, there are a large number of papers that deal with different aspects of funerary behaviour and/or present a smaller number of mortuary

[3] For a more detailed discussion on the Padea-Panagjurski Kolonii group see Chaps. 5 and 6, where it is pointed out that the existence of this group corresponds with the results of this study.

finds. For instance, Torbov has published a series of articles discussing different items that commonly appear in the Late Iron Age graves of North-Western Bulgaria: swords (Torbov 2000), battle knives (Torbov 1997, 2005a), spears (Torbov 2003), chain-mails (Torbov 2004), horse bits (Torbov 1998a), spurs (Torbov 1998b), or belt buckles (Torbov 2005b). Torbov was preceded by Nikolov who worked on the same area. In various articles and small booklets, Nikolov described the archaeological discoveries from North-Western Bulgaria, sometimes focusing on the Late Iron Age funerary finds from a larger area (Nikolov 1965, 1990) and at other times concentrating on one particular location, very briefly presenting all the archaeological evidence from that place (Nikolov 1961, 1964, 1967, 1969, 1971). Some of the same information can be found in the much older work of Popov, who put together many of the prehistoric discoveries from Bulgaria (Popov 1921, 1923, 1930). Similar to Nikolov, Nicolăescu-Plopşor gathered the Late Iron Age funerary finds from the South-West of Romania. Since most of the graves constituted accidental finds, usually few details were available apart from an approximate listing of the grave-goods, accompanied sometimes by drawings (Nicolăescu-Plopşor 1945). Sîrbu has also written a number of papers in which particular Late Iron Age funerary practices and grave types are discussed, but most of the ideas that he presents are a condensed reiteration of the various parts of his 1993 book (cf. Sîrbu 1985, 1986, 1994, 1997). Nonetheless, in some of his collaborative articles, wider topics are debated and the data that he brings is corroborated with other kinds of archaeological evidence (cf. Sîrbu and Arsenescu 2006) or with information relating to larger geographical areas (cf. Sîrbu et al. 1999; Sîrbu and Rustoiu 1999, 2006; Sîrbu and Ştefănescu 2008). Besides the above authors, numerous other scholars have written occasional papers that deal with different aspects of Late Iron Age funerary behaviour from smaller or larger regions (e.g., Moscalu 1977; Popović 1989; Kuzmanov 2005; Niculiţă 2007; Egri and Rustoiu 2008; Jetović and Ljuština 2008). The usual structure of such articles involves presenting a particular interpretation and then briefly introducing the funerary finds that concur with such a scenario (cf. Gergova 2006; Comşa 2010).

By far the most numerous are the papers and volumes that deal with the mortuary discoveries from a specific site, aiming to provide a simpler or more elaborate description and interpretation of those particular finds. In case of the articles, the text, pictures, and drawing are focussed almost exclusively on the grave-goods, especially their shape, size, and analogies, giving only minimal details regarding the spatial positioning of the different funerary elements (e.g., Todorović 1967; Tudor 1968; Nikolov 1981; Moga 1982). A notable exception is a paper by Vulpe (1976) where the author gives considerable details regarding the tumuli from Popeşti and briefly describes a series of unpublished similar graves. Additionally, the recent article of Teleagă et al. (2014) provides a very detailed account of the tumulus burials of Cugir. In very few instances, the publications were accompanied by annexes or separate articles that present, in a highly technical manner, the anthropological details of the deceased (e.g., Nicolăescu-Plopşor and Ricuşiţa 1969; Botezatu and Miu 1989). When the site contained a large number of mortuary finds, or when they were excavated as part of a larger investigation project that concentrated mainly on settlement remains, the publication took the form of a monograph. In such situation, there was generally a tendency to give more contextual data and more interpretation, connecting the different discoveries from the site to each other (e.g., Todorović 1972; Jovanović 1988; Ursachi 1995; Sîrbu et al. 2007).

1.3 Justification of Study

The existence of this study can be justified by the data sample, the question, and the innovative method.

In this volume, the funerary data from the entire area is employed for a broader comparison, an endeavour which has not been previously attempted since nearly all studies were either locally or nationally focussed. The breaking down of research by national borders is not surprising, given that archaeologists in the three countries, in common with nearly all European states, are strongly focussed on researching the past in their countries' territory. The modern borders are especially strong in the case of Late Iron Age research, since this particular period was considered divided into ethnic units that correspond spatially with today's states: Getae or Dacians in Romania, Scordisci in Serbia, and Thracians in Bulgaria. The communist regimes from the three countries, which only permitted limited circulation of people and information, were obviously a contributing factor as well. This separation was accentuated by the aggressive integration of the Dacians in the national narrative of Romania starting from the 1920s, but especially during the 1970s and 1980s, which legitimated a monopoly of this past by Romanian scholars (Popa 2013, 2015, 2016). Finally, one also needs to take into account the strong language barrier that exists between Romania, on the one hand, and Bulgaria and Serbia, on the other. Serbian and Bulgarian are linguistically close, meaning that researchers from both sides of the borders should be able to read each other's work without great difficulty, although even in this case cross-border projects are rare.

This volume deals with a topic that has yet to be tackled through a direct analysis of archaeological material. Questions of identity, particularly large group identity, are nearly entirely absent in studies of the Late Iron Age covering the Eastern Carpathian basin and the Lower Danube because the answers are assumed to be obvious given the ancient written sources that provide vague ethnic names. Identity has only been touched upon significantly in a study by Egri (2008), although her research concerned a much larger area and was aimed particularly at identity-forming practices of conviviality.

The main analysis procedure employed in this volume represents a new approach to comparing large burial data sets. The statistical algorithm used to compare the graves among each other has been developed specifically for this purpose and was given a large degree of flexibility which gives it strong paradigmatic potential. This algorithm is coupled with modelling techniques, particularly a series of clustering procedures, which allow for the graves to be grouped according to the funerary ritual and grave-good characteristics. Although modelling has been employed before in our discipline for grouping archaeological data,[4] it has not been used in such a manner and was never coupled with a similarity algorithm created especially for dealing with such kinds of information.

1.4 Structure of Volume

The volume has been structured in six chapters, with the first and the last forming the introduction and conclusion. Each of the rest deals with particular aspects relating to theory, data, method, results description, and interpretation. Each chapter is further divided into sections and subsections in order to facilitate the reading of the text and understanding of the main argument.

It should be noted that the discussion of theory does not form a chapter of its own. Rather, the different ideas relating to archaeological, anthropological, or sociological theory are introduced with the data or method to which they are directly linked. This particular approach has been adopted because it reflects the way in which the question of this study was tackled.[5] Theory, data, and method were developed together through a continuous feedback loop. As the burial data was gathered, particular theories relating to funerary archaeology were found to be useful for understanding how the mortuary ritual was played out. The type of information, as well as its resolution, also influenced which theoretical aspects relating to identity were employed since not all ideas could be adapted for the interpretation of low-resolution funerary data.[6] Yet, identity theory is more closely connected to the methodology, since the statistical methods used were developed and applied to follow the main principles of group identity.[7] However, only particular identity ideas were implementable statistically, determining their selection. Consequently, the theoretical aspects relating to mortuary ritual are introduced together with the burials that form the database of this study, while the issues pertaining to identity theory are discussed with the statistical method. Additionally, minor ideas about group identity are brought forward during the interpretation of the results to justify particular lines of thinking.

[4] Whitley (1991) has also used cluster analysis for interpreting mortuary information. For more recent examples of similar modeling techniques in archaeology see the work of Nakoinz (2010a, b, 2013).

[5] Through this strategy the divorce between theory, data and method is also avoided, a recurring issue of archaeological papers.

[6] Such an approach to archaeological theory, focusing on deploying theoretical ideas which contribute to an understanding of particular, contextually bounded issues, rather than just working with large theory blocks, has been advertised by people like Hegmon (2003) and Bintliff (2011).

[7] The method was also designed especially for the graves of the Eastern Carpathian basin and the Lower Danube dating to the Late Iron Age, accounting for their particular characteristics. But the use of different modelling techniques influenced in turn the choice of data, since not all the graves could be used in the end for the analysis. Therefore, data and method are also connected through a feedback loop.

Following this brief introduction, in Chap. 2 of the volume, the mortuary data is presented along with some ideas relating to funerary practices. The first section of the chapter is reserved for a theoretical discussion regarding funerary archaeology and mortuary practices in general, pointing out that graves are considered in this study to be a proxy of both the individual beliefs of the deceased and, or especially, of the community from which he or she was drawn. In the second section, the spatial and chronological dimensions of the data are outlined, thus providing the general limits of this study. Also in this part, the issue of the surprisingly small number of graves from this period, when compared to other intervals of time, is discussed. The third section is reserved for describing how the graves were recorded and structured and which data issues influenced this process, specifically the low resolution. Grave-goods, in particular, form the topic of the fourth section. For the grave objects, a hierarchically organized, categorical description was employed, combining functional and typological characteristics. The theoretical foundations for such a choice are discussed here along with a wide array of values taken by the categorical variables that serve to characterize the grave items.

Chapter 3 sets out to describe the methodology used in this volume. The first section is concerned with theories of identity, paying particular attention to group identity, which represents the main interest of this study. A special attention is given to the same other principle that stands at the basis of all identity constructions and forms the main idea behind the statistical analysis of this study. The second section contains the description of the analysis procedures, the statistical and spatial analysis. Much of this section refers to the newly developed similarity algorithm, implemented in R, describing the logic behind the various calculations and providing the most important equations that are employed. The main modelling procedures are also introduced, including the validation indexes used to verify internally the results. This is followed by a description of the main exploratory techniques, run in SPSS, which help to validate further the outcome, but also understand and interpret the resulting patterns. The last part of this section gives an account of how ArcGIS is deployed in order to produce a basic spatial analysis of the graves, which is coupled with the statistical results. The third and final section is meant to address briefly the numerous trials required to obtain valid results, mentioning the various parameters that influence the outcome, which required repeated adjustments in the search for a stable solution.

Chapter 4 contains a description of the statistical results obtained after running the analysis. The chapter starts with a presentation of the exact values produced when running the internal validation techniques on the final results. It is argued that while the index values do not give full assurance that the statistical results are not artificial, their fuzzy character corresponds well with the expectations of the employed identity theory. After establishing the validity of the results, the statistical groups provided by the cluster analysis are individually described, dwelling on their main characteristics as well as their spatial expanse. The final part deals with the small number of graves that could not be clustered, giving a possible explanation and interpretation of the situation.

Chapter 5, the last before the conclusions, represents the main interpretation, and thus the largest, chapter of this volume. Its first section contains the separate interpretation of each statistical group, based on their characteristics and geographical distribution. The relevance of each cluster in terms of group identity can only be revealed when compared with the other clusters, since identity is itself constructed on the same-other dichotomy. Hence, the interpretation takes the form of a detailed comparison, where each cluster is set against every other cluster. Following all the comparisons, the main group identity types found to relate to the clusters are discussed, showing why some interpretations, mainly those of status identity, are more likely than any other. The second section gives a macro analysis of the results, focussing on two large supra-groups observed during the group comparison. It is pointed out that the two supra-groups indicate two radically different regional identities which had little points of overlap. The few sites where the supra-groups appeared together are discussed individually, showing that these were either cases of erroneous clustering or of hybridity. The third section takes a micro approach to the results by discussing each of the geographical regions from the study area. This allows for an in-depth interpretation of the identity dynamics that occur at a regional or even at a local level, as well as for the identification of strongly localized group identities.

Chapter 6 represents the conclusion of this volume, in which the results of the analysis are corroborated with existing studies and with ancient written records to produce an overall interpretation of the political and identity developments of the Eastern Carpathian basin and the Lower Danube during the Late Iron Age. In the first section, it is shown that the clusters and supra-groups uncovered in this study correspond with the interpretation proposed for the political and religious development of this area. However, the results also indicate the existence of an important social rift, rooted in a deep group identity division, within the large political entity that dominated the area between the first century BC and first century AD. In the second section, it is discussed whether any of the identity solidarities that were determined correspond with the names Getae and Dacians provided by ancient writers. The relative geographical coordinates provided by Strabo coincide with the East-West division that characterizes the two supra-groups identified through the statistical analysis. However, an identification of the supra-groups with ethnic units cannot be sustained beyond resonable doubt.

References

Babeş, M. (1990). Daci sau romani? Etnogeneza românească între ştiinţă şi plăsmuire. *Alternative '90, 1*(7), 20–21.

Berciu, D. (1981). *Buridava dacică*. Bucureşti: Academiei.

Bintliff, J. (2011). The death of archaeological theory? In J. Bintliff & M. Pearce (Eds.), *The death of archaeological theory?* (pp. 7–22). Oxford: Oxbow.

Botezatu, D., & Miu, C. (1989). Studiul scheletelor in mormintele de la Brad aparţinând perioadei dacice. *Carpica, 20*, 297–304.

Comşa, A. (2010). Geto-Dacians and the after world. In I. Cândea (Ed.), *The Thracians and their neighbours in antiquity. Studia in honorem Valerii Sîrbu* (pp. 133–139). Brăila.
Costea, F. (2002). *Dacii din sud-estul Transilvaniei înaintea şi în timpul stăpânirii romane*. Braşov, Editura C2Design.
Crişan, I. H. (1986). *Spiritualitatea geto-dacilor : Repere istorice*. Bucureşti: Albatros.
Crişan, I. H. (1993). *Civilizaţia geto-dacilor*. Bucureşti: Meridiane.
Daicoviciu, H. (1972). *Dacii* (Ediţie revăzută şi completată.). Bucureşti: Editura Enciclopedică Română.
Egri, M. (2008). *Communal identity and provincial integration in the Lower Danube: An archaeological study of ceramics (late 1st century BC – early 2nd century AD)* (PhD Thesis). University of Cambridge, Cambridge.
Egri, M., & Rustoiu, A. (2008). The social significance of conviviality in the Scordiscian environment. In V. Sîrbu & D. L. Vaida (Eds.), *Funerary practices of the Bronze and Iron Ages in Central and South-Eastern Europe. Proceedings of the 9th International Colloquium of Funerary Archaeology* (pp. 83–93). Mega: Cluj-Napoca.
Florea, G. (2011). *Dava et oppidum. Débuts de la genèse urbaine en Europe au deuxième âge du Fer*. Cluj-Napoca: Acadèmie Roumaine. Centre d'Études Transylvaines.
Gergova, D. (2006). The tumular embankment in the burial rites and cosmogony of the Thracian Getae. The cosmic egg. *Istros, 13*, 85–94.
Glodariu, I., & Iaroslavschi, E. (1979). *Civilizaţia fierului la daci (sec. II î.e.n. - I e.n.)*. Cluj-Napoca.
Glodariu, I., Iaroslavschi, E., & Rusu, A. (1988). *Cetăţi şi aşezări dacice în Munţii Orăştiei*. Bucureşti: Sport-Turism.
Gostar, N., & Lica, V. (1984). *Societatea geto-dacică de la Burebista la Decebal*. Bucureşti: Junimea.
Hausmair, B. (2015). *Am Rande des Grabs. Todeskonzepte und Bestattungsritual in der frühmittelalterlichen Alamannia*. Leiden: Sidestone Press.
Hegmon, M. (2003). Setting theoretical egos aside: issues and theory in North American archaeology. *American Antiquity, 68*(2), 213–243. doi:10.2307/3557078.
Jetović, M., & Ljuština, M. (2008). Some Thracian elements from the Iron Age tumular graves in Novi Pazar Area (South-Western Serbia). In V. Sîrbu & I. Stângă (Eds.), *The Iron Gates region during the Second Iron Age. Settlements, necropolises, treasures* (pp. 38–56). Drobeta Turnu-Severin; Craiova: Editura Universitaria.
Jovanović, B. (1988). *Gomolava: Naselje Mlađeg Gvozdenog Doba. Late La Tène settlement*. Novi Sad: Vojvođanski muzej.
Kuzmanov, M. (2005). The horse in the Thracian burial rites. *Helis, 4*, 98–107.
Matei, A. V., & Pop, H. (2001). Măgura Moigradului-zonă sacră (sec. I î.e.n.) şi aşezare dacică fortificată (sec. I e.n.) In E. Iaroslavschi, V. Crişan, G. Florea, & G. Gheorghiu (Eds.), *Studii de istorie antică : Omagiu profesorului Ioan Glodariu* (pp. 253–277). Deva: Muzeul National de Istorie a Transilvaniei.
Moga, V. (1982). Morminte dacice de incineraţie la Teleac. *Apulum, 20*, 87–91.
Moscalu, E. (1977). Sur les rites funéraires des Getó-Daces de la plaine de Danube. *Dacia N.S., 21*, 329–340.
Nakoinz, O. (2010a). Kulturelle Räume der älteren Eisenzeit in Südwestdeutschland. In D. Krausse & D. Beilharz (Eds.), *'Fürstensitze' und Zentralorte der frühen Kelten : Absclußkolloquium des DFG-Schwerpunktprogramms 1171 in Stuttgart, 12.-15. Oktober 2009* (pp. 317–332). Stuttgart: Konrad Theiss.
Nakoinz, O. (2010b). Concepts of central place research in archaeology. In H.-R. Bork (Ed.), *Landscapes and human development: The contribution of European archaeology. Proceedings of the International Workshop 'Socio-Environmental Dynamics over the Last 12,000 Years: The Creation of Landscapes (1st-4th April 2009)* (pp. 251–264). Bonn: In Kommission bei Habelt.
Nakoinz, O. (2013). *Archäologische Kulturgeographie der ältereisenzeitlichen Zentralorte Südwestdeutschlands*. Kiel: Habelt.
Nicolăescu-Plopşor, C. S. (1945). Antiquités celtiques en Olténie. *Dacia, 11–12*, 17–33.

Nicolăescu-Plopşor, D., & Ricuşiţa, C. (1969). Caracterizarea antrolologică şi morfobiologică a scheletelor din complexul funerar de la Orlea (sec. II-I î.e.n). *Revista Muzeelor, 1*, 69–73.

Niculiţă, I. (2007). Contributions made to the study of the burial rite performed by the communities inhabiting East of the Carpathians in 3rd c. B.C. - 3rd c. A.D. *Acta Terrae Septemcastrensis, 6*(1), 71–73.

Nikolov, B. (1961). *Altimir prez vekovete: Istoricheski ocherk.*

Nikolov, B. (1964). *Arheologicheski pametnitsi vav Vrachansko.* Vratsa.

Nikolov, B. (1965). Thrakische Denkmäler in Bezirk Vraca. *Bulletin of the Institute of Archaeology, 28*, 163–202.

Nikolov, B. (1967). *Krushovitsa.* Vratsa: [Okrŭzhen Muzeĭ].

Nikolov, B. (1969). *Galatin.* Vratsa, [Okrŭzhen Muzeĭ].

Nikolov, B. (1971). *Sofronievo.* Vratsa: [Okrŭzhen muzeĭ].

Nikolov, B. (1981). Sépultures thraces près du village Sofronievo, département de Vraca. *Arheologija, 22*(3), 30–41.

Nikolov, B. (1990). Trouvailles thraces de la Bulgarie du Nord-Ouest. *Arheologija, 32*(4), 14–26.

Oltean, I. A. (2007). *Dacia: Landscape, colonisation and romanisation.* London: Routledge.

Popa, C. N. (2013). The trowel as chisel. Shaping modern Romanian identity through the Iron Age. In V. Ginn, R. Enlander, & R. Crozier (Eds.), *Exploring prehistoric identity. Our construct or theirs?* (pp. 164–174). Oxford: Oxbow.

Popa, C. N. (2015). Late Iron Age archaeology in Romania and the politics of the past. *Dacia N.S., 59*, 337–361.

Popa, C. N. (2016). The significant past and insignificant archaeologists. Who informs the public about their 'national' past? The case of Romania. *Archaeological Dialogues, 23*(1), 28–39.

Popov, R. (1921). Materiali za prouchvane na halstattskata i la-tenska culturi v Bulgaria i Makedonia. *Godishnik na Narodniya Arheologicheski Muzey v Sofia, 1*, 152–182.

Popov, R. (1923). Predistorichen otdel. *Vodach za Narodniya muzey v Sofia*, 50–115.

Popov, R. (1930). *Култура и животъ на предисторическия човѣкъ въ България. Часть II. Метална епоха ... Съ 68 обр. въ текста..* (Vols 1–2). *София.*

Popović, P. (1989). The Late Iron Age on the territory of Djerdap. *Starinar, 40–41*, 165–176.

Preda, C. (1986). *Geto-dacii din bazinul Oltului inferior: Dava de la Sprincenata.* Bucuresti.

Protase, D. (1971). *Riturile funerare la daci şi daco-romani.* Editura Academiei Republicii Socialiste România.

Rustoiu, A. (1996). *Metalurgia bronzului la daci: (sec. II î. Chr. - sec. I d. Chr.) Tehnici, ateliere şi produse de bronz.* Bucureşti: Institutul Român de Tracologie, Ministerul Învăţământului.

Rustoiu, A. (2002). *Războinici şi artizani de prestigiu în Dacia preromană.* Cluj-Napoca: Nereamia Napocae.

Rustoiu, A. (2005). The Padea-Panagjurski Kolonii group in South-Western Transylvania (Romania). In H. Dobrzańska, J. V. S. Megaw, P. Poleska, & Z. Woźniak (Eds.), *Celts on the margin: Studies in European cultural interaction 7th Century BC—1st Century AD. Dedicated to Zenon Woźniak* (pp. 109–120). Institute of Archaeology and Ethnology of the Polish Academy of Sciences: Kraków.

Sanie, S. (1999). *Din istoria culturii şi religiei geto-dacice* (Ediţia a 2-a, revăzută şi adăugită.). Iaşi: Editura Universităţii 'Al. I. Cuza'.

Sîrbu, V. (1985). Ritualuri şi practici funerare la geto-daci în sec. II îen. – I en. *Istros, 4*, 89–126.

Sîrbu, V. (1986). Rituels et pratiques funéraires des gèto-daces IIe siècle av. n.è - Ier siècle de n.è. *Dacia N.S., 30*(1–2), 91–108.

Sîrbu, V. (1993). *Credinţe şi practici funerare, religioase şi magice în lumea geto-dacilor (pornind de la descoperirile arheologice din Câmpia Brăilei).* Galaţi: Porto-Franco.

Sîrbu, V. (1994). Morminte tumulare din zona Carpato-Dunăreană (sec. I î. d. Chr. – I d. Chr.) *Istros, 7*, 123–160.

Sîrbu, V. (1997). Sacrifices humains et pratiques funéraires insolites dans l'areal thrace du Hallstatt et du La Tène. In *Prima epocă a fierului la gurile Dunării şi în zonele Circumpontice. Lucrările colocviului internațional, septembrie 1993, Tulcea.* (pp. 193–221). Tulcea: Institutul de Cercetări Eco-Muzeale.

Sîrbu, V., & Arsenescu, M. (2006). Dacian settlements and necropolises in Southwestern Romania (2nd c. B.C.-1st c. A.D.). In V. Sîrbu & S. A. Luca (Eds.), *The society of the living – the community of the dead (from Neolithic to the Christian Era). Proceedings of the 7th International Colloquium of Funerary Archaeology* (Vol. 1, pp. 163–186). Sibiu: Muzeul Național Brukenthal.

Sîrbu, V., & Rustoiu, A. (1999). Découvertes funéraires Géto-Daces du Sud-Ouest de la Roumanie (150-50av.J.C.) In M. Vasić (Ed.), *Le Djerdap - les Portes de Fer a la deuxiéme moitie du premier millenaire av. J. Ch. jusqu aux guerres daciques. Kolloquim in Kladovo-Drobeta-Tr. Severin* (pp. 77–91). Arheološki institut: Beograd.

Sîrbu, V., & Rustoiu, A. (2006). Funerary practices of the Geto-Dacians of the 2nd Century BC – 1st Century AD. In V. Lungu, G. Simion, & F. Topoleanu (Eds.), *Pratiques funéraires et manifestations de l'identité culturelle (Âge du Bronze et Âge du Fer)* (pp. 199–228). Tulcea: L'Institut de Recherches Éco-Muséologiques.

Sîrbu, V., & Ştefănescu, R. (Eds.). (2008). *Funerary practices in Central and Eastern Europe (10th c. BC - 3rd c. AD).* Brăila: Istros - Muzeul Brăilei.

Sîrbu, V., Rustoiu, A., & Crăciunescu, G. (1999). Descoperiri funerare din La Tène-ul târziu din zona Porţilor de Fier. *Thraco-Dacica, 20*(1–2), 217–230.

Sîrbu, V., Luca, S. A., Roman, C., Purece, S., Diaconescu, D., & Cerişor, N. (2007). *Vestigiile dacice de la Hunedoara/The Dacian vestiges in Hunedoara.* Sibiu: Muzeul Naţional Brukenthal.

Ştefan, A. S. (2005). *Les guerres daciques de Domitien et de Trajan: Architecture militaire, topographie, images et histoire.* Roma: Ecole française de Rome.

Strobel, K. (1998). Dacii. Despre complexitatea mărimilor etnice, politice şi culturale ale istoriei spaţiului Dunării de Jos. *Studii şi Cercetări de Istorie Veche şi Arheologie, 49*(1), 61–95.

Tasić, N. (Ed.). (1992). *Scordisci and the native population in the Middle Danube region.* Belgrade: Balkanološki institut SANU.

Teleagă, E., Bălăşescu, A., Soficaru, A., & Schoch, W. (2014). Die Scheiterhaufen aus Cugir und Tarinci. Ein Beitrag zu den Bestattungssitten der Balkanhalbinsel und des vorrömischen Dakiens in der Spätlatènezeit. *Praehistorische Zeitschrift, 89*(2), 305–336.

Theodossiev, N. (2000). *North-Western Thrace from the fifth to first centuries BC.* Oxford: Archaeopress.

Todorović, J. (1967). Les nécropoles prehistoriques de Rospi Ćuprija à Belgrade. *Starinar, 18*, 193–200.

Todorović, J. (1968). *Kelti u Jugoistocnoj Evropi.* Beograd.

Todorović, J. (1972). *Praistorijska Karaburma I – nekropola mlađeg željeznog doba* (Vol. 1). Beograd.

Torbov, N. (1997). Krivi trakiyski nozhove ot III v.pr.Chr. – I. v., otkriti v Severozapadna Bulgaria. *Izvestiya na Muzeite v Severozapadna Bulgaria, 25*, 15–45.

Torbov, N. (1998a). Trakiyski youzdi ot III v.pr.Chr. – I. v., otkriti v Severozapadna Bulgaria. *Izvestiya na Muzeite v Severozapadna Bulgaria, 26*, 11–42.

Torbov, N. (1998b). Spurs from the 2nd century BC – 1st century AD found in Northwestern Bulgaria. *Archaeologia Bulgarica, 2*(1), 54–63.

Torbov, N. (2000). Swords from II-I centuries BC found in Northwestern Bulgaria. *Izvestiya na Muzeite v Severozapadna Bulgaria, 28*, 11–34.

Torbov, N. (2003). Spear points and tips from North-Western Bulgaria (3rd – 1st c BC). *Izvestiya na Muzeite v Severozapadna Bulgaria, 29*, 51–68.

Torbov, N. (2004). Chain-mails from Northern Bulgaria III – I c. BC. *Archaeologia Bulgarica, 8*(2), 57–69.

Torbov, N. (2005a). Curved Thracian knives from North-Western Bulgaria (widespreading, date and origin). In T. Stoyanov, M. Tonkova, C. Preshlenov, & C. Popov (Eds.), *Heros Hephaistos. Studia in honorem Liubae Ognenova-Marinova* (pp. 358–367). Faber: Veliko Tŭrnovo.

Torbov, N. (2005b). Toki ot kolan i kolani-verizhki, otkriti na teritoriyata, zakliyuchena mezhdu rekite Timok i Iskar. In G. Kitov & D. Dimitrova (Eds.), *Zemite na Bulgaria. Lyulka na trakiyskata kultura* (pp. 208–214). Sofia: Universitetsko izdatelstovo 'Sv. Kliment Ohridski'.

Tudor, E. (1968). Morminte de luptători din a doua epocă e fierului descoperite la Rastu. *Studii şi Cercetări de Istorie Veche, 19*, 517–526.

Ursachi, V. (1995). *Zargidava: Cetatea dacică de la Brad*. Bucureşti: Caro Trading.

Vulpe, A. (1976). La nécroplole tumulaire gète de Popeşti. *Thraco-Dacica, 1*, 193–215.

Vulpe, A., & Zahariade, M. (1987). *Geto-dacii în istoria militară a lumii antice*. Bucureşti: Editura Militară.

Whitley, A. J. M. (1991). *Style and society in Dark Age Greece: The changing face of a pre-literate society 1100-700 BC*. Cambridge: Cambridge University Press.

Woźniak, Z. (1974). *Wschodnie pogranicze kultury Lateńskiej*. Ossolińskich: Zakład Narodowy im.

Chapter 2
Final Resting Place: The Archaeological Data

2.1 Death and Burial

2.1.1 Theoretical Concepts About Death: The Potential of Burials in Archaeology

Death is an important part of human existence, a reality that is encountered by all communities and every person, which through its very nature is difficult to handle. People have an almost natural fear of it or at least anxiety about it.[1] For this reason, a wide series of cultural practices are in place to allow individuals and communities to deal with the inevitable confrontation with death and to separate it from the world of the living. These can be grouped under the umbrella description of funerary or mortuary practices.

Funerary practices are generally extremely ritualized. There is usually a precise list of strictly prescribed activities that need to be performed by the mourners at the death of an individual, accompanied by a series of taboos. These rituals are regularly sustained by a wide spectrum of religious and afterlife beliefs that provide a narrative of an individual's existence after death. Some have argued that the ritualization of death is a consequence of people's inability to deal with this moment and accept it as a naturally recurring event (Ariès 2004, p. 41).

Death, in reality, occurs twice: once in the biological sphere and once in the social sphere (Hasenfratz 1983; for ethnographic examples see Barley 1998). Biological death is an instant event; it has basically no temporality attached to it, although determining its exact timing varies culturally mainly based on medical knowledge (Hoof and in der Schmitten 1995). Social death, on the other hand, takes

[1] However some studies have shown that the fear of death develops in children only after the ages of 3–5, for which reason it may be argued that it is, at least partly, also a culturally learned attitude (Becker 2004, pp. 24–25).

C. N. Popa, *Modelling Identities*, Quantitative Archaeology and Archaeological Modelling, https://doi.org/10.1007/978-3-319-63267-4_2

various amounts of time, in some cases stretching over several years and can be considered a process.[2] Hence, once a person dies, he/she does not instantly also cease to be a socially active member of the community (see Fahlander 2008; Gansum 2008).[3] Instead, the deceased is removed from the social sphere through the funerary ritual itself. Sometimes this ends with the disposal of the corpse. However, this is not always the case, as there are instances where the dead only truly depart from the living community following a ritual event that can take part some years after death (cf. Robb 2007: 290–291).

Death is, thus, very much a social loss that throws a community off balance; it is as much a social trauma as it is an emotional one. Through funerary practices, this loss is acknowledged and dealt with (Hakenbeck 2004, p. 41). The highly ritualized character of mortuary practices fixes the steps that need to be followed at such a ceremony, although there is some room for variation to account for different elements such as circumstances of death (Robb 2007, p. 288, 2013). This high ritualization means that generally there are precise roles for the mourners and other participant community members.[4] Order is created through this almost automatized behaviour, which gives a sense of stability in a time of social anxiety.

Given the social stabilizing role of the funerary ritual, one can infer that social relationships are played out throughout its duration (Parker Pearson 1982, p. 101). The mourners, deceased, and participant community members are entangled in a mesh of social relationships which gets expressed during the mortuary ritual. The death of a community member risks disintegrating the system of social relationships, causing potential chaos (Goody 1962, p. 26; Hertz 1960). However, the funerary ritual is a highly structured event when people are expected to know how to behave; a specific range of resources, for instance, phrases, bodily movements, and material symbols, are expected to be mobilized in ways appropriate to each group of individuals taking part in a funeral (Mizoguchi 1992, p. 40). This creates a well-controlled social context in which social roles are played out, refuting the potential destabilizing effect caused by the death of a community member and affirming the group's social equilibrium. As a result, the relationships that exist within a community are reinforced during the funerary ritual, though it also provides an arena for them to be challenged by the participants (Parker Pearson 1982, p. 102).

Assuming that the social roles played out throughout a mortuary ritual correspond exactly to those existing in society would, however, be erroneous. It is generally thought that funerary practices provide an idealized version of the community, meaning that distortions of smaller or larger intensity regularly occur (Parker Pearson 1982, p. 112). These are to be expected since social relationships are not the

[2] Some scholars make a distinction between primary and secondary mortuary rituals, according to their temporal relationship to the physical death (Chesson 2001: 8, note 1).

[3] In this sense there are scholars which have argued for an agency of the dead and of the dead body (Williams 2004).

[4] Kan (1989, p. 125) differentiates between the mourners and other participants, which he sees as having opposite roles.

only ones that influence the playing out of funerary rituals; a second major component is given by afterlife beliefs (see Hausmair 2015, pp. 33–58).

The interplay of social relationships and afterlife beliefs in the construction of funerary rituals has often been acknowledged, but there is little consensus between scholars as to the impact of each. Some scholars, such as Binford (1971), O'Shea (1981, 1984), or more recently Brather (Brather 2008; Brather-Walter and Brather 2012), keep a large emphasis on the importance of social relationships. Others, however, consider religious and afterlife beliefs to have primacy (e.g., Hallam and Hockey 2001). Only rarely has the influence of both been mapped out thoroughly. A remarkable exception is the study of Carr (1995), where the author does a wide cross-cultural study testing different ideas coming from both sides. He concludes that both ideas of the afterlife, which he calls philosophic-religious beliefs, and social relationships have an equal impact on the funerary ritual and the treatment of the dead body, with the latter often becoming more prominent as social complexity increases.

The funerary ritual is also a time when identities get expressed since these are inherently constructed through social relationships (see Chap. 3). Multiple layers of identity expression can be determined. This includes firstly the identity of the mourners and other participants of the event. Secondly, there is the identity of the dead person which is usually based largely on his/her personal identity. However, the particular aspects of the deceased's social persona (sensu Binford 1971) that get expressed during the mortuary ritual are determined by the mourners since they are the ones preparing the body.[5] Consequently, the deceased is assigned a constructed identity, adequate for this particular event, which in some cases involves his/her individuality getting dissolved within a common group membership (cf. Stoddart 2015). Finally, there is a larger community identity. This is embedded in every choice made throughout the mortuary ritual, as this event, together with the activities that it entails, consists an identity-forming process. The fact that particular mortuary practices accompany the death of particular individuals represents an identity-defining characteristic of the deceased's community. There is a proper way[6] of dealing with the dead, a mutually agreed way of behaving at such an event, specific material items that are involved, all of which are governed to a substantial degree by the cultural traditions to which the ritual participants adhere.

The actual preparation of the deceased body and of the grave represents a materialization of the funerary ritual. The burial itself is what archaeologists find; it provides the material remains that are used in the present to reconstruct the social relationships and/or afterlife beliefs in effect during the funerary ritual of past people. Given the focal point occupied by the dead body and grave preparation, burial

[5] This idea has been pointed out through the well-known expression: "The dead do not bury themselves" (Parker Pearson 1999a, p. 3).

[6] Or a number of proper ways.

remains are, at least in part, representative of the funerary ritual as a whole, although there are many elements which are certainly lost as they do not get material form (e.g., songs, bodily postures) or do not get placed in the grave. At the same time, archaeologists obtain a simplified image from burials since they appear to provide snapshot, an instant, while in fact they are the outcome of a laborious mortuary ritual with temporality assigned to it.

The objects uncovered in burials, generally referred to as grave-goods, have been given particular attention by archaeologists. The grave-goods may be personal objects of the deceased[7] or they can represent gifts given by the mourners or other funeral participants. In many instances, the objects deposited are previously used, although it can also happen that they are made specifically for this occasion (cf. Olivier 1999). Grave-goods can be intentionally destroyed before being placed in the burial; some may even be ritually "killed".[8] Lastly, burials can also include containers of food and drink, placed with the dead or consumed during funerary feasts (Parker Pearson 1999a, pp. 7–10). All these objects are carefully selected by the mourners and funeral participants and are thus indicative of the deceased's and community members' social relationships and afterlife beliefs.

Numerous studies have shown that burials constitute a valuable data source for inferring social relationships. The papers of Parker Pearson (1982, 1993, 1999a, b) remain fundamental in revealing the potential of funerary data for archaeologists. By looking at body treatment, grave preparation, and the choice of grave-goods, one gets an insight into the social norms that came into play during the funerary ritual and the social relationships that were materialized through it.

Burials have also traditionally been employed by archaeologists for studies of identity, particularly status, and ethnic affiliation. Arguably, there have been numerous problems in reading burials through an ethnic lens, since it often resulted in the splitting of mortuary remains according to the ethnic typology of their grave-goods.[9] Similar simplistic interpretations were sometimes produced when the ritual preparations and grave-goods were purely analysed in terms of their economic value, which was used as a direct measure for the social status of the deceased. Nevertheless, there is also a broad spectrum of identity studies that employ burials to produce much more critical analyses, pointing out the numerous layers of identity of the deceased, mourners, and community as a whole that get expressed during the preparation of burials (Hakenbeck 2007, 2011; Hausmair 2015; Kuijt 2008; Lucy 2002). Mortuary remains are thus a good choice of data for questions of identity, provided that a critical attitude is taken both towards death and burial, and identity construction.

[7] Yet even the deceased's personal belongings are chosen by the mourners.

[8] Such a scenario can be proposed for instance for many of the swords uncovered in Late Iron Age graves. These are often found to be double or triple folded, which can only be the outcome of a deliberate act associated with funerals (e.g. Nikolov 1981).

[9] For a critique of ethnic approaches to funerary evidence see the studies of Brather (2000, 2002, 2004).

2.1.2 *Practical Arguments for Using Burials*

The potential of burials for producing a narrative about past identity is the main reason to employ this particular data type in my study of Late Iron Age group identity, but there is also an important practical motivation: data publication. Many of the excavations that have been carried out throughout the twentieth century in South-East Europe suffer in terms of publication quality. There are numerous cases of sites that have been excavated for several years, sometimes even decades, without receiving a minimal level of publication. This phenomenon tends particularly to affect settlements. Even when a monograph gets published, the information is often so vague and unreliable, that it makes the publication virtually unusable.[10] Generally, burials suffer less from that problem.

It is much more likely for mortuary remains to get published than settlements. This may have to do with an affinity that archaeologists have with human remains. It may also be related to the size of the excavation and sheer amount of data. There is no doubt that many settlements occupy large areas—though there are also big cemeteries—and thus a more sustained effort is required to process all the archaeological material and give it an adequate publication and interpretation. In addition, burials are generally considered to be closed contexts, with limited or no subsequent intervention. They principally contain material items that were in use at a particular moment in time, for which reason they have been used far more widely than settlement evidence for establishing typological and chronological frameworks. Most burials also allow staged, measured analysis, where parts neatly form elements of a whole. This is programmatically easier to deal with than a complex interrelated settlement with difficult stratigraphy. Whatever the reason, burials have received more attention than other kinds of archaeological evidence, although this does not mean that all mortuary finds are well-published. Many of them have only a minimal level of publication and there are cases of funerary discoveries from decades ago that are still in museum deposits awaiting attention.

2.2 Data Limits and Overview

In order to sort through the vast archaeological information available for the Late Iron Age of South-East Europe in an efficient manner, it was necessary to decide on some guiding rules for selecting the burials appropriate for analysis. These rules were deduced from the research question and the issues that led to its formulation. One of the key issues was to establish the relationship between the Late Iron Age

[10] A well-known example in this sense is Berciu's monograph, *Buridava dacică* (Berciu 1981). It has been pointed out that much of the stratigraphic interpretation as well as the proposed chronology are faulty. Similarly, many of the artefacts uncovered are wrongly dated and typologized and much of the archaeological information that the author uses for his interpretation is inaccurate (Babeş 1982).

people of present-day Romania and their contemporaries to the South, South-West, and West. For this reason, the boundaries were extended well beyond the traditional national boundaries in order to transcend any problems created by modern frontiers and to allow the internal spatial patterning to be unaffected by artificial modern limits. Given the geographical and chronological boundaries embedded in the formulation of this problem, these spatial and temporal limits were employed as a starting point for the current study.

2.2.1 Spatial Limits

The geographical areas for this study were, however, not strictly fixed a priori. While there were some general initial boundaries in mind, these were altered constantly as the data were gathered and as various issues were encountered and dealt with (when possible). Such a process is natural in research, as there is a constant degree of feedback between the actual process of data gathering and interpretation. Some limitations were introduced as a consequence of academic time constraints, forcing in some cases the exclusion of regions (e.g., South-East Slovakia and the Upper Tisza basin in South-West Ukraine) which initially were planned to be included.

Consequently, the spatial limits were roughly set to the territory of Romania—which can be thought as being the core area for this study—and the Southern and Western neighbouring regions that presented evidence of intense contact with this core—meaning parts of Bulgaria, Serbia, and Hungary.[11] The term contact is defined as any form of direct interchange between members of different communities (cf. Schortman and Urban 1998; Silliman 2005),[12] in present-day Romania and those found to the South and West.

These territories were not considered in their full extent for this study. The region of Dobrudja from Romania, which borders the Black Sea, was excluded, because of its strong cultural connection with the Greek World caused by the ancient Greek colonies established in the area as far back as the seventh century BC (Avram and Babeş 2000). The intense contact undoubtedly had a profound impact on the identity of the people coming from this region, introducing a different issue—that of relations with Greek colonies—which fell outside the scope of this

[11] There are also signs of contact with the Late Iron Age people of present-day Romania to the North-West, meaning the Upper Tisza basin in South-West Ukraine and South-Eastern Slovakia, as well as the East and North-East, corresponding to Southern Ukraine and the Republic of Moldova. However these regions were not incorporated into the study as it would introduce a series of new variables, revolving around cultural contact with the area of the so-called Przeworsk culture, which would enlarge the discussion beyond the possibilities of one study.

[12] This requirement was the main principle for determining how much from the areas South and West of Romania to include. Unfortunately this rule still left room for ambiguity, as sometimes it was entirely up to interpretation whether or not there was enough evidence for contact. On the other hand, such situations are not uncommon in our discipline since archaeology is not an exact science but an interpretative one.

study. A similar argument could be made for much of Eastern and Southern Bulgaria (Emilov 2007a, b).

As for Serbia, only the evidence from the Central and Northern parts of the country was considered. This roughly corresponds to the region around the Danube River, present-day Belgrade, and Vojvodina. South of these regions, there was little evidence of burial practices during the chronological period of interest (see below) and also only scarce signs of contact with the Late Iron Age people from present-day Romania (Jovanović 1985).

The territory of Hungary presented a different problem. Despite this area being intensely settled during the Late Iron Age, there was virtually no funerary evidence that could be attributed to the period of interest to this study (see below) (Hellebrandt 1999; Horvath et al. 1987). For this reason, even though initially it was planned to include this part of Europe in the analysis, it was not possible to do so.

Therefore, the study area can be summarized as the Northern half of South-East Europe, or more precisely, the Eastern Carpathian basin and the Lower Danube. This corresponds to the following modern territorial units: Romania without the region of Dobrudja, North-Western Bulgaria, Central, and Northern Serbia (Fig. 1.1).[13]

2.2.2 *Chronological Limits*

The time frame was more strictly defined by the research question than the geographical limits, although some deviations were permitted because of the lack of more accurate dating for the funerary evidence. Nonetheless, the aim was to include the burials that were dated between the middle of the second century BC and the end of the first century AD, which according to the updated Reinecke relative chronology corresponds approximately to the La Tène C2-D (Božić 1981, 2008, pp. 119–147; Guštin 1984) or Late La Tène.

There were several reasons for choosing this particular time interval. The first one had to do with the scope of this study. For this period, archaeologists had suggested the existence of clearly individualized ethnic units, especially in the case of Romania (Crişan 1993; Daicoviciu 1981), an idea which my research sought to question. Thus, it seemed obvious to focus on the time which some researchers consider to be "classic" when referring to Late Iron Age Romania (cf. Babeş 1988; Glodariu 2001).

Secondly, this was the chronological interval that corresponded to important social and political phenomena, both in this region, but also across much of temperate Europe. In the Eastern Carpathian basin, the start of this period saw a change in material culture patterns in Transylvania, which some consider to be caused by a

[13] In the case of North-West Bulgaria, the denomination North-West Thrace was preferred to refer to the region throughout the volume, because the main source for this area, Theodossiev's study (2000), employs this terminology.

movement of population into that region during the first half of the second century BC (Rustoiu 2002, pp. 33–40). This was also the time when important political formations appeared, culminating with a so-called kingdom that had its centre in South-West Transylvania at the site of Sarmizegetusa Regia (Daicoviciu 1981). The emergence of such political formations in this area was simultaneous with the development of large settlement sites, named *davae*, which are considered to have reached a nearly urban stage (Florea 2011).[14] In the rest of temperate Europe, from Hungary to Southern France, these events were paralleled by the appearance of *oppida*, very large settlements with fortifications that often enclosed areas measuring hundreds of hectares (Collis 1984; Fichtl 2000).

In addition to the above political and social changes, the Late La Tène was a time when the Roman Empire was expanding into much of Europe, including the Balkans and the Carpathian basin (Boardman et al. 2001). This put significant pressure on the Iron Age inhabitants, substantially for military reasons, as they came into direct, intense, and sometimes violent contact with a powerful *other*. The continuous presence of the Roman Empire was a factor that shaped the existence of Iron Age people (cf. Wells 1998: 276). Considering that this was also the period when significant political and organizational changes were taking place, it is safe to say that at this time the Eastern Carpathian basin and the Lower Danube was a volatile world where power and social relations were constantly strained and renegotiated. Various communities came together, willingly or not, under weak or powerful leaders, only to be engulfed by even larger political formations or to be again separated as these entities crumbled. It has been pointed out that, in such circumstances, when communities are put under large amounts of pressure, questions of identity come to the fore and take expression in the different elements of social life (Graves-Brown and Jones 1996). These ideas also hold true for Late Iron Age Europe (cf. Derks 2009: 421–422), making this period a good candidate for a study of identity and the choice for this study.

Finally, there was also a very practical reason for choosing the middle of the second century BC to the end of the first century AD and not a shorter period or some variation of it. Since the chronology of many Late Iron Age sites from South-East Europe is highly inexact, numerous finds could only be loosely dated to this relatively wide time interval. Hence, choosing to work with this time frame allowed for an easier identification of material which had the appropriate dating and avoided delicate problems of chronology that probably cannot be answered. Nonetheless, in the cases where a more accurate chronology was determined, the dating was recorded and employed in the interpretation.

[14] It should be mentioned that using the urban-rural dichotomy in the case of Late Iron Age settlement sites is not always useful, since the two terms refer to settlements typical of the Mediterranean world. Forcing them onto temperate Europe only limits our interpretations.

2.2.3 *Void of Burials*

The Late La Tène was also a period of important changes in terms of funerary rituals. The first half of the second century BC saw a rapid shift across temperate Europe to a funerary ritual that left no archaeological trace. From the Black Sea to the Atlantic Ocean, the large Late Iron Age cemeteries, so typical for the fifth, fourth, and third centuries BC (La Tène A–La Tène C1), came to an abrupt end, replaced by what can be called a "void of burials" (Spânu 2002, p. 103). Some have suggested that this phenomenon can be explained as a dissolution of the individual person into the collective, which may be observed also in the settlement patterns, with the rise of large *oppida* and *davae* (Wells forthcoming). This situation contrasts highly with that from the final part of the Early Iron Age (Hallstatt C2-D) when large tumulus burials, such as those found at Vix or Hochdorf, dotted the landscape, emphasizing the individual person rather than the collective (Knüsel 2002; Olivier 1999).

The disappearance of burials was, however, not total. While the vast majority of people did indeed resort to a burial rite which left no archaeological traces, groups of burials could occasionally still be encountered. Such was the case of the cemeteries found near the *oppida* of Titelberg (Metzler-Zens et al. 1999) and Bibracte (Quinn 1995), although the number of graves uncovered represented only a very small fraction of the estimated population of the two settlements. Thus, while the number of graves did indeed decrease radically, burials did not entirely disappear.

The area of the Eastern Carpathian basin and the Lower Danube shares this pattern of a scarcity of funerary evidence for the Late La Tène. While there is no estimate for the entire area at this point, Sîrbu calculated that, of all the burials identified on the modern territory of Romania dating from the fifth century BC to the third century AD, those that can be placed between the second century BC and the first century AD represent only about 2% (Sîrbu 1993, p. 22). The number that Sîrbu proposed for the La Tène C2-D is considerably smaller than the one I employ in my research, as he left out of his calculations a series of discoveries for different reasons. Moreover, several new burials have been uncovered since he made his study. Nonetheless, his estimate gives a good relative approximation of the impact that this phenomenon had in Romania and it can probably be extended to much of South-East Europe albeit with a margin of error.

2.2.4 *Burials in the Void*

Despite this huge drop in funerary finds, there were still enough burials to be found for a comprehensive study. For the present analysis, the graves of 370 individuals were used, derived from 314 burial contexts. This discrepancy appeared because there were burials in which more than one individual was interred. In this study, a very simple, purely conventional distinction was made between burial and grave. A burial is the place where one or more individuals have been laid to rest, while a grave corresponds to one individual only. Thus, a burial can contain several graves.

The burials came from 139 sites spread across modern Romania, Bulgaria, and Serbia (Annex A.1).[15] The number of sites is so high because many of them contained just a single isolated grave. However, in a few cases, large cemeteries were identified. An important necropolis was discovered at the sites of Karaburma and Rospi Ćuprija, two neighbouring quarters of present-day Belgrade. At Karaburma, a total of 96 Iron Age graves were uncovered, but only 33 of them were dated in the time interval of interest for this study (Todorović 1972). Immediately next to Karaburma, another series of Late Bronze Age and Iron Age burials were identified at Rospi Ćuprija (Todorović 1963a, b, 1967).[16] Eight of the graves discovered there had the right chronological parameters to be included in the current study.

The cemetery that gave the largest numbers of graves for this study came from the relatively recent site of Hundeoara–Grădina Castelului (Sîrbu et al. 2007a; b). Located on a plateau in South-West Transylvania, next to a contemporary settlement and just in front of a large medieval castle, the site was dated in its entirety to the La Tène C2-D. It produced a total of 53, generally well-recorded, graves for this study. The deceased, most of whom were very small children, were inhumed or cremated.

A considerable number of graves came also from the sites of Orlea—23 graves (Comşa 1972), Brad—19 graves (Ursachi 1995), and Popeşti—11 graves (Popescu and Vulpe 1982; 1976; Vulpe and Gheorghiţă 1979; Vulpe 1955, 1959). The rest of the sites gave less than 10 graves each for the study. Fifteen of them produced only two graves and 95 had only one such find.

2.3 Data Organization

2.3.1 Data Issues

A major problem was faced in the making of this study: the poor quality of the data. A large part of the burials employed had a very low quality of recording, both in terms of funerary ritual details, such as burial shape, depth, exact localization, etc., and their grave-goods. Often part of the burial inventory was not recorded or only briefly mentioned. This was especially the case with ceramic vessels. In many instances, there was just the mention that ceramic vessels were present in the graves, without any description, picture, or even quantity. This grave-good bias did not occur with other items such as weapons, which were reasonably well-recorded in what were probably most cases. This contrast between weapons and vessel

[15] The large majority of the graves (58.8%) were uncovered in Romania, followed by Bulgaria (22.5%) and Serbia (18.7%).

[16] Karaburma and Rospi Ćuprija represent undoubtedly the same archaeological site. The distinction comes from the two different names attributed to these quarters of Belgrade.

recording can be easily guessed by running a simple frequency analysis: 47.3% of all graves contained weapons, while only 41.4% were recorded as containing vessels. Such a ratio between weapons and ceramic vessels is extremely unlikely to reflect actual field finds since ceramic vessels generally represent some of the most common objects found during excavations.

The structure of the database employed in this study, as well as the method of analysis, was designed to minimize this bias. By devising a hierarchical approach to grave-good recording and by shifting emphasis to specific grave elements, it was possible to extract the maximum amount of information from such low-resolution data and produce results that pass validation tests. Moreover, the presence of recording biases was taken into account when producing the interpretation of the results.

However, it was also necessary to abandon the use of data that initially were desirable for the analysis. Details regarding proximity to settlements or water sources, which were employed on a smaller sample (Popa 2012, 2014), could not be utilized when all graves were analysed together, since such information was missing in too many cases and could seriously distort the analysis. Other information relating to the funerary ritual, such as grave shape, depth, or the presence of animal offerings, was also put to one side since the recording of these elements was very sporadic. The same stood true for the age and sex of the deceased.[17] A series of similar problems were encountered when dealing with the inventory of these burials. Initially, it was planned to include a long list of details regarding object positioning, integrity, exposure to fire, object treatment, or decoration. Unfortunately, none of the above could be employed in the end for the analysis as these characteristics could not be determined in many cases because of poor records.

2.3.2 Data Structure

All details of each burial, including those that did not end up in the final analysis, were recorded in a specially designed database, prepared in Microsoft Access 2010. This involved creating numerous interrelated tables, forms, queries, and reports in order to allow for easy data storage, data viewing as well as data export. While in many cases it was possible to obtain the desired structure by employing Microsoft Access' standard options, sometimes it was necessary to implement SQL code, especially in the case of the forms and queries. Microsoft SQL or PostgreSQL would have been a more robust and flexible software solution, albeit far less user-friendly. However, I felt that, for the data at hand, Microsoft Access was able to account for most of the options that I required.

In order to allow for easy filtering of the information, individual details were stored in separate variables or fields. This means that the data were divided in sepa-

---

[17] Sex and age were, however, deliberately not included in the initial analysis for reasons discussed in the following chapter.

Level Number	Table Name			
LEVEL 1	burials			
LEVEL 2	inhumations	cremations	cenotaphs	unknowns
LEVEL 3	inventory			

Fig. 2.1 List of main tables arranged by level

rate table columns, or even in separate tables, each of which recorded a particular type of information, for example, grave depth. Such a division gave the possibility to compare individual grave elements between them, to identify whether they formed specific patterns of variation, and to observe whether their variation was related to that of other grave components.

Since the data were stored in several tables, it was necessary to relate them to one another according to a specific variable that each pair of related tables had in common. This represented a number that was assigned conventionally to each burial and grave,[18] generally called the primary key. The presence of primary keys permitted one to know from which exact burial and grave each piece of information was derived.

The data were stored in six main tables which related to each other in a hierarchal manner, arranged in three levels, reflecting the order in which the data were entered and the data type (Fig. 2.1). The burials table was situated on the first hierarchical level, in which general details relating to the burial were stored, such as location, whether it was flat or tumulus, etc. Four tables sat on the second level in which details relating to the treatment of the body were entered as well as more precise grave information. The distinction between these tables was made according to the way the body was treated, when a body was present at all. Hence, the four tables on level two corresponded to: inhumation, cremation, cenotaph, and unknown.[19] This division was necessary since different details were recorded depending on how the body was treated. For example, for an inhumation one would enter the position of the skeleton, whether it was intact or whether the bones were found in anatomic position, while in the case of a cremation it was necessary to note whether the pyre was identified and whether the bones had been left on the pyre or deposited in a separate spot. For cenotaphs or unknown grave types, no such information existed. After entering the information relating to the treatment of the body, the grave-good details were inserted in one large inventory table situated on the third hierarchical level. In this table, details about each individual grave-good from each grave were recorded.

[18] Burials and graves had different numbers due to the distinction that was made between them.

[19] All the graves where, due to poor data recording, there was uncertainty regarding the treatment of the body, went in the unknown table. However, for the analysis, the likely treatment was assumed, based on physical proximity and similarity to other graves.

The data tables from different hierarchical levels were related to each other through one-to-many relationships.[20] This means that each entry from the burials table situated on level one corresponded to one or more entries from the four tables situated on level two and each of these correspond to one or more entries from the inventory table which was on level three. For instance, one of the tumulus burials from Brad contained a cremation grave as well as two inhumation graves, each of which contained one or more grave-goods. The general details regarding the burial positioning were recorded in the burial table on level one. This entry was related to three other entries on level two, one from the cremations table and two from the inhumations table, containing details about the treatment of the body and more detailed grave information. Finally, each of the three graves was related to the objects found in them and which were separately entered in the inventory table situated on level three.

Besides the six data storage tables, there were a series of auxiliary tables that were used in order to standardize the content of some variables and avoid the occurrence of errors. This means that for some variables only predefined values could be entered, which were fixed by auxiliary tables containing all the possible values that the target variables could take. Such an artifice was employed for fields that stored location information, but also for those that kept the sex and age of the deceased. This method proved especially useful when it came to recording the functional and typological parameters of the grave-good objects (see Sect. 2.4 of this chapter).

2.3.3 *Tables Description*

All the data were stored in Microsoft Access tables. However, these tables were only accessed—for input, modification, and browsing—through specially programmed forms that allowed for a good control over the inputted information. Each data table had its own form[21] and they were connected to one another in a similar fashion to their tables. The operator shifted from the burials form to one of the grave forms and then to the inventory form by using a series of buttons programmed in each of them.[22] The choices made in the higher level forms were used to filter the options in the lower level ones. Hence, browsing through already existent data, the operator

[20] The necessity to implement such relationships was what forced the development of this three-tiered recording system, since otherwise it would not have been possible to express such relationships between the different entries of one table.

[21] Thus there was a burials form, an inhumations form, a cremations form, a cenotaph form, an unknown ritual form and of course an inventory form.

[22] The level two and three forms could only be accessed through the forms situated at one level higher. It was not possible to access the grave forms without having accessed the burials form before and having selected which exact burial one is working on. This allowed for a good control over data structure and integrity.

could only view in the inventory form the items from the grave selected in one of the grave forms and which corresponded to the burial chosen in the burial form.

The burials table was the first one to receive information when a new entry was made and contained 18 variables. The first of these was the *burial number*,[23] which is a number that was given to each burial to function as a primary key for the table. This number could not be entered by the user during the data entry process. Instead, it was automatically completed through a code that was programmed into the form and assigned to run every time a new entry was made. This avoided the human error factor in completing this crucial table field.[24]

The first three variables that were completed when making a new entry in the burials table served to fix the relative geographical position of the burial: *country*, *region*, and *location* (site name or nearest locality). The values for the country and region variables were linked to an auxiliary table containing all the possible options available for the spatial extent of the study.

The next variable to be completed was *grave type*. In this case, there were three possible options: flat, tumulus, or construction. If the grave type was tumulus, two more variables were completed when possible: *tumulus diameter* and *tumulus height*. The option construction was only introduced because in the case of three burials of the total sample, an obvious stone or wood structure was found to cover them.[25] While it could be that some form of construction covered other burials as well, they were not signalled by the teams conducting the excavations.[26]

After *grave type*, the *ritual type* was entered. The available options were: inhumation, cremation, cenotaph, unknown, and multiple. The first four values of this variable are self-explanatory; the fifth value, multiple, refers to the situations where within the same burial there were two or more individuals who received different ritual treatment.

Next, there were two yes/no options. The first one was the variable *multiple burials*. If this variable received the value yes, it meant that at least two different graves, with the same or different ritual types, were present within the same burial.[27] If it took the value no, then only one individual was deposited in that burial. The second yes/no variable was *generic entry*. If this value was selected, it meant that the entry was based on very loose information and many of its details were approximated.

---

[23] To allow the names of variables to be easily identified they are *italicized* in the text. For a similar reason, the fixed values taken by variables are underlined but only when directly referred to.

[24] This is the variable through which the entries made in this table connected to the ones from level two. Thus, any error in completing it resulted in a major mixing of information.

[25] These are the two graves from Cetăţeni (Măndescu 2006) and the one signalled at Sprâncenata (Preda 1986).

[26] Nonetheless since only three burials were entered with *grave type* construction this particular value had a minimal impact on the analysis results.

[27] The information of the *multiple* variable is different from the multiple option of *ritual type*. The former records whether two or more graves appeared in the same burial, like two inhumations, or an inhumation and a cremation, while the latter only stores the cases when a burial contained at least two graves in which the body was differently treated, such as an inhumation and a cremation.

This situation only occurred in nine cases[28] and was considered necessary since otherwise information that could prove useful would have been left entirely out of the analysis.

The following two variables related again to the relative position of the burials. The first one, *river proximity,* was used to give an appreciation of how close the findspot was from a major water presence—not necessarily a river, although usually it referred to one. The available options were banks, near, far, unknown. The second variable was called *settlement proximity* and positioned the grave in relation to a contemporary settlement. The choices were: inside, near, far, unknown. The extreme relativity of the two variables, despite having developed clear principles as to when each value was assigned, made them unusable for the actual analysis of the entire sample, although they were included later in the interpretation process.

The recording of the more or less exact geographical position was attempted using the following three variables: *latitude*, *longitude,* and *height*. The coordinates referred to the findspot or to the locality that gave the name to the site and not to the actual coordinates of each individual burial.[29] For this reason, the latitude and longitude were recorded using only three decimals since adding more would not have actually given a better localization. The height was recorded only loosely, without any decimals, using freely available satellite imagery. The purpose of these variables was to allow for large-scale spatial analysis using ArcGIS.

The following variable was called *observations* and contained, as the name suggests, any further notes on the burial that may be important and could not be included in one of the already mentioned variables. This was followed by *bibliography*, where the references related to that specific burial were placed. Finally, there was also a *burial image* variable which gave the possibility to insert any pictures, drawings, or plans of the burial available from publications.

After completing the burials table, another set of data was entered in one of the tables from level two. According to the value of the *ritual type* variable, from level one, a different table was completed on level two, although part of the variables they contained were the same. In the inhumation table, there was firstly an *inhumation number* variable which was used to relate it to the grave inventory table.[30] Afterwards, the *intact* variable recorded whether the skeleton was found intact,

[28] The graves came from the following localities: Liubichevats (Bilievina) (Theodossiev 2000, p. 127), Mala Vrabitsa (Konopishte) (Popović 1992a; Theodossiev 2000, p. 128), Sofronievo (Nikolov 1972; Theodossiev 2000, p. 136), Vajuga (Popović 1987, pp. 154–155, 1992a, b; Theodossiev 2000, p. 142), Zhivovtsi (Theodossiev 2000, p. 148), Gruia (Pârvan 1928, pp. 38–40; Nicolăescu-Plopşor 1945), Padea (Bondoc 2008) and two from Spahii (Gherghe 1978, 1983, 2008).

[29] Hence if two or more burials originated from the same site they received the same coordinates.

[30] The variable *inhumation number*, just like *burial number*, but also *cremation number*, *cenotaph number* and *unknown grave number*, were not manually entered. It took its values automatically through a code programmed within the forms associated with the tables of each variable. The automatic numbering of Microsoft Access was not chosen due to discrepancies in numbering that appeared if an entry was deleted.

having the options yes/no/unknown. In the *bone connection,* the articulation of the body was recorded as: anatomic position, partially anatomic position, non-anatomic position, not stated. Following this was the skeleton *position* and *orientation,* which were filled out in a manner that best described the state of the human remains.[31] If the *ritual* type variable of level one was completed with cremation, then it was required to enter values in the cremations table on level two. This table incorporated, besides the *cremation number* variable, a *location of ashes* and *location of incineration* variable, in which values relevant to the variable names were entered. Then the *pyre identification* variable was completed with the values yes/no/unknown. Finally, the tables for cenotaphs and unknown grave type had only the *cenotaph number* and *unknown grave number* as unique variables to them. There were additionally a number of variables which occurred in all four tables of level two. The first of these was *grave shape*, having the options rectangular, circular, oval, irregular, and not stated. Next, there was *grave dimension*, where the approximate metric measurement of the grave could be entered and an *offerings* field, where any food offerings discovered in the grave, had to be included, including animal bones. This was followed by three variables that fixed the chronology. The first one was a simple text *chronology* variable where rough, absolute time intervals were entered.[32] It was complemented by *chronology start* and *chronology end* in which exact numerical values were put in, corresponding to the limits of the time period.[33] There was also a yes/no *inventory* field, an *observation* variable in which any further information deemed as important was added and a/an *inhumation/cremation/cenotaph/unknown grave image* variable. Finally, there was the *burial number* variable which recorded the same value as the primary key variable *burial number* from the corresponding burials table entry on level one. Besides all the above, the inhumation and cremation had three extra variables. Two of them had to do with the age of the deceased: *exact age* and *age*. The first one could be completed in reference to the age in years at the time of death (e.g., 20–30 years, 40 years etc.), while for the second one the options referred to the anthropological age class newborn, child, adolescent, adult, elder, and unknown.[34] The third vari-

[31] If a list of values was not given then the variable could take whatever value—this includes text—best described the archaeological finds. However, when giving details about the skeleton, the general terminology employed was that proposed by Sprague (2005).This lack of exact data input control was accepted in these cases because of the large number of values that the variables could take. In addition, such variables were never planned to be included in the actual analysis, but were only consulted during the interpretation process.

[32] For example first century BC to first century AD.

[33] So if the rough date was first century BC to first century AD then *chronology start* would be −100 and *chronology end* 100. These exact values were useful for carrying out basic chronological calculations.

[34] Standard anthropological distinction were made between these values (Herrmann et al. 1990, p. 52) with small alterations. Newborn refers to neonate, although the age was extended to the interval 0–1 years instead of the standard 0–0.5 years since the data recording often did not allow for a better differentiation. Also, the infans 1 and infans 2 categories were compressed in the child option for the same reason.

able recorded the sex of the deceased using the options: male, possibly male, female, possibly female, and unknown.[35]

The last table to be completed was that of the inventory on level three. For each grave-good, regardless of the *ritual type*, a separate entry was made. The entries were ordered according to *inventory number*, which got its values automatically through a code embedded in the entry form. There was also a/an *inhumation/cremation/cenotaph/unknown grave number*, which was used to relate each particular grave-good to its corresponding grave from one of the four tables of level two. Following this, there were four variables which fixed the function and approximate typology of the object. They were ordered hierarchically and had the conventional names *category 1*, *category 2*, *category 3*, and *category 4*; their values were fixed by a large auxiliary table and are discussed in detail in the following subsection of this chapter. Then the *number of objects* was entered; this generally took the value 1, except for special cases.[36] It was followed by *location of object*, where the relative location of the object was inserted. The *material* or material combination of the object was also entered. The values were fixed by an auxiliary table which consisted of a long list that included different kinds of metals, but also clay, glass, bone, amber, etc. The state of the object was given in the *intact* variable as yes/no/unknown and any secondary signs of burning were stored through the values of the *burned* variable—which could be completed with yes, no, or unknown. Similar values could be given to the *decoration* variable. The next variable, named *folded*, recorded whether the grave-good was folded or not, although this usually applied only to weapons[37]; the available options were yes, no, unknown, and not applicable. Finally, there were three variables used basically to describe the grave-good: *object description*, *object dimensions*, and *observations*. Additionally, there was an *object image* variable which was used to store the drawings and pictures of the item.

[35] Due to the small number of graves containing sex information, for the final interpretation the option of possibly male was often equated with male and that of possibly female with female.

[36] Generally each object received a separate entry. However, when the number of objects was unknown the value −1 was entered. This was often the case when the site reports mentioned that a number of sherds where identified, without stipulating exactly how many vessels they came from. Another case when objects were grouped together in one entry was when it was obvious that they formed together one single item. This happened for example when several beads where found in a grave; they were grouped in one entry describing a bead necklace, unless there were indications otherwise.

[37] This variable was introduced because it was observed that an important amount of the weapons appearing in the graves of the Eastern Carpathian basin and the Lower Danube during the Late La Tène were folded before being deposited. Recording this information in a separate variable gave the possibility to identify any patterns which incorporated this practice.

2.3.4 *Queries and Reports*

In order to visualize the data better, given that they were spread out in six different tables, combined Microsoft Access queries and reports needed to be utilized. Reports were especially useful in this respect as they allowed for the visualization of the images attached. Hence, with the help of reports and by applying filters, it was possible to view, in one report, all the items that corresponded to criteria that were of interest: for instance, one could view all the weapons, or specific kind of weapons, such as swords, which were found in the cremation graves of Serbia.

Queries became especially useful when it was time to prepare the data for export. Since the main analysis was conducted in R and SPSS (see Chap. 3), it was necessary to combine all the tables into a single large one which would permit for the entire data to be exported in an easy manner. Through a query, all the relevant data, 33 variables in total, were combined. In this resulting table, each entry (each row) corresponded to an inventory item. However, all the important information from the burial and grave tables was kept as well and was repeated for each grave-good.[38] Also, in the newly created export table, a new numbering system was inserted based on the grave itself and not on the burial. This is because the level of the analysis was fixed at grave level (level two)—since these contained only one individual—and not at the burial level (level one).

2.4 Object Categorization

The main variables which described inventory items were *category1*, *category 2*, *category 3*, and *category 4*. These functioned on a hierarchical basis, going from very general at level one, to very particular at level four. This model for organizing data is similar to the one developed in parallel by Nakoinz (2012) for recording chronological information and which has been shown to have many advantages. In the case of this study, however, there was a further hierarchy established between function and type. The first two variables referred to the function[39] of an item, whereas the following two referred to its shape as determined by the typological classification.

[38] Therefore if a grave had five objects placed as grave-goods, then the data from the burial and grave tables would appear five times. However, if the grave did not have any inventory, all the burial and grave data would still be included in the final table, but it would only appear once.

[39] This represented the function that the object had before it was deposited in the burial. However, in establishing the function one had to take into account the assemblage that was suggested by the burial goods with which it was deposited, as well as other funerary practice elements.

2.4.1 Theoretical Principles

Function was given primacy over shape because of the question of interest in this study, that of identity, and because of the theory of identity that is employed (see Chap. 3). Identity is born out of practice and is constructed through our engagement with the physical reality that surrounds us (Jones 1999, p. 226). In a very simplistic manner, similar identities will be signalled by similar practices given that identity is based on the same other principle.[40] Therefore, it was necessary to postulate the similarity of the practices of past people based on the material remains uncovered. Focussing on function rather than shape allowed for an easier consideration of the practices that an object, and thus also the people that used it, was involved in. For example, characterizing an object as a drinking vessel gives more insight in this regard than describing it as a cup with flared out lip and raised handle.

Another point that needs considering is that similar practices do not require typologically similar items, just objects that can fulfil broadly a similar function, at least in that particular context. People can enact the same practices with a different array of items and the similarity between the two practices will be recognized by its participants as long as there are enough elements in common. Hence, for people to share a common identity, it is not necessary for them to be involved in perfectly similar practices,[41] but rather to participate in practices that they acknowledge as being the same. Of course, this does not mean that anyone involved in practices that are at least somewhat alike will share a full spectrum of similar identity. Two ironsmiths may recognize each other as being the same since they practice a similar craft using probably mostly similar items; but there are many more elements involved, such as details about how some of the items are used, in which order and at which particular moment, etc. However, given the poor resolution of the data available for this study, such nuances were very hard to grasp, if at all.[42]

Practices, thus, incorporate a fluid set or assemblage of items; considering function before shape makes it easier for these assemblages to be identified. Since such sets are constructed around the idea of how a practice is conducted—e.g., the proper way of drinking wine (cf. Egri 2008)—looking at function gives the possibility to identify whether assemblages of objects that present typological differences relate to similar practices. Assemblages have their own internal structure (Robb 2004), which characterize their general functional parameters in a given context; by focussing on these relatively constant aspects, rather than on fluid item shapes, these recurring sets are pinpointed. This procedure ultimately results in the identification of similar practices.[43]

---

[40] This is undoubtedly an oversimplification of how identity functions, but in the case of low resolution archaeological data such artifices need to be employed (see Chap. 3 for a full argument).

[41] Similar practices from the point of view of a distant observer, such as an archaeologist.

[42] Such level of identity finesse is in general extremely difficult to access using the archaeological record alone.

[43] It can often happen that we might not be able to fully understand what exactly those practices were. Nonetheless, for the question posed in this study such identification is not obligatory.

Nonetheless, shape was also incorporated in the recording process through the four category variables, though it was placed hierarchically on a lower level than function. The object types, together with their more particular variations, complement the functional parameters to signal the full spectrum of shape variation that pertains to those parameters. Variations of this kind play a crucial role in determining nuances relating to certain practices. If such nuances are observed to correlate with other factors, like geographical occurrence, then they may imply a localized way of carrying out certain practices, thus suggesting strongly rooted localized identities. Alternatively, some object types may prove to be very constant, appearing repeatedly in the same functional combination regardless of their localization. In this case, the presence of those particular items may have been pivotal for specific practices. On the whole, considering shape in such a manner avoids the trap of directly linking material culture shape to identity, but at the same time recognizes the role it plays in sculpting it, since determining patterns of shape variation is vital for tearing through complex multi-layered identities.

2.4.2 Construction of Categories

The values of the four main variables used to describe grave-goods were built up as the data was explored and entered into the database, not fixed *a priori*. The process started with the conception of a very rough sketch of the variable values based on a small data sample analysed in a previous study (Popa 2010). Starting from that, with each burial and each item included in the database, these initial values were added to and/or modified. This continued until the last entry was made. The values were thus constructed organically and evolved as the database grew. The scope of this method was to obtain a good characterization of the variety of object types, one which fitted the material in the best possible manner given the research question. Hence, the values obtained are not valid as a large-scale archaeological material characterization; they are intricately linked to their context—the particular funerary context, but also the general geographical and chronological limits. These values only make sense for the data that they have been developed as they are symbiotic to that data. The method represents thus a hermeneutic circle (Gadamer 1989, pp. 266–267)[44] since the variable values were continually added to or replaced as the data were explored and understood.

The method used to develop the four variables functioned also as a validation technique according to hermeneutic reasoning (Gadamer 1989, p. 268). After completing the entire database and running the analysis, the results were evaluated. If the results provided no discernable pattern or one that was extremely unexpected, it was due to an error introduced in the process of categorizing the data, including the grave-goods, or one that appeared in the weight parameters of the analysis (see

[44] This concept comes out of the work of Heidegger (1962) and was elaborated upon in anthropology by Geertz (1975).

Category 1	weapon					
Category 2	offensive					defensive
Category 3	sword		battle knife	spear	arrowhead	
Category 4	type 1	type 2				

Fig. 2.2 Example of pyramidal structure for weapon

Chap. 3). Both of these could be caused by a gap between the way in which Iron Age people perceived and incorporated the segment of reality used for this analysis into their cultural milieu and the way in which it was recorded and dealt with through the database and analysis parameters. Fine-tuning these parameters, so that the two views corresponded more closely, led to clearer results which, through interpretation, gave a plausible account of the past.[45]

2.4.3 *Variables Description: General Information*

The four variables, *category 1*, *category 2*, *category 3,* and *category 4*, were designed to work with one another. They took their values from an auxiliary table in which their values were arranged hierarchically; combined with a code implemented in the inventory entry form, it fixed the exact values that each variable could take, filtering out the choices for the lower level variables as the higher level values were selected. In other words, for each value taken by *category 1*, there were only a fixed number of choices available for level *category 2*. The same relationship existed between *category 2* and *category 3* as well as between *category 3* and *category 4*. The total number of choices increased as one moved down the hierarchical ladder, giving a pyramidal structure for the combined values of the four variables.

One of the primary concerns in developing this four-tiered variable system was for it to work with the low-resolution data available for this study. The variables were designed to permit the extraction of a maximum amount of information from the cases where details were entirely lacking.[46] Each of the four variables presented an increasing level of detail. Thus, a minimal level of information allowed for the completion of *category 1*; as more detail was provided, more variable values could be entered. To complete the value of *category 4,* the exact shape of the item needed to be known (Fig. 2.2). This was usually possible only if a drawing or picture was available and preferably also a good description of the item. This method gave the

[45] Of course numerous other validation techniques were deployed, such as checking for the statistical validity of the results (see Chap. 3). However, despite all the verification, unless someone develops an improved version of Asimov's chronoscope (1990), the veridical quality of any interpretation can never be proven irrefutably.

[46] The lack of information refers here to the absence of grave-good descriptions and drawings or pictures from the original publication of the studied sites.

possibility to employ a large body of data with extremely bad publication and recording which otherwise would have had to be discarded.

2.4.4 Variables Description: Functional Categories

Category 1 referred to very general functions that the grave-goods may have been involved in. The possible values for it were: adornment or clothing accessory, coin, horse gear, tool, vessel or vessel implement, weapon, other and unidentified object. The last two entries referred to values that were not used in the analysis: any object that was unrecognizable was inserted as an unidentified object; any object that was identifiable but had an unknown function or a singular appearance was put as other.[47]

All objects that related directly to the human body were placed under adornment or clothing accessory. This means that, although not suggested by the name, toiletry objects were also included here. Consequently, the choices for *category 2* were in this case toiletry and costume. The toiletry option corresponded to all objects that were meant to have a direct effect on the body, but were not actually placed on it—for example mirrors—while the costume option referred to items that were placed directly on the body for aesthetic or practical reasons (or both)—for instance belts.

The coin option is self-explanatory. No functional sub-division was identified in any case; thus, the only possible value for *category 2* was also coin.

Horse gear corresponded to all objects that were involved in horse riding, placed either on the horse or on the rider—e.g., horse bit for the former and spurs for the latter. For *category 2,* a division was made between the items that had a purely practical riding function and those that incorporated a parade dimension—such as a gilded harness.

The tool option corresponded to the items that respected the broadest definition of this term—facilitate manual or mechanical labour—and were not included in other categories. Given the wide range of possibilities, there were six options for *category 2* whose names describe what they stand for: agriculture, cutting, metalworking, perforating, sharpening, and weaving.

Vessel or vessel implement included pottery, metal vessels, and all other objects that were normally associated with them—for instance *simpula*. They were divided on level two in drinking, eating and cooking, lighting, and finally storage. In this case, it was often quite difficult to settle on the function fulfilled by some vessels. Part of the problem was solved by creating the hybrid category eating and cooking, although many issues still remained. Undoubtedly, some vessels could have been used to perform various tasks. In some instances, by examining the item, it was pos-

[47] Given the type of analysis employed (see Chap. 3), it was opted to put as other very particular objects, those that did not present even remote similarities with anything in the database. This is because they made no contribution to the final outcome but instead added noise during the statistical analyses, making it harder to interpret the results. The decision was taken only after having run the analysis several times with the unique objects in their separate categories and observing the effects.

sible to tell how the object was actually utilized—for instance, a tumbler could serve for drinking and also for lighting; however, if employed for lighting, traces of secondary burning should often be visible, thus giving a good indicator for differentiation. In other cases, differentiation was much more difficult. Categorical values were assigned then based on the common associations that the object was regularly found in and which probably indicated its "normal" use (sensu Robb 2004).

The final option for *category 1* was weapon. In this category, all objects that functioned as weapons or that were incorporated in weapon costumes were put together. The possible values for *category 2* were: costume, defensive, offensive, and hunting. The costume option was introduced in order to place sword chains, as these appeared in several instances. These items were not placed in the costume category of adornment or clothing accessory because they were clearly related to the weapon panoply; the presence of sword chains did not make sense outside of their relation with weapons. The defensive option was reserved for items whose main function was to protect their user from an aggressor—for instance a shield—and offensive was employed for objects that served to harm a possible adversary—such as a sword. Finally, the hunting option was introduced to explain the rare appearance of arrowheads in otherwise weapon-less graves.[48]

2.4.5 Variables Description: Typological Categories[49]

category 3 and *category 4* are variables developed to describe the shape variation observed in grave inventories. The first variable referred to generic shapes—such as necklace, horse bit, pitcher, or sword—while the second one fixed further differentiation, where possible, by differentiating between types—e.g., sword type 1, sword type 2—based on a series of characteristics.

Fixing the values for *category 3* was generally not very problematic, since distinctions could usually be made in a relatively straightforward manner. For instance, the possible values for costume adornments or clothing accessories were: belt, bracelet, bead necklace, earring, fibula, lunar necklace, and ring. Of course, in some cases, it was slightly more difficult to make such distinctions. In those situations, guiding rules, relating to some particular shape elements, were fixed based on the whole body of data, although contextual differences were made as well. One such case was establishing whether an object should be recorded as a knife, which went in the category cutting tools, or a battle knife, which corresponded to offensive weapons. It was observed that generally the latter were much larger than the former, especially in terms of their length. This principle worked in most situations, yet uncertainties

[48] Arrowheads could thus also be introduced as an offensive weapon. The difference was made contextually, based on whether or not at least one other type of weapon was present in the grave.

[49] Due to the large number of options available for *category 3* and *category 4*, over 140 (!) for the latter, it has been opted to discuss in the text, with examples, the main principles used to fix the values of the two variables and introduce some of the main issues encountered in their development. Nevertheless, a full list of the values taken by these variables, along with those of *category 1* and *category 2*, can be found in the Annex A.2.

still arose. In those cases, contextual differences were made. It was noticed that in most instances, battle knives were accompanied by at least one other type of offensive or defensive weapon, while for cutting knives this generally did not hold true.[50] Based on this observation, the differentiation between knife and battle knife in the few difficult cases was made through the presence or absence of other weapon types.

For some vessel types, a different artifice was employed. It was noticed that a number of items that were inconsistently referred to in publications using different terms presented a great deal of similarities. The decision was taken to group these into what can be called hybrid categories, such as bowls and porringers, *situlae* and cauldrons, cups and tumblers, or *kantharos*-like vessels. Employing this strategy presented a major advantage: it allowed one to insert a value in *category 3* even in the cases where no proper description and/or image of the item was given.[51] Hence, even if it was not possible to know exactly what an author referred to when he/she mentioned the presence of a bowl in a grave, it was still possible to give a value to *category 3* since the range of objects that could possibly be referred to with that term was covered by bowls and porringers. Of course, in the absence of a picture or drawing, no value would be assigned to *category 4* unless no further differentiation could be made at that level or the exact shape was known.

In other instances, however, despite some objects being identified through particular terms by publication authors, it was decided not to insert any value in *category 3* since the argument for such a categorization was unconvincing. Moreover, considering the other inventory items as well as further grave parameters, it would produce extremely unusual combinations. This was the case of the so-called gold pendant from the flat cremation burial of Kumano (Sladić 1987) (Fig. 2.3). Both the original publication and a later one (Theodossiev 2000, p. 124) identified the object in a similar manner. While this item certainly constituted an adornment incorporated in some kind of costume, it is doubtful whether it was indeed a pendant.[52] This suspicion is supported by the unusual grave-good combination. Together with it were also a battle knife, two spearheads, and three other vessels. A similar combination of grave elements, especially when considering ritual details, is unique in the database; even the weapons-pendant necklace association alone had only three other occurrences, all of which were not flat burials but tumulus ones.[53] This very unusual combination triggered the algorithm employed for the analysis to isolate

[50] In the final database, 92 of the 102 graves that contained a battle knife had also at least one other type of defensive or offensive weapon. As for cutting knives, 15 of the 24 graves that included knives did not have any weapons.

[51] There was a second advantage, that of reducing the variation existing in *category 3*. While this was especially a necessity for *category 4*, as it will be discussed in the following paragraphs, the idea was the same: reducing variation made it easier to identify patterns of similarity.

[52] While it is not questioned that in other contexts it may have been considered a pendant, the context in which it was found did not send to a practice where it was considered in such a manner.

[53] This combination appeared in one of the tumulus graves from Altimir (Nikolov 1965)—although the identification of the pendant in that case is also rather uncertain due to intense burning—, in another one coming from Popeşti (Vulpe 1976)—a rich grave, containing a very large number of grave-goods—and finally a tumulus from Piscu Crăsani (Sîrbu 1994, pp. 125–126; Vulpe 1976, pp. 205–206)— although in this case the weapon was defensive, a bronze trimming that probably came from a helmet.

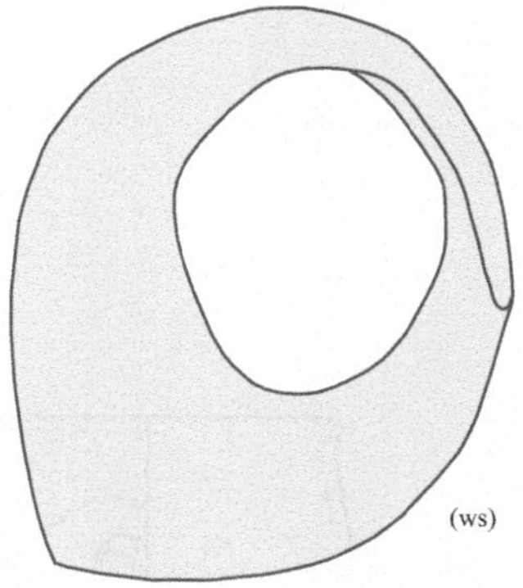

Fig. 2.3 Kumano "pendant" (after Sladić 1987, p. 22, Fig. 7)

this grave. Confronted with such facts, it was decided to complete only *category 1* and *category 2* with adornment or clothing accessory and costume, respectively, leaving empty the typological variables. Taking this course of action incorporated my doubt about the object and solved the problem of the grave's unusualness.

The issues with developing and completing *category 4* were slightly different since it dealt with small object differences. A main idea was to incorporate as much of the observed differences as possible without falling into particularism. The establishment of too many types would make it very difficult to apply the analysis method employed in this study (see Chap. 3) since comparing graves between one another would then produce too little similarity. On the other hand, using too general categories would have the opposite effect, a lack of variation. Therefore, it was necessary to find a balance without forcing the data.

For some objects, previously devised object typologies were employed. This was only possible if the typologies were developed specifically for the Late La Tène of the Eastern Carpathian basin and the Lower Danube, as otherwise it was found that they generally failed to explain the variation observed in the material record.[54] As a result, the only typologies that could be employed directly were those established by Rustoiu for earrings (1996, pp. 102–105) and fibulae (1997), by Torbov for swords (2000) and spurs (1998), and by Werner for horse bits (1988).[55] In several other cases, it was possible to give values to *category 4* based loosely on already established typologies, by making smaller or larger modifications so that they fit

[54] An example of this is Brunaux and Lambot's work (1987) in which the authors construct a typology of some La Tène weapons and weapon implements. While it was initially planned to rely heavily on this volume, in the end the categorization could only be deployed, with adaptation, in the case of shields.

[55] Nonetheless, not the entire spectrum of their typologies was employed since it was found that sometimes the level of variation used was too detailed. This is why, in the case of the fibulae and horse bits, subtypes were not used—such as 2A—but only the large group types.

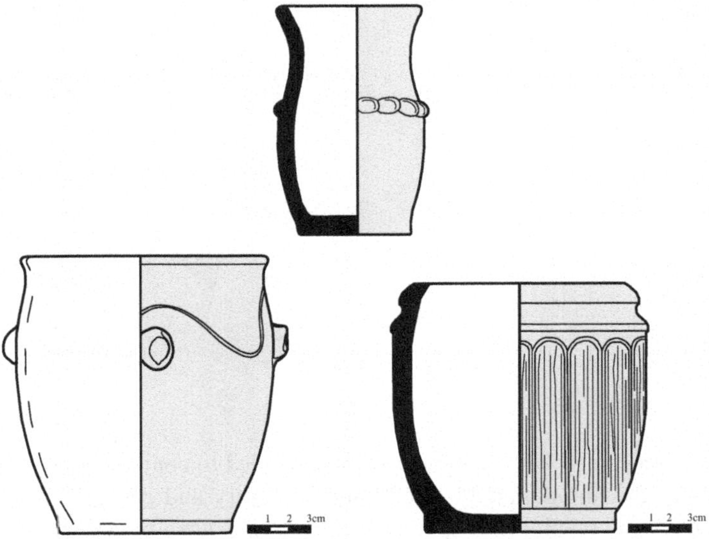

Fig. 2.4 Jar types examples: (1) type 1 from Brad (after Ursachi 1995, p. 590, pl. 363/7); (2) type 2 from Mala Vrabitsa (Aymana) (after Stalio 1986, p. 46, Fig. 36); (3) type 3 from Karaburma (after Todorović 1972, T. XV, grave 39/7)

with the database items. Thus, the typology of bracelets and that of pendant necklaces was based on Rustoiu (1996, pp. 93–102, 121–128), that of belts was based on Babeş (1983), that of helmets on Pflug (1989), and the one for shields on Brunaux and Lambot (1987, pp. 130–131).

A number of objects required the development of a personalized typology based on the grave-goods entered in the database. At times, this was relatively easy to do and did not require the establishment of extremely rigorous parameters, as the differences were simple to spot, making the types easily identifiable—for example this was the case of jars (Fig. 2.4) or scissors (Fig. 2.5). In other instances, this proved to be more difficult, as the exact differences were harder to identify and required a set of differentiation parameters. These generally referred to the presence or absence of various elements and their positioning—for instance, handles or shoulders in the case of vessels[56]—, the shape of particular elements—like a straight neck for vessels, rhombic blade for spears, and concave or convex cutting edge for battle knives—, as well as the proportion between different quantifiable parameters—like that between the height of a vessel and its maximum width. In this manner, it was possible to define *category 4* values for vessels such as jugs (Fig. 2.6) or fruit-bowls (Fig. 2.7), but also weapons like battle knives (Fig. 2.8) or spears (Fig. 2.9).

[56]The term vessels refers to the value vessel or vessel implement of *category 1*. Similar shortened versions of the values taken by variables are employed in several other cases as well.

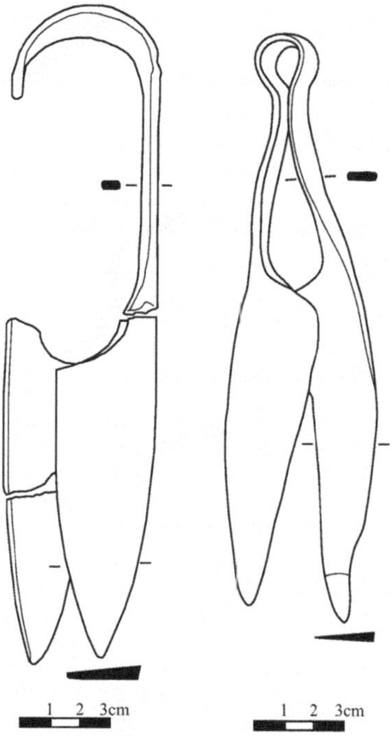

Fig. 2.5 Scissors types examples: (1) type 1 from Karaburma (after Todorović 1972, T. XXVII, grave 92/3); (2) type 2 from Karaburma (after Todorović 1972, T. I, grave 4/4)

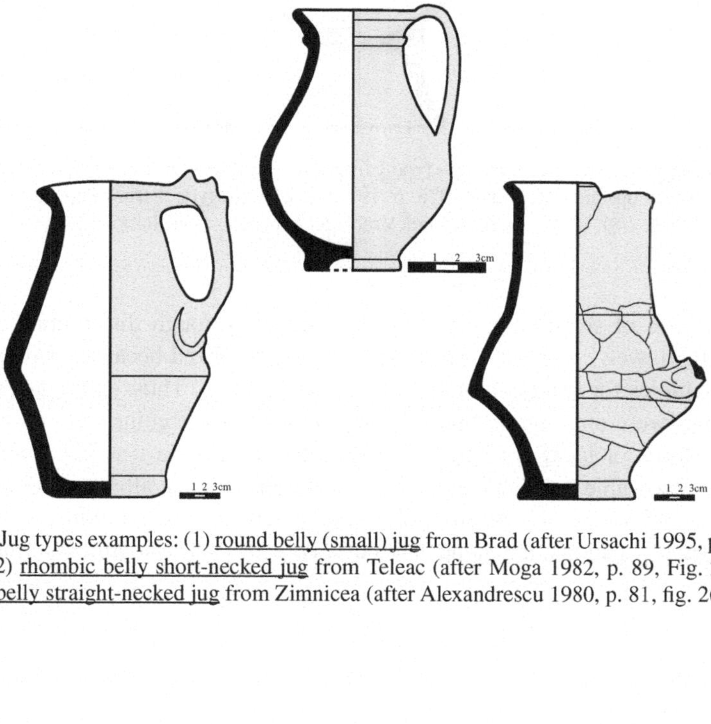

Fig. 2.6 Jug types examples: (1) round belly (small) jug from Brad (after Ursachi 1995, p. 586, pl. 355/5); (2) rhombic belly short-necked jug from Teleac (after Moga 1982, p. 89, Fig. 2/1a); (3) rhombic belly straight-necked jug from Zimnicea (after Alexandrescu 1980, p. 81, fig. 26/2)

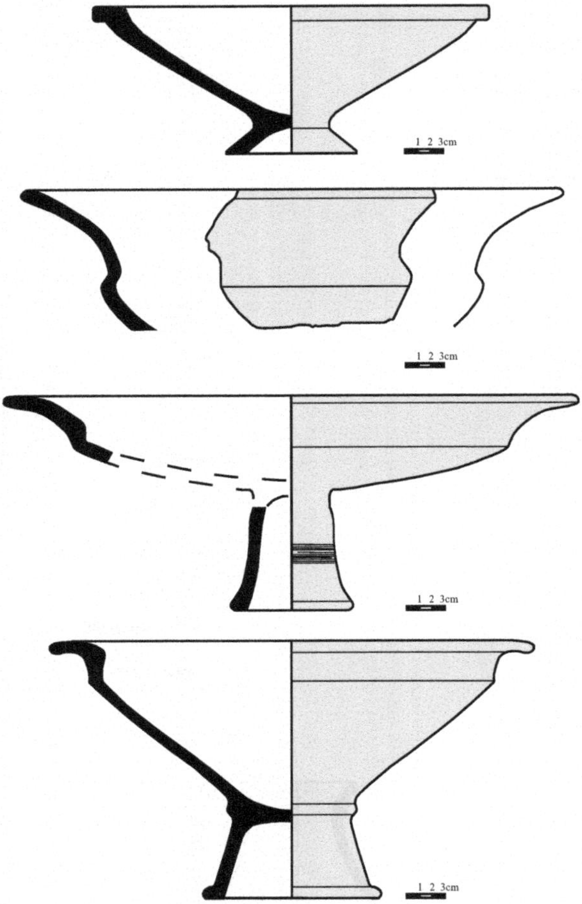

Fig. 2.7 Fruit-bowl types examples: (1) type 1 from Lăceni (after Moscalu 1977, p. 331, fig. 3/2); (2) type 2 from Popeşti (after Vulpe 1976, p. 199 Fig. 7/7); (3) type 3 from Popeşti (after Vulpe 1976, p. 199 Fig. 7/8); (4) type 4 from Mala Vrabitsa (Aymana) (after Stalio 1986, p. 46, fig. 32).

In the case of some *category 3* values, only very rough differentiations were made at the lower, *category 4*, level. This usually occurred because there were not enough samples for making a more intricate partitioning. Thus, eating and cooking implements were only divided into *patera* and fork, while coins were classified as dinar, Histrian, or local emission. Finally, sometimes there was not enough item variation observable to be able to make any differentiation at all at the bottom level, or there were too few object samples or objects with a good recording in the database. In such situations, the value entered in *category 4* was identical to the one in

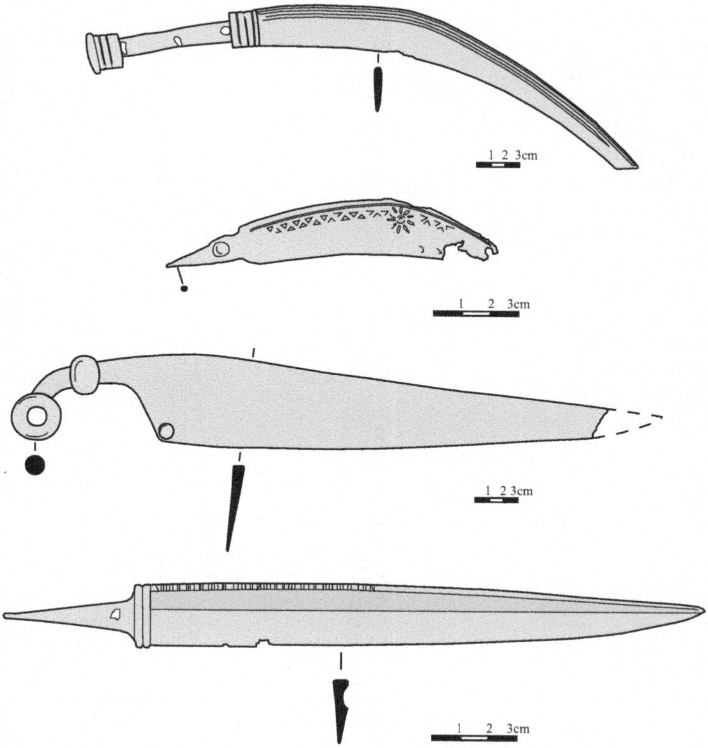

Fig. 2.8 Battle knife types examples: (1) type 1 from Golenţi (after Nicolăescu-Plopşor 1945, pl. IV/7); (2) type 2 from Ajmana (after Stalio 1986, p. 47, fig. 40); (3) type 3 from Ritopek (after Todorović 1973, p. 81, Fig. 7); (4) type 4 from Rospi Ćuprija (after Todorović 1963b, Y52 2(2), Fig. 10)

category 3 so as to signal that there was too little divergence in terms of object shape. This occurred, for instance, with cutting knives or weapon belt chains.

The four category system used to describe the grave-goods, together with all other variables employed to store and characterize the funerary data, is symbiotic with the methodology of this study, which is described in the following chapter. The different variables were designed to permit easy comparison of their values, which allowed for similarities and differences between graves to be easily established. Furthermore, through their definition, most variables were aimed at identifying particular practices rather than material variation, a fundamental element when working with identity-related questions.

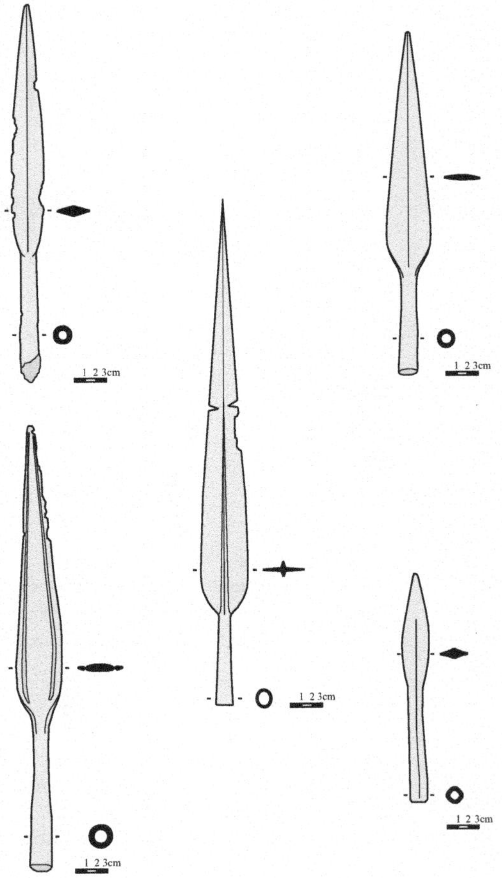

Fig. 2.9 Spear types examples: (1) type 1 from Dubova (after Spânu 2002, p. 85, Fig. 1/2); (2) type 2 from Ritopek (after Todorović 1973, p. 81, Fig. 5); (3) type 3 from Karaburma (after Todorović 1972, T. XXXII, grave 105/3); (4) type 4 from Karaburma (after Todorović 1972, T. XXXVI, grave 137/8); (5) type 5 from Padea (after Bondoc 2008, p. 156, Fig. 6/16)

References

Alexandrescu, D. (1980). La nécropole gete de Zimnicea. *Dacia N.S., 24*, 19–126.

Ariès, P. (2004). The hour of our death. In A. C. G. M. Robben (Ed.), *Death, mourning, and burial: A cross-cultural reader* (pp. 40–48). Oxford: Blackwell.

Asimov, I. (1990). The dead past. In *The complete stories* (Vol. 1, pp. 3–40). London: HarperCollins.

Avram, A., & Babeş, M. (Eds.). (2000). *Civilisation Grecque et cultures antiques périphériques: Hommage à Petre Alexandrescu à son 70e anniversaire*. Bucarest: Editura Enciclopedică.

Babeş, M. (1982). Review of Buridava dacică (Dumitru Berciu). *Studii şi Cercetări de Istorie Veche şi Arheologie, 33*(2), 250–257.

Babeş, M. (1983). Paftalele Latène târzii din sud-estul Europei. *Studii şi Cercetări de Istorie Veche şi Arheologie, 34*(3), 196–221.

Babeş, M. (1988). Descoperiri funerare şi semnificaţia lor în contextul culturii geto-dacice clasice. *Studii şi Cercetări de Istorie Veche şi Arheologie, 39*(1), 3–32.

Barley, N. (1998). *Tanz ums Grab*. Stuttgart: Klett-Cotta.

Becker, E. (2004). The terror of death. In A. C. G. M. Robben (Ed.), *Death, mourning, and burial: A cross-cultural reader* (pp. 23–31). Oxford: Blackwell.

Berciu, D. (1981). *Buridava dacică*. Bucureşti: Academiei.

Binford, L. R. (1971). Mortuary practices: Their study and potential. In J. A. Brown (Ed.), *Approaches to the social dimension of mortuary practices* (pp. 6–29). Washington, DC: Society for American Archaeology.

Boardman, J., Griffin, J., & Murray, O. (Eds.). (2001). *The Oxford illustrated history of the Roman world*. Oxford: Oxford University Press.

Bondoc, D. (2008). Descoperirile de epocă La Tène de la Padea, jud. *Dolj. Studii şi Cercetări de Istorie Veche şi Arheologie, 59–60*, 137–163.

Božić, D. (1981). Relativna Kronologija mlajše železne dobe v Jugoslovanskem Podonavju. *Arheološki vestnik, 32*, 315–347.

Božić, D. (2008). *Late La Tène-Roman cemetery in Novo mesto : Ljubljanska cesta and Okrajno glavarstvo. Studies on fibulae and on the relative chronology of the Late La Tène period*. Ljubljana: Narodni muzej Slovenije.

Brather, S. (2000). Ethnische Identitäten als Konstrukte der frühgeschichtlichen Archäologie. *Germania, 78*, 139–177.

Brather, S. (2002). Ethnic identities as constructions of archaeology: The case of the Alamanni. In A. Gillett (Ed.), *On barbarian identity: Critical approaches to ethnicity in the Early Middle Ages* (pp. 149–176). Turnhout: Brepols.

Brather, S. (2004). Ethnische Interpretationen in der frühgeschichtlichen Archäologie. In *Geschichte, Grundlagen und Alternativen*. Berlin: W. de Gruyte.

Brather, S. (2008). Kleidung, Bestattung, Identität. Die Präsentation sozialer Rollen im frühen Mittelalter. In S. Brather (Ed.), *Zwischen Spätantike und Frühmittelalter. Archäologie des 4. bis 7. Jahrhunderts im Westen* (pp. 237–273). New York: de Gruyter.

Brather-Walter, S., & Brather, S. (2012). Repräsentation oder Religion? Grabbeigaben und Bestattungsrituale im frühen Mittelalter. In N. Krohn & S. Ristow (Eds.), *Wechsel der Religionen - Religion des Wechsels: Tagungsbeiträge der Arbeitsgemeinschaft Spätantike und Frühmittelalter* (pp. 121–143). Hamburg: Kovac.

Brunaux, J.-L., & Lambot, B. (1987). *Guerre et armement chez les Gaulois 450–52 av. J.-C.* Editions Errance: Paris.

Carr, C. (1995). Mortuary practices: Their social, philosophical-religious, circumstantial, and physical determinants. *Journal of Archaeological Method and Theory, 2*, 105–200.

Chesson, M. S. (2001). Social memory, identity, and death: An introduction. In M. S. Chesson (Ed.), *Social memory, identity, and death: Anthropological perspectives on mortuary rituals* (pp. 1–10). Naperville, IL: American Anthropological Association.

Collis, J. (1984). *Oppida: Earliest towns North of the Alps*. Sheffield: Department of Prehistory and Archaeology.

Comşa, E. (1972). Contribuţie la riturile funerare din secolele II-I îen., din sud-estul Olteniei (mormintele de la Orlea). *Apulum, 10*, 65–78.

Crişan, I. H. (1993). *Civilizaţia geto-dacilor*. Bucureşti: Meridiane.

Daicoviciu, H. (Ed.). (1981). Studii dacice. Cluj-Napoca: Dacia.

Derks, T. (2009). Ethnic identity in the Roman frontier. The epigraphy of Batavi and other Lower Rhine tribes. In T. Derks & N. Roymans (Eds.), *Ethnic constructs in antiquity: The role of power and tradition* (pp. 239–282). Amsterdam: Amsterdam University Press.

Egri, M. (2008). *Communal identity and provincial integration in the Lower Danube: An archaeological study of ceramics (late 1st century BC – early 2nd century AD)*. PhD thesis. University of Cambridge, Cambridge.

Emilov, J. (2007a). La Tene finds and the indigenous communities in Thrace. Interrelations during the Hellenistic period. *Studia Hercynia, 11*, 57–75.

Emilov, J. (2007b). Foreign impulses and local responses in Hellenistic Thrace after the Celtic raids. *Jubileus, 6*, 141–153.

Fahlander, F. (2008). A piece of the mesolithic. Horizontal stratigraphy and bodily manipulations at Skateholm. In F. Fahlander & T. Oestigaard (Eds.), *The materiality of death: Bodies, burials, beliefs* (pp. 29–46). Oxford: Archaeopress.

Fichtl, S. (2000). *La ville Celtique: Les oppida de 150 av. J.-C. à 15 ap. J.-C.* Paris: Errance.
Florea, G. (2011). *Dava et oppidum. Débuts de la genèse urbaine en Europe au deuxième âge du Fer*. Cluj-Napoca: Acadèmie Roumaine. Centre d'Études Transylvaines.
Gadamer, H.-G. (1989). *Truth and method*. (J. Weinsheimer & D. G. Marshall, Trans.) (Second, revised edition.). London: Sheed & Ward.
Gansum, T. (2008). Reproduction and relocation of death in Iron Age Scandinavia. In F. Fahlander & T. Oestigaard (Eds.), *The materiality of death: Bodies, burials, beliefs* (pp. 141–146). Oxford: Archaeopress.
Geertz, C. (1975). On the nature of anthropological understanding: Not extraordinary empathy but readily observable symbolic forms enable the anthropologist to grasp the unarticulated concepts that inform the lives and cultures of other peoples. *American Scientist, 63*(1), 47–53. doi:10.2307/27845269.
Gherghe, P. (1978). Cercetările arheologice de salvare efectuate în necropola şi aşezarea geto-dacică de la Turburea-Spahii. *Litua. Studii şi Cercetări, 1*, 15–31.
Gherghe, P. (1983). Cercetări şi descoperiri arheologice cu privire la civilizaţia geto-dacică pe teritoriul judeţului Gorj. *Arhivele Olteniei, 2*, 49–73.
Gherghe, P. (2008). The necropolis and the Geto-Dacian settlement of the Turburea locality, Spahii village, Gorj county. In V. Sîrbu & I. Stângă (Eds.), *The Iron Gates region during the Second Iron Age. Settlements, necropolises, treasures* (pp. 140–149). Drobeta Turnu-Severin; Craiova: Editura Universitaria.
Glodariu, I. (2001). Civilizaţia geto-dacă din a doua jumătate a secolului al II-lea a. Chr. până la începutul secoului al II-lea p. Chr. In M. Petrescu-Dîmboviţa & A. Vulpe (Eds.), *Istoria Românilor. Moştenirea timpurilor îndepărtate* (Vol. 1, pp. 725–797). Bucureşti: Enciclopedică.
Goody, J. (1962). *Death, property and the ancestors: A study of the mortuary customs of the Lodagaa of West Africa*. London: Tavistock.
Graves-Brown, P., & Jones, S. (1996). Introduction. Archaeology and cultural identity in Europe. In P. Graves-Brown, S. Jones, & C. Gamble (Eds.), *Cultural identity and archaeology: The construction of European communities* (pp. 1–24). London: Routledge.
Guštin, M. (1984). Die Kelten in Jugoslawien. *Jahrbuch des Römisch-Germanischen Zentralmuseums Mainz, 31*, 305–363.
Hakenbeck, S. (2004). Ethnic tensions in early medieval cemeteries in Bavaria. *Archaeological Review from Cambridge, 19*(2), 40–55.
Hakenbeck, S. (2007). Situational ethnicity and nested identities: New approaches to an old problem. *Anglo-Saxon Studies in Archaeology and History, 14*, 19–27.
Hakenbeck, S. (2011). Roman or barbarian? Shifting identities in early medieval cemeteries in Bavaria. *Post - Classical Archaeologies, 1*, 37–66.
Hallam, E., & Hockey, J. L. (2001). *Death, memory and material culture*. New York: Berg.
Hasenfratz, H.-P. (1983). Zum sozialen Tod in archaischen Gesellschaften. *Jahrbuch für Universalgeschichte, 34*, 126–137.
Hausmair, B. (2015). *Am Rande des Grabs. Todeskonzepte und Bestattungsritual in der frühmittelalterlichen Alamannia*. Leiden: Sidestone Press.
Heidegger, M. (1962). *Being and time*. (J. MacQuarrie & E. Robinson, Trans.). London: SCM Press.
Hellebrandt, M. (1999). *Celtic finds from Northern Hungary*. Budapest: Akadémiai Kiadó.
Herrmann, B., Grupe, G., & Hummel, S. (1990). Prähistorische Anthropologie: Leitfaden der Feld- und Labormethoden. Bern: Springer.
Hertz, R. (1960). *Death and the right hand*. Aberdeen: Cohen & West.
Hoof, J., & in der Schmitten, J. (1995). Kritik der „Hirntod"-Konzeption. In J. Hoof & J. in der Schmitten (Eds.), *Wann ist der Mensch tot? Organverpflanzung und „Hirntod"-Kriterium* (pp. 153–252). Hamburg: Rowohlt.
Horvath, L., Kelemen, M. H., Uzsoki, A., & Vadász, É. (1987). *Corpus of Celtic finds in Hungary. Vol. I: Transdanubia*. Budapest: Akademiai Kiado.

Jones, S. (1999). Historical categories and the praxis of identity: The interpretation of ethnicity in historical archaeology. In P. P. A. Funari, M. Hall, & S. Jones (Eds.), *Historical archaeology: Back from the edge* (pp. 219–232). London: Routledge.

Jovanović, A. (1985). Dazische Gräberformen in Obermoesien. *Materijali, 20*, 127–140.

Kan, S. (1989). *Symbolic immortality: The Tlingit potlatch of the nineteenth century*. London: Smithsonian Institution Press.

Knüsel, C. J. (2002). More Circe than Cassandra. The princess of Vix in ritualized social context. *European Journal of Archaeology, 5*(3), 275–308.

Kuijt, I. (2008). The regeneration of life: Neolithic structures of symbolic remembering and forgetting. *Current Anthropology, 49*(2), 171–198.

Lucy, S. (2002). Burial practice in early medieval Eastern England: Constructing local identities, deconstructing ethnicity. In S. Lucy & A. J. Reynolds (Eds.), *Burial in early medieval England and Wales* (pp. 72–87). London: The Society for Medieval Archaeology.

Măndescu, D. (2006). *Cetăţeni: Staţiunea geto-dacă de pe valea Dâmboviţei superioare*. Brăila: Editura Istros.

Metzler-Zens, N., Metzler-Zens, J., & Méniel, P. (1999). *Lamadelaine : Une nécropole de l'oppidum du Titelberg*. Luxembourg: Musée National d'Histoire et d'Art.

Mizoguchi, J. (1992). A historiography of a linear barrow cemetery: A structurationist's point of view. *Archaeological Review from Cambridge, 11*(1), 39–50.

Moga, V. (1982). Morminte dacice de incineraţie la Teleac. *Apulum, 20*, 87–91.

Moscalu, E. (1977). Sur les rites funéraires des Getó-Daces de la plaine de Danube. *Dacia N.S., 21*, 329–340.

Nakoinz, O. (2012). Datierungskodierung und chronologische Inferenz – Techniken zum Umgang mit unscharfen chronologischen Informationen. *Praehistorische Zeitschrift, 87*(1), 189–207.

Nicolăescu-Plopşor, C. S. (1945). Antiquités celtiques en Olténie. *Dacia, 11–12*, 17–33.

Nikolov, B. (1965). Thrakische Denkmäler in Bezirk Vraca. *Bulletin of the Institute of Archaeology, 28*, 163–202.

Nikolov, B. (1972). Trakiyski grobni nahodki vav Vrachansko. *Arkheologiia, 14*(3), 53–68.

Nikolov, B. (1981). Sépultures thraces près du village Sofronievo, département de Vraca. *Arheologija, 22*(3), 30–41.

O'Shea, J. (1981). Social configurations and the archaeological study of mortuary practices: A case study. In R. Chapman, I. Kinnes, & K. Randsborg (Eds.), *The archaeology of death* (pp. 39–52). Cambridge: Cambridge University Press.

O'Shea, J. M. (1984). *Mortuary variability: An archaeological investigation*. London: Academic Press.

Olivier, L. (1999). The Hochdorf 'princely' grave and the question of the nature of archaeological funerary assemblages. In T. Murray (Ed.), *Time and archaeology* (pp. 109–138). London: Routledge.

Parker Pearson, M. (1982). Mortuary practices, society and ideology: An ethnoarchaeology study. In J. Hodder (Ed.), *Symbolic and structural archaeology* (pp. 99–114). Cambridge: Cambridge University Press.

Parker Pearson, M. (1993). The powerful dead: Archaeological relationships between the living and the dead. *Cambridge Archaeological Journal, 3*, 203–229.

Parker Pearson, M. (1999a). *The archaeology of death and burial*. Stroud: Sutton.

Parker Pearson, M. (1999b). Food, sex and death: Cosmologies in the British Iron Age with particular reference to East Yorkshire. *Cambridge Archaeological Journal, 9*(1), 43–69.

Pârvan, V. (1928). *Dacia: An outline of the early civilizations of the Carpatho-Danubian countries*. Cambridge: The University Press.

Pflug, H. (1989). *Antike Helme*. Köln: Rheinland-Verlag.

Popa, C. N. (2010). A new framework for approaching Dacian identity. In S. Berecki (Ed.), *Iron Age communities in the Carpathian basin* (pp. 395–423). Cluj-Napoca: Mega.

Popa, C. N. (2012). Till death do us part. A statistical approach to identifying burial similarity and grouping. The case of the Late La Tène graves from the Eastern Carpathian basin. In S. Berecki (Ed.), *Iron Age rites and rituals in the Carpathian basin* (pp. 401–412). Târgu Mureş: Mega.

Popa, C. N. (2014). The quest for group identity in Late Iron Age Romania. Statistical reconstruction of groups based on funerary evidence. In C. N. Popa & S. Stoddart (Eds.), *Fingerprinting the Iron Age* (pp. 108–122). Oxford: Oxbow.

Popescu, E., & Vulpe, A. (1982). Nouvelles découvertes du type Ferigile. *Dacia, 26*, 77–114.

Popović, P. (1987). *Le monnayage des Scordisques; Les monnaies et la circulation monétaire dans le centre des Balkans*. Belgrade: IVe-Ier siècle av.n.è.

Popović, P. (1992a). Italische Bronzegefässe im Skordiskergebiet. *Germania, 70*(1), 61–74.

Popović, P. (1992b). Celtic cemeteries in the Iron Gates area. In N. Tasić (Ed.), *Scordisci and the native population in the Middle Danube region* (p. 58). Belgrade: Balkanološki institut SANU.

Preda, C. (1986). *Geto-dacii din bazinul Oltului inferior: Dava de la Sprincenata*. Bucuresti: Editura Academiei Republicii Socialiste România.

Quinn, D. S. (1995). La nécropole de la Croix du Rebout: premieres perspectives. Bulletin intérieur/Association française pour l'étude de l'âge du fer, *13*, 62–66.

Robb, J. (2004). The extended artefact and the monumental economy: A methodology for material agency. In E. DeMarrais, C. Gosden, & C. Renfrew (Eds.), *Rethinking materiality: The engagement of mind with the material world* (pp. 131–139). Cambridge: McDonald Institute for Archaeological Research.

Robb, J. (2007). Burial treatment as transformations of bodily ideology. In N. Laneri (Ed.), *Performing death: Social analyses of funerary traditions in the ancient Near East and Mediterranean* (pp. 287–298). Chicago: Oriental Institute of the University of Chicago.

Robb, J. (2013). Creating death: An archaeology of dying. In S. Tarlow & L. N. Stutz (Eds.), *The Oxford handbook of the archaeology of death and burial*. Oxford: OUP Oxford.

Rustoiu, A. (1996). *Metalurgia bronzului la daci: (sec. II î. Chr. - sec. I d. Chr.) Tehnici, ateliere şi produse de bronz*. Bucureşti: Institutul Român de Tracologie, Ministerul Învăţământului.

Rustoiu, A. (1997). *Fibulele din Dacia preromană (sec. II î.e.n. - I e.n.)*. Bucureşti: Institutul Român de Tracologie, Ministerul Educaţiei Naţionale.

Rustoiu, A. (2002). *Războinici şi artizani de prestigiu în Dacia preromană*. Cluj-Napoca: Nereamia Napocae.

Schortman, E., & Urban, P. (1998). Culture contact structure and process. In J. G. Cusick (Ed.), *Studies in culture contact: Interaction, culture change, and archaeology* (pp. 102–125). Carbondale: Center for Archaeological Investigations, Southern Illinois University.

Silliman, S. (2005). Culture contact or colonialism? Challenges in the archaeology of native North America. *American Antiquity, 70*(1), 55–74.

Sîrbu, V. (1993). *Credinţe şi practici funerare, religioase şi magice în lumea geto-dacilor (pornind de la descoperirile arheologice din Câmpia Brăilei)*. Galaţi: Porto-Franco.

Sîrbu, V. (1994). Morminte tumulare din zona Carpato-Dunăreană (sec. I î. d. Chr. – I d. Chr.) *Istros, 7*, 123–160.

Sîrbu, V., Luca, S. A., & Roman, C. (2007a). Tombs of Dacian warriors (2nd – 1st C. BC) found in Hunedoara–Grădina Castelului (Hunedoara county). *Acta Terrae Septemcastrensis, 7*(1), 155–177.

Sîrbu, V., Luca, S. A., Roman, C., Purece, S., Diaconescu, D., & Cerişor, N. (2007b). *Vestigiile dacice de la Hunedoara/The Dacian vestiges in Hunedoara*. Sibiu: Muzeul Naţional Brukenthal.

Sladić, M. (1987). A tomb of a warrior from the village of Kumane near Veliko Gradište. *Viminacium, 2*, 19–23.

Spânu, D. (2002). Un mormânt de epocă târzie de la Dubova. *Studii şi Cercetări de Istorie Veche şi Arheologie, 52–53*, 83–132.

Sprague, R. (2005). *Burial terminology: A guide for researchers*. Lanham, MD: AltaMira Press.

Stalio, B. (1986). Le site préhistorique Ajmana à Mala Vrbica. In V. Kondić (Ed.), *Đerdapske sveske* (Vol. 3, pp. 27–50). Beograd.

Stoddart, S. (2015). Mediating the dominion of death in prehistoric Malta. In C. Renfrew, M. J. Boyd, & I. Morley (Eds.), *Death rituals social order and the archaeology of immortality in the ancient world* (pp. 130–137). Cambridge: Cambridge University Press. http://dx.doi.org/10.1017/CBO9781316014509.009.

Theodossiev, N. (2000). *North-Western Thrace from the fifth to first centuries BC*. Oxford: Archaeopress.

Todorović, J. (1963a). *Rospi Ćuprija. Nécropole de l'époque de La Tène à Beograd*. Bonn: R. Havelt Verlag.

Todorović, J. (1963b). Rospi Ćuprija. Nécropole de l'époque La Tène à Beograd. *Inventaria Archaeologica, 6*.

Todorović, J. (1967). Les nécropoles prehistoriques de Rospi Ćuprija à Belgrade. *The Star, 18*, 193–200.

Todorović, J. (1972). *Praistorijska Karaburma I – nekropola mlađeg željeznog doba* (Vol. 1). Beograd.

Todorović, J. (1973). Une tombe double de guerriers scordisques à Ritopek. *Starinar, 24–25*, 79–83.

Torbov, N. (1998). Spurs from the 2nd century BC – 1st century AD found in Northwestern Bulgaria. *Archaeologia Bulgarica, 2*(1), 54–63.

Torbov, N. (2000). Swords from II-I centuries BC found in Northwestern Bulgaria. *Izvestiya na Muzeite v Severozapadna Bulgaria, 28*, 11–34.

Ursachi, V. (1995). *Zargidava: Cetatea dacică de la Brad*. Bucureşti: Caro Trading.

Vulpe, R. (1955). Şantierul arheologic de la Popeşti. *Studii şi Cercetări de Istorie Veche, 6*(1–2), 239–269.

Vulpe, R. (1959). Şantierul arheologic de la Popeşti. *Materiale şi Cercetări Arheologice, 6*, 307–324.

Vulpe, A. (1976). La nécroplole tumulaire gète de Popeşti. *Thraco-Dacica, 1*, 193–215.

Vulpe, A., & Gheorghiţă, M. (1979). Şantierul arheologic Popeşti. com. Mihăileşti, jud. Ilfov. Raport preliminar asupra rezultatelor din campania anilor 1976-1977. *Cercetări arheologice Muz. Istorie România, 3*, 95–105.

Wells, P. S. (1998). Identity and material culture in the later prehistory of Central Europe. *Journal of Archaeological Research, 6*(3), 239–298. doi:10.1023/A:1022828421770.

Wells, P. S. (forthcoming). Monuments and cultural landscapes: Memory, agency and practice in prehistoric Europe. In S. Stoddart (Ed.), *Gardening time. Reflections on memory, monuments and history in Sardinia and Scotland*. Oxford: Oxbow.

Werner, W. M. (1988). *Eisenzeitliche Trensen an der Unteren und Mittleren Donau*. Munchen.

Williams, H. (2004). Death warmed up: The agency of bodies and bones in Early Anglo-Saxon cremation rites. *Journal of Material Culture, 9*, 263–291.

Chapter 3
The Working Apparatus: Identity and Statistics

The theoretical tools are intimately linked to the data employed for this study. The ideas about identity produce a theoretical framework within which the question addressed in this book is answered through an interpretation of the data patterns signalled by the practical tools. The relationship between data and identity theory can thus be characterized as being dialectic in nature. On the one hand, data characteristics (e.g., data type, resolution) influence the theoretical tools that are deployed, particularly which nuances or elements of identity theory offer possibilities to answer the proposed question. On the other hand, the theoretical framework determines which specific sets of data are chosen, and how these data are recorded and grouped together.

The practical tools also share a direct connection with the data. These tools represent mainly statistical procedures directly applied to the data so as to obtain patterns which are then interpreted to answer the proposed research question. A dialectic relation between method and data is implicit in this case as well. The data characteristics directly influence the choice of method, since only a limited number of statistical procedures are suitable for dealing with low-resolution funerary information. Conversely, the statistical method requires the data to be ordered in a specific manner before they can be analysed. Additionally, some particular cases may not be responsive to the analysis, causing them to be excluded or discussed separately.

The two types of tools are themselves interdependent, heavily reliant on one another. The theory and method were designed in parallel, each feeding into the other as they were developed. Ideas of identity stand at the foundation of the similarity algorithm and determine the choice of modelling techniques, in the form of clustering procedures. However, the results obtained from applying the practical tools are introduced through a feedback loop back into the ideas of identity that are deployed. This is because the theoretical framework needs to allow for the outcome of the analysis to be interpreted in a way that answers the research question.

C. N. Popa, *Modelling Identities*, Quantitative Archaeology and Archaeological Modelling, https://doi.org/10.1007/978-3-319-63267-4_3

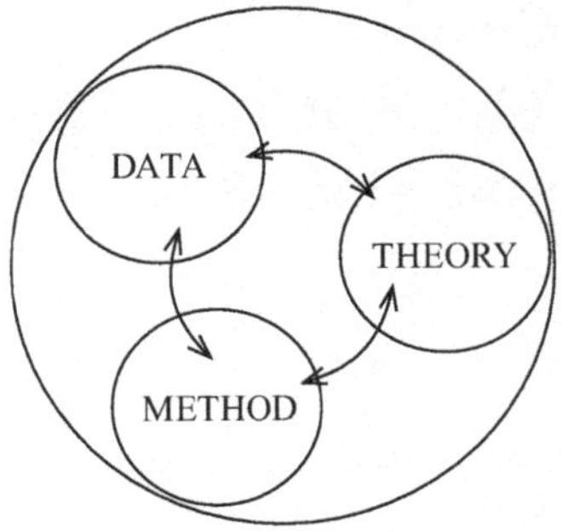

Fig. 3.1 Visualization of data, method, and theory feedback loop

Therefore, theory, method, and data are all closely linked into what may be thought of as a symbiotic relationship (Fig. 3.1). The definition and functioning of each of them is heavily dependent on the other two and any change made to one of the components has a reverberating impact on the rest.

3.1 The Theoretical Tools: Identity Theory

3.1.1 Identity Theory Concepts in Archaeology

Identity is generally understood as the essence of who an individual or a group is in relation to a larger social context; it defines what is unique about that individual or group (Wells 1998, p. 242). Therefore, it relates to the ways in which social actors distinguish themselves in their relation with other such actors (Jenkins 1996, p. 4).

In the fields of archaeology and anthropology, the term identity is often closely linked to that of ethnicity. Hobsbawm (1992, p. 4) considers that ethnicity refers to "a readily definable way of expressing a *real* (sic) sense of group identity which links the members of "we" because it emphasizes their differences from "them". What they actually have in common besides not being "them" is not clear…". Hence, it can be said that ethnicity refers to a specific type of group identity. It is difficult to say how ethnic identity is different from any other group identity; while it is quite an easy task to say what ethnicity is not, it is almost impossible to define what it really is, although the popular perception is more or less the opposite (Hakenbeck 2004a, p. 4). Weber singles out some of its binding elements, by saying that ethnicity is based "on a subjective belief in…common descent because of similarities in physical type or of customs or both, or because of memories of colonization and migration", though he also adds that ethnicity does not itself constitute a group, but "facilitates group formation of any kind, particularly in the political sphere" (Weber 1978, p. 389). Many identity studies have been dedicated to the study and identification of ethnicity (e.g., Barth 1969a; Eriksen 1993; Banks 1996; Demoule 1999; Lucy 2005), including through the archaeological record (e.g.,

Jones 1997; Hakenbeck 2004b; Roymans 2004; Erciyas 2005; Bouzek and Domaradzka 2007; Jovanović 2008; Derks and Roymans 2009). The only reason for this seems to be that ethnicity is the main "imagined community" (Anderson 1991) based on which modern nations were formed. Why this type of identity should be given so much importance when studying the past, especially when dealing with antiquity and prehistory, is hard to say (see Popa and Stoddart 2014).

The use of the terms identity and ethnicity throughout the twentieth century has varied considerably, and this variation can be linked to the three theoretical schools of archaeology: culture-historical, processualist, and post-processualist (Trigger 2006).

In the culture-historical period, in the first half of the twentieth century, there were usually no studies that dealt directly with identity and ethnicity from a sociological point of view and no difference was made between the two concepts. The existence of ethnic identity at any point in the past was considered to be a historical given, for which reason the concept was employed implicitly in archaeological studies on a wide scale. The general idea was that archaeological cultures corresponded to ethnically distinct groups of people, leading to the image of a prehistoric landscape populated by monolithic cultural entities that gradually evolved in time. The two main authors who introduced and developed these concepts were Kossinna and Childe (Jones 1997) and some of their points can still be widely encountered in much of European archaeology. This approach to identity has been named primordial by some (Di 2013, p. 376).

As the ideas about archaeological cultures changed in the Anglophone area as a response to the attacks of Binford (1962, 1968), so did the perspectives on identity and ethnicity. Studies that dealt with identity as a social phenomenon started to be integrated at this point, but the focus was principally on ethnicity as a research topic rather than identity since the two terms were still seen as largely coincident. The dominant view, mainly based on the work of Barth (1969b), became that identities are malleable, changing according to circumstances so as to fit people's interests. Identities are given form through a series of boundaries which are actively maintained, but also manipulated by people in order to coincide with their economic or social interest. In this view, the direct relationship between material culture and ethnicity was questioned to a certain degree, but not denied. Identities were conceived as constantly being "instrumentalized" which made them somewhat divorced from the person and arguably reduced to the status of tools. For this reason, this theory has come under attack as being too functionalist and ignoring many of the personal aspects that come into play in the formation and expression of identity (Jones 1997). The "instrumentalist approach", as it has been called (Graves-Brown and Jones 1996; Jones 1996, 1997), gained in popularity mainly during the period when much of archaeological works from the UK and US were following the so-called processualist framework, which stressed the purely "scientific" nature of archaeology, with all its implications, such as the importance of functionality, objectivity, and generalizations. While many of those thoughts have been abandoned, Barth's ideas remain today highly influential as there are hardly any identity studies which do not cite his work. Moreover, in the past 15 years, much of the critique launched against this view has been integrated, leading to much more nuanced approaches. Such studies now also clearly acknowledge the distinction between identity in general and ethnicity as a particular type of group identity (Barth 2000; Cohen 2000).

With the birth of post-processualism and the rise of ideas about the subjectivity and relativity of archaeological knowledge, new ways of thinking about identity were introduced. The separation between the concept of identity and ethnicity became instated, as numerous studies emerged regarding various kinds of identity, such as class, gender, or religion, demoting ethnicity to being solely such a particular type. The end result is that there appears to be no clear-cut way of getting to identity through archaeology, each author choosing to build their own framework in their studies. The general trend is, however, to use Bourdieu's (1977) theory of practice by linking the formation and expression of identity to the *habitus* (Babić 2005; Díaz-Andreu 2005; Hakenbeck 2004a; Jones 1996, 1997, 1999). Thus, identity is built using the same principles that are active within the *habitus*, and just like them, is constructed and reinforced through everyday practice and is objectified through material engagement (Tilley 2006). Furthermore, since material culture shapes and is itself shaped by the same governing principles, and at the same time, represents one of the means through which identity is manifested, it is possible to study the identity of past people by examining the overlapping patterns that result from the archaeological record.[1] The general rule is that all these elements vary from one context to the other, as the expression of identity is modified according to the social principles which are active in that particular situation. There is, however, a problem linked to the construction of identity which has not yet been answered and that has led to the splitting of research into two groups of scholars. Most authors consider that the formation of an identity is principally a subjective phenomenon, that it is built on the similarities that one has with the other members of a group, placing the differences in relation to other groups in a secondary position (Graves-Brown 1996; Jones 1996, 1999; Lucy 2005; Shennan 1989). In contrast, partly inheriting the ideas of the "instrumentalist theory", some think that it is primarily the product of the marking of difference and exclusion, rather than the sign of an identical, naturally constituted unity (Hall 1996). This division roughly corresponds to that signalled by Di (2013, pp. 375–376), with regard to the isolationist and interactionist approaches. Whatever the answer might be, it is quite clear that when working with this topic one needs to bear in mind that identity markers signal both sameness and difference at the same time (Popa 2010).

A small variation of the above approach can be postulated by employing recent theoretical developments. It involves integrating ideas regarding inter-human interaction and human-object relationships, suggested by Latour (2005), as well as concepts regarding person and individual introduced through theories of personhood (Fowler 2004; Strathern 1999). In this view, identity is indeed fluid and personal, but

[1] The fundamental problem in accessing identity purely through material culture is that objects can no longer be considered simple identity signifiers, though they can have significance in terms of identity; however this significance exists only within a known and communicable frame of reference (Hakenbeck 2004a, p. 3).

it is at the same time entirely relational, meaning that it is based on the relations established with others. People do not define identity through themselves, but through the relationships that they establish with other people, regardless whether they are conceived as different or the same. Consequently, speaking about identity makes sense only in the context of these relationships since, outside of them, it does not exist. In this scenario, material culture plays an important role since many relationships are mediated or indeed defined through objects (cf. Robb 2004). Identity, thus, becomes open for study by archaeologists, since through the archaeological record one encounters a part of the material remains that were involved in identity-defining relationships. The task is to place the objects in the relationships that they were part of and reconstruct the network of relations that defined people's identities.

3.1.2 *Identity: Directly Implementable Ideas*

Identity, in itself, is a very broad and all-encompassing term which raises significant difficulties when seeking to apply it to the concrete archaeological record. A major issue is the existence of multiple types of identities that an individual can hold: family, social, religious, class, state, etc. Additionally, following on the point of Jovanović (2005, p. 77), there is a vertical hierarchy of identities according to their level of generality and which function concomitantly (e.g., local, regional, ethnic, national). In order to account for all of these possibilities, one would require an enormous amount of information provided by high-resolution data. Archaeologically, we rarely have access to that level of information.

As described in the previous chapter, the data employed for this study suffer severely from low resolution. This requires a significant alteration of the working theory so as to be able to deploy it with such kinds of data. Consequently, it has been opted to focus on group identity rather than identity in general, since the latter is usually associated with the individual level and necessitates very fine data recording to be accessed. Additionally, the individual dimension is of little interest in this study, given the question that is tackled.

I define group identity as a feeling of togetherness that an indefinite number of people share and which they feel differentiates them from other groups or people. What exactly binds these people together is unknown to us as observers. The vague nature of group identity following this definition is obvious. It is its generality that makes the concept employable when dealing with low-resolution archaeological data and when no prior knowledge exists regarding the particular types of group identities that found their expression in the material record of the investigated contexts. Nevertheless, the definition still presents difficulties in terms of its applicability. In order for these ideas on group identity to be employable, it is necessary to establish a series of theoretical pillars that allow for direct methodological implementation.

The first of these pillars is that group identity is constructed, expressed, and maintained through practice, an idea deployed in the data recording strategy. The grave-good items that served in the analysis were recorded using a four-tiered hierarchical system of variables that incorporated both their function and shape. This recording procedure shifted the emphasis from the object itself to the practices that the objects were involved in (see Chap. 2, Sect. 2.4).

The second theoretical pillar is that group identity has at its very core the same-other principle. This comes out of the idea that identity is based on qualities that people see themselves as sharing with some, as well as elements they consider as distinguishing them from others (Canuto and Yaeger 2000, p. 2). This basic principle is enacted through practice and objectified through the material record which should allow archaeologists to recognize it (Allison 2008, pp. 41–42). Its implementation comes in the form of a similarity algorithm that compares the funerary practices, which are then grouped based on their similarities and differences using clustering procedures (see Sect. 3.2 of this chapter).

Uncovering practice similarities and differences represents an important step, but such patterns of resembling practices cannot be equated with group identity since not all elements of commonality are necessarily connected to identity formation and expression. It is at this point that the third theoretical pillar is useful: group identity is overdetermined. Overdetermination is a theory of irreducibility, in which a given phenomenon (e.g., group identity) is conceptualized as an effect produced by a potentially infinite number of contributing and interacting phenomena, none of which are both necessary and sufficient (Voss 2008, p. 4). Therefore, the third theoretical pillar refers to the multidirectional character of group identity. For an observed pattern of practice similarity or difference to be significant in terms of group identity, it is necessary to uncover other elements, independent of the analysis, which show a similar pattern. When such a pattern correspondence is found, the likelihood of coincidence, though not unthinkable, becomes rather low. It is then possible to postulate, with reasonable certainty, that the practices being focused did indeed participate in the construction and expression of group identity. Furthermore, given that some of the independent variables may hold more precise information, they can offer hints at the particular types of group identities manifested in the investigated contexts. This logic is followed in the interpretation of the clustering results, as the clusters are compared with additional information not included in the analysis, such as spatial positioning of the graves, age and sex of the deceased, contemporary settlement organization, written sources, etc. (see Chaps. 5 and 6).

The three pillars are combined to create a cohesive archaeological approach to group identity. Their capacity for methodological application helps bridge the gap between method and theory that characterizes a large number of identity studies from archaeology. Nevertheless, the approach can be criticized for reducing group identity to a somewhat bare-bone concept.

3.2 The Practical Tools

The practical tools chosen for this study are statistical analysis and spatial analysis. Statistical procedures, summed up under the term comparative contextual modelling or contextual statistical analysis, were used in order to put into practice a basic concept of group identity: the same-other dichotomy. This was implemented through the statistical package R using an algorithm that was developed specifically for this study. Based on the results of this algorithm, cluster analysis was applied to obtain possible groupings of the burial data. These groupings were then examined with exploratory techniques, using the statistical programme SPSS, in order to observe the elements that have led to such a grouping. Finally, a simple spatial analysis was run, with the help of ArcGIS, in order to observe the spatial dynamics of the obtained grave groups within the geographical area of the study.

3.2.1 Statistical Analysis: Theoretical Considerations

Before describing the statistical procedure, it is necessary to put forward a series of theoretical considerations regarding statistical analysis. These refer to what statistics can actually do and how its results can be used by archaeologists.[2]

First of all, statistical analysis is only a tool. Archaeologists apply this tool to data in order to reveal possible patterns. However, statistical methods cannot actually say what the patterns represent. Explaining what a pattern means is purely a process of interpretation which is done entirely by the researcher. This point is true for both exploratory or descriptive techniques (e.g., histogram, principal component analysis) and for model-based ones (e.g., Bayesian methods, agent-based modelling).

Secondly, statistical analysis should always be done with a question in mind (Shennan 1997, p. 216). Most of the time, plunging blindly into data with statistical methods will give results which are either absolutely useless or which cannot be employed since it is not possible to know what they actually reflect. This point is especially true for modelling techniques. In the case of exploratory methods, it often happens that they are used without a clear question; this may actually prove useful, especially if there are easily identifiable patterns to be found in the data. Nonetheless, even in this case, having a specific question to ask the data greatly increases the possibility of getting useful results.

Finally, statistics are not objective. There are at least two layers of subjectivity that one has to bear in mind.

The first one is linked to data recording since every statistical algorithm uses a database. The form of the database can be broadly limited by the chosen method, but the actual values recorded within it are a matter of choice. Choices are present everywhere in the database (e.g., deciding between a mug and a jug). Therefore, it has to be remembered that a computer can only calculate what it is told to calculate.

The second layer is linked to the statistical algorithm itself. Any algorithm is written by a person and the choices that the programmer makes when conceiving the algorithm have of course a direct impact on the results. Indeed, these choices are made to the best knowledge of the programmer, and the programmer can be an archaeologist or at least someone who is familiar with archaeological work, but in

[2] Some of these ideas can be found in the introduction of *Statistics in Archaeology* by Baxter (2003, pp. 1–18). They can also be found in one of my previous publications (Popa 2012, p. 402).

the end these are decisions which shape the outcome of the analysis. A computer can only calculate how it is told to calculate.

However, these ideas should not discourage archaeologists from employing statistical analysis. They are meant rather to guide those who use it or are thinking of using it and to make it clear what statistics can and cannot do. Statistics can show patterns, but cannot determine what these patterns mean; it can help to answer questions, but only if these are asked beforehand; it can give a useful result, but this result will not be the objective output of a machine.

3.2.2 Statistical Analysis: The Use of R

R was utilized in order to run the main part of the statistical analysis. There are two important reasons for using this particular piece of software. First of all, R is very flexible, which means that it can work with any type of data, allowing one to specify exactly what type of analysis it should conduct. Secondly, R is open source, which means that there is no need to pay for a license in order to use it; moreover, it also implies that there is a large community that constantly creates statistical packages for it. The major drawback is that R is not very user-friendly; everything is done by writing script into a console and creating functions or employing previously designed ones. Therefore, one needs to have knowledge of computer programming in order to use it as well as an understanding of the powerful statistical functions and methods contained in its numerous statistical packages.

R was employed in this study for running a series of statistical procedures in two steps, each of which are discussed separately. The first step consists of a similarity algorithm programmed by me specifically for the dataset employed in this study. The second step consists of several cluster analysis methods.

However, before running the similarity algorithm, it was necessary to choose the variables on which to run the statistics. This meant deciding what information from the database, described in the previous chapter, could actually serve for the analysis. The variables chosen to fulfil this purpose were: *burial type*, *ritual type*, *multiple burial*, *category 1*, *category 2*, *category 3*, *category 4*, and *material*. These specific variables were chosen for two reasons. Firstly, because it was considered that they are relevant for the question that is being asked about the manifestation of group identity in the funerary record. Secondly, because these variables passed the integrity test, whose threshold was set at 70%. This means that at least 70% of the graves on which the statistical analysis was run contained information in these variables. Thus, a maximum of 30% of information was accepted to be missing. The only exception was *category 4* for which 39.5% of the data were missing. To account for the lack of data, less emphasis was placed on this variable and constant checks were made so that no patterning occurs based on the missing information.[3]

[3]Although methodologically it would have been correct to leave out this variable, it was considered that the data that it holds is too valuable to be left out of the analysis.

It should be noted that the variables related to age, sex as well as the geographical position were intentionally left out. This is because it was decided to keep these as independent variables which were crosschecked at the end with the result of the cluster analysis, using SPSS. This artifice gave the possibility to inspect whether age and sex were relevant in regard to identity manifestation and whether the funerary display of identity changed according to region. In this way, the manifestation of these specific types of identities could be singled out. If these variables had been introduced in the actual cluster analysis, such observations would have no longer been possible. For instance, if sex had been considered in the analysis, then the similarity algorithm, and of course also the cluster analysis, would have determined that the graves belonging to individuals of the same sex were rather similar to one another. This means that the entire analysis would have started with the premise that the graves containing individuals of the same sex had a certain degree of similarity. Conversely, leaving the information related to sex out of the cluster analysis gave the possibility to verify whether the sex of the deceased had an influence on the choices made by the mourners during the mortuary ritual without assuming beforehand that it did. For example, if sex had been considered as a variable in the analysis and the clustering algorithm would have determined that the graves can be split in two groups, each of different sex, then it would have been highly problematic to infer that gender identity was being expressed in the funerary record since this assumption would have already been made. On the other hand, if the same result had been obtained without using sex as a variable in the cluster analysis, then it would have been safe to affirm that one was dealing with the expression of gender identity embedded in the mortuary ritual. Ultimately, to put it in very simple terms, the difference between using sex as a variable or not can be translated as my taking the decision that sex was an important identity element or seeing whether the mourners took that decision.

3.2.2.1 The Similarity Algorithm

The similarity algorithm was born out of the need to quantify how similar or different the graves were to each other (Drennan 1996, pp. 271–283). Hence, it involved putting into numbers the empirical observations that are made when comparing two graves. Such a transformation was necessary since many statistical procedures, including cluster analysis, can only operate with numerical values.

While there are numerous similarity algorithms in existence, none of them would work with the data employed in this study. Most similarity algorithms were developed to work with either continuous or binary data (Drennan 1996, pp. 271–283; Everitt et al. 2011, pp. 43–69). Continuous data refer to the recording of numbers, which could be the expression of measurements. The classical way of calculating the similarity, or in this case the dissimilarity index, is by employing a simple *Euclidean distance*. Binary data, on the other hand, refers to variables that contain 0 or 1 values, 0 referring to absence and 1 to presence. In this case, there are several possible calculations of the similarity depending on the question that is being asked and on what the data stands for. Nevertheless, the most common methods are *Simple Matching* and *Jaccard's Coefficients* (Drennan 1996, pp. 277–279). The data for this study are, however, neither continuous nor binary, but categorical (Agresti 1990), meaning that each variable can contain different independent values. It is often suggested that categorical variables should be transformed into binary ones, but in doing so much of the information necessary for answering identity questions would be lost. Alternatively, a large number of binary variables could be created, one for each of the possible values taken by the categorical variables. This has the effect of greatly increasing data complexity, due to an exponential increase in the number of variables. When such a transformation is not possible, methods for comparing categorical data have been proposed (Agresti 2007), but usually they require a specific structure of the data which again does not fit with the one that is used in this study. This situation created the necessity to construct a new similarity algorithm with the ability to process the specific type of data available for this study and mimic a particular way of approaching the burial information.

The similarity algorithm received as input the raw data and gave as output a dissimilarity or distance matrix. The algorithm involved numerous operations and several phases. Each of them is detailed below.

The first step was to import all the data into R from the Microsoft Access database. This was done through a table in which each entry corresponded to an inventory item that also contained all the ritual information associated with the grave from which it came. Hence, the table unfortunately contained a large amount of redundant ritual information.

Next, from the imported data, the relevant variables were extracted. This means that a copy of the data was made containing only the variables that would be employed in the actual cluster procedure.

This step was followed by the controlled transformation of the data into numerical values. The data held in each of the analysed variables were converted from string type to integer type. For instance, the variable *ritual type*, which could contain as values inhumation, cremation, cenotaph, or unknown, was converted to contain the values 1, 2, 3, or −1, each of these corresponding to the initial ritual types. −1 was used for all variables when data was missing. It was opted to do a controlled transformation of the variables instead of allowing R to do so intrinsically because it was required to know exactly what numerical values correspond to the initial information. This was needed for the later stages of the similarity algorithm when there was the possibility of assigning different weights to the variables as well as the values that they contain.

After all the used variables were converted to numerical data, the algorithm calculated separately the similarity of the graves based on the ritual information and the same similarity based on the grave-goods.

Calculating the similarity based on ritual was rather straightforward. Each grave was compared one by one to all other graves using the three variables relating to ritual: *burial type*, *ritual type,* and *multiple burial*. Depending on the weight attributed to each variable, a value was obtained to characterize how similar all the graves were to one another. The condition for two variables to add to the similarity was for them to contain the same value, a value which had to be different from -1, meaning that there had to be information regarding that particular aspect of the grave. By applying this condition to each variable, the algorithm determined a number between 0 and the sum of all the weights assigned to the variables. For example, if a weight of 1 was attributed to each variable, then the similarity index between two graves was between 0 and 3, since there are three variables. This similarity index was then standardized by dividing the index by the maximum possible value, the sum of all the weights, which in this example was 3. This operation transformed all the indexes into a value between 0 and 1, with 0 meaning that the two compared graves were completely different and 1 that they were identical. For the algorithm to give consistent results, the same weight had to be assigned to the variables during all the grave comparisons. Therefore, it was not possible to run half of the graves with a set of assigned weights and run the other half with a different set of weights. The only way to achieve such an operation would have been to split the data initially into two data sets and run the analysis separately on them, each time with the different set of weights. The designation of weights to the variables was done on a purely empirical basis. The choice had to do largely with the question at hand, but it may also be based on observations done beforehand. For instance, if the placing of the grave next to a river was observed a priori to be very important, then more weight could be put on the variable recording that particular information. It has been observed that the best results were achieved by running the algorithm a great number of times with different sets of weights. The results thus obtained were then compared, choosing the one that gave the clearest patterns and that had weight values best fitting with the question being asked.

Calculating the similarity between graves based on the funerary inventory was more complex, involving several operations. The basic functioning principle was similar to what was described above: each grave was compared to each other grave in order to calculate a value characterizing their similarity. However, the comparison of two graves involved two steps. Firstly, each grave-good from the first grave was compared with all the other grave-goods from the second grave based on the inventory-related variables: *category 1*, *category 2*, *category 3*, *category 4*, *material*. The outcome of all these comparisons was a matrix of m by n components, with m representing the total number of grave-goods from the first grave and n the total number of grave-goods from the second grave. In a similar way to the result from the ritual information comparison, the values contained in the matrix were between 0 and the sum of all the weights assigned to the variables, with the addition of variable values weights.

The weighing system in the case of the grave-good comparisons was more complex than when dealing with the ritual variables. This is because, for the grave-goods, the algorithm allowed weights to be attributed not only to variables, but also to individual variable values.[4] Therefore, it was possible to instruct the algorithm that, for specific values taken by some variables, it should introduce an additional figure in

[4] The algorithm allows for individual weights to be attributed to ritual variables as well, but this was not found to be necessary for running the dataset used in this study.

the similarity index calculation.[5] This extra figure could also be negative, but its absolute value could not be higher than that of the weight attributed to the variable to which it belonged. This meant that each similarity identified between two graves had to add a minimum positive value to the similarity index. For example, if a weight of 3 was added to the *category 3* variable, then the minimum weight that could be assigned to one of its values was −2. On the other hand, if a positive weight was attributed instead, there was no fixed upper threshold. What this weighing procedure achieved was to give the option to increase or reduce the importance of specific types of grave-goods in the overall grave comparisons, integrating any observations made empirically on the data. It also allowed for the results to be fine-tuned so as to be made clearer, in those cases where a pattern was discovered based on particular grave-good combinations, but too much statistical noise hindered its precise identification. Finally, through such a weighting system, it was possible to test particular scenarios regarding the importance of specific items in terms of group identity.

The second step in calculating the similarity between two graves, after the variable and variable values weights were summed up, was to identify the maximum value of the similarity index based on the grave-goods comparisons. This was done by choosing a number of values from the matrix resulting from the first step and adding them together while respecting the following conditions:

1. It was only possible to choose one value from each row and one value from each column of the matrix.[6]
2. The number of values chosen from the matrix had to be equal to the minimum between m and n, with m and n referring to the number of columns and rows of the matrix.

The first condition was the essential one as the second came as a corollary from it. Basically, what the conditions refer to was that each grave-good could be used only once in the sum. For instance, if one grave would contain a sword and a fibula and another one two swords and a fibula, then the sum that gave the similarity between the graves would contain the comparison between the sword from the first grave and only one of the swords from the second grave (Fig. 3.2).

Choosing the values from the matrix that gave the maximum sum based on those conditions was a rather complex endeavour. Luckily, this problem had already been encountered before and had been resolved through a combinatory optimization algorithm, the so-called Hungarian method (Kuhn 1955). Unfortunately, although methodologically correct, implementing Kuhn's solution added a large number of extra operations that needed to be run with each comparison that was done between every two graves. This ended up greatly increasing computational time. For this

[5] Only a small number of variable values were attributed an extra weight. For the rest, the default 0 value was in place, meaning that most of them added to the calculation only the weight that corresponded to their variables.

[6] It should be noted that unless m and n were equal, there were a number of rows or columns, depending on whether m or n was bigger, from which no values were chosen. This number was equal to the absolute value of $m - n$ (i.e. $|m - n|$).

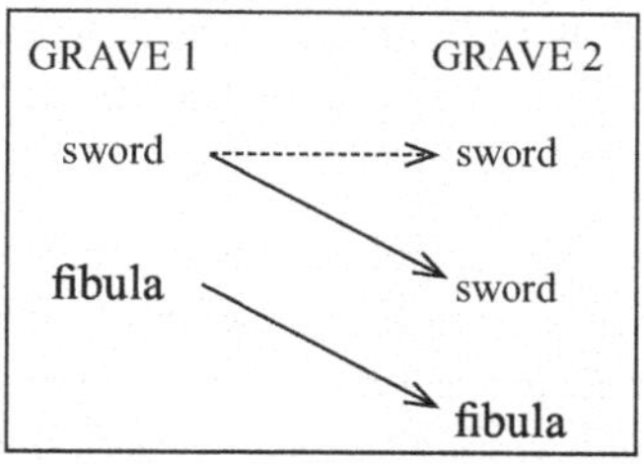

Fig. 3.2 Visualization of grave-goods comparison. The *dotted line* comparison is not considered due to double use of sword from grave 1

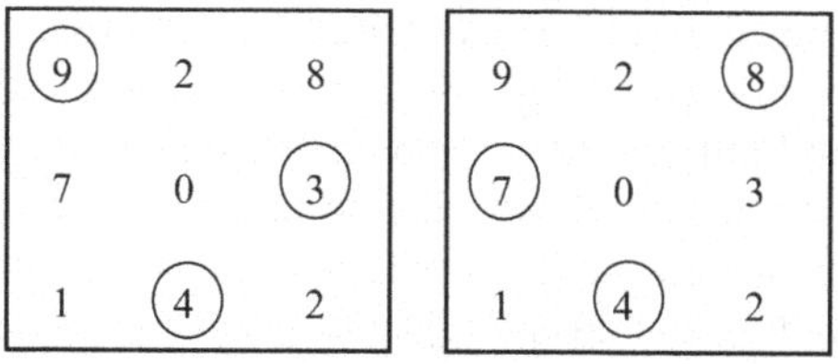

Fig. 3.3 Example where choosing highest value per column/row (*left*) does not produce the maximum sum. The values that give the maximum sum are encircled in the right matrix

reason, an easier solution was opted for. The solution was to go through all the columns or all the rows, depending on whether m or n was smaller, choosing each time the maximum value while respecting the first condition. The problem with this approach was that it did not necessarily produce each time the maximum sum (Fig. 3.3). However, after running the entire statistical procedure with both computational procedures, no actual differences were spotted between the two. Therefore, although possible errors were introduced through the second method, these did not affect the final outcome of the analysis in an observable manner.

After the sum was determined, the next step was to standardize the result as in the case of the ritual similarity calculation, which was done by dividing the computed sum by the maximum between two cumulated weight indexes. These indexes were computed by summing up, for each grave, the weight of the variables describing all of its grave-goods as well as any potential weights associated with the values of those variables. Hence, the mathematical calculation can be expressed using the equation:

$$S_{i,j} = \frac{\mathrm{Sum}_{i,j}}{\max\left(w_i, w_j\right)}$$

where

$S_{i,j}$ is the final calculated standardized similarity based on grave-goods between grave i and grave j

$\mathrm{Sum}_{i,j}$ is the maximum sum based on grave-goods calculated between grave i and grave j

w_i is the cumulated weight index for grave i, calculated as the total sum of the weights assigned to the variables and the variable values used to describe the grave-goods of grave i

w_j is the cumulated weight index for grave j, calculated as the total sum of the weights assigned to the variables and the variable values used to describe the grave-goods of grave j

The result obtained was between 0 and 1, with 0 meaning that the two graves were completely different and 1 that they were identical. It should be noted that, because a choice was made to use the maximum between the two cumulated weight indexes in the above equation, the value of 1 for $S_{i,j}$ could only be encountered when the two graves had the same number of grave-goods and their corresponding weights were equal. Such a choice was considered necessary in order to get cases of absolute similarity (i.e. a value of 1 for $S_{i,j}$) only in instances where the graves were truly identical, even though $\mathrm{Sum}_{i,j}$ could never be larger than the minimum between the two cumulated weight indexes. However, if $\min(w_i,w_j)$ were to be used instead in the above equation, then some cases of partial similarity could also show as complete resemblance. To illustrate this point, let us take again two graves, the first with a sword and a fibula and the second with two swords and a fibula. Also, let us assume that the corresponding items have exactly the same characteristics and that each object has a total weight of 1 associated with them. On comparing the grave-goods, all the items from the first grave give full similarity to those of the second, producing a figure of 2, equal to the cumulated weight index of the first grave. When $\min(w_i,w_j)$ is used in the equation above, then $S_{i,j}$ calculates as 1, suggesting that the two graves are completely identical, which they are obviously not. On the other hand, when $\max(w_i,w_j)$ is employed, then $\mathrm{Sum}_{i,j}$ is divided by the higher cumulated weight index of the second grave, which is 3, meaning that $S_{i,j}$ takes a value of 0.66. In this manner, the presence of the second sword counts as an element of dissimilarity (Fig. 3.4).

After all these calculations were done, the outcome was two similarity matrices, one based on the ritual variables, the other one based on the grave-goods. At this point, there was the option either to run the clustering statistics individually on one of the two matrices, or to run them on the combined results. If it was chosen to run the clustering on them separately, then the remaining operation was to turn the similarity matrices into dissimilarity or distance matrices (Shennan 1997, pp. 222–227). Transforming a similarity into a dissimilarity index is usually done in one of two ways:

$$D_{i,j,} = 1 - S_{i,j}$$

or

$$D_{i,j,} = \sqrt{1 - S_{i,j}}$$

where

$S_{i,j}$ is the final calculated standardized similarity between grave i and grave j
$D_{i,j}$ is the dissimilarity index or distance between grave i and grave j

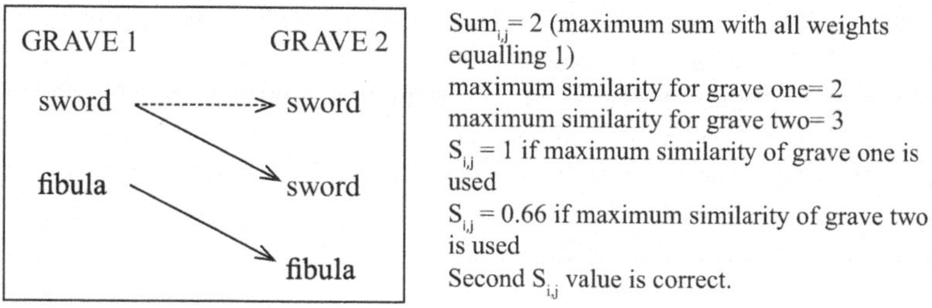

Fig. 3.4 Example justifying the use of the maximum weight for standardization

The difference between the two equations is that the second one renders the graves more similar, or to be correct, less dissimilar, to one another. The distance matrices thus obtained had the following properties:

1. Each row and each column corresponded to a grave. In other words, the matrices were square, meaning that they had the same number of rows and columns.
2. The value from row number *i* and row number *j* corresponded to the dissimilarity index between grave *i* and grave *j*.
3. All the values contained were between 0 and 1, with 0 meaning identical and 1 completely different (so the opposite of a similarity index).
4. The matrices were symmetrical to their primary diagonal. This can be translated in $m_{i,j}$ being equal to $m_{j,i}$, where $m_{i,j}$ is the value located on column *i* and row *j* and $m_{j,i}$ is the value located on column *j* and row *i*. In other words, the dissimilarity index obtained from comparing grave *i* to grave *j* was the same as comparing grave *j* with grave *i*.

If instead of running the cluster analysis independently on ritual and grave-good similarities it was chosen to run it on the two indexes put together, then it was required to combine the two matrices into one. The most direct way of doing this would have been to employ a simple arithmetical mean:

$$S_{i,j} = \frac{R_{i,j} + G_{i,j}}{2}$$

where

$S_{i,j}$ is the final total calculated standardized similarity between grave *i* and grave *j*
$R_{i,j}$ is the final calculated standardized similarity between grave *i* and grave *j* based on the ritual variables
$G_{i,j}$ is the final calculated standardized similarity between grave *i* and grave *j* based on the grave-goods

Using such an equation would have put an equal amount of importance on both ritual and grave-goods. While this looks at first glance acceptable, it would actually have created serious inconsistencies in the results. For instance, if there were two graves which were identical as far as the ritual variables were concerned, but each had only one object as inventory and those objects were different, this would have produced a similarity index of 0.5. If the two graves had instead ten objects each, and again all objects were completely different, then the algorithm would have given the same result, 0.5. But such a computation would not have reflected the data; instead, the algorithm should have determined that the two graves containing only one object each were far more similar than the graves containing ten objects each. To make the algorithm function in such a manner, a weighted rather than an arithmetical mean was introduced:

$$S_{i,j} = \frac{R_{i,j} + \alpha \times G_{i,j}}{\alpha + 1}$$

where

$S_{i,j}$ is the final total calculated standardized similarity between grave i and grave j
$R_{i,j}$ is the final calculated standardized similarity between grave i and grave j based on the ritual variables
$G_{i,j}$ is the final calculated standardized similarity between grave i and grave j based on the grave-goods
α is a parameter that varies according to the maximum number of grave-goods

The α parameter from the equation above had the role to regulate how much the two components, the ritual and the grave-good similarity, counted in the final similarity index. The parameter varied according to the maximum number of grave-goods present in the two graves. The value that it took was calculated on a purely empirical basis. Nevertheless, as a general rule, when the two compared graves had a small number of objects, then α took values that were smaller than 1. Alternatively, when they had large quantities of grave-goods, α became bigger than 1. When α took values that were smaller than 1, the ritual similarity weighed more than the grave-good similarity; conversely, when α was higher than 1, the grave-good similarity weighed more. For the case when α equalled 1, both components counted 50% and the equation transformed into an arithmetical mean.

Finally, after calculating the value of the similarity index, the last step was to transform it into a dissimilarity index and thus obtain the dissimilarity or distance matrix. The procedure was identical to the one described for the individual ritual and grave-good matrices.

3.2.2.2 The Clustering Procedure

Clustering algorithms are used in order to determine the possible groupings of data cases,[7] meaning, in a more general manner, that they are employed for classification (Everitt et al. 2011). It is a procedure that mimics one of human mind's fundamental ways of dealing with complicated variability: categorizing, or putting things into

[7] For this analysis the cases refer to graves.

groups (Drennan 1996, p. 309). Cluster analysis is largely an empirical method; there is little theoretical backing for the results obtained (cf. Hennig and Liao 2013: 315–318). Therefore, it is extremely important to verify clustering results by using different validation procedures. On the other hand, this lack of control over the clustering mechanism gives a large advantage to modelling techniques since they are able to group cases without requiring a preconceived classification system.[8]

There are various algorithms for clustering, all of them operating on a similarity or dissimilarity matrix calculated from the original data. Each clustering algorithm tends to give a certain group structure due to its internal mechanism. This implies that certain clustering patterns can be more readily identified with some algorithms, while with other ones it can prove to be significantly more difficult. For example, simple linear patterns will be easiest to identify with a Single Linkage Hierarchical Algorithm. On the other hand, because of the rigidity of clustering procedures, every method will arrange the data into a particular kind of grouping construction, thus forcing the data structure. For instance, Hierarchical Clustering in general will force the data into a hierarchical structure.

Consequently, to overcome the issues of the different clustering algorithms, but at the same time to take advantage of their potentially different outcomes, it was decided to employ several methods, giving the possibility to explore the alternative grouping scenarios that could occur. The results thus obtained were validated individually as well as by comparing them to each other.

In choosing the clustering procedures, there was an important limiting factor: the need for them to work with a pre-calculated distance matrix. Most R clustering algorithms, while operating on a distance matrix, require the original data to be provided. These data have to contain either continuous or binary variables, based on which the distance matrix is implicitly calculated using standard methods.[9] However, in this study the distance matrix was calculated through the separate similarity algorithm, given the categorical nature of the variables. Consequently, it was not possible to use any of the clustering procedures that calculated the distance matrix themselves. This significantly decreased the available options.

The first clustering algorithm deployed is by far the most commonly used one: Hierarchical Cluster Analysis or Agglomerative Nesting (Agnes). The wide use of this method has led some authors practically to identify cluster analysis with it (Drennan 1996, pp. 309–320). The algorithm functions in an agglomerative manner, working in multiple steps to combine into a cluster the cases that are most similar. At each stage, the most similar cases are grouped together or added to an already existing group. The end result is a hierarchical tree in which the bottom levels are the most similar and the top levels contain the cases that are furthest apart. The easiest way to display such results is through a dendrogram.

There are several types of possible hierarchical procedures based on the similarity principle which is employed during the numerous steps of the algorithm. The

[8] Examples of the latter are typological classifications, where cases are place into groups according to pre-established criteria.

[9] See previous subsection for a discussion of those methods.

most widely used types are: Single Linkage or nearest neighbour; Complete Linkage or furthest neighbour; and Average Linkage. Additionally, Ward, Centroid, Median, and McQuitty methods can also be used (Everitt et al. 2011, pp. 73–78). Each of these different Hierarchical Clustering methods can, and often do, give potentially different results. Deciding on which one to use cannot be done in advance except in very few cases. The soundest way is to run the algorithm using all the methods, or at least the three main ones, and then observe which produces the clusters that are best defined and at the same time the easiest to interpret (Drennan 1996, pp. 315–316). In this study, Average Linkage, and sometimes Complete Linkage, gave the most solid results. The R functions used for clustering were *hclust* from the *stats* package (Team R 2011) and *agnes* form the *cluster* package (Maechler et al. 2011).

A method closely related to Hierarchical Clustering, and which was highly responsive to the data used in this study, is Divisive Analysing Clustering (Diana). This technique works principally in the same manner as regular hierarchical procedures, but in an opposite way since, rather than being agglomerative, it is divisive in nature. The procedure starts by placing all the cases into one large group and then, through multiple steps, divides the group, or the most dissimilar group if it is not at the first step, based on the dissimilarity matrix. The output is a hierarchical tree resembling the one obtained through agglomerative algorithms (Kaufman and Rousseeuw 2005, pp. 253–277). In R, the function used for divisive clustering was *diana* from the *stats* package.

Hierarchical Clustering procedures do not have as direct outcome the group membership of each case from a dataset, but, as already mentioned, they give a hierarchical tree. In order to obtain an actual grouping of the cases, it is necessary to cut the tree. This literally refers to drawing a line on the hierarchical tree under which all cases that belong to the same branch are considered as being part of one group (Fig. 3.5). Deciding where to draw the line is usually done by pure observation (Drennan 1996, p. 316), although there are guiding principles which help to determine the optimum cut height such as the so-called "elbow" rule (Tibshirani et al. 2001). After examining the dendrogram, in order to cut the tree, it is necessary either to provide the similarity value for cases to be included in the same group or to give the number of groups that one wants to have.

In R, there is a statistical package that contains functions which help to determine the optimum number of clusters: the *Dynamic Tree Cut* package (Langfelder et al. 2008). The main function from this package is *cutreeDynamic*, which implements novel dynamic branch cutting methods for detecting clusters in a dendrogram, depending on their shape and the distance matrix. Given the complexity of the hierarchical trees obtained in this study, this function was often employed for cutting the dendrograms, though empirically based cuts were also used.

The second clustering technique utilized was Partitioning Around Medoids (PAM), which is a more robust version of the model-based K-Means method (Everitt and Hothorn 2009, pp. 322–323). The main principle of Partitioning Around Medoids is to construct an optimum set of clusters around a specified number of optimally chosen cluster centres (Kaufman and Rousseeuw 2005, pp. 68–123). The cluster centres are determined so that they minimalize the sum of dissimilarities to

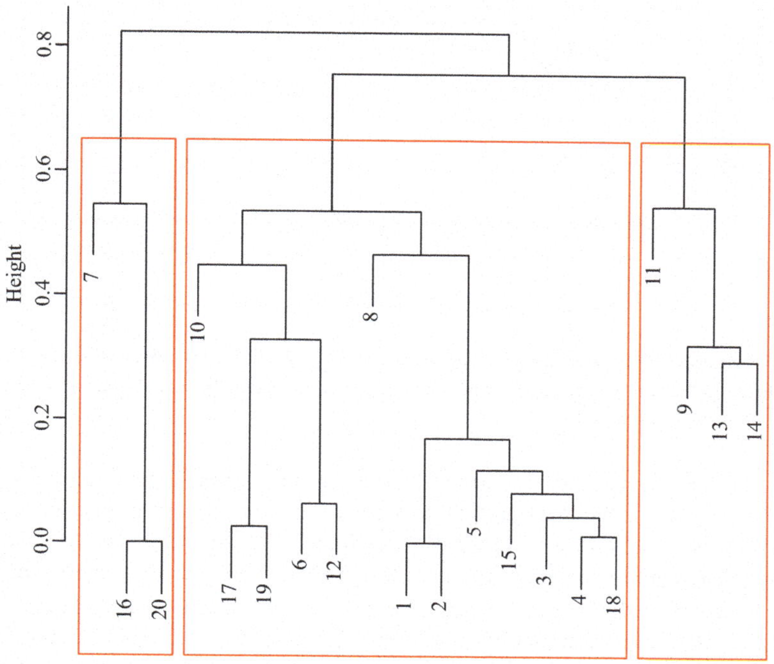

Fig. 3.5 Example dendrogram generated for 20 graves from the database using Average Linkage. The *red blocks* delimit three clusters obtained by cutting the tree at a height of 0.6

their closest neighbours. Afterwards, each case is assigned to the closest cluster. The number of clusters normally needs to be given initially by the user. However, by using the R function *pamk* from the *fpc* package (Hennig 2013), it is only required to specify a cluster interval, for instance between two and ten clusters, and the algorithm selects the solution that is considered to be optimal based on an internal cluster validation method, silhouette calculation. The algorithm returns the cluster membership of each data case, offering the possibility of displaying the solution as a two-dimensional graph (Fig. 3.6).

The third clustering method deployed was Fuzzy Clustering (Abonyi and Feil 2007; Everitt et al. 2011, pp. 242–249). This method requires for the number of clusters that are assumed to exist to be specified in advance. The algorithm returns, for every case of the database, the probability of it being part of each of the clusters. This method thus allows for a more refined observation of how well-delimited the groups are and how much overlap occurs between them. Moreover, based on the calculated probabilities, the procedures can identify whether the number of clusters provided corresponds with the data, or whether their number was smaller.[10] The R function that performs fuzzy clustering is *fanny* from the *cluster* package; it is largely based on the method described by Kaufman and Rousseeeuw (2005, pp. 164–196).

[10] The procedure cannot signal the existence of more clusters than what it was given.

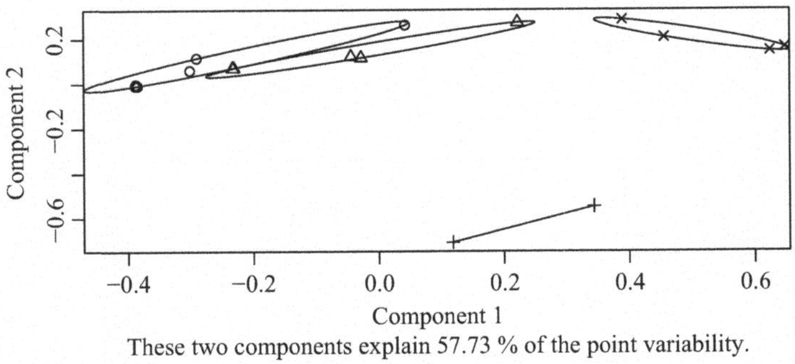

Fig. 3.6 Example of two-dimensional graph generated by PAM for 20 graves from the database. The graves belonging to the same cluster are represented using the same symbols and circled together or connected by a line

In addition to the three clustering methods, a Multidimensional Scaling tool was used to help visualize the clusters and their relationships. The purpose of this method, also known as Principal Coordinates Analysis, is to produce an n-dimensional graphic representation of the cases based on how similar or different the cases are to each other (Drennan 1996, pp. 285–297). The basic principle is that the cases that are more similar will be placed closer to one another in the n-dimensional graph, while the ones that are dissimilar will be placed at a larger distance. Hence, the similarity of the cases is proportional to the distance between them in the graph. The ideal situation is for the graph to have only two dimensions, since such a representation can more easily be read. The results of PAM were represented in this manner in Fig. 3.6. Unfortunately, when a low number of dimensions are used, the correlation between the points corresponding to each case on the graph and the similarity between the cases becomes weaker. That is why more than two dimensions sometimes need to be employed, but such graphical representations are harder to read and interpret. In this study, the *metaMDS* function from the *vegan* statistical package of R was used (Oksanen et al. 2013), which does a Nonmetric Multidimensional Scaling with Stable Solution from Random Starts. This function has the enormous advantage that, unlike most multidimensional scaling algorithms, it is adapted to work with nonmetric data, which is the type of data used in this study. At the same time, it is considered to be a very robust method that can produce highly accurate results (Minchin 1987).

The solutions obtained from applying the four algorithms described above were validated to confirm that a good and robust solution was obtained. First of all, the results obtained from the clustering methods were internally validated using *silhouette* width measurements (Rousseeuw 1987) and the *Dunn coefficient* (Dunn 1974). The *silhouette* determines for each individual case a coefficient between −1 and 1 by comparing the separation of that case from its cluster against the cluster's heterogeneity. If the index is higher than 0, then it is likely that the case is well-clustered; conversely, if the index is negative, then the case is probably badly clustered (Everitt et al. 2011, pp. 128–129; Kaufman and Rousseeuw 2005, pp. 83–102). This index

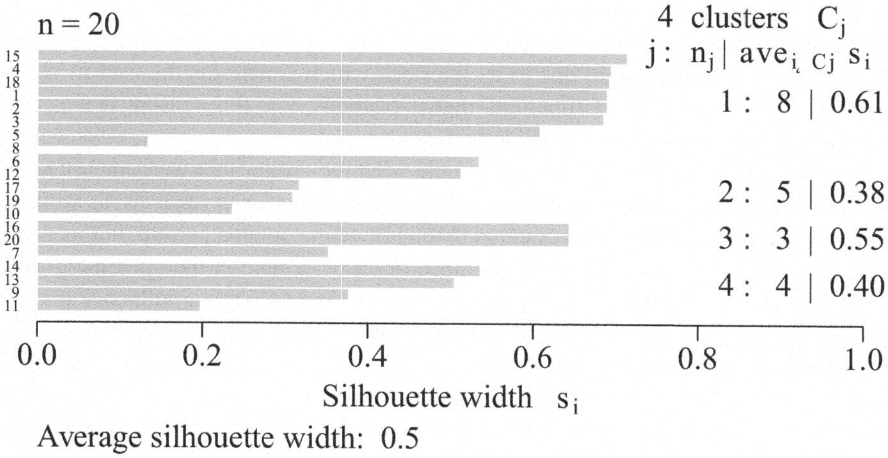

Fig. 3.7 Graphical representation of the PAM silhouette values for the 20 clustered graves

is commonly represented graphically as it allows one to observe easily any problems with the groups as well as individual cases (Fig. 3.7). The *Dunn coefficient* is used to complete the *silhouette* results. It is an index that gives a result between 0 and 1, with 0 meaning that very fuzzy clusters were obtained and 1 implying that crispy solutions were determined (Everitt et al. 2011, p. 246). Given the nature of the calculation that it computes, *Dunn coefficient* requires for the clusters to be extremely well-separated in order for it to produce a high value. Consequently, it can often give low values even for solid results, if the clusters do not have very clear borders or are not entirely differentiated (Halkidi et al. 2001, pp. 130–131).

Besides computing the two indexes for internal validation, the clustering solutions were externally validated by comparing them to each other. This involved merging the clustering results into a single matrix and examining this matrix to identify how similar or different the outputs were. A good measure of this similarity was the *adjusted Rand index* (Everitt et al. 2011, pp. 264–265; Hubert and Arabie 1985; Miligan and Cooper 1986).

3.2.3 Statistical Analysis: The Use of SPSS

The results obtained from running the similarity and clustering algorithms were exported to SPSS together with the initial data. SPSS was employed in order to validate further the clustering results and to determine the elements that were characteristic of each of the identified groups.

It was decided to move the data from R to SPSS for this step of the analysis because of the more user-friendly interface of the latter program. SPSS allows for easy visualization of the results in a tabular and graphical form. Therefore, it is optimal for doing descriptive statistics, such as frequency calculations and cross-tabulations. However, SPSS behaves poorly when more complex analyses are required, as it is highly rigid due to its interface which constrains the user to work with the limited number of functions that it contains. For this reason, it was not practical to use the program for the actual cluster analysis.

Instead, SPSS was deployed to understand what the groups that were identified in R stood for. Hence, all the variables that were used in the cluster analysis, as well as individual variable values, were counted in relation to the obtained group. In this way, it was possible to observe the preponderance of each variable in the outcome of the clustering and to check whether the absence of data had a dramatic influence on the results. For instance, if one of the groups contained all the graves for which there was no information related to *material*, then it was highly likely that the clustering was incorrect, as the absence of data was a reason for which those graves were identified as being similar to each other. Besides looking at individual variables, several variables and variable values were taken together and cross-tabulated with the group numbers to identify whether they had a tendency to occur together as sets in the graves.

At this step, the independent variables that were left out of the cluster analysis, such as *age*, *sex*, *chronology*, or *geographical position*, were brought in. Their distribution across the different clusters was examined so as to identify whether certain values were predominating in particular groups. Such a method can help to pin point specific types of identities that were manifested in the funerary ritual (e.g., gender identity, regional identity). For some of these variables, such as *age* or *sex*, much information was lacking, but this dearth did not affect the results, as the variables did not contribute to the clustering outcome.

3.2.4 Spatial Analysis: The Use of ArcGIS

ArcGIS was used to observe the geographical distribution of the graves, of the individual variable values, and of the groups obtained through clustering. The generated map was also compared to the two-dimensional graph produced by the Multidimensional Scaling tool.

In order to obtain a map of the region, satellite imagery was employed. The satellite images were taken from the ASTER Global Digital Elevation Model (Aster GDEM2),[11] which provides the data free of charge. A large number of images needed to be downloaded so as to cover the entire area under study. They were mosaicked together and georeferenced in ArcGIS. Afterwards, hydrological information was added; the data were obtained from the European Union Catchment Characterization and Modelling project.[12] Finally, the computed map, containing all these elements, was cut so as to correspond exactly to the boundaries of the region from where the data derive.

[11] http://gdem.ersdac.jspacesystems.or.jp/

[12] http://ccm.jrc.ec.europa.eu/php/index.php?action=view&id=23

On the geographical map thus obtained, the location of the graves from the database was plotted. The location of the graves was in most cases very vague, with just the nearest locality being mentioned. Hence, the exact positioning of the graves could not be determined. Nonetheless, because the aim was not to have very detailed spatial analysis, this did not represent a major obstacle. The geographical coordinates were obtained in most cases through Google Maps; all the graves were then georeferenced in ArcGIS.

After the geographical distribution was obtained, statistical data was added. Each of the computed groups was plotted to observe whether they corresponded to narrow or wide areas or whether they overlapped with certain geographical regions. Particular attention was given to the interaction between the different groups: whether several groups appeared in a small area, whether certain groups appeared often together, or whether they were never present in the same region. Moreover, the importance of geographical features was also considered, especially in the case of mountain ranges, rivers, or lakes. It was examined whether such features delimited the extension of the grave groups, in which case they could correspond to identity barriers. Besides plotting the clusters, individual variables, variable groups as well as their values were charted when deemed necessary. This helped to understand the dynamic of group identity as it allowed for the identification of barriers that were being maintained or zones of intense mixture.

A final procedure was to compare the geographical distribution of the graves and of the groups with a two-dimensional graph generated by the Multidimensional Scaling tool.[13] Such a comparison was useful for further investigating the role played by geographical distance in the coagulation of the identified groups. In this sense, it was possible to observe whether the groups that were statistically dispersed on the graph were similarly dispersed geographically. In addition, it gave the option to note whether the groups and graves that were found to be very far or very close to each other statistically presented themselves in a similar manner when plotted on the map. All of these calculations and observations were basically aimed at analysing the relationships between the statistical and the geographical distance (e.g., directly proportional, inversely proportional, non-proportional).

3.3 The Road to the Results

The final results of the analysis, presented in the following chapter, were not obtained from the first trial. It was necessary to run the analysis many hundreds and even thousands of times. After every run, the results were checked for statistical and empirical validation and adjustments were made to improve them.

In the first run, no weight was added to any of the funerary ritual or grave-goods variables and variable values. Also, the α parameter from the ritual and grave-good

[13] For similar comparison see the studies of Nakoinz (Nakoinz 2009, 2013; Nakoinz and Steifen 2008).

combination equation was left in its default position, namely 1, for all cases. This resulted in a split based purely on the funerary ritual data, since the similarity given by those variables was always higher than that of the grave-good variables due to a lower number of choices available for each of them. Thus, it was necessary to change α to a higher value. Moreover, its value had to change according to the number of grave-goods contained by the graves under comparison.[14] After numerous trials, it was established that the best outcome was obtained when α took values between 2.5 and 4, depending on the maximum number of items contained in the compared graves. The results produced using these α values were not determined purely by the funerary ritual variables, but rather a balance was struck between them and the grave-good variables.

Unfortunately, the clustering algorithms were still far from giving results that could pass validation. Very faint groupings could already be intimated, although their exact number was still uncertain. The main concern thus became to assign weights to each variable and, when necessary, to specific variable values in order to clarify those initial patterns. All of these weights thus represented parameters that influenced the results. However, given their large number and the virtually infinite possible values that they could take, it required a long number of trials until an acceptable result was reached. This procedure basically represented a fine-tuning of the analysis to the cultural framework that was in place for the Late La Tène communities of the Eastern Carpathian basin and the Lower Danube. The analysis parameters which corresponded to the desired cultural framework had to be assessed through a trial-and-error method that ran in an iterative loop until no further improvement could be achieved. The best way to describe this procedure is through the analogy of a complex radio which has to be tuned in to a faint radio signal. The analysis constitutes the actual radio and the analysis parameters are its numerous knobs which can be turned up or down to adjust the frequency. When the radio is first turned on, a weak signal, full of interference, can be heard in the background. The task is to rotate the knobs so as to reduce the background noise and make the radio signal clearer. Yet, the user has no knowledge of which exact knobs need to be adjusted and by which value. My solution was to rotate each knob individually, or several at a time if deemed appropriate, and hear whether the signal is becoming stronger or weaker. This is repeated until either the background noise is entirely gone or until it is brought to a level that cannot be reduced further. In a very similar manner, the analysis parameters of the statistics were adjusted numerous times, followed by an evaluation of the results and thus of the effects of those adjustments. If the results were improved, then that particular solution was flagged as the new basis for further adjustments; if not, then the previous best solution was kept. This procedure was repeated numerous times, until the results passed validation procedures and until any further adjustments of the parameters were found to decrease rather than increase the statistical validation indexes and solution quality.[15]

[14] The argument for this can be found in the previous section of this chapter.

[15] Therefore it cannot be stated for certain that the best solution was reached; it is doubtful that a perfect outcome even exists. The only thing that can be said is that all attempts to improve that particular result, within a reasonable time limit, failed.

The adjustments made to the analysis parameters were, however, not done entirely randomly—although at times gradual, random modifications from a given solution were also utilized—but rather through informed, structured guesses. Most of the parameter changes were based on observations made in SPPS. Using basic exploratory procedures, such as frequency calculations or cross-tabulations, the output of the R analysis was examined for the variables and/or variable values that could strengthen the result and those that added noise. If some variables and/or some of their values contributed to clearer clusters, then a higher weight was put on them at the next run of the analysis. On the other hand, if the reverse was true, then their weight was reduced. For instance, it was observed that in terms of grave-goods, most clusters mainly differentiated themselves based on the values of *category 1* and especially *category 2*. As a result, a higher emphasis was placed on the two variables, particularly on the second. On the other hand, most values of *category 4* and *material* were found to be shared relatively equally across several groups. This had the effect of an increased similarity between graves that appertained to different clusters; this meant more noise and less clear results. Consequently, the weight of those variables was reduced. A similar logic was also applied to individual variable values. Using such data-informed observations, it was deduced which variables and variable values needed to have their weight adjusted and in which direction (up or down). Yet, the exact weight figures were not inferable. For that, it was necessary to assign different values to each and pick the one that produced the best outcome. This entire procedure was repeated every time a new optimal solution was reached.

In the process of adjusting the weights of variables and variable values, two things needed to be constantly checked for: the effect of missing values and the impact of high weights. Since the data quality was very poor, most variables had at least some missing values. Despite the similarity algorithm not utilizing missing values in the grave comparisons, they undoubtedly still influenced the outcome of the analysis.[16] Hence, it was necessary to check the impact that they had on the results. This meant verifying whether missing values served as a basis for clustering.[17] If in the case of a variable this was found to be true, then it was necessary to reduce the weight of that variable so as to counterbalance the missing values effect. The variables and variable values that had very high weights assigned to them also needed to be controlled. In that case, it was normal that some clusters were defined and, at least to some extent, based on those variables and variable values; the issue was one of magnitude. If their weights were too high, it could happen that much or all of the clustering was based solely on one specific variable or one of its values, minimizing the role of all other analytical elements. When this was observed, the solution was simply to reduce the very high weights until the effect disappeared. By continuously scanning for these two issues, which were otherwise not identified

[16] For this reason, the extent of the missing values was a factor that influenced the choice of variables for the statistical analysis, as stated in the previous subsection of this chapter.

[17] In other words, it was observed whether the graves that had variables with missing values were clustered in a specific group or whether they were dispersed among several/all groups.

through internal validation procedures,[18] it was ensured that the results were not artificially created by the user or poor data.

3.3.1 Weight Calibration Example

For the purpose of illustrating how the weight calibration functions, a series of steps are illustrated in which the weight of grave-good variables and variable values is adjusted. At each step, the justification for any weight modifications is introduced, along with the clustering results of applying those weights and the evaluation of that particular solution. While in some cases those steps followed directly one after the other in the analysis procedure, in other instance there may have been a series of additional intermediary steps, most of which involved results that were negatively evaluated. Nevertheless, the steps still exemplify how the calibration of the weight parameters was achieved on a practical level. The clustering procedure used was PAM, since it allowed for an easy evaluation of solutions with a large range of clusters. However, when particularly promising results were obtained by PAM, the solution was compared against the outcome of hierarchical clustering.

3.3.1.1 Step 0

Step 0 represents the starting point for this example. The ritual weights were fixed in previous steps to 7 for *burial type*, 10 for *ritual type,* and 5 for *multiple burial*, since these values were found to give the best results to that particular point. The grave-good variables were each given a weight of 1 and no weight was placed on any of the individual variable values. This implies that no calibration was done to any of the variables used to compare the objects deposited in the graves.

At this point, by far the largest silhouette values were obtained for three clusters (Table 3.1). However, this particular clustering was not very helpful since the results basically showed a splitting into inhumations without grave-goods, inhumations with grave-goods, and cremation graves (Table 3.2). The wish was at this point to increase the silhouette values in order to obtain solutions with a higher number of clusters, if possible. To do this, it was necessary to find a way of splitting the three groups (Fig. 3.8).

[18]The internal validation procedures were quite misleading in this regard. Usually the clustering results based on missing data, and especially those determined by high weights, produced good validation indexes. Furthermore, fixing the issues mainly gave results with lower validation values.

Table 3.1 Silhouette values for steps 0–8

No. of clusters	PAM clustering silhouette figures								
	Step 0	Step 1	Step 2	Step 3	Step 4	Step 5	Step 6	Step 7	Step 8
2	0.273	0.278	0.291	0.262	0.256	0.272	0.280	0.270	0.280
3	0.315	0.335	0.343	0.331	0.257	0.341	0.348	0.339	0.352
4	0.222	0.284	0.324	0.322	0.167	0.331	0.329	0.328	0.349
5	0.234	0.246	0.281	0.278	0.209	0.279	0.281	0.282	0.288
6	0.241	0.263	0.289	0.275	0.215	0.276	0.277	0.283	0.290
7	0.235	0.258	0.285	0.263	0.214	0.267	0.272	0.276	0.283
8	0.229	0.242	0.283	0.261	0.213	0.260	0.263	0.273	0.270
9	0.208	0.243	0.292	0.239	0.209	0.252	0.261	0.265	0.270
10	0.203	0.257	0.290	0.252	0.219	0.252	0.259	0.259	0.269

3.3.1.2 Step 1

There was no obvious step to take in order to split groups 1 and 3. Hence, it was decided to start by raising the weight on *category 1* to 3, while leaving all the other weights constant. This gave the possibility to observe the effect of putting emphasis on this particular variable.

Unfortunately, the effects on the results were minimal with the silhouette values barely increasing for most clustering solutions (Table 3.1). Nonetheless, some positive effects could be observed, since the silhouette values for more than three clusters did indeed increase. However, the actual results of the weight increase were not clearly visible because the value assigned to *category 1* was still rather small. Thus, it was deemed necessary to further increase the weight on that variable for the effects to be observed.

3.3.1.3 Step 2

For the next step, it was decided to further increase the weight on *category 1* to 10. While this was a large weight increase, it gave the possibility to assess the actual effect of raising the weight on this particular variable. For further solutions, the weight could be reduced, if it was found to influence the results too much.

The PAM clustering revealed a significant increase in silhouette values over the previous two steps (Table 3.1). This effect was particularly observable for clustering solutions involving three groups or more. Therefore, it was deduced that increasing the weight on *category 1* had the desired effect.

3.3.1.4 Step 3

For the next step, the effect of adding weight on *category 2* was tested. The weight on *category 1* was reset to 0, while that of *category 2* was raised to 10. Increasing the weight by small values produced minimal results as was the case in step 1.

Table 3.2 Step 0 *object category 1* values by *ritual type* for the three groups PAM solution

	PAM group							
	1			2		3		
	Cenotaph	Cremation	Inhumation	Cremation	Inhumation	Cenotaph	Cremation	Inhumation
	Count	Count	Count	Count	Count	Count	Count	Count
Adornment or clothing accessory	1	5	51	0	0	2	85	4
Coin	0	0	0	0	0	1	1	0
Horse gear	0	0	0	0	0	2	69	2
Tool	0	0	5	0	0	0	40	4
Vessel and vessel implement	0	2	9	0	0	4	131	6
Weapon	0	0	3	0	0	5	161	5

The counts refer to number of graves rather than number of objects

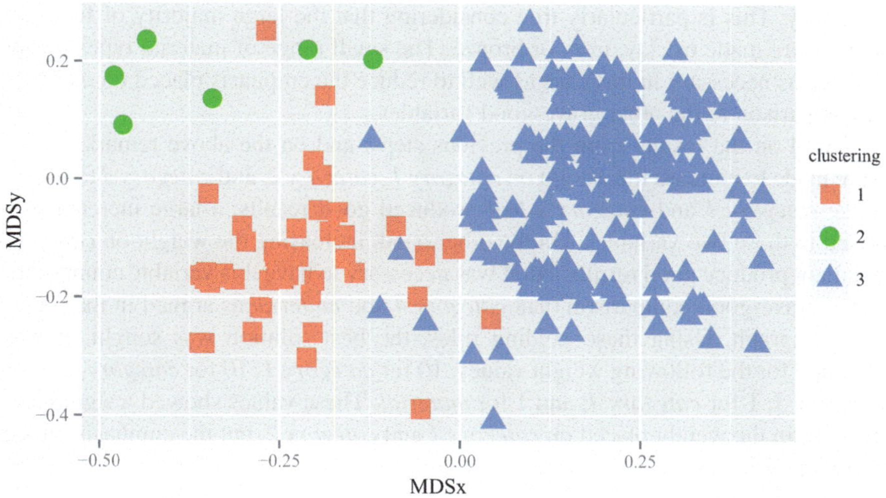

Fig. 3.8 2D representation of step 0 PAM results using MetaMDS

Therefore, it was opted to increase the weight to 10 in order to clearly observe the results and to have an outcome comparable to that from step 2.

The clustering results saw once again a significant increase in silhouette values, similar to that from step 2 (Table 3.1). This indicated that increasing the weight on *category 2* produced more robust groups, and thus, it was a good option to place significant emphasis on this variable.

3.3.1.5 Step 4

The effect of increasing the weight on *category 3* was also tested. The weights on *category 1* and *category 2* were once again reset to 0. Using the same logic and procedure as that from the previous step, the weight on *category 3* was raised to 10.

The clustering results revealed a decrease in silhouette values when compared to those obtained at step 0 (Table 3.1). This indicated that *category 3* should not be emphasized much since it had the effect of reducing the robustness of the clustering solutions.

3.3.1.6 Step 5

The weight on *category 4* was not tested for its effect when increased because 39.5% of the data for this variable was missing, which would certainly create clustering based on the lack of data. It was actually desired to decrease the emphasis on this variable in comparison to the other three grave-good category variables. Increasing the weight on *material* was also not implemented because it is unlikely that the material of the grave-goods constituted a principal element in terms of identity similarity. This is particularly true considering that the large majority of funerary items were made of clay, iron, or bronze. The small range of material types meant that it was necessary in this case as well to reduce the emphasis placed on *material* in comparison to the other grave-good variables.

Based on the results from the previous steps, and on the above remarks, trials were made to increase the weight on *category 1*, *category 2*, and *category 3* together. Since *category 1* and *category 2* had produced good results, a large increase was added to these two variables. On the other hand, increasing the weight on *category 3* did not produce good results, but it was necessary to have this variable count more in the grave-good comparison than *category 4* and *material* as argued in the previous paragraph. Using these guiding rules, the best solution was sought. It was obtained for the following weight values: 10 for *category 1*; 10 for *category 2*; 5 for *category 3*; 1 for *category 4*; and 1 for *material*. These values showed a significant increase in the weight placed on *category 1* and *category 2*, but the emphasis on the two variables was far lower than that from steps 2 and 3, given that the sum of all the variable weights was used for normalizing the comparison results.

The silhouettes obtained at this step were higher than those from the steps before for several of the clustering solutions (Table 3.1). It is interesting to note that the silhouette value for the four cluster solution rose all the way to 0.33, just 0.01 from the value obtained in the case of three clusters, although these figures were not far from those of step 3. Nevertheless, this solution was tested for its correspondence with the results of hierarchical clustering. A dendrogram was thus produced using the Diana procedure, which was cut with the dynamic tree method. This resulted in five rather than four groups and several graves were not clustered at all. This solution had very little resemblance to that of PAM, indicating that a good solution was not reached. Nevertheless, the PAM silhouette values suggest that the three initial clusters were closer to being split, meaning that steps in the right direction were being made. This could also be guessed, albeit with difficulty, when comparing the multidimensional scaling results obtained at step 0 and step 5 (Fig. 3.9).

3.3.1.7 Step 6

In order to further improve the results, it was necessary to start applying weights to the different variable values. For this procedure, the results and variable weights from step 5 were used as a first basis. In the particular steps exemplified here, no further modifications of the variable weights took place. However, for the fine-tuning of the final results, additional changes were still implemented.

The three groups clustering result from step 5, which had the highest silhouette, was explored using exploratory procedures in SPSS in order to find ways of improving it. The aim was to split the already obtained groups using the weighing mechanism and produce results with acceptable silhouettes. One strategy was to find values which appeared in a balanced percentage in one group, preferably between 25 and 75%, and were not found in many of the graves from other groups. Increasing the weigh on this value allowed for the initial group to be more easily split by the

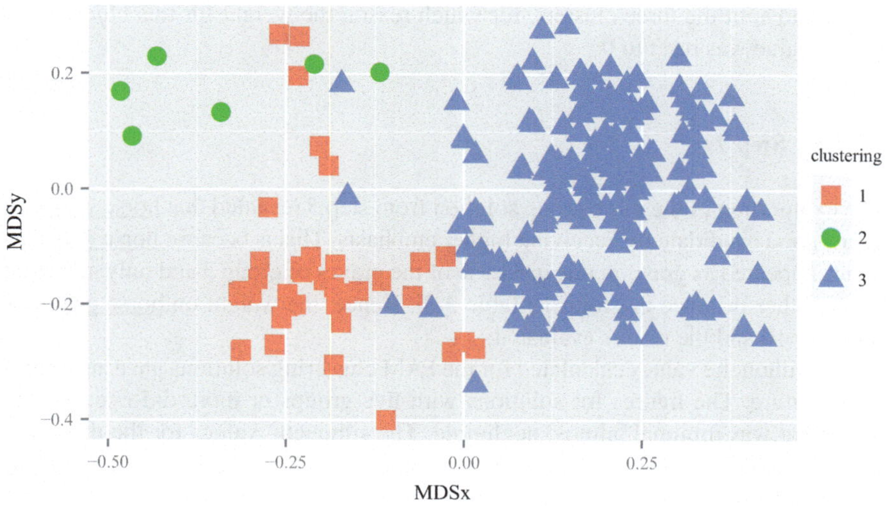

Fig. 3.9 2D representation of step 5 PAM results using MetaMDS

Table 3.3 Step 5 *object category 1* values the three groups PAM solution

	PAM group		
	1	2	3
	Percent	Percent	Percent
Adornment or clothing accessory	87.9%	13.8%	38.1%
Coin	0.0%	0.0%	0.9%
Horse gear	1.7%	0.0%	31.9%
Tool	10.3%	2.5%	18.1%
Vessel and vessel implement	20.7%	6.3%	59.7%
Weapon	5.2%	2.5%	74.8%

The percentages refer to number of graves rather than number of objects

clustering procedures. However, if that value also occurred in other groups, it could have the opposite effect and reduce the silhouette values, since it made the graves from different clusters more similar to one another. This procedure was carried out starting with the values of *category 1* and continued with those of the other variables in decreasing hierarchical order.

Looking at the distribution of the *object category 1* values, it was decided to increase the weight placed on vessels, since they were found in 59.7% of the group 3 graves (Table 3.3). However, raising the weight on vessels to 10 only produced a minimal increase of the silhouette values for some of the clustering solutions. It actually added to the robustness of the three clusters solution and decreased the silhouette for the four clusters result (Table 3.1). This may be due to the fact that vessels were also found in a significant percentage in the graves of group 1. Therefore, this increase in emphasis on vessels did not have the desired effect of helping to split the three clusters, for which reason the weight for this *object category 1* value was reset to 0.

3.3.1.8 Step 7

The exploration of the three group solution from step 5 revealed that horse gear was also a good candidate for receiving higher emphasis. This is because horse gear elements appeared as grave-goods in 31.9% of the graves of group 3 and only appeared in one other instance in group 1 (Table 3.3). Hence, the weight on horse gear was raised to 10 and the results evaluated.

The silhouette values calculated for the PAM clustering solutions gave an ambivalent picture. The figures for solutions with five groups or more did rise, but the increment was minimal, almost negligible. The silhouette values for the three and four cluster solutions decreased by a small amount (Table 3.1). It was decided that these results were not convincing enough to justify the increase in weight. Therefore, all the *object category 1* weights were once again reset to 0.

3.3.1.9 Step 8

Adornments and clothing accessories and weapons were the only other values that could have the desired effect when emphasized. However adornments appeared in large quantities in both groups 1 and 3, suggesting that they were probably not a good choice in terms of weight increase. On the other hand, weapons were found almost only in group 3 (Table 3.3). There was another indication that weapons were the right choice. As previously remarked, for the clustering results obtained at step 5, the four groups solution had a silhouette value that was only 0.01 smaller than that of the three groups solution (Table 3.1). When the four groups solution was explored, it was found that cluster three from the three groups solution had been split into two groups based mostly on the presence or absence of weapons (Table 3.4). Hence, to increase the silhouette and facilitate clustering in more than three groups, it was necessary to place more emphasis on weapons.

Table 3.4 Step 5 *object category 1* values the four groups PAM solution

	PAM group			
	1	2	3	4
	Percent	Percent	Percent	Percent
Adornment or clothing accessory	93.3%	0.0%	30.5%	53.6%
Coin	0.0%	0.0%	1.3%	0.0%
Horse gear	0.0%	0.0%	44.8%	4.8%
Tool	8.3%	0.0%	15.6%	23.8%
Vessel and vessel implement	6.7%	0.0%	44.2%	95.2%
Weapon	5.0%	0.0%	99.4%	21.4%

The percentages refer to number of graves rather than number of objects

Raising the weight on weapons to 10 did indeed produce positive results, leading to a significant increase in the silhouettes figures for clustering solutions having four groups or more. The solution with four and three clusters had nearly an identical silhouette value at this point (Table 3.1). Furthermore, the six clusters solution reached a silhouette value of 0.29.

3.3.1.10 Steps 8+

The distribution of the *category 1* values did not show any other potential for weight increase, for which reason possible candidates were sought for the weights of the other grave-good variables. Through numerous other steps, the silhouette values were gradually increased until no better solution was obtained. It should be mentioned that this involved changing several of the weight values established in the steps illustrated here, since it was found that different figures gave better solutions when combined with the weights of other variable values.

The outcome of all these procedures was a series of grave clusters which were interpreted in terms of group identity. However, before such an interpretation was possible, it was necessary to separately characterize each of the clusters in terms of funerary ritual elements, grave-goods, and geographical spread, as well as have the results validated using internal and external methods. All of this represents the focus of the following chapter.

References

Abonyi, J., & Feil, B. (2007). *Cluster analysis for data mining and system identification*. Basel: Birkhäuser.

Agresti, A. (1990). *Categorical data analysis*. New York: Wiley.

Agresti, A. (2007). *An introduction to categorical data analysis* (2nd ed.). Hoboken, NJ: Wiley-Interscience.

Allison, J. R. (2008). Exchanging identities. Early Pueblo I red ware exchange and identity North of the San Juan River. In M. Varien & J. M. Potter (Eds.), *The social construction of communities: Agency, structure, and identity in the Prehispanic Southwest* (pp. 41–68). Lanham: Rowman & Littlefield Publishers.

Anderson, B. (1991). *Imagined communities: Reflections on the origin and spread of nationalism*. London: Verso.

Babić, S. (2005). Status identity and archaeology. In M. Díaz-Andreu, S. Lucy, S. Babić, & D. Edwards (Eds.), *The archaeology of identity: Approaches to gender, age, status, ethnicity and religion* (pp. 67–85). London: Routledge.

Banks, M. (1996). *Ethnicity: Anthropological constructions*. London: Routledge.

Barth, F. (1969a). *Ethnic groups and boundaries: The social organization of culture difference*. Boston: Little, Brown and Company.

Barth, F. (1969b). Introduction. In F. Barth (Ed.), *Ethnic groups and boundaries: The social organization of culture difference* (pp. 9–38). Boston: Little, Brown and Company.

Barth, F. (2000). Boundaries and connections. In A. P. Cohen (Ed.), *Signifying identities. Anthropological perspectives on boundaries and contested values* (pp. 17–36). London: Routledge.

Baxter, M. (2003). *Statistics in archaeology*. Chichester: John Wiley & Sons.

Binford, L. R. (1962). Archaeology as anthropology. *American Antiquity, 28*, 217–225.

Binford, L. R. (1968). Archaeological perspectives. In L. R. Binford & S. R. Binford (Eds.), *New perspectives in archaeology* (pp. 5–32). Chicago: Aldine.
Bourdieu, P. (1977). *Outline of a theory of practice*. Cambridge: Cambridge University Press.
Bouzek, J., & Domaradzka, L. (2007). Tradition of ethnic identity in the funeral rites during the history of the Roman Empire: The case of Thrace. *Acta Terrae Septemcastrensis, 6*(1), 43–48.
Canuto, M.-A., & Yaeger, J. (2000). Introducing an archaeology of communities. In M.-A. Canuto & J. Yaeger (Eds.), *The archaeology of communities: A New World perspective* (pp. 1–15). London: Routledge.
Cohen, A. P. (2000). Introduction: Discriminating relations – identity, boundary and authenticity. In A. P. Cohen (Ed.), *Signifying identities. Anthropological perspectives on boundaries and contested values* (pp. 1–13). London: Routledge.
Demoule, J. (1999). Ethnicity, culture and identity: French archaeologists and historians. *Antiquity, 73*, 190–198.
Derks, T., & Roymans, N. (Eds.). (2009). *Ethnic constructs in antiquity: The role of power and tradition*. Amsterdam: Amsterdam University Press.
Díaz-Andreu, M. (2005). Gender identity. In M. Díaz-Andreu, S. Lucy, S. Babić, & D. Edwards (Eds.), *The archaeology of identity: Approaches to gender, age, status, ethnicity and religion* (pp. 13–43). London: Routledge.
Di, H. (2013). Approaches to the archaeology of ethnogenesis: Past and emergent perspectives. *Journal of Archaeological Research, 21*(4), 371–402.
Drennan, R. D. (1996). *Statistics for archaeologists: A commonsense approach*. New York: Plenum.
Dunn, J. C. (1974). Some recent investigations of a new fuzzy partitioning algorithm and its application to pattern classification problems. *Journal of Cybernetics, 4*, 1–15.
Erciyas, B. D. (2005). Ethnic identity and archaeology in the Black Sea region of Turkey. *Antiquity, 79*, 179–190.
Eriksen, T. H. (1993). *Ethnicity and nationalism: Anthropological perspectives*. London: Pluto Press.
Everitt, B., & Hothorn, T. (2009). *A handbook of statistical analyses using R*. New York: CRC Press.
Everitt, B., Landau, S., Leese, M., & Stahl, D. (2011). *Cluster analysis* (5th ed.). Chichester: Wiley.
Fowler, C. (2004). *The archaeology of personhood: An anthropological approach*. London: Routledge.
Graves-Brown, P. (1996). All things bright and beautiful? Species, ethnicity and cultural dynamics. In P. Graves-Brown, S. Jones, & C. Gamble (Eds.), *Cultural identity and archaeology: The construction of European communities* (pp. 81–95). London: Routledge.
Graves-Brown, P., & Jones, S. (1996). Introduction. Archaeology and cultural identity in Europe. In P. Graves-Brown, S. Jones, & C. Gamble (Eds.), *Cultural identity and archaeology: The construction of European communities* (pp. 1–24). London: Routledge.
Hakenbeck, S. (2004a). Reconsidering ethnicity: An introduction. *Archaeological Review from Cambridge, 19*(2), 1–6.
Hakenbeck, S. (2004b). Ethnic tensions in early medieval cemeteries in Bavaria. *Archaeological Review from Cambridge, 19*(2), 40–55.
Halkidi, M., Batistakis, Y., & Vazirgiannis, M. (2001). On clustering validation techniques. *Journal of Intelligent Information Systems, 17*(2–3), 107–145.
Hall, S. (1996). Introduction: Who needs 'identity'? In S. Hall & P. du Gay (Eds.), *Questions of cultural identity* (pp. 1–17). London: Sage.
Hennig, C. (2013). fpc: Flexible procedures for clustering. Retrieved from http://CRAN.R-project.org/package=fpc
Hennig, C., & Liao, T. F. (2013). How to find an appropriate clustering for mixed-type variables with application to socio-economic stratification. *Journal of the Royal Statistical Society: Series C (Applied Statistics), 62*(3), 309–369. doi:10.1111/j.1467-9876.2012.01066.x.
Hobsbawm, E. J. (1992). Ethnicity and nationalism in Europe today. *Anthropology Today, 8*(1), 3–8.
Hubert, L., & Arabie, P. (1985). Comparing partitions. *Journal of the Classification, 2*, 193–218.
Jenkins, R. (1996). *Social identity*. London: Routledge.

Jones, S. (1996). Discourses of identity in the interpretation of the past. In P. Graves-Brown, S. Jones, & C. Gamble (Eds.), *Cultural identity and archaeology: The construction of European communities* (pp. 62–80). London: Routledge.

Jones, S. (1997). *The archaeology of ethnicity: Constructing identities in the past and present.* London: Routledge.

Jones, S. (1999). Historical categories and the praxis of identity: The interpretation of ethnicity in historical archaeology. In P. P. A. Funari, M. Hall, & S. Jones (Eds.), *Historical archaeology: Back from the edge* (pp. 219–232). London: Routledge.

Jovanović, B. (2005). The challenge of plural identity. *Balcanica, 36*, 71–83.

Jovanović, B. (2008). Ethnic relations within the tribal community of the Scordisci. In V. Sîrbu & I. Stângă (Eds.), *The Iron Gates region during the Second Iron Age. Settlements, necropolises, treasures* (pp. 57–62). Drobeta Turnu-Severin; Craiova: Editura Universitaria.

Kaufman, L., & Rousseeuw, P. J. (2005). Finding groups in data: An introduction to cluster analysis. Chichester: Wiley.

Kuhn, W. (1955). The Hungarian method for the assignment problem. *Naval Research Logistic Quarterly, 2*, 83–97.

Langfelder, P., Zhang, B., & Horvath, S. (2008). Defining clusters from a hierarchical cluster tree: The Dynamic Tree Cut package for R. *Bioinformatics, 24*(5), 719–720. doi:10.1093/bioinformatics/btm563.

Latour, B. (2005). *Reassembling the social: An introduction to actor-network-theory*. Oxford: Oxford University Press.

Lucy, S. (2005). Ethnic and cultural identities. In M. Díaz-Andreu, S. Lucy, S. Babić, & D. Edwards (Eds.), *The Archaeology of identity: Approaches to gender, age, status, ethnicity and religion* (pp. 86–109). London: Routledge.

Maechler, M., Rousseeuw, P., Struyf, A., Hubert, M., & Hornik, K. (2011). *cluster: Cluster analysis basics and extensions*.

Miligan, G. W., & Cooper, M. C. (1986). A study of the comparability of external criteria for hierarchical cluster analysis. *Multivariate Behavioral Research, 21*, 41–58.

Minchin, P. R. (1987). An evaluation of the relative robustness of techniques for ecological ordination. *Vegetatio, 69*, 89–107. doi:10.2307/20038106.

Nakoinz, O. (2009). Zentralortforschung und Zentralörtliche Theorie. *Archäologisches Korrespondenzblatt, 39*(3), 361–380.

Nakoinz, O. (2013). *Archäologische Kulturgeographie der ältereisenzeitlichen Zentralorte Südwestdeutschlands*. Kiel: Habelt.

Nakoinz, O., & Steifen, M. (2008). Zwischen den Fürstensitzen der Hallstattzeit- Das Projekt "Siedlungshierarchien und kulturelle Räume. *Starigard. Jahresbericht des Fördervereins des Instituts für Ur- und Frühgeschichte der Christian-Albrechts-Universität Kiel, 9*, 91–105.

Oksanen, J., Blanchet, F. G., Kindt, R., Legendre, P., Minchin, P. R., O'Hara, R. B., et al. (2013). *vegan: Community ecology package*. Retrieved from http://CRAN.R-project.org/package=vegan

Popa, C. N. (2010). A new framework for approaching Dacian identity. In S. Berecki (Ed.), *Iron Age communities in the Carpathian basin* (pp. 395–423). Cluj-Napoca: Mega.

Popa, C. N. (2012). Till death do us part. A statistical approach to identifying burial similarity and grouping. The case of the Late La Tène graves from the Eastern Carpathian basin. In S. Berecki (Ed.), *Iron Age rites and rituals in the Carpathian basin* (pp. 401–412). Târgu Mureş: Mega.

Popa, C. N., & Stoddart, S. (2014). Fingerprinting the European Iron Age. Historical, cultural and intellectual perspectives on identity and ethnicity. In C. N. Popa & S. Stoddart (Eds.), *Fingerprinting the Iron Age* (pp. 323–331). Oxford: Oxbow.

Robb, J. (2004). The extended artefact and the monumental economy: A methodology for material agency. In E. DeMarrais, C. Gosden, & C. Renfrew (Eds.), *Rethinking materiality: The engagement of mind with the material world* (pp. 131–139). Cambridge: McDonald Institute for Archaeological Research.

Rousseeuw, P. J. (1987). Silhouettes: A graphical aid to the interpretation and validation of cluster analysis. *Journal of Computational and Applied Mathematics, 20*, 53–65.

Roymans, N. (2004). *Ethnic identity and imperial power: The Batavians in the early Roman Empire*. Amsterdam: Amsterdam University Press.

Shennan, S. (1989). Introduction: Archaeological approaches to cultural identity. In S. Shennan (Ed.), *Archaeological approaches to cultural identity* (pp. 1–32). London: Routledge.

Shennan, S. (1997). *Quantifying archaeology* (2nd ed.). Edinburgh: Edinburgh University Press.

Strathern, M. (1999). *Property, substance and effect: Anthropological essays on persons and things*. London: Athlone.

Team R. (2011). *R: A language and environment for statistical computing*. Vienna. Retrieved from http://www.R-project.org/

Tibshirani, R., Walther, G., & Hastie, T. (2001). Estimating the number of clusters in a data set via the gap statistic. *Journal of the Royal Statistical Society: Series B (Statistical Methodology), 63*(2), 411.

Tilley, C. (2006). Objectification. In C. Tilley, W. Keane, S. Küchler, M. Rowlands, & P. Spyer (Eds.), *Handbook of material culture* (pp. 60–71). London: Sage.

Trigger, B. G. (2006). *A history of archaeological thought* (2nd ed.). Cambridge: Cambridge University Press.

Voss, B. L. (2008). *The archaeology of ethnogenesis: Race and sexuality in colonial San Francisco*. London: University of California Press.

Weber, M. (1978). In G. Roth & C. Wittich (Eds.), *Economy and society: An outline of interpretive sociology* (Vol. 1). Berkeley: University of California Press.

Wells, P. S. (1998). Identity and material culture in the later prehistory of Central Europe. *Journal of Archaeological Research, 6*(3), 239–298. doi:10.1023/A:1022828421770.

Chapter 4
A Complex Answer. Results Description

4.1 General Description and Validation

The final results were obtained from a sample of 364 graves after six were taken out due to the noise they were introducing into the clustering procedure. The solution was converged upon by two clustering procedures: Partitioning Around Medoids (PAM) (Kaufman and Rousseeuw 2005, pp. 68–122) and Divisive Analysis Clustering (Diana) (Kaufman and Rousseeuw 2005, pp. 253–279), cut using a hybrid dynamic cut procedure (Langfelder et al. 2008). The two results were very similar, as they presented an adjusted Rand index of 0.7788 (Hubert and Arabie 1985).

The largest internal validation values were produced by PAM for three groups. This result had an average silhouette of 0.3789 and a Dunn index of 0.12, but did not coincide with the outcome of any other clustering procedure. Instead, convergence was obtained for the second best results that PAM produced, which showed the existence of seven clusters. This result had an average silhouette of 0.3622 and a Dunn index of 0.0879.

The results of Diana were cut using hybrid dynamic cut into seven groups, although eight burials could not be clustered in this case. The calculated silhouette was 0.365 and the Dunn index was 0.081. In this case, no better results could be obtained using this procedure; it was not possible to produce a solution of three clusters like the one produced by PAM.

The results of PAM and Diana presented a large degree of similarity, shown by the 0.7788 value calculated for the adjusted Rand index. In practice, this meant that besides the eight burials that could not be clustered by the second method, the two analyses only differed in 34 other instances (Table 4.1).

The other clustering procedures did not produce results that could be employed. They all had lower silhouette and Dunn index values and produced a different number of groups. When compared with the results of PAM or Diana, the average Rand index was usually lower than 0.6. The only exception was the outcome produced through Agglomerative Nesting (Agnes) using Average Linkage (Kaufman

C. N. Popa, *Modelling Identities*, Quantitative Archaeology and Archaeological Modelling, https://doi.org/10.1007/978-3-319-63267-4_4

Table 4.1 Comparison of the count of graves pertaining to each cluster according to PAM and Diana

		Diana								
		1	2	3	4	5	6	7	NA	Total
PAM	1	49	0	0	0	0	0	0	2	51
	2	14	36	0	0	0	0	0	0	50
	3	0	0	62	0	0	0	0	4	66
	4	0	2	0	48	2	0	1	0	53
	5	0	0	0	13	67	0	0	0	80
	6	0	0	0	0	1	25	1	2	29
	7	0	0	0	0	0	0	35	0	35
Total		63	38	62	61	70	25	37	8	364

The *underlined* figures show differences. Column NA refers to the non-clustered graves of Diana

and Rousseeuw 2005, pp. 199–252). When cut with the hybrid dynamic cut procedure, it gave nine groups which averaged at a silhouette of 0.345. However, the average Rand index was only 0.67 with the clustering results of PAM and 0.64 with those of Diana. On the other hand, the results yielded by fuzzy clustering were especially poor, as the silhouette values did not even get as high as 0.15 regardless of the number of groups that it was programmed to find.

Therefore, the final results employed for interpretation are the ones produced by PAM, coinciding largely with those of Diana (Annex A.3 and A.4). The validation parameters, silhouette and Dunn index, gave figures that are reasonable, but not entirely reassuring. There are no precise instructions for the values that these parameters should take in order to be sure that the clusters obtained are real. A silhouette value between 0.36 and 0.37 suggests that the groups obtained are probably the product of patterns that are present in the data, although the artificial nature of the clusters cannot be fully rejected. The Dunn index figure is even less reassuring. There could be multiple reasons for these relatively uncertain values. The first one, which seems most likely, has to do with the nature of the clusters. Some of the obtained groups were rather well-defined, but most of them were very fuzzy; in some cases, it was difficult for the clustering algorithm to distinguish between two groups. While from a clustering perspective this is not a desirable situation,[1] in terms of the identity question from this study such an outcome is actually expected and welcomed. There is little doubt that during the Late Iron Age of the Eastern Carpathian basin and the Lower Danube, just like today, very clearly bounded identity groups did not exist in most cases. There was a lot of middle ground and entanglement since people did not live in voids, but in a world of interactions. This fuzziness made it difficult for the clustering algorithms to identify a border between

[1] It has been pointed out that that internal clustering validation techniques have major difficulties with clusters that are not well separated from one another (Legány et al. 2006). This is augmented in the context of this study by the limitation of using validation measures that only require the distance matrix as input and not the original data.

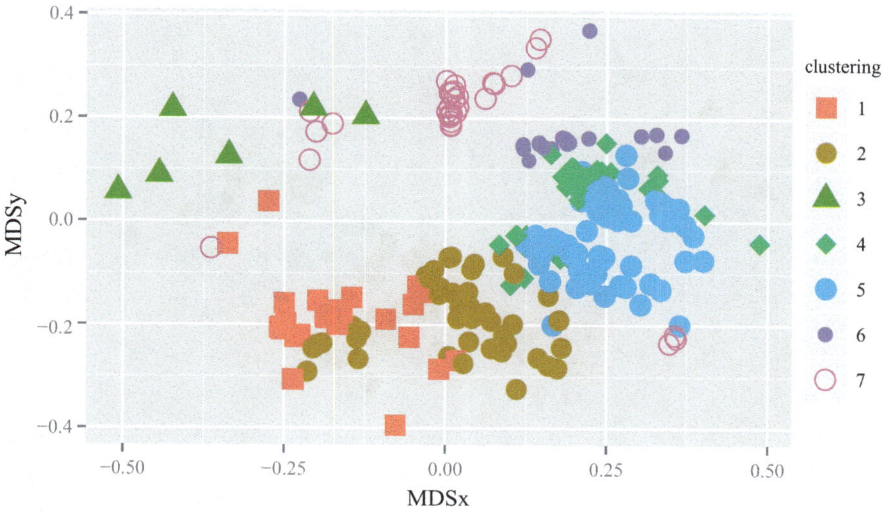

Fig. 4.1 2D representation of PAM results using MetaMDS

one group and another in terms of funerary practices. Following the validation logic of the hermeneutic circle, such results fit well with expectations, indicating that they could be valid, at least in the framework that was deployed (Gadamer 1989, p. 267). A second reason for the uncertain validation values could be the actual inexistence of any clusters. This scenario is improbable since very close results were produced by two different clustering procedures, PAM and Diana. Additionally, the result given by a third method, Agnes, also resembled, to a degree, the outcome of PAM and Diana; some of the groups of the former function were actually almost identical with those produced by the latter two. Moreover, when the clusters are displayed in a 2D graph using multidimensional scaling, the differentiation of the groups is rather obvious (Figs. 4.1 and 4.2); moreover, plotting the results of Agnes easily reveals their resemblance to those of PAM and Diana (Fig. 4.3). Finally, the characterization of each cluster uncovers the main elements that make them (see below) and implicitly demonstrates the existence of a logic on which this clustering was done.

On the whole, there are enough arguments to consider the result of PAM and Diana as both statistically and empirically valid. The groups are fuzzy and sometimes hard to differentiate from one another, affecting the values of the internal validation indexes. But it is this fuzziness that makes the clusters credible since authentic group identities are fluid and interwoven. This characteristic is one of the main features that comes out of the description of the groups below.[2]

[2] In the description of the groups the results of PAM are given primacy over those of Diana since it was found that the outcome of PAM is somewhat more rigorous when looking at the elements that were put in each cluster. Nonetheless, in the cases where there were significant differences between PAM and Diana, for instance groups 1 and 2, both results are equally introduced.

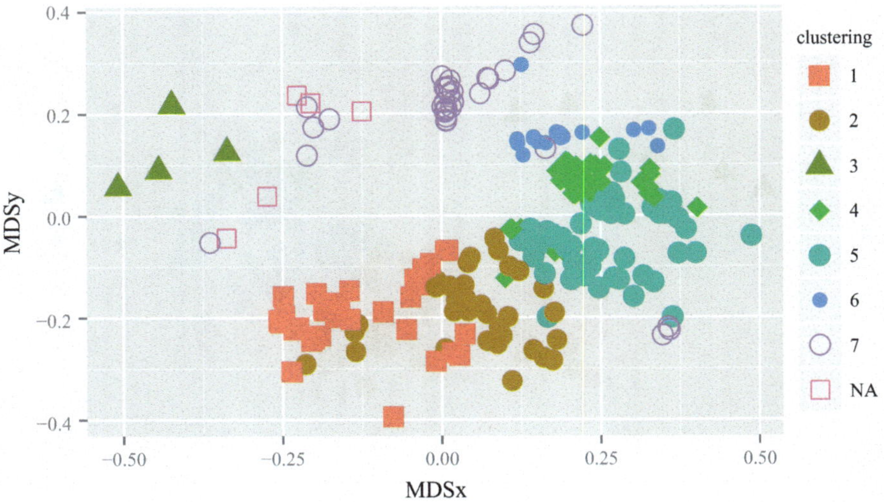

Fig. 4.2 2D representation of Diana results using MetaMDS. NA refers to non-clustered graves

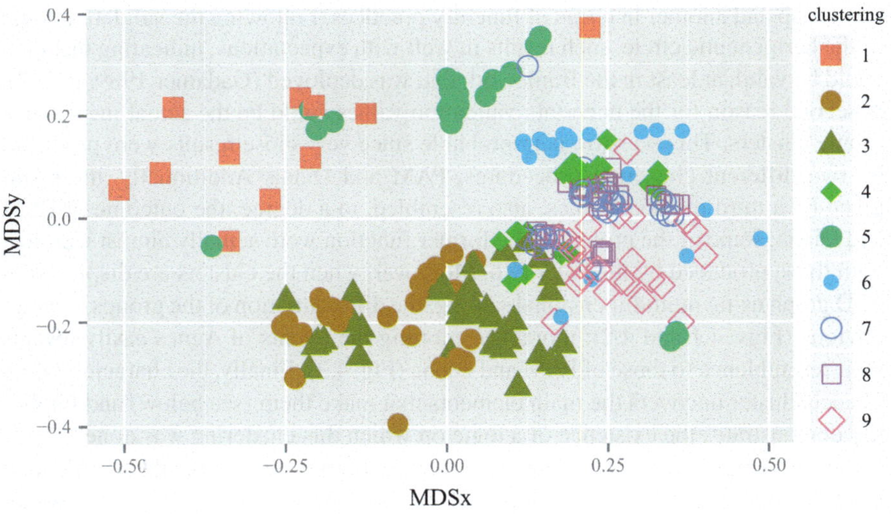

Fig. 4.3 2D representation of Agnes results using MetaMDS

4.2 Group 1

Group 1 contained 51 graves according to the PAM clustering and 63 according to Diana. The difference between the two appears because Diana added 14 graves to group 1 that PAM put in group 2; additionally, two graves that PAM incorporated in group 1 could not be clustered using Diana. This suggests that group 1 bears significant resemblance to group 2, a fact which is confirmed statistically since the separation index between the two was just 0.2 in the case of PAM and 0.24 in the case of Diana.

The cluster consisted of mainly flat inhumations. According to PAM, only seven cremations were included; Diana group 1 contained 14 cremations. There were also a small number of tumulus graves—six tumuli included in the PAM group and eight in the Diana one. The distinction between single and multiple burials seems not to have been important in this case, since the cluster included an almost equal number of both. All the graves were either close to water sources or directly on the banks of a river. Similarly, many graves were found near a settlement; however, a significant number were actually entirely included in one (Table 4.2).

Since most of the graves contained inhumations, it was possible to determine the age of the deceased in a considerable number of cases. The large majority of the skeletons were found to belong either to newborns or to children, although there were also some adults. On the other hand, sex could only be determined in very few instances and the proportion between male and female did not appear to be significant (Table 4.3).

All graves had grave-good items, but usually in small quantities—on average two items per grave. One of the main features of this group seems to have been the presence of adornments or clothing accessories since all graves—with the exception of two in the case of PAM—contained such items, but no more than one. All of these adornments represented costume elements. Other types of objects were found in very small quantities if at all: there were some graves containing vessels—eight according to PAM and 14 according to Diana—and some that had tools—seven graves. The vessels, which may be underrepresented due to recording biases, were employed for either storage, drinking, or eating and cooking; most of the tools were

Table 4.2 Group 1 PAM and Diana counts for *grave type*, *ritual type*, *multiple burials*, *river proximity*, and *settlement proximity* variable

		Count PAM	Percent PAM	Count Diana	Percent Diana
Grave type	Construction	1	2.0	1	1.6
	Flat	44	86.3	54	85.7
	Tumular	6	11.8	8	12.7
Ritual type	Cenotaph	1	2.0	1	1.6
	Cremation	7	13.7	14	22.2
	Inhumation	43	84.3	48	76.2
Multiple burials	No	25	49.0	31	49.2
	Yes	26	51.0	32	50.8
River proximity	Banks	15	29.4	17	27.0
	Near	36	70.6	46	73.0
Settlement proximity	NA	1	2.0	2	3.2
	Inside	17	33.3	20	31.7
	Near	32	62.7	40	63.5
	Far	1	2.0	1	1.6

Table 4.3 Group 1 PAM and Diana counts for *age* and *sex* variables

		Count PAM	Percent PAM	Count Diana	Percent Diana
Age	NA	12	23.5	17	27.0
	Newborn	10	19.6	12	19.0
	Child	16	31.4	20	31.7
	Adolescent	4	7.8	4	6.3
	Adult	9	17.6	10	15.9
Sex	NA	36	70.6	45	71.4
	Female	6	11.8	9	14.3
	Male	9	17.6	9	14.3

used for cutting or perforating. Objects from the category weapons or horse gear consisted singular appearances (Tables 4.4 and 4.5).[3] It is interesting to note that the quantity of grave-goods was very small. Thus, even though most graves had adornments or clothing accessories, their number was only slightly higher than that of the total number of individuals, meaning that the large majority of graves contained only one such item. Solely in the case of Diana, there were eight graves that had two adornments or clothing accessories (Table 4.6). The distribution of tools described a similar situation to adornments or clothing accessories. In contrast, the figure for vessels or vessel implements was quite high considering the number of graves in which they were found. This effect was produced by the three inhumations coming from the site of Gomolava.[4] In terms of the actual object shapes, the most common appearance was that of bead necklaces—mainly simple spherical ones, pendant necklaces—especially bucket-pendants,[5] and fibulae. There were also occurrences of belts and bracelets, although in smaller quantities.[6]

To sum up, it seems that the common type of grave for group 1, which can be thought as the model,[7] is the flat inhumation, placed either near or inside a settlement,

[3] In the case of Diana three graves with weapons were included. It should be noted however that in two of these instances—one grave from Altimir (Theodossiev 2000, p. 106) and one from Kalimanitsa (Theodossiev 2000, p. 118)—there were no actual weapons present in the graves but rather belt chains. The third case—Liubichevats (Bilievina) (Theodossiev 2000, p. 127)—constituted a situation where the identification of the item as a weapon could not be definitely confirmed.

[4] Three individuals—an adult male, an adult female and a child—were found placed together in a pit inside the settlement of Gomolava in what seems to have been a simultaneous burial (Jovanović 1988, pp. 53–57, 175–176). They were placed on and/or covered with sherds coming from at least eight vessels. There was also a fibula just under them. Given this situation it would not have been correct to assign the items with any one individual since they were clearly meant for all three. It was thus thought that it would be more appropriate to enter the material with each of the three, although this created an instance of tripled data.

[5] The bucket-pendants probably functioned as protective amulets and contained organic materials, such as seeds, flowers, animal hair or bones etc. (Egri and Rustoiu personal comment) (Fig. 4.4).

[6] The distribution of vessels is not discussed due to their small number and the important distortion effect produced by the tripled data from the three graves of Gomolava.

[7] The term model is employed in this context to refer to a hypothetical ideal grave of the cluster, one that contains all or most of the characteristics which define the group.

Table 4.4 Count of *object category 1* for PAM and Diana group 1

		Count PAM	Percent PAM	Count Diana	Percent Diana
Object Category 1	NA	1	1.9	0	0.0
	Adornment or clothing Accessory	49	96.0	63	100.0
	Horse gear	1	1.9	1	1.5
	Tool	7	13.7	7	11.1
	Vessels and vessel implement	8	15.6	14	22.2
	Weapon	1	1.9	3	4.7

The counts and percentages refer to number of graves rather than number of objects

Table 4.5 Count of *object category 2* for PAM and Diana group 1

				Count PAM	Percent PAM	Count Diana	Percent Diana
Object Category 1	Adornment or clothing accessory	Object Category 2	NA	1	1.9	1	1.5
			Costume	49	96	63	100.0
	Horse gear	Object Category 2	NA	1	1.9	1	1.5
	Tool	Object Category 2	NA	1	1.9	1	1.5
			Agriculture	1	1.9	1	1.5
			Cutting	3	5.8	2	3.1
			Metalworking	1	1.9	1	1.5
			Perforating	2	3.9	2	3.1
			Weaving	0	0.0	1	1.5
	Vessels and vessel implement	Object Category 2	NA	4	7.8	6	9.5
			Drinking	1	1.9	5	7.9
			Eating and cooking	0	0.0	3	4.7
			Storage	3	5.8	5	7.9
	Weapon	Object Category 2	NA	0	0.0	1	1.5
			Costume (W)	1	1.9	2	3.1

The counts and percentages refer to number of graves rather than number of objects

possibly also near a water source, and containing a small number of adornment or clothing accessories and occasionally vessels.

Examining the geographical spread of this cluster (Fig. 4.5), it is remarkable to note that with the exception of four graves, in the case of the PAM grouping, and eight graves, in the case of the Diana grouping, all the finds came from North of the Danube River and East of the Danube gorges, roughly the area surrounding the Carpathian Mountains arch and corresponding to the modern territory of Romania. The idea that this cluster is more or less centred on the Carpathians is further reinforced by the observation that the finds that appeared outside of this zone, the graves from Bulgaria and Serbia, represent the Southern and Eastern extremities of the

Table 4.6 Count of number of *object category 1* items for PAM and Diana group 1

	No. of objects	PAM Count	Diana Count
Adornment or clothing accessory	0	2	0
	1	49	55
	2	0	8
Coin	0	51	63
Horse gear	0	50	62
	1	1	1
Tool	0	44	56
	1	5	5
	2	1	1
	3	1	1
Vessels and vessel implement	0	43	49
	1	3	8
	2	2	3
	8	3	3
Weapon	0	50	60
	1	1	3

The PAM and Diana counts refer to number of graves rather than number of objects

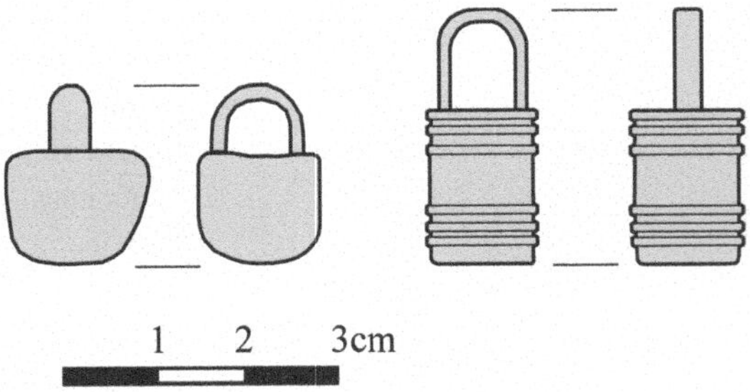

Fig. 4.4 Example of bucket-pendants from Ocnița (after Berciu 1983, p. 34, Fig. 2)

group, placed well outside the distribution area of the other graves, especially in the case of the PAM grouping. The size of this geographical spread of cluster 1 is considerable even when leaving out the graves from Bulgaria and Serbia. On the other hand, over half of the finds came from only two sites: Brad (Moldova) and Hundeoara-Grădina Castelului (Western Transylvania). Brad also represents the Northern limit of the group and is very close to its Eastern limit, whereas the site of Hunedoara-Grădina Castelului constitutes the Western limit, if the graves coming from Serbia are excluded. It should be noted also that, given especially the geographical distribution of the PAM group, the number of funerary finds decreases the further one goes from the mountains, as most graves followed very closely the line of the Carpathian arch. Ultimately, the spatial analysis suggests that cluster 1 describes a pattern of funerary practices that were shared over a relatively large area having at its centre the Carpathian Mountains arch, rarely crossing South of the Danube or East of the Danube gorges.

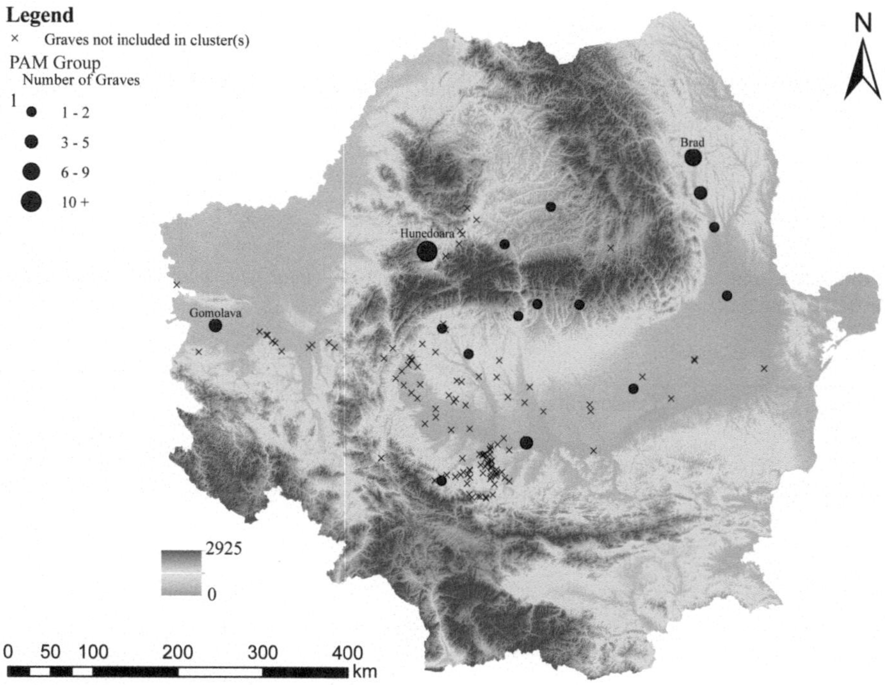

Fig. 4.5 Geographical spread of group 1. The points are placed according to the PAM clustering only because of minimal differences with Diana

4.3 Group 2

Group 2 was made of 50 graves according to the PAM clustering and 38 according to Diana. The 12 grave difference appears to be a product of a number of graves assigned to group 1, instead of group 2 by Diana. As mentioned in the description of group 1, this is the effect of a substantial similarity between the two clusters.

The group consisted mainly of flat cremations, although there were also a number of tumulus cremations and flat inhumations, especially given the PAM clustering (Table 4.7). The large majority of the graves came from single burials and were located either near or on the banks of a river/water source. In addition, most graves were located in the vicinity of a settlement (Table 4.8). Since the dominant ritual was cremation, there were very little data relating to the age and sex of the deceased, and thus no useful information could be extracted from these variables.

All graves contained relatively small quantities of items, but nonetheless more than the graves of group 1. As with the previous cluster, the presence of adornments or clothing accessories seems to have been fundamental, as they appeared in all instances. However, unlike the graves of group 1, more than 70% had two or more of these items, the large majority of which were costume elements, although there

Table 4.7 Cross-tabulation of grave type and ritual type for PAM group 2

		Ritual type			
		Cenotaph	Cremation	Inhumation	Total
Grave type	Construction	0	1	0	1
	Flat	0	27	11	38
	Tumular	1	9	1	11
Total		1	37	12	50

Table 4.8 Group 2 PAM and Diana counts for *grave type*, *ritual type*, *multiple burials*, *river proximity*, and *settlement proximity* variables

		Count PAM	Percent PAM	Count Diana	Percent Diana
Grave type	Construction	1	2.0	1	2.6
	Flat	38	76.0	27	71.1
	Tumular	11	22.0	10	26.3
Ritual type	Cenotaph	1	2.0	1	2.6
	Cremation	37	74.0	32	84.2
	Inhumation	12	24.0	5	13.2
Multiple burials	No	42	84.0	36	94.7
	Yes	8	16.0	2	5.3
River proximity	Banks	14	28.0	13	34.2
	Near	33	66.0	22	57.9
	Far	3	6.0	3	7.9
Settlement proximity	NA	7	14.0	6	15.8
	Inside	4	8.0	0	0.0
	Near	39	78.0	32	84.2

were also two items of toiletry, namely two mirrors.[8] Vessels appear to have been also very important, as they were present in more than 65% of cases. Most of these graves just contained one vessel, although a significant number had two or more. The majority were either drinking or eating and cooking vessels, although there were also nine graves containing storage vessels and three that had lighting vessels. Almost a quarter of the graves also contained tools, nearly all of which were cutting tools, namely knives. Likewise, a quarter of the group 2 graves had weapons, mostly defensive, but also offensive or used for hunting. Finally, five graves contained horse gear riding elements, most of which were spurs (Tables 4.9 and 4.10).

The range of adornment and clothing accessories was considerable. The most numerous items by far were brooches—36 fibulae coming from 28 graves according to PAM and 33 fibulae coming from 25 graves according to Diana. There was a lot of variation in the type of fibulae as no specific type dominated. Nonetheless, the

[8] One of these came from a tumulus cremation found next to the settlement of Poiana (Sîrbu 1993, pp. 72–73; Vulpe 1976, pp. 208–210) and the other from a flat cremation at Zimnicea (Alexandrescu 1972, p. 19, 1980, p. 26).

Table 4.9 Count of *object category 1* for PAM and Diana group 2

		Count PAM	Percent PAM	Count Diana	PAM Diana
Object Category 1	Adornment or clothing accessory	50	100.0	38	100.0
	Horse gear	5	10.0	5	13.1
	Tool	12	24.0	11	28.9
	Vessels and vessel implement	33	66.0	29	76.3
	Weapon	12	24.0	12	31.5

The counts and percentages refer to number of graves rather than number of objects

Table 4.10 Count of *object category 2* for PAM and Diana group 2

				Count PAM	Percent PAM	Count Diana	Percent Diana
Object Category 1	Adornment or clothing accessory	Object Category 2	NA	2	4.0	3	7.8
			Costume	50	100.0	38	100.0
			Toiletry	2	4.0	2	5.2
	Horse gear	Object Category 2	NA	1	2.0	1	2.6
			Riding	4	8.0	4	10.5
	Tool	Object Category 2	Cutting	11	20.0	11	28.9
			Perforating	1	2.0	1	2.6
			Weaving	1	2.0	0	0.0
	Vessels and vessel implement	Object Category 2	NA	12	24.0	11	28.9
			Drinking	16	32.0	14	36.8
			Eating and cooking	15	30.0	14	36.8
			Lighting	3	6.0	3	7.8
			Storage	9	18.0	8	21.0
	Weapon	Object Category 2	NA	1	2.0	0	0.0
			Costume (W)	1	2.0	0	0.0
			Defensive	5	10.0	5	13.1
			Hunting	3	6.0	3	7.8
			Offensive	2	4.0	4	10.5

The counts and percentages refer to number of graves rather than number of objects

most common ones were the type 2 and type 20.[9] Besides brooches, there were more than ten graves that contained bracelets, bead necklaces, pendant necklaces, or belts. In each case, the most common type was: bracelet type 6,[10] simple spherical bead necklace or beads "with eyes", bucket-pendants, and type 1 belts.[11]

[9] These two types, like with all other fibula types, refer to the ones proposed by Rustoiu with the same number (1997).

[10] The type 6 bracelet was circular in section and consisted of a double bar—on its entire circumference or just half of it—which was occasionally ribboned. The ends were simple or flattened (Fig. 4.6).

[11] This belt type was defined by Babeş (1983).

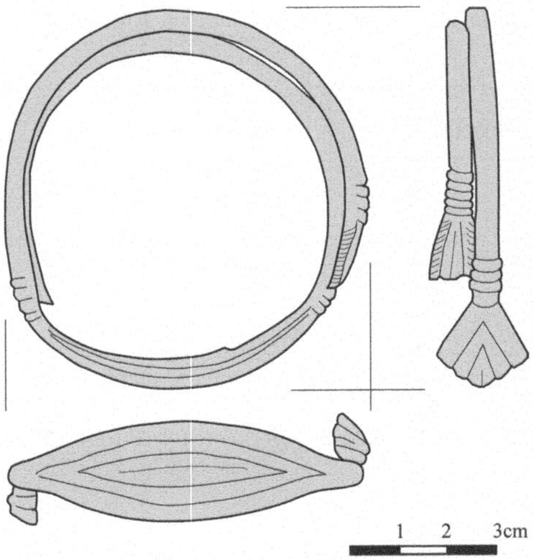

Fig. 4.6 Example of type 6 bracelet from Rospi Ćuprija, burial 30 (after Todorović 1963, Y52 2(1), Fig. 2)

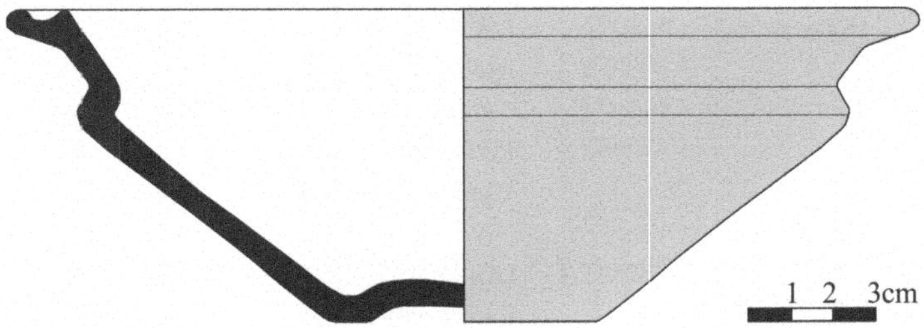

Fig. 4.7 Example of type 1 porringer from Kostolac, burial 2 (after Jacanović 1997, p. 129, Table 1/2)

Fourteen different vessel shapes were found in the graves of group 2. Only five of these made their appearance in more than five graves: cups and tumblers, jugs, bowls and porringers, fruit-bowls, and finally amphorae. Of the specific shapes, the type 1 porringer had the biggest occurrence (eight graves) (Fig. 4.7); amphorae were found in six graves but more exact types were lacking in this case.

As for the weapon shapes that appeared in this cluster, they were: one belt chain, three chain-mails, two type 2 helmets,[12] three hunting arrows, and two battle knives—one of which was of type 1.[13]

Based on the grave-good and funerary ritual elements, the typical grave of group 2 was the single flat cremation, although the use of inhumation and tumuli was not unusual. Grave-goods always included adornments or clothing accessories, usually more than one, and very often had one or more vessels. In rare cases, cutting knives could also appear, as well as weapons.

[12] This type was defined by Rustoiu (1996, p. 148).

[13] The type 1 battle knife had a convex curved blade and back (Fig. 2.8).

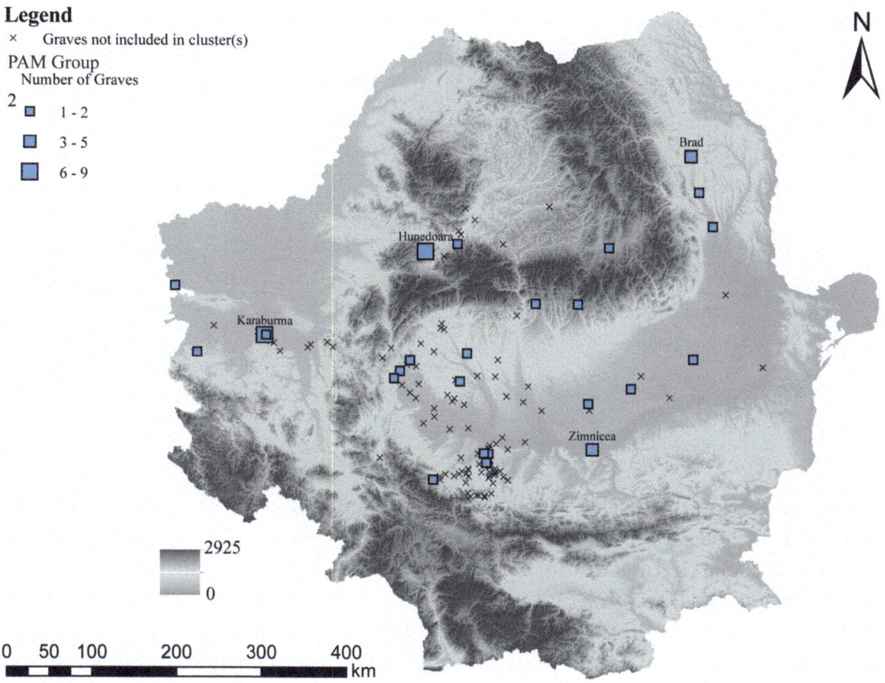

Fig. 4.8 Geographical spread of group 2. The points are placed according to the PAM clustering only because of minimal differences with Diana

The geographical spread of the graves was very vast, even larger than that of group 1 (Fig. 4.8). Most of the graves still came from the regions surrounding the Carpathian Mountains, especially from Moldova, Muntenia, and Western Transylvania, but an almost equal number were placed in Central Serbia as well as North-West Thrace (Table 4.11). The sites that gave the most burials were those of Karaburma (Central Serbia), Hundeoara-Grădina Castelului (Western Transylvania), Brad (Moldova), and Zimnicea (Muntenia). The distribution of these four sites, each located in a different regions, is another good indicator for the wide spread of the graves of group 2. Hence, unlike cluster 1, the funerary finds were distributed in this case almost evenly over nearly the entire study area, suggesting a pattern of funerary practices that was shared by communities spread throughout the whole of the Eastern Carpathian Basin and the Lower Danube.

4.4 Group 3

Group 3 consisted of 66 graves according to PAM and 62 following the clustering of Diana. The four grave difference appears because PAM placed in this group four graves that could not be clustered through the Diana algorithm.

Table 4.11 Regional distribution of group 2 according to PAM and Diana

		Count PAM	Percent PAM	Count Diana	Percent Diana
Region	Central Serbia	9	18.0	9	23.7
	Moldova	8	16.0	4	10.5
	Muntenia	10	20.0	8	21.1
	Oltenia	2	4.0	1	2.6
	NW Thrace – East	6	12.0	5	13.2
	NW Thrace – West	6	12.0	5	13.2
	Transylvania – East	1	2.0	1	2.6
	Transylvania—West	7	14.0	4	10.5
	Vojvodina	1	2.0	1	2.6
	Total	50	100.0	38	100.0

This group was made nearly exclusively of flat inhumations. More than two thirds of the graves came from multiple burials. They were placed near or on the banks of a river/water source. In addition, they were situated close to a contemporary settlement, although nearly a third (20 graves) were found within an actual settlement. This value is very high when compared to the other clusters; except for group 1 which also had a high count of graves located inside a settlement (17 graves), all the other clusters had a maximum of five graves, or none at all, coming from within the limits of a contemporary settlement (Table 4.12).

Since most of the deceased were inhumed, a good amount of information relating to age was available. According to the anthropological analysis, the graves contained a nearly equal numbers of newborns, children, and adults and a smaller number of adolescents. Thus, the age at death was overall low. Unfortunately, sex was determined only in 11 cases, giving a five to six ratio between male and female (Table 4.13). As a result of this low number, there is little that one can say in terms of the role of sex and gender in defining the characteristics of this group.

Only five of the graves of this cluster contained grave-goods, and in all cases, it was an object that could not be identified. This means that a characteristic of group 3 was the absence of any grave-good items. Consequently, the typical grave of this cluster was the flat inhumation, coming usually from a multiple burial and containing no grave-good items.

Group 3 corresponds spatially, with no exception, to the geographical area North of the Danube and East of the Danube Gorges—thus, the graves were all found in the modern territory of Romania (Fig. 4.9). However, they were spread throughout all the different regions of this zone, although most graves came from Western Transylvania and Oltenia which is a product of the two large funerary sites from Hundeoara-Grădina Castelului and Orlea (Table 4.14). Unlike cluster 1, the graves did not seem to follow closely the line of the Carpathian Mountains arch, as several graves were found far in the plane of Muntenia or close to the Danube valley. Hence, the area that corresponds to this group was quite large, suggesting a widely shared North Danubian burial practice.

Table 4.12 Group 3 PAM counts for *grave type*, *ritual type*, *multiple burials*, *river proximity*, and *settlement proximity* variables

		Count	Percent
Grave type	Construction	1	1.5
	Flat	64	97.0
	Tumular	1	1.5
Ritual type	Cremation	4	6.1
	Inhumation	62	93.9
Multiple burials	No	20	30.3
	Yes	46	69.7
River proximity	NA	1	1.5
	Banks	21	31.8
	Near	44	66.7
Settlement proximity	NA	2	3.0
	Inside	20	30.3
	Near	44	66.7

Table 4.13 Group 3 PAM counts for *age* and *sex* variables

		Count PAM	Percent PAM
Age	NA	18	27.3
	Newborn	16	24.2
	Child	15	22.7
	Adolescent	6	9.1
	Adult	11	16.7
Sex	NA	55	83.3
	Female	6	9.1
	Male	5	7.6

4.5 Group 4

Group 4 included 54 graves according to PAM and 61 according to the Diana clustering. The difference between the two appears for the following reasons: PAM added to group 4 five graves that Diana distributed in groups 2, 5, and 7; Diana placed 13 graves in group 4 which PAM put in group 5. This confusion of the two clustering algorithms appears because clusters 4 and 5 are remarkably similar, as shown by the separation index between the two which was less than 0.1, both in the case of PAM and Diana.[14]

Cluster 4 was made mostly of flat cremations, although a quarter of the burials were tumular. All of the graves, with one exception, came from single burials. Similarly, nearly all of them were placed either near or on the banks of a river/water source. In addition, more than half were located near a contemporary settlement, although this information could not be recorded for a significant number of graves

[14]The same observation can be made when looking at the 2D graph produced using multidimensional scaling (Figs. 4.1 and 4.2).

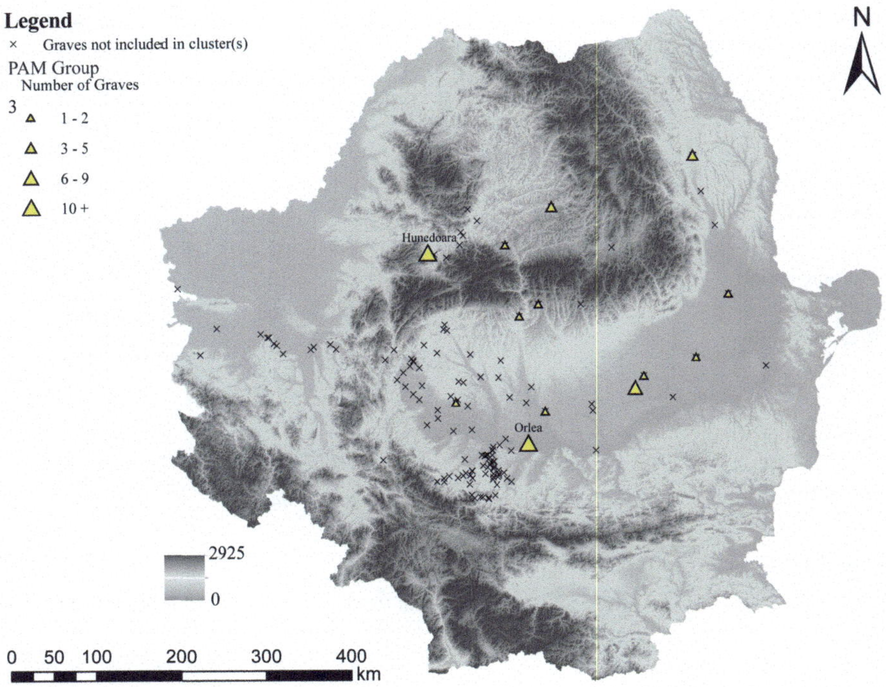

Fig. 4.9 Geographical spread of group 3. The points are placed according to the PAM clustering only because of minimal differences with Diana

Table 4.14 Regional distribution of group 3 according to PAM

		Count PAM	Percent PAM
Region	Moldova	4	6.1
	Muntenia	11	16.7
	Oltenia	22	33.3
	Transylvania—Centre	3	4.5
	Transylvania—West	26	39.4

(Table 4.15). Since nearly all of the deceased were cremated, there was virtually no information relating to age or sex.

All the graves contained grave-goods. The major element in the case of group 4 was the presence of weapons since they appeared in all cases, with one exception in the PAM clustering; most graves had two such items. In a small number of cases, three weapons were present but not more than that. Four graves included by PAM had just one item of weaponry. Nearly all the weapons were offensive, although Diana incorporated in this cluster seven graves with defensive weapons.[15] Apart for these, just under half of the graves had vessels, which were used either for drinking,

[15] The difference appeared mainly because PAM did not include any graves that contained shields in group 4 while Diana did not make this separation.

Table 4.15 Group 4 PAM and Diana counts for *grave type*, *ritual type*, *multiple burials*, *river proximity*, and *settlement proximity* variables

		Count PAM	Percent PAM	Count Diana	Percent Diana
Grave Type	Flat	38	71.7	46	75.4
	Tumular	15	28.3	15	24.6
Ritual type	Cenotaph	1	1.9	0	0.0
	Cremation	49	92.5	58	95.1
	Inhumation	3	5.7	3	4.9
Multiple burials	No	52	98.1	60	98.4
	Yes	1	1.9	1	1.6
River proximity	NA	2	3.8	2	3.3
	Banks	16	30.2	18	29.5
	Near	34	64.2	38	62.3
	Far	1	1.9	3	4.9
Settlement proximity	NA	17	32.1	20	32.8
	Inside	1	1.9	1	1.6
	Near	33	62.3	34	55.7
	Far	2	3.8	6	9.8

eating and cooking, or storage. Usually, only one vessel with this function would be placed in each grave, although two or more drinking or eating and cooking vessels could also be encountered. However, one cannot exclude a possible bias in terms vessel recording. Adornments or clothing accessories did not appear in large numbers—in 11 graves according to PAM and 8 according to Diana. These were all costume elements and, with one exception in the case of PAM, only one was found in each grave. A similar situation could be encountered in the case of tools, although they were discovered in slightly fewer graves—seven according to PAM and nine in the clustering of Diana—and were also, with one exception, single occurrences in funerary assemblages. The tools were used mostly for cutting, but also sharpening and in agriculture. Lastly, among the grave-goods, there were also horse gear riding elements. A significant distinction appeared in this case between PAM, which inserted 12 graves with horse gear, and Diana, which placed 20 graves that had such items. This difference was caused by the fuzzy boundary between groups 4 and 5. With the exception of three graves, only one horse gear element per grave was included in the funerary assemblages (Tables 4.16 and 4.17).

The weapon types that appeared most often in cluster 4 were as follows: spears—more than 80%[16] of the graves contained one, usually a type 1 or 2 and less often

[16] In general, when percentages are used instead of exact numbers in the description of the groups, it is because these are nearly identical in the case of the PAM and Diana clustering, although the exact number of graves may differ slightly.

Table 4.16 Count of *object category 1* for PAM group 4

		Count PAM	Percent PAM	Count Diana	Percent Diana
Object Category 1	Adornment or clothing accessory	11	20.3	8	13.1
	Horse gear	12	22.2	20	32.7
	Tool	7	12.9	9	14.7
	Vessels and vessel implement	24	44.4	24	39.3
	Weapon	53	98.1	61	100.0

The counts and percentages refer to number of graves rather than number of objects

Table 4.17 Count of *object category 2* for PAM group 4

				Count PAM	Percent PAM	Count Diana	Percent Diana
Object Category 1	Adornment or clothing accessory	Object Category 2	Costume	11	20.3	8	13.1
	Horse gear	Object Category 2	Riding	12	22.2	20	32.7
	Tool	Object Category 2	Agriculture	1	1.8	1	1.6
			Cutting	6	11.1	7	11.4
			Sharpening	1	1.8	2	3.2
	Vessels and vessel implement	Object Category 2	NA	13	24.0	16	26.2
			Drinking	9	16.6	7	11.4
			Eating and cooking	8	14.8	5	8.1
			Storage	5	9.2	4	6.5
	Weapon	Object Category 2	NA	1	1.8	1	1.6
			Defensive	1	1.8	7	11.4
			Offensive	52	96.2	60	98.3

The counts and percentages refer to number of graves rather than number of objects

type 3[17]; battle knives, present in over 60% of the cases, mostly type 1; and swords, found in about half of the graves, both type 1 and 2. Apart from these, arrowheads were discovered in a few instances; also, one grave had a chain-mail together with a type 2 helmet. According to the Diana clustering, there were also six graves that

[17] Type 1 spear refers to a spearhead that was oval in shape and that extended to its maximum width in a point situated in the top two thirds of the blade. The profile of the blade was flat, rhombic or with a central ridge. Type 2 spear refers to a spearhead that had an elongated shape and that extended to its maximum width in a point situated in the bottom one third of the blade. The profile of the blade was flat, rhombic or with a central ridge. Type 3 spear refers to a spearhead that had a nearly triangular shape and that extended to its maximum width in a point situated in the bottom one third of the blade. The profile of the blade was always rhombic (Fig. 2.9).

contained a shield (Table 4.18).[18] It is interesting to note that, with very few exceptions, no two weapons of the same type were present in the same grave.

In terms of vessels, there was considerable variation in their shape. The most frequent were bowls and porringers, especially the porringer type 1, but also jugs. Other vessels appeared in less than three graves or only once.[19] With two exceptions, the adornments or clothing accessories were fibulae, half of which were of type 4. As for the tools, three burials contained a cutting knife and another three had a scissor; a cutting axe and a sickle appeared in one grave each. Finally, all cases of horse gear referred to horse bits.[20] Three of these graves contained additionally a buckle for attaching the saddle.

There are a couple of recurring associations among the grave-goods. One of them is that, with the exception of six graves, swords and battle knives did not appear in the same assemblage; on the other hand, when a sword and battle knife were placed together a spear was not present,[21] even though the sword and spear were regularly part of the same assemblage. Another observation is that seven out of the eight graves that had a fibula also had a vessel and six of these also contained a sword. And finally, tools and horse gear were never part of the same grave assemblages.

To sum up, the common type of grave for group 2 was the single flat cremation containing at least two different kinds of offensive weaponry, but never more than three such items. Usually, a spear would form one of the weapon elements. The grave could also include one or several vessels, but rarely other items. Thus, one of the main characteristic was the lack of other grave-goods besides weapons and vessels. This gave the graves a rather sober and militaristic appearance.

The spatial distribution of this cluster shows an emphasis on the Western part of the Lower Danube (Fig. 4.10). Most graves came from the Eastern side of North-West Thrace and from Oltenia; a significant number were found in Central Serbia as well. The geographical spread is, thus, much smaller than that of groups 1, 2, and 3. The centre was undoubtedly the area just East of the Danube gorges, South as well as North of the river. There were two additional site concentrations: a larger one along the same river but West of the Danube gorges in Central Serbia, and a smaller one in Western Transylvania. Furthermore, PAM included in this group tumulus number one from Popeşti which clearly stands out in terms of its positioning. Analysing its grave-goods, which consisted of eight vessels and one spearhead (Vulpe 1976, pp. 193–194), it seems that the grave was wrongly placed by the clustering algorithm in this group. The spatial patterning thus suggests that group 4 refers to a funerary practice that was shared over a relatively limited area just East of the Danube gorges, although it was also evident in some pockets in Central Serbia, as well as, to a smaller degree, in Western Transylvania.

---

[18] Unfortunately in most of these cases it was not possible to determine the exact type of shield.

[19] As noted in Chap. 2, the shape and exact type of vessels could often not be determined due to poor recording.

[20] Every grave contained a maximum of one horse bit. Unfortunately their type could only be identified in four cases. These were two type 16, one type 1 and one type 5 as defined by Werner (1988).

[21] The one exception in this case is the grave of Cetate in the region of Oltenia where a sword, battle knife and spear were found together. (Nicolăescu-Plopşor 1945, pp. 19–20).

Table 4.18 Count of *object category 4* weapons for PAM and Diana group 4

						Count PAM	Percent PAM	Count Diana	Percent Diana
Object Category 2	NA	Object Category 3	NA	Object Category 4	NA	1	1.8	1	1.6
	Defensive	Object Category 3	Chainmail	Object Category 4	Chainmail	1	1.8	1	1.6
			Helmet	Object Category 4	Helmet type 2	1	1.8	1	1.6
			Shield	Object Category 4	NA	0	0.0	5	8.1
				Object Category 4	Shield type 2	0	0.0	1	1.6
	Offensive	Object Category 3	Arrowhead	Object Category 4	Arrowhead	2	3.7	2	3.2
			Battle knife	Object Category 4	NA	7	12.9	9	14.7
					Battle knife type 1	17	31.4	20	32.7
					Battle knife type 2	4	7.4	4	6.5
					Battle knife type 3	5	9.2	6	9.8
			Spear	Object Category 4	NA	19	35.1	22	36.0
					Spear type 1	8	14.8	12	19.6
					Spear type 2	11	20.3	10	16.3
					Spear type 3	5	9.2	7	11.4
					Spear type 4	0	0.0	1	1.6
					Spear type 5	1	1.8	1	1.6
			Sword	Object Category 4	NA	10	18.5	16	26.2
					Sword type 1	6	11.1	7	11.4
					Sword type 2	7	12.9	9	14.7

The counts and percentages refer to number of graves rather than number of objects

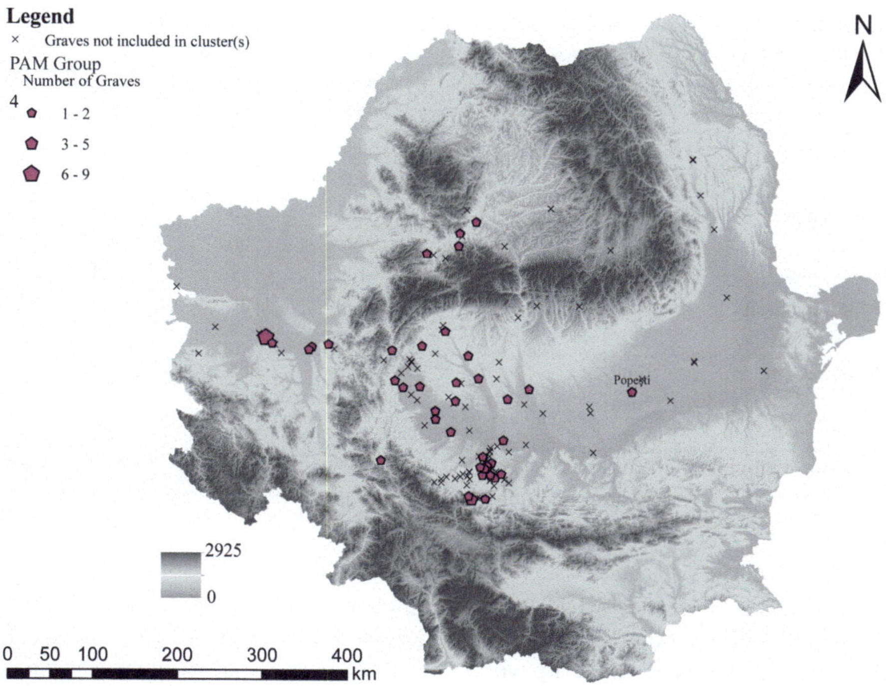

Fig. 4.10 Geographical spread of group 4. The points are placed according to the PAM clustering only because of minimal differences with Diana

4.6 Group 5

Group 5 is the largest cluster of all, containing 80 graves according to PAM and 70 according to Diana. The difference appears because, as mentioned previously, groups 4 and 5 are statistically very close to one another, and thus, Diana placed 13 graves in group 4 that PAM included in group 5. In addition, Diana added to group 5 two graves that were included in group 4 by PAM and another one which was placed in group 6.

Cluster 5 contained both flat and tumulus cremations, although the latter were only a third of the total. With the exception of two graves, all of them came from single burials. Apart for a small number of graves, they were placed either near or on the banks of a water source. The large majority was also near to a settlements, though never inside. A small number were also located far from any settlement, but this figure was higher than that of any other group (Table 4.19). Since nearly all of the deceased were cremated, there was virtually no information relating to age or sex.

Table 4.19 Group 5 PAM and Diana counts for *grave type*, *ritual type*, *multiple burials*, *river proximity*, and *settlement proximity* variables

		Count PAM	Percent PAM	Count Diana	Percent Diana
Grave type	Flat	52	65.0	42	60.0
	Tumular	28	35.0	28	40.0
Ritual type	Cenotaph	1	1.3	3	4.3
	Cremation	78	97.5	66	94.3
	Inhumation	1	1.3	1	1.4
Multiple burials	No	78	97.5	68	97.1
	Yes	2	2.5	2	2.9
River proximity	Banks	29	36.3	25	35.7
	Near	44	55.0	40	57.1
	Far	7	8.8	5	7.1
Settlement proximity	NA	17	21.3	14	20.0
	Near	52	65.0	49	70.0
	Far	11	13.8	7	10.0

The graves of cluster 5 had by far the highest number of grave-goods when compared with the other groups, averaging at more than seven items per grave.[22] As expected, due to its similarity with group 4, the presence of weapons was paramount in this cluster, appearing in all instances. Moreover, the large majority of graves had either three or four elements of weaponry, and in some cases, even more. Diana, however, included two graves that had only one weapon. Apart for two instances, all graves contained offensive weapons, nearly always two or three. Nevertheless, there were also a large number of defensive weapons: they appeared in 60% of the graves. Only one defensive weapon was normally placed in graves; the exceptions were eight graves which contained two or three such objects (Table 4.20).

Just like in cluster 4, around half of the graves of group 5 contained vessels, a figure which is probably affected by recording biases. Most vessels were used for drinking or eating and cooking, and less for storage. However, unlike cluster 4, the grave assemblages of group 5 included numerous other objects. Nearly half of the graves had adornments or clothing accessories. Most of these were costume elements, but there were also two items of toiletry: a mirror and a razor. Usually, only one such object was discovered in the graves, although in almost a third of cases two or more were encountered. The situation was similar for horse gear elements. Horse riding implements were found in more than half of the graves and in two cases parade objects were deposited.[23] A smaller number of graves, around 20%, had tools.

[22] On average the tumulus graves of this group had a larger quantity of grave-goods than the flat graves.

[23] The two cases referred to here are tumulus number two from Cugir which contained, among other things, a gilded harness and a cart (Crişan 1980; Teleagă et al. 2014), and the tumulus of Costeşti-Cetăţuie which had a cart (Gheorghiu 2005, p. 208).

Table 4.20 Count of number of *object category 1* weapons for PAM and Diana group 5

	Number of Objects	Count PAM	Percent PAM	Count Diana	Percent Diana
Costume (W)	0	75	93.8	65	92.9
	1	5	6.3	5	7.1
Defensive	0	32	40.0	28	40.0
	1	40	50.0	34	48.6
	2	4	5.0	4	5.7
	3	4	5.0	4	5.7
Hunting	0	80	100.0	70	100.0
Offensive	0	2	2.5	2	2.9
	1	5	6.3	6	8.6
	2	17	21.3	13	18.6
	3	40	50.0	33	47.1
	4	7	8.8	7	10.0
	5	3	3.8	3	4.3
	6	5	6.3	5	7.1
	8	1	1.3	1	1.4

The PAM and Diana counts refer to number of graves rather than number of objects

Table 4.21 Count of *object category 1* for PAM and Diana group 5

		Count PAM	Percent PAM	Count Diana	Percent Diana
Object Category 1	Adornment or clothing accessory	38	47.5	39	55.7
	Coin	2	2.5	2	2.8
	Horse gear	43	53.7	36	51.4
	Tool	15	18.7	13	18.5
	Vessels and vessel implement	43	53.7	41	58.5
	Weapon	80	100.0	70	100.0

The counts and percentages refer to number of graves rather than number of objects

Most of them served for cutting, but there were also a small number that served for sharpening. Finally, two graves, one from Popeşti (Vulpe 1976, pp. 201–203) and another from Costeşti-Cetăţuie, each contained a coin (Gheorghiu 2005, p. 208) (Tables 4.21 and 4.22).

The weapon shapes found most often in the group 5 graves were: spears—in 90% of the graves, about a third of which were of type 1, although all other types also appeared in smaller quantities, battle knives—in approximately 75% of the graves, half of which were type 1 and a fifth type 3[24], swords—in about 60% of the

[24] The type 3 battle knife had a straight or slightly concave blade and back (Fig. 2.8).

Table 4.22 Count of *object category* 2 for PAM and Diana group 5

				Count PAM	Percent PAM	Count Diana	Percent Diana
Object Category 1	Adornment or clothing accessory	Object Category 2	Costume	37	46.2	38	54.2
			Toiletry	2	2.5	2	2.8
	Coin	Object Category 2	Coin	2	2.5	2	2.8
	Horse gear	Object Category 2	Parade	2	2.5	2	2.8
			Riding	42	52.5	35	50.0
	Tool	Object Category 2	Agriculture	1	1.2	1	1.4
			Cutting	12	15.0	11	15.7
			Perforating	3	3.7	3	4.2
			Sharpening	3	3.7	2	2.8
	Vessels and vessel implement	Object Category 2	NA	21	26.2	17	24.2
			Drinking	22	27.5	24	35.2
			Eating and cooking	16	50.0	18	25.7
			Lighting	1	1.2	1	1.4
			Storage	8	10.0	9	12.8
	Weapon	Object Category 2	Costume (W)	5	6.2	5	7.1
			Defensive	48	60.0	42	60.0
			Offensive	78	97.5	68	97.1

The counts and percentages refer to number of graves rather than number of objects

graves, most of which were of type 2, and shields—in just under 60% of the graves.[25] In a few instances, other weapons or weapon-related items appeared: chain-mails, helmets, sword chains, *saurotes*, and arrowheads. It is interesting to note that, just like in group 4, the same weapon shape rarely appeared twice in the same grave. The only exception was in the case of spears, since approximately 30% of the graves had two or more of these (Table 4.23).

The most commonly reoccurring vessels were bowls and porringers—especially the porringer type 1—, fruit-bowls, and jugs. In the case of adornments and clothing accessories, the most numerous were fibulae—more than a third of such items, mainly of type 2, bracelets—just over a fifth of the adornments; usually of type 6, and belts—nearly a fifth of all, with no particularly dominant type. The large majority of horse gear was in the form of horse bits, half of which were of type 16. There were also a small number of spurs, mostly of type 1. Finally, the few tools found were mostly scissors, especially of type 2, cutting knives and sharpening stones.

Given the high number of grave-goods, there were many item combinations, though one particular assemblage stood out. Nearly half of the group 5 graves had a spear, a battle knife, and a sword. Swords and battle knives were almost always in this combination. A high majority of these graves contained horse gear as well.

[25] In the case of shields in most cases it was not possible to establish the exact type. Nonetheless a quarter of all the shields were of type 1, which corresponds to Brunaux and Lambot's type 15 (1987, pp. 130–131).

Table 4.23 Count of *object category 4* weapons for PAM and Diana group 5

						Count PAM	Percent PAM	Count Diana	Percent Diana
Object Category 2	Offensive	Object Category 3	Arrowhead	Object Category 4	Arrowhead	3	3.7	3	4.2
			Battle knife	Object Category 4	NA	16	20.0	14	20.0
					Battle knife type 1	30	37.5	27	38.5
					Battle knife type 2	6	7.5	6	8.5
					Battle knife type 3	12	15.0	10	14.2
					Battle knife type 4	2	2.5	2	2.8
			Sauroter	Object Category 4	Sauroter	2	2.5	2	2.8
			Spear	Object Category 4	NA	27	33.7	24	34.2
					Spear type 1	27	33.7	23	32.8
					Spear type 2	10	12.5	11	15.7
					Spear type 3	7	8.7	6	8.5
					Spear type 4	9	11.2	8	11.4
					Spear type 5	7	8.7	7	10.0
			Sword	Object Category 4	NA	23	28.7	17	24.2
					Sword type 1	10	12.5	9	12.8
					Sword type 2	21	26.2	17	24.2
	Costume (W)	Object Category 3	Belt chain	Object Category 4	Belt chain	5	6.2	5	7.1
	Defensive	Object Category 3	Chainmail	Object Category 4	Chainmail	8	10.0	8	11.4
			Helmet	Object Category 4	NA	2	2.5	2	2.8
					Helmet type 1	1	1.2	1	1.4
					Helmet type 2	1	1.2	1	1.4
			Shield	Object Category 4	NA	32	40.0	27	38.5
					Shield type 1	11	13.7	11	15.7
					Shield type 2	2	2.5	1	1.4
					Shield type 3	2	2.5	2	2.8

The counts and percentages refer to number of graves rather than number of objects

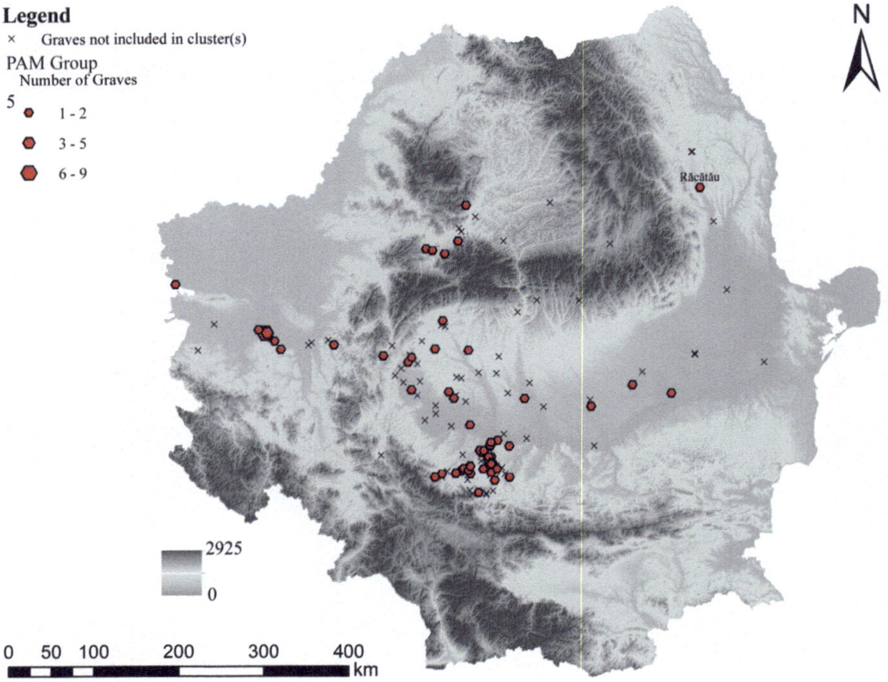

Fig. 4.11 Geographical spread of group 5. The points are placed according to the PAM clustering only because of minimal differences with Diana

More than half also incorporated a shield. The assemblage of spear, battle knife, and sword was found in both tumulus and flat graves, although the latter were slightly more numerous in group 5. However, overall, it was more likely for the set to appear in tumulus graves than in flat graves. 21% of the tumuli from the database contained the combination of these three items, while the same objects were found together only in 7.2% of the flat graves.

In summary, the typical grave of group 5 was a single flat or tumulus cremation containing three or four items of weaponry among which there was usually a spear, a battle knife, and a sword. In addition, a shield could appear as well as horse gear elements. The grave could also include vessels as well as adornments or clothing accessories.

In terms of the geographical distribution, nearly half of the graves came from North-West Thrace. There were also a significant number of graves placed in Central Serbia as well as some in Oltenia (Fig. 4.11, Table 4.24). A small amount came from Western Transylvania and Muntenia. There was also one grave from Răcătău (Moldova) placed in this group due to the possible presence of two pieces of chain-mail, probably coming from one object only, in tumulus number one (Căpitanu 1986, pp. 119–120). The presence of those two pieces seems highly unusual[26]; this idea is

[26] Their presence is even more unusual given that the graves coming from Moldova do not normally have any kind of weapons.

Table 4.24 Regional distribution of group 5 according to PAM and Diana

		Count PAM	Percent PAM	Count Diana	Percent Diana
Region	Central Serbia	16	20.0	14	20.0
	Moldova	1	1.3	1	1.4
	Muntenia	4	5.0	5	7.1
	Oltenia	9	11.3	7	10.0
	NW Thrace—East	38	47.5	30	42.9
	NW Thrace—West	4	5.0	4	5.7
	Transylvania—West	6	7.5	7	10.0
	Vojvodina	2	2.5	2	2.9

also supported by the results of the cluster and spatial analysis which clearly indicate the grave as an outsider of cluster 5. Regardless of this, the group referred to a funerary practice which was shared mostly in a very limited area South of the Danube, although smaller pockets appeared also North of the river and in Central Serbia.

4.7 Group 6

Group 6 is the smallest of all groups. It had 29 graves according to PAM and 25 according to Diana. The difference of four graves appears because PAM included in this cluster one grave that Diana added to group 5, another one that it put in group 7 and two more that could not be clustered using the latter method.

Nearly, all of the graves of group 6 were flat cremations and came from single burials. In the large majority of cases, they were placed either near or on the banks of a river/water sources as well as near a contemporary settlement, but never actually inside one (Table 4.25). Just like with the other cremation graves groups, age and sex data was generally missing.

The graves of cluster 6 had very small grave assemblages, usually only two items. It was defined, just like groups 4 and 5, by the presence of weapons in all graves, apart for one.[27] However, unlike the previous two clusters, the graves of group 6 never had more than one item of weaponry. The weapons were always offensive according to Diana, although PAM also placed three graves with hunting weapons. The graves did not include any adornments or clothing accessories and, with one exception, no tools.[28] About a third of the graves contained one or two vessels used for drinking, eating and cooking, or storage. Just like in many of the

[27] The one instance where no weapon appeared was grave number one from Oriahovo. However in this case it seems likely that a weapon was actually initially present since the grave was destroyed through ploughing and next to it there was another grave containing weapons (Nikolov 1993, pp. 18–22).

[28] The exception was in this case the grave of Gorna Kremena which contained a sharpening stone (Domaradzki and Nikolov 1982).

Table 4.25 Group 6 PAM and Diana counts for *grave type*, *ritual type*, *multiple burials*, *river proximity,* and *settlement proximity* variables

		Count PAM	Percent PAM	Count Diana	Percent Diana
Grave type	Flat	24	82.8	22	88.0
	Tumular	5	17.2	3	12.0
Ritual type	Cenotaph	2	6.9	0	0.0
	Cremation	25	86.2	25	100.0
	Inhumation	2	6.9	0	0.0
Multiple burials	No	27	93.1	25	100.0
	Yes	2	6.9	0	0.0
River proximity	Banks	9	31.0	9	36.0
	Near	18	62.1	14	56.0
	Far	2	6.9	2	8.0
Settlement proximity	NA	7	24.1	7	28.0
	Near	20	69.0	16	64.0
	Far	2	6.9	2	8.0

Table 4.26 Count of *object category 1* for PAM and Diana group 6

		Count PAM	Percent PAM	Count Diana	Percent Diana
Object Category 1	Horse gear	12	41.3	11	44.0
	Tool	1	3.4	1	4.0
	Vessels and vessel implement	9	31.0	7	28.0
	Weapon	28	96.5	24	96.0

The counts and percentages refer to number of graves rather than number of objects

other groups, a recording bias relating to vessels may be in effect. Nearly, half of the graves had one to three pieces of horse gear (Tables 4.26 and 4.27).

The weapon and horse gear items are the only ones worth mentioning in terms of their shape since little information was given about the vessels. The weapons found in the group six graves were spears, swords, or battle knives. PAM also included three graves with hunting arrows. Most of the spears were of type 1, although there was also one grave with a type 3 and one with a type 4 spear. Similarly, most of the battle knives were of type 1. Swords, however, were of type 1 as well as type 2. As for the horse gear elements, they were either horse bits or spurs. There was never more than one horse bit per grave. Most of these were of type 16, though a type 14 and a type 15 also appeared. As for the spurs, they were of type 1 or type 2 and could appear alone in a grave or in groups of two.

In terms of associations, one can observe that horse gear and vessels were rarely found in the same grave, although this may be an artefact of the bias against the recording of vessels. However, as expected, the two different horse

Table 4.27 Count of *object category 2* for PAM and Diana group 6

				Count PAM	Percent PAM	Count Diana	Percent Diana
Object Category 1	Horse gear	Object Category 2	Riding	12	41.3	11	44.0
	Tool	Object Category 2	Sharpening	1	3.4	1	4.0
	Vessels and vessel implement	Object Category 2	NA	8	27.5	7	28.0
			Drinking	1	3.4	0	0.00
			Eating and cooking	2	6.8	1	4.0
			Storage	1	3.4	0	0.00
	Weapon	Object Category 2	Hunting	3	10.3	0	0.00
			Offensive	25	86.2	24	96.0

The counts and percentages refer to number of graves rather than number of objects

gear elements, spurs and horse bits, appeared together, although more graves had horse bits than spurs.[29]

Summing up, the model for group 6 was the single flat cremation grave. It had a simple grave assemblage that always included weapons and could also contain horse gear elements. On rare occasions, vessels could also appear, though they may have been more common than was recorded. Just like in cluster 4, the graves of this group give a sober, militaristic impression.

The geographical distribution shows that the graves of group 6 were present practically only in two neighbouring regions North-West Thrace and Oltenia (Fig. 4.12, Table 4.28). In isolated cases, such graves appeared in Western Transylvania, while PAM also placed, probably wrongly, a tumulus grave from Poiana (Moldova) in group 6.[30] It is thus quite clear that the burial practices referred to by this group was limited to a small area just East of the Danube gorges, both South and North of the river.

4.8 Group 7

Group 7 contained 35 graves according to PAM and 37 according to Diana. The difference of two graves appears because Diana included in this cluster one grave which PAM placed in group 4 and another one which it put in group 6.

The large majority of the graves were flat cremations. However, there were also a small number of flat inhumations and tumulus cremations. Nearly, all came from single burials. Most of them were placed near or on the banks of a river/water source

[29] It seems likely that all graves containing horse bits also had spurs, but due to their small dimensions they did not survive or were overlooked during excavation.

[30] This was tumulus number two from Poiana (Vulpe 1976, pp. 208–210).

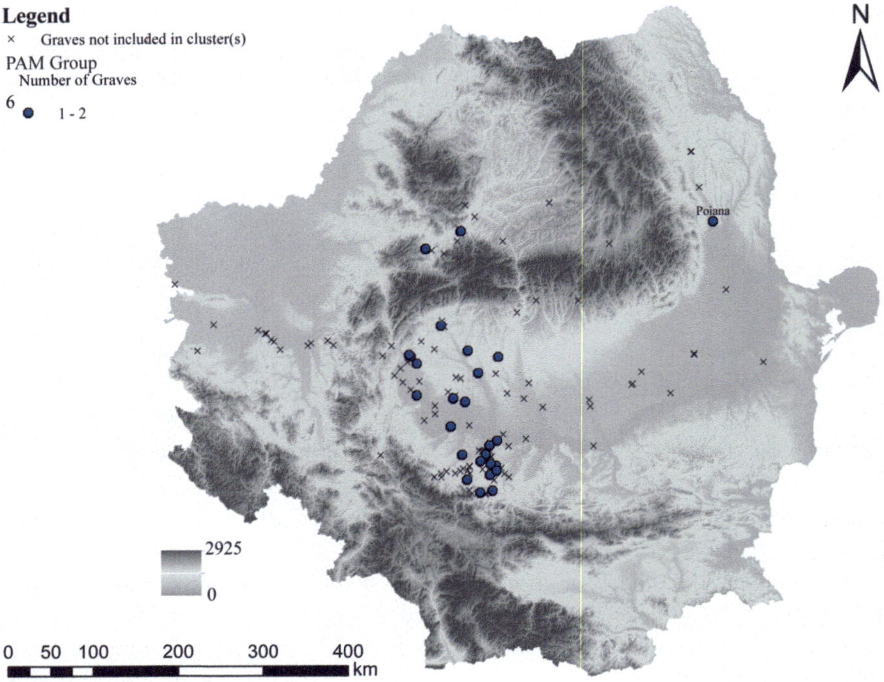

Fig. 4.12 Geographical spread of group 6. The points are placed according to the PAM clustering only because of minimal differences with Diana

Table 4.28 Regional distribution of group 6 according to PAM and Diana

		Count PAM	Percent PAM	Count Diana	Percent Diana
Region	Moldova	1	3.4	0	0.0
	Oltenia	12	41.4	12	48.0
	NW Thrace—East	13	44.8	12	48.0
	Transylvania—West	3	10.3	1	4.0

as well as close to a contemporary settlement. Five graves were found within the actual limits of a settlement (Table 4.29).

The grave assemblage of the group 7 graves consisted almost entirely of vessels; most of them included two or more. Nearly, 60% contained drinking vessels and around half had cooking or eating vessels; storage vessels were found in about a quarter of them. No grave had any adornments or clothing accessories or horse gear elements. According to PAM, there were no graves with weapons either. However, Diana included two graves that contained a weapon each—one grave from Kostolac that had a sword (Jacanović 1997) and another from Poiana that included an arrowhead (Vulpe 1976, pp. 208–210). Finally, seven graves contained tools, used mainly for cutting, but also sharpening, weaving, and in agriculture (Tables 4.30 and 4.31).

Table 4.29 Group 7 PAM and Diana counts for *grave type, ritual type, multiple burials, river proximity,* and *settlement proximity* variables

		Count PAM	Percent PAM	Count Diana	Percent Diana
Grave type	Flat	30	85.7	31	83.8
	Tumular	5	14.3	6	16.2
Ritual type	Cenotaph	0	0.0	1	2.7
	Cremation	29	82.9	30	81.1
	Inhumation	6	17.1	6	16.2
Multiple burials	No	34	97.1	36	97.3
	Yes	1	2.9	1	2.7
River proximity	NA	0	0.0	0	0.0
	Banks	17	48.6	18	48.6
	Near	16	45.7	17	45.9
	Far	2	5.7	2	5.4
Settlement proximity	NA	2	5.7	2	5.4
	Inside	5	14.3	5	13.5
	Near	28	80.0	30	81.1

Table 4.30 Count of *object category 1* for PAM and Diana group 7

		Count PAM	Percent PAM	Count Diana	Percent Diana
Object Category 1	Tool	7	20.0	7	15.2
	Vessels and vessel implement	35	100.0	37	80.4
	Weapon	0	0.00	2	4.3

The counts and percentages refer to number of graves rather than number of objects

Table 4.31 Count of *object category 2* for PAM and Diana group 7

				Count PAM	Percent PAM	Count Diana	Percent Diana
Object Category 1	Tool	Object Category 2	Agriculture	1	2.9	1	2.7
			Cutting	4	11.4	4	10.8
			Sharpening	2	5.7	2	5.4
			Weaving	1	2.9	1	2.7
	Vessels and vessel implement	Object Category 2	NA	13	37.1	14	37.8
			Drinking	20	57.1	21	56.7
			Eating and cooking	14	40.0	15	40.5
			Lighting	2	5.7	2	5.4
			Storage	9	25.7	10	27.0
	Weapon	Object Category 2	Hunting	0	0.0	1	2.7
			Offensive	0	0.0	1	2.7

The counts and percentages refer to number of graves rather than number of objects

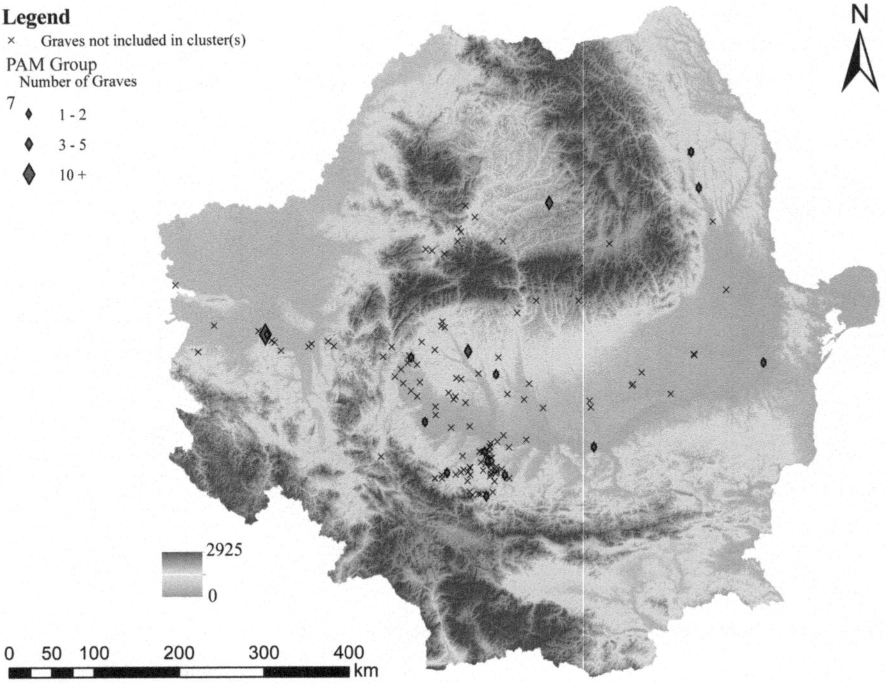

Fig. 4.13 Geographical spread of group 7. The points are placed according to the PAM clustering only because of minimal differences with Diana

In terms of object shape, most of the vessels were bowls and porringers, especially the porringer type 1, cups and tumblers, jugs, and *kantharos*-like vessels. Except for a few cases, two vessels of the same shape, or even of the same function, did not appear in the same grave. As for the tools, these were two cutting knives, two sharpening stones, two sickles, two spindle whorls, and a scissor.

In conclusion, the typical graves of group 7 were the single flat cremations which had as grave-goods two or more vessels and sometimes tools.

The geographical spread of group 7 is very wide. Most of the graves came from Central Serbia, but overall they do not appear to be bound to any particular region (Fig. 4.13, Table 4.32). Hence, several graves were placed in Oltenia or North-Western Thrace, but also Muntenia, Moldova, and Transylvania. Thus, it can be said that the burial practice linked to this group was shared over a very large area, although it was predominantly encountered West of the Danube gorges.

4.9 Partially Clustered Graves

As already mentioned, there were eight graves which could not be clustered using the dendrogram produced by Diana and cut with the hybrid dynamic tree cut method. All the graves came from Romania: one from Cepari (Popescu and

Table 4.32 Regional distribution of group 7 according to PAM and Diana

		Count PAM	Percent PAM	Count Diana	Percent Diana
Region	Central Serbia	14	40.0	14	37.8
	Moldova	3	8.6	4	10.8
	Muntenia	2	5.7	2	5.4
	Oltenia	7	20.0	7	18.9
	NW Thrace—East	6	17.1	6	16.2
	NW Thrace—West	0	0.0	1	2.7
	Transylvania—Centre	3	8.6	3	8.1

Vulpe 1982), two from Corlate (Nicolăescu-Plopşor 1945, pp. 20–23), four from Hunedoara-Grădina Castelului (Sîrbu et al. 2007), and one from Sighişoara-Wietenberg (Rustoiu et al. 1993). Unlike Diana, PAM was able to cluster them in the following manner: two in group 1, four in group 3, and another two in group 6.

All of the graves were flat; four were cremations and four were inhumations. Just two of them, one from Cepari and one from Hunedoara-Grădina Castelului did not contain any grave-goods. The rest had items placed in the graves, but in small numbers; generally, the objects were extremely degraded and thus their shape or function remained unknown. This may be the reason for which Diana did not succeed in placing them in any of the seven groups.

Overall, there does not seem to be anything special related to these eight graves. It is highly likely that Diana did not succeed in clustering them purely because there was insufficient information about them, although there were probably other graves with equally poor data. Nonetheless, in the case of the eight graves, given the data that was available for them, Diana could not find sufficient similarity so as to include them in any of the seven clusters that it defined.

4.10 Non-clustered Graves

Six entries from the database were not employed in the final analysis. This is because the clustering algorithms found it difficult to add the six graves to any group. Including them produced results with a lot of noise which did not pass the validation procedures. Of the six entries left out of the analysis one came from Padea, one from Radovene, one from Brad, one from Răcătău, and two from Biala Slatina.

The grave from Padea actually represented a generic entry for the numerous funerary discoveries that were uncovered accidentally by local farmers when planting vineyards between 1966 and 1968 (Bondoc 2008). Numerous spearheads were found then, as well as some swords, battle knives, cutting knives, fibulae, horse bits, coins, and vessels, all of which came from an unknown number of flat cremation graves. Unfortunately, the exact association of those objects was not recorded and the attempt to reconstruct at least a generic assemblage for those graves obviously did not succeed.

At Radovene, Theodossiev (2000, p. 134) signalled the existence of five tumuli. One of them, based on its grave assemblage, was dated to the Late La Tène, while the others were attributed to more recent phases, either the second to third centuries AD or the Middle Ages. The Iron Age grave was only partially excavated. It contained no traces of human remains. The grave-goods included only horse gear, namely a horse bit and a number of bronze fittings. While the grave could have been a cenotaph, the reduced level of information did not allow the clustering algorithms to group the grave in any manner.

The two graves from Brad and Răcătău were published as tumulus cenotaphs with no grave-goods (Sîrbu 1994, p. 128; Ursachi 1995, pp. 107–110). They were each part of two small tumulus cemeteries associated with two settlements situated close to one another, along the Siret River in Moldova. The other tumuli from Brad and Răcătău were not much different from the two; some of them were cenotaphs while others were cremation graves; none of which had many grave-goods. However, since these were the only two cenotaphs in the whole database without any items, the clustering algorithms were not able to group the two with other graves, thus resulting in them being greatly separated from all the other.[31]

The final two graves, from Biala Slatina, were found together 2 km South of the town, in the Liubomir locality (Theodossiev 2000, p. 108). Both of them were tumuli and part of a group of five such graves uncovered at the same spot. Just like the grave of Radovene, they contained only horse gear elements: horse bits, harness rings, and *phalerae*. The algorithms were not able to cluster adequately graves that had only such items, instead signalling their unique character. This may be an indication either that the graves were not recorded adequately—which is undoubtedly true, though the same can be said about most of the graves from the database—or that they were linked to a phenomenon that was separated from other funerary finds. Although there are too few data to propose a suitable theory, it could be that such finds were in fact not human but horse burials, a situation not unheard of, given the important role played by horses in the Balkan Iron Age (cf. Kuzmanov 2005).

Summing up, the 370 graves used in this study were placed into seven groups, plus six non-clustered graves. Every group was characterized by a specific set of elements, though most had a considerable degree of internal variation. The next step is to compare the groups among them, to observe how much they overlapped or differed and provide an identity interpretation of these observations. This represents the main focus of the following chapter.

References

Alexandrescu, D. (1972). Morminte din perioada mai tîrzie a necropolei getice de la Zimnicea. *Crisia, 2*, 15–26.

Alexandrescu, D. (1980). La nécropole gete de Zimnicea. *Dacia, 24*, 19–126.

[31] The lack of any human remains and grave-goods raises the question of whether these were indeed graves or the result of some other activity.

Babeş, M. (1983). Paftalele Latène târzii din sud-estul Europei. *Studii şi Cercetări de Istorie Veche şi Arheologie, 34*(3), 196–221.

Berciu, D. (1983). Mormintele de înhumaţie de la Ocniţa-Buridava. *Thraco-Dacica, 4*(1–2), 32–38.

Bondoc, D. (2008). Descoperirile de epocă La Tène de la Padea, jud. Dolj. *Studii şi Cercetări de Istorie Veche şi Arheologie, 59-60*, 137–163.

Brunaux, J.-L., & Lambot, B. (1987). *Guerre et armement chez les Gaulois 450–52 av. J.-C.* Paris: Editions Errance.

Căpitanu, V. (1986). Cercetările arheologice de la Răcătău, jud. Bacău. *Materiale şi Cercetări Arheologice, 16*, 109–120.

Crişan, I. H. (1980). Necropola dacică de la Cugir. *Apulum, 18*, 81–87.

Domaradzki, M., & Nikolov, B. (1982). Spasitelni razkopki na trakiyska nadgrobna mogila pri s. Gorna Kremena, Vrachanski okrag. *Arheologicheski Otkritiya i Razkopki prez 1981 g*, 86.

Gadamer, H.-G. (1989). *Truth and method.* (J. Weinsheimer & D. G. Marshall, Trans.) (Second, revised edition.). London: Sheed & Ward.

Gheorghiu, G. (2005). *Dacii pe cursul mijlociu al Mureşului (sfârşitul sec. II a. Ch. - începutul sec. II p. Ch.).* Cluj-Napoca: Mega.

Hubert, L., & Arabie, P. (1985). Comparing partitions. *Journal of the Classification, 2*, 193–218.

Jacanović, D. (1997). Late La Tène site 'Dunavac' in Kostolac. *Glasnik, 13*, 127–134.

Jovanović, B. (1988). *Gomolava: Naselje Mlađeg Gvozdenog Doba. Late La Tène settlement.* Novi Sad: Vojvođanski muzej.

Kaufman, L., & Rousseeuw, P. J. (2005). *Finding groups in data: An introduction to cluster analysis.* New York: Wiley.

Kuzmanov, M. (2005). The horse in the Thracian burial rites. *Helis, 4*, 98–107.

Langfelder, P., Zhang, B., & Horvath, S. (2008). Defining clusters from a hierarchical cluster tree: the Dynamic Tree Cut package for R. *Bioinformatics, 24*(5), 719–720. doi:10.1093/bioinformatics/btm563.

Legány, C., Juhász, S., & Babos, A. (2006). Cluster validity measurement techniques. In *AIKED'06: Proceedings of the 5th WSEAS international conference on artificial intelligence, knowledge engineering and data bases* (pp. 388–393). Stevens Point, WI: World Scientific and Engineering Academy and Society (WSEAS).

Nicolăescu-Plopşor, C. S. (1945). Antiquités celtiques en Olténie. *Dacia, 11-12*, 17–33.

Nikolov, B. (1993). Settlements and finds from the Bronze and Iron Ages in the vicinity of the town of Oriahovo. *Izvestiya na Muzeite v Severozapadna Bulgaria, 21*, 11–26.

Popescu, E., & Vulpe, A. (1982). Nouvelles découvertes du type Ferigile. *Dacia, 26*, 77–114.

Rustoiu, A. (1996). *Metalurgia bronzului la daci: (sec. II î. Chr. - sec. I d. Chr.) Tehnici, ateliere şi produse de bronz.* Bucureşti: Institutul Român de Tracologie, Ministerul Învăţământului.

Rustoiu, A. (1997). *Fibulele din Dacia preromană (sec. II î.e.n. - I e.n.).* Bucureşti: Institutul Român de Tracologie, Ministerul Educaţiei Naţionale.

Rustoiu, A., Comşa, A., & Lisovschi-Cheleşanu, C. (1993). Practici funerare în aşezarea dacică de la Sighişoara-Wietenberg (observaţii preliminare). *Ephemeris Napocensis, 3*, 81–95.

Sîrbu, V. (1993). *Credinţe şi practici funerare, religioase şi magice în lumea geto-dacilor (pornind de la descoperirile arheologice din Câmpia Brăilei).* Galaţi: Porto-Franco.

Sîrbu, V. (1994). Morminte tumulare din zona Carpato-Dunăreană (sec. I î. d. Chr. – I d. Chr.) *Istros, 7*, 123–160.

Sîrbu, V., Luca, S. A., Roman, C., Purece, S., Diaconescu, D., & Cerişor, N. (2007). *Vestigiile dacice de la Hunedoara/The Dacian vestiges in Hunedoara.* Sibiu: Muzeul Naţional Brukenthal.

Teleagă, E., Bălăşescu, A., Soficaru, A., & Schoch, W. (2014). Die Scheiterhaufen aus Cugir und Tarinci. Ein Beitrag zu den Bestattungssitten der Balkanhalbinsel und des vorrömischen Dakiens in der Spätlatènezeit. *Praehistorische Zeitschrift, 89*(2), 305–336.

Theodossiev, N. (2000). *North-Western Thrace from the fifth to first centuries BC.* Oxford: Archaeopress.

Todorović, J. (1963). Rospi Ćuprija. Nécropole de l'époque La Tène à Beograd. *Inventaria Archaeologica, 6.*

Ursachi, V. (1995). *Zargidava: Cetatea dacică de la Brad.* Bucureşti: Caro Trading.

Vulpe, A. (1976). La nécroplole tumulaire gète de Popeşti. *Thraco-Dacica, 1*, 193–215.

Werner, W. M. (1988). Eisenzeitliche Trensen an der Unteren und Mittleren Donau. Munchen.

Chapter 5
From Large to Small. Results Discussion

5.1 Discussion of the Statistically Derived Groups[1]

5.1.1 General Groups Overview

The interpretation of the outcome of the cluster analysis is not at all straightforward. An easily interpreted result would have consisted of clearly differentiated groups in terms of their characteristics and preferably also strict geographical separation. Were that the case, determining identity boundaries as well as inferring the possible nature of such identities would have been a simple task. Yet such an outcome would have been artificial from a modern theoretical perspective, since nearly all studies point toward the fluid nature of identity. People may feel that they share a common identity with a specific group, but the way that *sameness* is exhibited varies according to a multitude of contextual factors, some of which may relate to personal preference or may be the result of differential interaction with members of other communities. The results of the statistical analysis confirm this scenario for the Late Iron Age of the Eastern Carpathian basin and the Lower Danube, since most groups presented a significant degree of overlap.

Hence, the primary observations for the seven clusters are that, even though they were quite varied, they were not clearly distinguishable from one another. While indeed there were groups which had little resemblance to each other, almost every group had at least one other with which it shared a series of features. The main idea, a conceptual model, of each group is definable for each cluster (see Chap. 4). However, most graves did not exactly follow the model, but presented a smaller or larger degree of variation, often giving them resemblance to other groups.[2] Such

[1] The interpretation of the results is based mainly on the results of PAM (see Chap. 4).

[2] It should also be noted that there may also be errors introduced through the clustering procedure, leading to some graves being placed wrongfully in a group. Some of these errors are signaled and, when possible, corrected in the different sections of this chapter.

C. N. Popa, *Modelling Identities*, Quantitative Archaeology and Archaeological Modelling, https://doi.org/10.1007/978-3-319-63267-4_5

situations occurred particularly when the cluster models presented similarities. In those cases, drawing the boundaries between one group and another was undoubtedly forced; it was done mainly as a result of the constraints produced by the method of analysis.[3]

Comparable issues were encountered when examining the geographical distribution. It is hard to perceive any clear boundaries appearing between the different groups; most of them coincided spatially to some degree. Some groups had an almost perfect overlap, such as groups 1 and 3 or 4 and 6, suggesting complementarity, while others only partially shared the same space. Therefore, as with the features of the groups, there was a lot of variation in terms of the geographical distribution, but some concentrations are observable and may have formed the core area for some clusters.

Building on these observations, it is interesting to note that, in general, the groups that were quite similar in terms of their characteristics also largely shared the same area. For instance, groups 4, 5, and 6, which were nearly all cremations and had as one of their prime features the presence of weapons, seem to have been centred on a North-South axis spanning from South-West Transylvania to North-West Thrace. A secondary axis can be observed when comparing groups 4 and group 5. It was orientated East-West and closely followed the course of the Danube River. Groups 1 and 3 also shared the same space, but were in other respects separate from those previously mentioned. These two clusters, both of which contained almost exclusively flat inhumations, were arranged around the Carpathian Mountains, following their contour quite closely. Finally, groups 2 and 7 had a very wide distribution, spreading practically across the entire geographical study area. Both of them were made mainly of flat cremations, but had considerable differences in terms of grave-goods. Based on these observations, it can be argued that two large supra-groups can be identified: one placed mainly in the East, consisting of groups 1 and 3, and the other found predominantly in the West, containing groups 4, 5, and 6 (Figs. 5.1 and 5.2). Groups 2 and 7 were scattered in the area of both supra-groups, maybe signalling some kind of overarching liaison group identity.

In order to grasp the possible group identities linked to the seven clusters, every group will be discussed through a comparison with the other groups. Since identity is built on the interplay between similarity and difference, producing an interpretation of each group based purely on their own features would be difficult and arguably faulty in terms of methodological approach, since a proper social understanding can only be gained when groups are compared with one another and integrated into the larger scenario. The closest analogy is that of a jigsaw puzzle. The place of each piece of the jigsaw can only be found by comparing each piece with all of the other pieces to find the precise ones that it joins and the ones that it does not match. Just looking at each individual piece in isolation does not take one closer to the solution. Hence, each group will be separately compared with all other groups and inter-

[3] An effect introduced by this situation, and already discussed in the previous chapter, is the difficulty in statistically validating the clustering results.

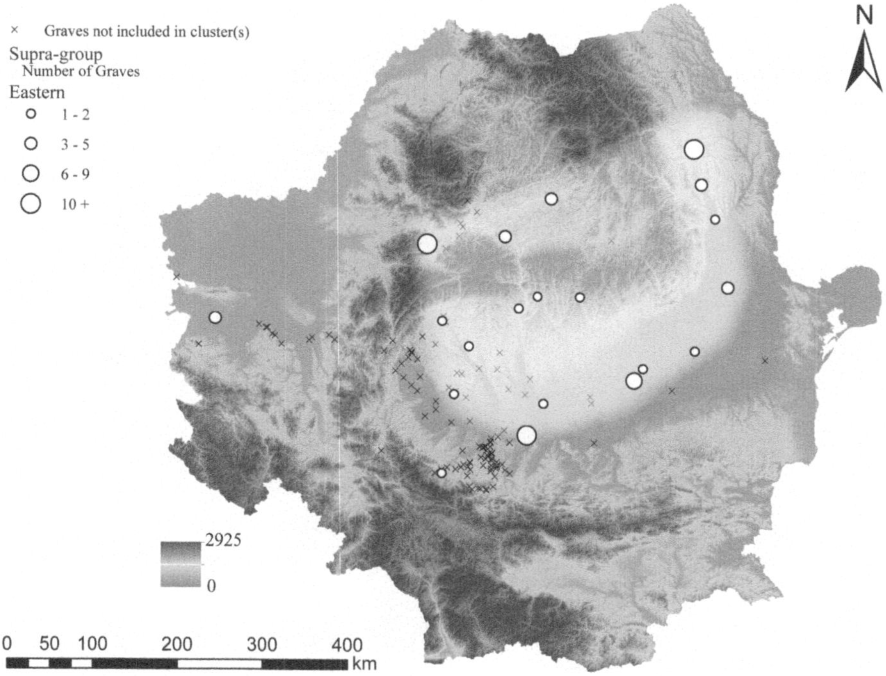

Fig. 5.1 Geographical distribution of Eastern supra-group with contour of main distribution area

preted based on observed overlap or differentiation, so that the most reasonable explanations can be proposed for the possible group identities linked to the funerary practice patterns.[4] The order in which the groups are discussed is chosen so as to facilitate their analysis, placing the groups with high resemblance one after the other. In this way, the similarities are easier to point out and comparison repetitions are reduced.

5.1.2 *Group 1*

Group 1, through its grave-goods, presents a large degree of similarity with group 2. Both of them are defined by the presence of adornments or clothing accessories, but only one such item was found in each of the graves of group 1, while more than two thirds of the graves of group 2 contained two or more such items. Additionally, a

[4] It should be noted that such an interpretation method unavoidably leads to a series of repetitions. In order to reduce such situations, some group characteristics will be intentionally omitted if they are not relevant to the comparison or if they were amply discussed in a different section.

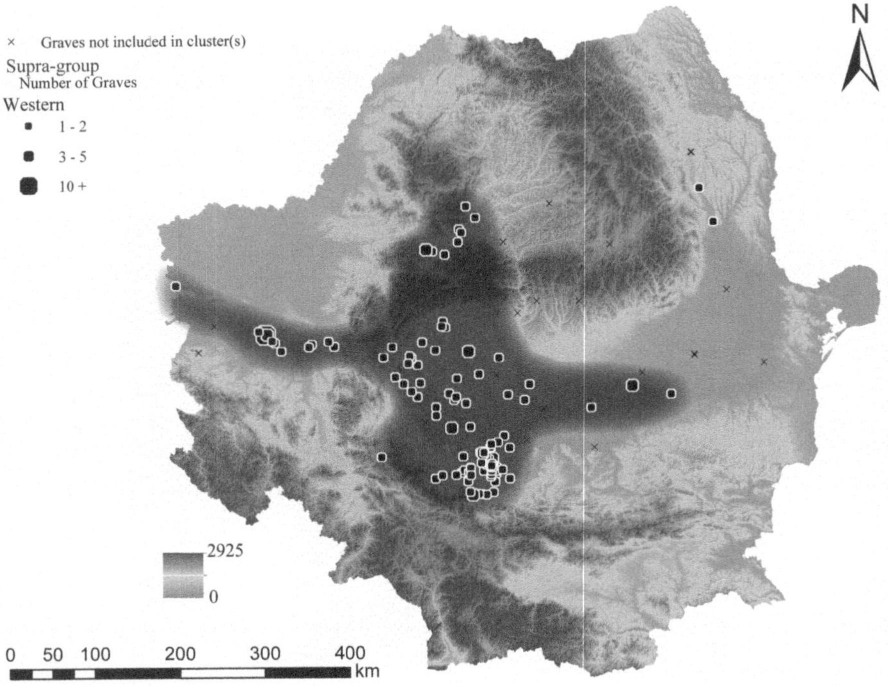

Fig. 5.2 Geographical distribution of Western supra-group with contour of main distribution area

variety of other objects, such as tools or vessels, were placed in many of the graves of group 2, but the graves of group 1 rarely contained any other items. In terms of specific adornment types, generally all objects appeared in much larger quantities among the grave-goods of group 2 and were found in more graves.[5] The single exception is given by bead necklaces: nearly a third of the graves of group 1 contained such an item, while they were only found in just over a fifth of the graves of group 2. Bead necklaces, along with fibulae, represent the only artefact types which had a significant presence in the graves of group 1, while in the case of group 2 there were also other object types which were found in at least a quarter of graves, such as bracelets or belts. Even though both groups 1 and 2 contained several graves with fibulae, it is interesting to note that apart from types 19 and 20, the exact fibula types differed (Table 5.1).

Many differences in the features of funerary ritual can be detected between the two clusters. The primary distinction is the general use of inhumation for the graves of group 1 and cremation for those of group 2. In addition, half of the group 1 graves came from multiple burials, while this was rarely encountered in group 2. Finally, one third of the graves of group 1 came from inside a contemporary settlement; in

[5] This last observation is significant since cluster 1 and 2 contained a nearly identical number of graves: there were 51 in group 1 and 50 in group 2.

Table 5.1 Count of fibula types per group

		PAM group			
		1	2	4	5
		Count	Count	Count	Count
Object Category4	Fibula type 1	1	0	0	0
	Fibula type 2	0	5	4	9
	Fibula type 3	0	2	0	0
	Fibula type 4	0	1	0	0
	Fibula type 6	0	0	0	1
	Fibula type 7	0	1	0	0
	Fibula type 10	0	1	0	0
	Fibula type 11	0	0	0	1
	Fibula type 16	0	2	0	0
	Fibula type 17	1	0	0	1
	Fibula type 19	2	1	0	0
	Fibula type 20	4	4	0	0
	Fibula type 28	0	1	0	0
	Fibula type 30	0	1	0	0
	Fibula type Gomolava	3	0	0	0
	Fibula type Vinkovci	0	0	0	1

Only the groups that contain fibulae are represented. Figures refer to number of objects

the case of group 2, this only happened in four instances. Therefore, while group 1 had important similarities with group 2 in terms of grave-goods, it differed to a large degree in terms of funerary ritual.

The spatial distribution of the two clusters shows that group 1 was included within the much broader geographical area of group 2. Although at first glance it appears that group 1 spread as far West and South as group 2, the finds from Gomolava, in Vojvodina, and Kalimanitsa, in North-West Thrace, sum up to only four graves and represented isolated cases (see Chap. 4). Those sites were obviously the exception rather than the rule, since generally group 1 graves did not appear South of the Danube or West of the Danube gorges. On the other hand, graves from group 2 were a regular appearance in those parts as well. Therefore, it can be safe to say that group 2 extended further South and West when compared to group 1 (Fig. 5.3). Nonetheless, the two groups coexisted in much of the same geographical space. Furthermore, graves from the two clusters were regularly encountered in the same site, such as at Brad (Ursachi 1995), Hundeoara-Grădina Castelului (Sîrbu et al. 2007b), or Popeşti (Popescu and Vulpe 1982).

Given the relationship between groups 1 and 2, it is possible that the burial practice patterns refer to a social status identity. Taking into account the sheer quantity of grave-goods and to a lesser extent the funerary ritual, it is conceivable that the individuals of group 1 were of a comparable but lower status than those of group 2. The use of inhumation in one cluster and cremation in the other may be the outcome

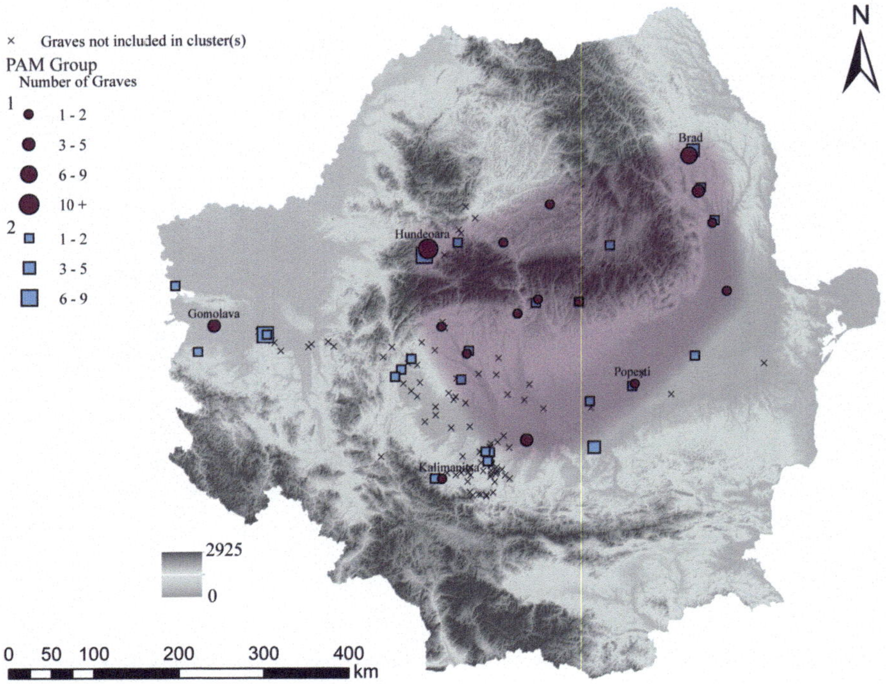

Fig. 5.3 Geographical distribution of PAM groups 1 and 2 with contour of group 1

of distinct afterlife beliefs. Nevertheless, in general, cremation involves more effort and organization than inhumation (cf. Williams 2004), which can suggest a comparable higher status for the deceased of group 2, although such a judgment does not stand by itself. However, considering also that half of the group 1 individuals came from multiple burials, and combined with the differences in grave-goods, a hierarchical division in terms of social status seems plausible.

The only other cluster that presents similarity to group 1 in terms of funerary ritual is group number 3. On the one hand, the two groups differ in terms of grave-goods, since group 3 graves basically had no contents except the human remains. However, considering that most of the graves of group 1 contained just one costume item, this difference in grave-goods does not appear too radical. On the other hand, the features of the funerary ritual make the two groups considerably alike. Both of them were formed mainly of flat inhumations. At least half of the graves came from multiple burials and were situated either near or, in many cases, within an actual settlement (Table 5.2). These characteristics are very significant since none of them apply to any other cluster, thus making groups 1 and 3 clearly stand out from all the others. Equally important is the geographical distribution since both groups appeared precisely in the same areas. Practically, apart from a number of cases, all the sites which contained graves from one group also had some from the other.

Table 5.2 All PAM group counts for *grave type*, *ritual type*, *multiple burials*, *river proximity*, and *settlement proximity* variables

		PAM group						
		1	2	3	4	5	6	7
		Count	Count	Count	Count	Count	Count	Count
Grave type	Construction	1	1	1	0	0	0	0
	Flat	44	38	64	38	52	24	30
	Tumular	6	11	1	15	28	5	5
Ritual type	Cenotaph	1	1	0	1	1	2	0
	Cremation	7	37	4	49	78	25	29
	Inhumation	43	12	62	3	1	2	6
Multiple burials	No	25	42	20	52	78	27	34
	Yes	26	8	46	1	2	2	1
River proximity	NA	0	0	1	2	0	0	0
	Banks	15	14	21	16	29	9	17
	Near	36	33	44	34	44	18	16
	Far	0	3	0	1	7	2	2
Settlement proximity	NA	1	7	2	17	17	7	2
	Near	32	39	44	33	52	20	28
	Inside	17	4	20	1	0	0	5
	Far	1	0	0	2	11	2	0

The funerary practices associated with groups 1 and 3 suggest the existence of group identities shared by members of the same communities. The difference between the two may be connected to some social status distinctions, but this were most likely minimal or entirely absent in most cases. Group 3 may have involved slightly altered concepts of the body, since in the case of many graves there was little apparent care for the deceased (see group 3 discussion). Nevertheless, the same situation was encountered in the case of many of the group 1 individuals (e.g., Şura Mică, Sîrbu 1986: 101–102).

Besides clusters 2 and 3, no other group presented significant similarities with group 1. Cluster 7 shared much of the same area with group 1, although it also extended much to the West, just like group 2. Yet it differed almost completely from group 1, both in terms of funerary ritual characteristics, as group 7 included cremations coming from single burials, and when considering the grave-goods, since the group 7 graves contained chiefly vessels and no adornments or clothing accessories. The only thing that can be thought as uniting them is the small number of grave-goods. However, the group 1 grave-goods incorporated primarily costume elements, objects that were probably of a personal nature, directly linked to the deceased and placed in direct contact with the body. In contrast, the grave-goods of group 7 were dissociated from the deceased. The vessels placed in the graves were probably linked to a particular funerary ritual practice and did not constitute personal belongings of the deceased. Despite these significant differences, the two clusters still appeared partly in

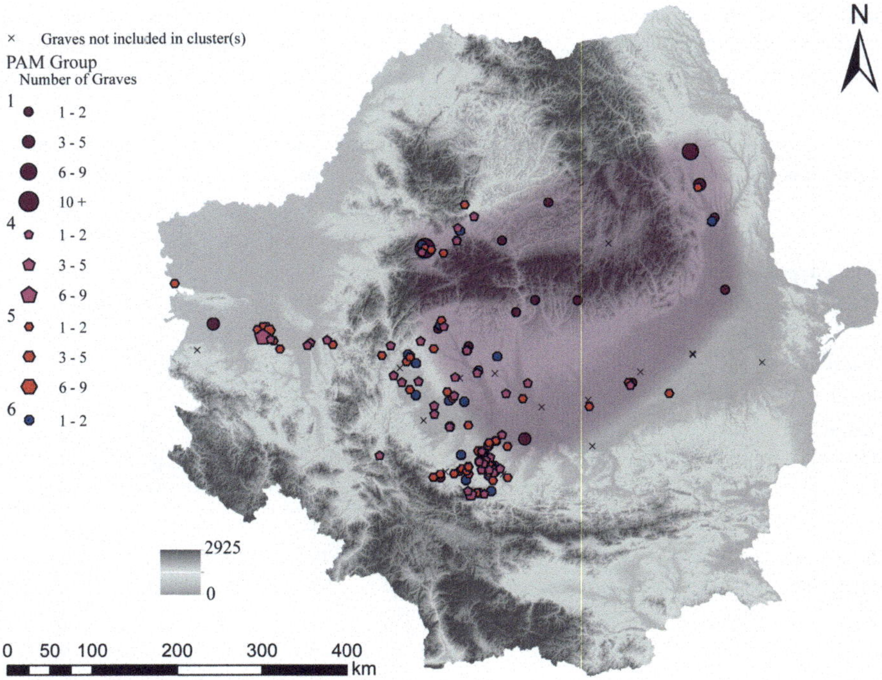

Fig. 5.4 Geographical distribution of PAM groups 1, 4, 5, and 6 with contour of group 1

the same geographical area. Consequently, the burial practice patterns of groups 1 and 7 signal considerably dissimilar group identities which were shared by people of the same communities. Just like with the previous two groups, they may have referred to different social status identities, although the relationships between the two is hard to determine since there are virtually no elements that the two had in common.

The remaining groups, 4, 5, and 6, differed in practically all aspects from group 1: they employed different funerary rituals, had nearly no common grave-goods, and presented little spatial overlap (Fig. 5.4). This quasi complete separation is significant in itself. These were people that lived in different geographical regions and engaged during funerals in different practices, with distinct forms of material culture. Therefore, through this comparison, a second identity dimension comes to the fore. Group 1 is not only linked to a specific social status identity, but also to a regional one, pointing to a situation of nested identities (cf. Hakenbeck 2007). People's identity was linked to the place that they saw themselves as occupying in society, but that specific position in society only existed in particular regions, namely Moldova, Muntenia, Transylvania, and parts of Oltenia. This conclusion is reinforced by the identical situation of group 3 (see below). There are of course regions where group 1, on the one side, and group 4, 5, and 6, on the other, overlapped: mainly South-West Transylvania, Eastern Oltenia, and partly Muntenia. However, this situation was to be expected of communities living so close to one another: there is always a contact zone; an area where the two merge, coexist, and become entangled.

5.1.3 Group 3

Group 3 has the largest similarity with group 1, especially in terms of funerary ritual and the geographical area in which they appeared. It has already been stated that the two clusters presumably refer to very similar group identities. The treatment of the deceased of these two groups, especially evident in the case of the cluster 3 graves, signals a distinct perception of the body, maybe as a simple physical vessel lacking an actual person. In some cases, several bodies appear to have been thrown in together in pits which were afterwards used for rubbish disposal, as was the case at Sighişoara-Wietenberg (Rustoiu et al. 1993) or at Orlea (Comşa 1972). Considering that the large majority of skeletons belonged to children, it may be that the individuals of group 3, and many of group 1, were considered to be social outcasts, people who were not perceived as actual community members, the children because of their age and the rest because of some other motive.[6] For this reason, many did not receive an actual burial; rather their bodies were simply disposed of. These individuals did not undergo a social death, but purely a physical one; their death probably did not represent a threat to the social equilibrium of the community who buried them (cf. Malinowski 2004) since no observable funerary context was created to give people the possibility to accept and interiorize the loss. Thus, the individuals of groups 3 and 1 were either not part of the social community or were considered to be already socially dead.

It is also possible that at least part of these individuals were in fact human sacrifices. According to this theory, sustained by some researchers (Sîrbu 1997), all skeletons found in non-funerary contexts, such as features that resembled rubbish pits, represent the outcome of ritual killing. The main argument for this theory is the poor treatment of the skeletons and the mentioning of this practice by late antique authors (e.g., Jordanes, *Getica*, V.41).[7] Additionally, there are somewhat analogous practices identified to the South of the Danube, dated between the fifth and third century BC, which some have interpreted as evidence of human sacrifice (Tonkova 2010). In spite of all these arguments, there are no osteological data to confirm the violent killing of these individuals. The few anthropological analyses that were carried out failed to show any clear sign of intentional violence (e.g., Nicolăescu-Plopşor, and Ricuşiţa 1969; Botezatu and Miu 1989). This of course does not rule out human sacrifice, since there are sacrificial techniques, such as strangulation, which do not necessarily leave any evidence on the bones. Nonetheless, without at least some form of anthropological evidence, this theory cannot be unequivocally embraced.

---

[6] The reasons for someone being seen as an outcast were probably varied. They may have been ostracized because of some activity that they carried out during their life or they may have been slaves since the existence of occasional slaves among the communities of the Eastern Carpathian basin was mentioned (Bodor 1981; Florea 2006; Gostar and Lica 1984). Alternatively, social exclusion could have been brought about by some diseases or disabilities, although the lack of extensive pathological data does not allow for confirmation.

[7] It should be mentioned that Jordanes wrote several hundred years later, although he had as sources writings that were chronologically closer to the Late La Tène.

Another alternative is that group 3 refers to a group of people for which there was a different perception of death. In such a tradition, the body and the person were clearly separated; once death occurred the body was not considered to be representative of the person anymore. Thus, the body may not have played an important role in the actual process of mourning and was simply disposed of. However, such a scenario does not seem very plausible and no ethnographic parallels for such behaviour could be found. One would expect such a radically different conception of death to be accompanied by other important differences. These people lived in the same settlements as the individuals of groups 2 or 7; they did not represent an isolated community. It seems hard to accept that, in what were probably small villages, such pregnant differences in the conception of death existed. Rather it is more likely that groups 1 and 3 were comprised of individuals that were perceived as social outsiders by a community which tapped broadly into a similar body of knowledge about death.

The ritual features typical of group 3 have partial parallels in some areas of Iron Age Europe. For instance, at the site of Danebury, in Southern Britain, Walker (1984) discusses the presence of numerous human bones in a number of apparent rubbish pits inside the large Iron Age settlement. She reaches a similar conclusion to the one proposed for cluster 3, that the deceased were most likely social outcasts. On the other hand, Carr and Knüsel (1997) consider the presence of such bones at several sites in Southern Britain, as being the result of excarnation practices, making their link with the position of the deceased in society harder to establish. However, the use of excarnation cannot be sustained for the funerary finds of group 3, since none of the signs that would indicate this practice was detected for the graves of this cluster, like animal gnawing on the bones or the generalized presence of incomplete, disarticulated skeletons (Carr and Knüsel 1997, p. 170). Rather, the mortuary finds of group 3 indicate a similar scenario to that proposed by Armit in his analysis of European Iron Age headhunting practices (Armit 2012). By integrating elements of personhood theory (Fowler 2004; Strathern 1999), he proposed that, at least in some instances, these functioned as practices of exclusion that served to reinforce the group identity of the communities which carried them out (Armit 2012, pp. 204–221). In a comparable manner, the individuals of group 3 were considered to be social outcasts; their exclusion, signalled through the treatment that they received in death, or rather the lack of treatment, reinforced their outsider status and thereby reaffirmed the solidarity of the community from which they were excluded.

The above observations are not valid for all cases. Some individuals received at least some attention during burial as there are occasional signs of funerary preparations. For instance, at Hunedoara-Grădina Castelului, the deceased, mostly children, were placed in shallow graves in rock niches which were at least partially prepared for the occasion.[8] However, nearly all graves were used at least a second time to make another inhumation, usually of another child but sometimes also of an

[8] Using natural scoops in the rock for placing bodies is not an uncommon practice (Parker Pearson 1999, p. 5). Nonetheless, there are no other such instances in the Late Iron Age of the Eastern Carpathian basin and the Lower Danube.

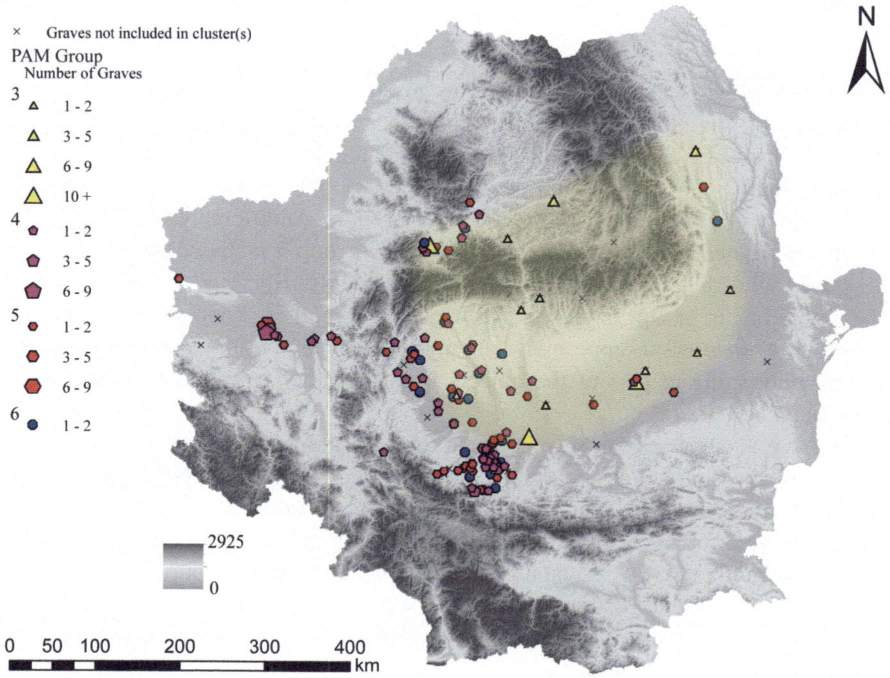

Fig. 5.5 Geographical distribution of PAM groups 3, 4, 5, and 6 with contour of group 3

adult. In such cases, the line between clusters 1 and 3 is again proven to be extremely blurry, as individuals from the two groups received a treatment that was practically identical.

Group 3 appears not only in the same area as group 1, but also that of groups 2 and 7, although the latter two extend much more to the West. However, both group 2 and 7 differ considerably from group 3 in terms of grave-goods and funerary ritual. Therefore, the same conclusion as with group 1 is the most likely—that the clusters relate to people with different social status identities.

When compared with groups 4, 5, and 6, once again a similar conclusion as with group 1 is reached. The clusters were nearly entirely separated from group 3, on grounds of grave-goods, funerary ritual, and geography (Fig. 5.5). Therefore, group 3 is linked to a group identity that was manifested in areas where the burial practices associated with groups 4, 5, and 6 were not encountered. It thus appears that, group 3 may also be linked to a regional identity. Considering that a similar supposition can be made about group 1 and that groups 1 and 3 shared a number of characteristics, including the spatial distribution, the existence of a regional identity seems extremely plausible. This identity spread over Moldova, Muntenia, Transylvania, and Eastern Oltenia. It is interesting to note that this is also the area where nearly all of the inhumations came from, which is to be expected given that groups 1 and 3 are the only ones which had in their model the use of inhumation. Given all these elements, one can conclude that the two clusters signal the existence of a larger supra-group identity (see Sect. 5.2).

5.1.4 Group 4

Group 4 presents a very close similarity to group 5. According to the average separation matrix, the clusters are more similar to one another than any of the other groups.[9] They were both defined by the use of flat and tumulus cremation graves in which weapons played a central role. However, group 4 included sets of two weapons, while in group 5 there were always three or more. Additionally, the weapons of group 4 were nearly exclusively offensive, while group 5 included a large number of graves with defensive weapons, especially shields. Horse gear elements were also numerous in group 5, but were comparatively rarer in group 4. On the whole, the group 4 grave-goods appear as a less complete version of those of group 5, containing only some or part of the objects from the latter but sharing all the basic elements.

The two clusters remain similar when their geographical spread is considered. Both of them occupied an area that can be defined mainly by a North-South axis running from South-West Transylvania to the North, through Oltenia, to North-West Thrace in the South. Additionally, there is one other axis running East-West along the Danube, although this orientation is clearer in the case of group 5, as the latter extends more in both directions. The region where group 4 graves were found was, thus, included in the area of group 5, although the latter also extended further over a narrow strip going from East to West.

Groups 4 and 5 likely referred to very close group identities which were manifested in a well-defined area. All facts point towards the individuals of group 4, having a status that was inferior to those of group 5, meaning that we may relate the two clusters to some sort of social status identity. The two groups of people were complementary in society and engaged to a large extent with the same material culture, at least in funerary contexts. Given the central position of weapons, the individuals were either warriors or had to be buried in a manner that emphasized martial abilities.

Groups 4 and 6 were also rather similar as they were virtually identical in terms of funerary ritual features. In addition, group 6 was defined through the presence of weapons among its grave-goods just like group 4. However, all group 6 graves contained only one such item, while those of group 4 had two or more. Nearly half of the grave-goods from group 6 also included horse gear, but practically no other items appeared. In contrast, horse gear only appeared in a quarter of the group 4 graves; instead, vessels were found in nearly half the cases. Sometimes adornments or clothing accessories were discovered in the graves of group 4, but they never occurred in those of group 6. In terms of geographical expansion, the two clusters had a near perfect overlap. The only difference is that group 4 graves were found additionally further West along the Danube, in Central Serbia (Fig. 5.6).

Based on their comparison, it can be concluded that the two clusters referred to warrior-orientated social identities. It is likely that the group 6 individuals enjoyed

[9] The cluster.stats R function calculates a separation of just 0.08 between the two.

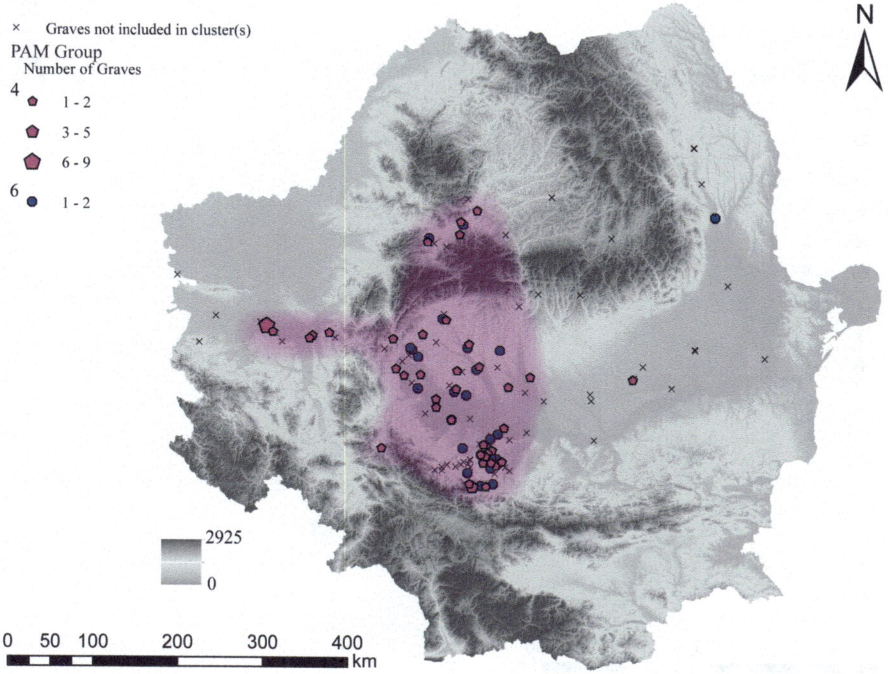

Fig. 5.6 Geographical distribution of PAM groups 4 and 6 with contour of group 4

a lower status than those of group 4, given the smaller number of weapons and the sheer lack of other grave-good items. It may also be that group 6 actually contains weapon graves for which only part of the original grave-goods was recovered, since many of the mortuary finds represent chance finds. While this seems like a reasonable explanation, the same observation can be made for many of the group 4 graves and thus the argument cannot be entirely trusted.

Group 4 shared the same funerary ritual elements also with clusters 2 and 7. However, there was a marked difference in terms of grave-goods since the latter two included no weapons. On the other hand, all of them contained vessels, though in smaller numbers in the case of group 4. Spatially, the cluster 4 graves were found in regions that are included in the larger area of groups 2 and 7 (Fig. 5.7). Therefore, the three clusters referred to burials practices that could be encountered in the same communities, but were not directly linked to one another. These may be linked to group identities which tapped into different material culture forms.

Finally, group 4 shared practically no elements in common with groups 1 and 3. There were marked distinctions in terms of funerary ritual and grave-goods. Groups 4 and 1 both had adornments or clothing accessories, although they appeared only in small numbers in the former. However, the object types found in the two groups were almost completely different. Group 1 had especially bead necklaces and fibulae. Group 4 did not include any bead necklaces and the few fibulae that it had were all of a different type than those of group 1 (Table 5.1). The differences between the

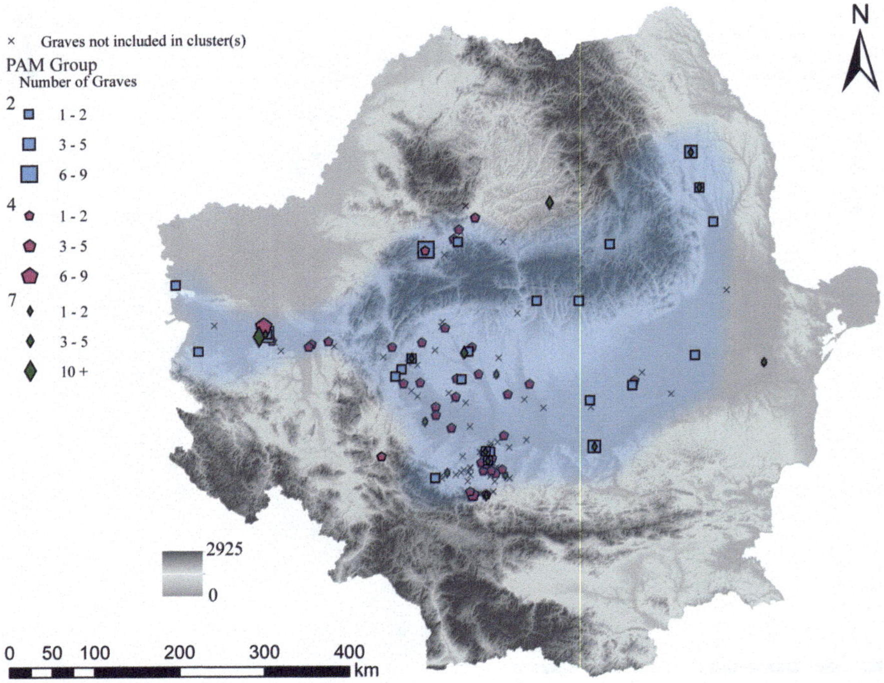

Fig. 5.7 Geographical distribution of PAM groups 2, 4, and 7 with contour of group 2

clusters persist when examining the spatial distribution, as was already pointed in the above sections on groups 1 and 3. The clusters only overlapped within a small strip in South-West Transylvania and Eastern Oltenia (Fig. 5.8).

Given all these elements, it seems likely that, in a similar fashion to clusters 1 and 3, group 4 related not only to a social status identity, as it came out of the comparisons with the other groups, but also to a regional identity. The boundaries of this regional identity corresponded largely to South-West Transylvania, Oltenia, North-West Thrace, and the Danube valley in Central Serbia. Considering the close relationship between this group and clusters 5 and 6, the regional identity also extended further West along the Danube, in parts of Vojvodina, as well as in some regions of Muntenia.

5.1.5 *Group 5*

As already described, group 5 has a very high degree of similarity with group 4. Based on the comparison of the two clusters, it was deduced that the burials of group 5 were of individuals that probably enjoyed a relatively high social status. The same conclusion can be reached by comparing groups 5 and 6. In this case, the difference between the clusters is much larger in terms of grave-goods, although

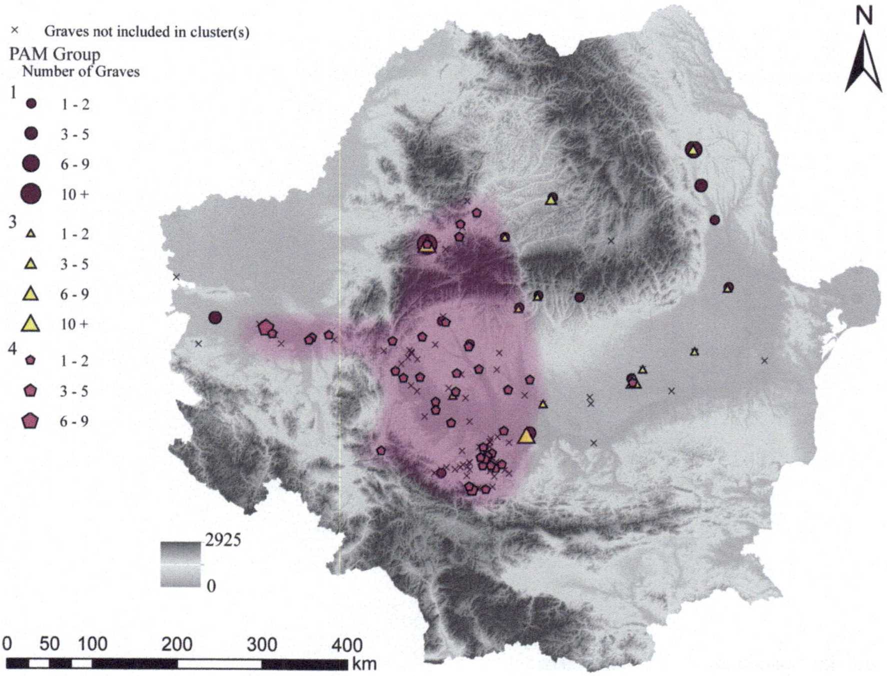

Fig. 5.8 Geographical distribution of PAM groups 1, 3, and 4 with contour of group 4

they still share the same funerary ritual elements. All category 1 grave-goods appeared in greater proportion and quantity in the graves of group 5 than in those of group 6. In terms of geographical spread, group 5 entirely incorporates the area of group 6. In addition, group 4 extends West along the Danube, into Central Serbia and Vojvodina, as well as West into Muntenia (Fig. 5.9).

Groups 2 and 7 exhibit less resemblance to group 5 due to grave-good differences, although they still largely share the same funerary ritual elements. This difference is based mostly on the lack of weapons, and to a degree, horse gear elements. All three clusters had vessels and groups 2 and 5 also contained adornments or clothing accessories. It is worth noting that groups 2, 5, and 7 are the only ones that had an overall ratio of vessels per grave higher than one. For cluster 7, this figure was even above two, although these numbers may be impacted by the recording bias relating to vessels. In terms of adornments or clothing accessories, the figures show a much higher value for group 2 (Table 5.3). However, in the case of both vessels and adornments, no remarkable discrepancies were observed in terms of the specific object types that were deposited. As for the geographical spread of the three clusters, groups 2 and 7 stretched over the entire area where the group 5 graves were found, but the former two also extended far more to the East (Fig. 5.10). Therefore, the burial practices linked to the three clusters were encountered in the same communities, which points again towards a possible manifestation of social status identity. It seems conceivable that group 5 individuals enjoyed a comparably higher

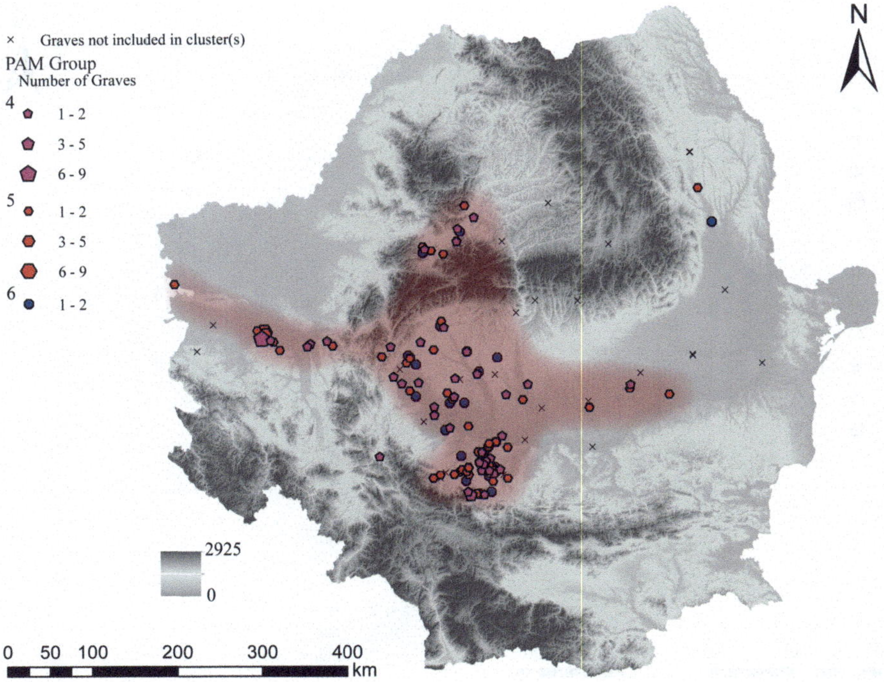

Fig. 5.9 Geographical distribution of PAM groups 4, 5, and 6 with contour of group 5

Table 5.3 Mean count of *adornments or clothing accessories* and *vessel or vessel implements* per grave according to PAM groups

	PAM group						
	1	2	3	4	5	6	7
	Mean	Mean	Mean	Mean	Mean	Mean	Mean
Adornment or clothing accessory	0.96	2.30	0.00	0.23	0.80	0.00	0.00
Vessels and vessel implement	0.61	1.46	0.00	0.94	1.40	0.41	2.29

status than those of group 7, but this is much more difficult to ascertain in regard to group 2. It may be that both enjoyed a reasonably high status, but employed different material culture forms, and thus, tapped into different practices, for the expression of their position.

In regard to clusters 1 and 3, the two illustrate the same differences from group 5 that they showed when compared to group 4. There is a large discrepancy in all three dimensions: funerary ritual, grave-goods, and geographical distribution.[10] This supports, like in the previous cases, the existence of separate regional identities.

The similarities and differences with clusters 4 and 6, together with the sheer quantity and value of the grave-goods, make group 5 certainly stand out from the

[10] However, in terms of spatial distribution, there is a larger overlap than in the case of group 4, since several group 5 graves were found in Muntenia.

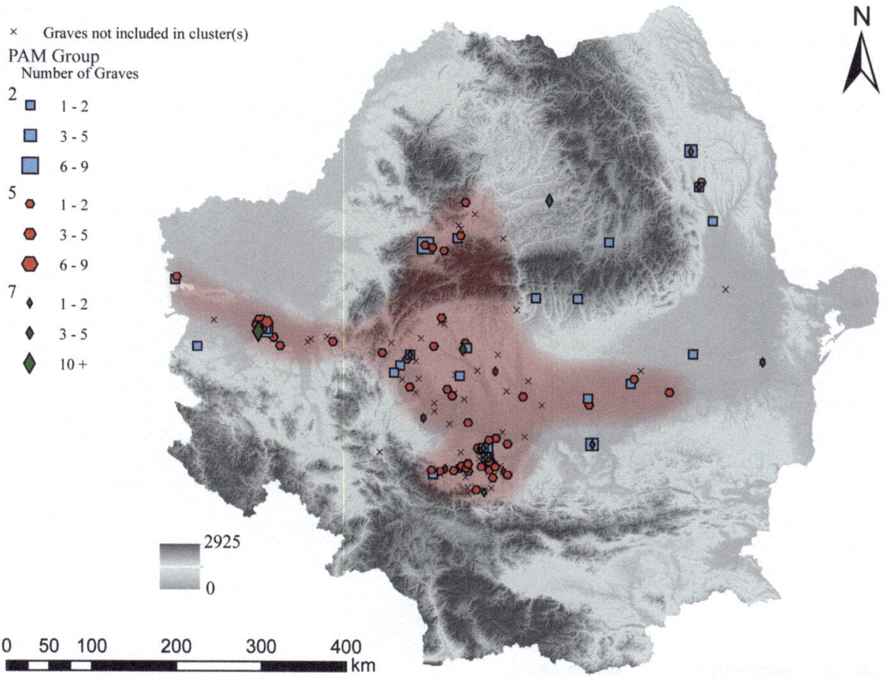

Fig. 5.10 Geographical distribution of PAM groups 2, 5, and 7 with contour of group 5

weapon-focussed groups. This distinct character can also be observed when compared to clusters 2 and 7. As a result, it is likely that group 5 refers to a very high-status warrior elite identity; these individuals may well have been local chiefdoms/warlords. Their graves suggest that they relied heavily on weapons as a display of their social position.

5.1.6 Group 6

Of the three weapons-dominated clusters, group 6 had by far the least objects, whether these weapons or other kind of items. Unlike the graves of groups 4 or 5, which always incorporated at least two or three weapons, those of cluster 6 never contained more than one such item. The weapons were in nearly half the cases accompanied by horse gear elements, a situation which is also encountered in group 5 but not in group 4. A third of the graves also had vessels, which is proportionally less than what was found in groups 4 and 5 where they appeared in nearly half the cases. Of course, like in the other groups, the possible bias relating to vessels recording may affect this observation. Overall, group 6 represents the least developed version of the warrior-like graves. Spatially, this group had the smallest expansion of all clusters, which is to be expected given that also in terms of actual numbers it

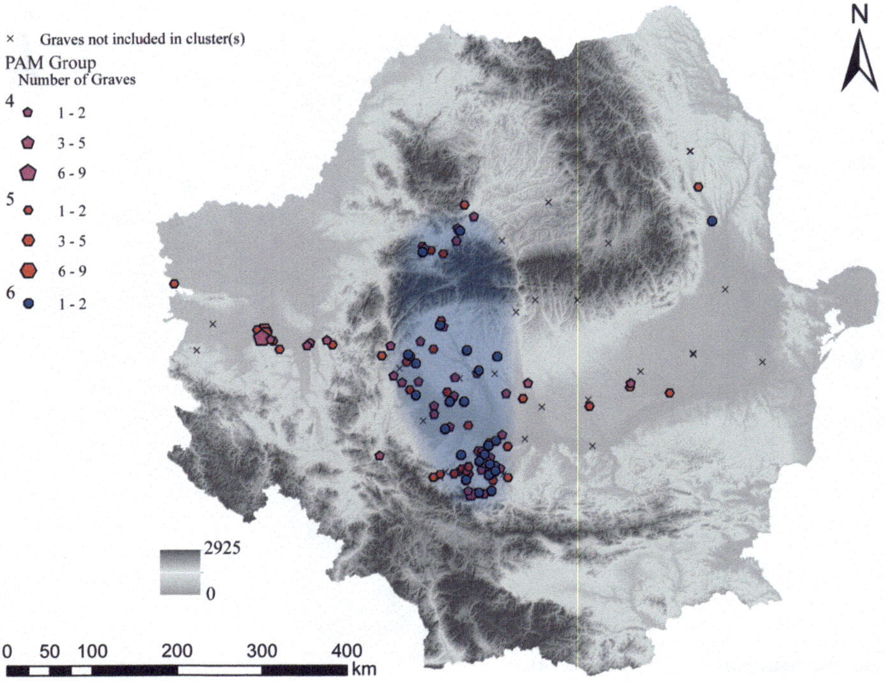

Fig. 5.11 Geographical distribution of PAM groups 4, 5, and 6 with contour of group 6

was by far the smallest. The graves are placed on the same North-South axis as those of group 4 or 5; unlike the two other weapon clusters, they cannot be encountered further West, in Central Serbia, or East, in Muntenia (Fig. 5.11). Thus, group 6 refers to a burial practice that accompanied those of groups 4 and 5. It may be connected to a less developed warrior-orientated identity, suggesting a social status inferior to that signalled by clusters 4 and 5.

Groups 2 and 7 compare with group 6 in the same manner that they did with the two other weapon-dominated clusters. Most of the elements that they share in common have to do with the funerary ritual elements, since the majority of the graves were single, flat, occasionally tumulus, cremations. On the other hand, the near lack of weapons or horse gear elements from groups 2 and 7 make the clusters different in terms of grave-goods. In addition, the group 6 graves did not contain any adornments or clothing accessories, which were the dominant grave-goods in the case of group 2. Geographically, the area where the group 6 graves were found is included in that of the other two clusters (Fig. 5.12), suggesting that these diverse burial practices were enacted by people living in the same communities, at least in some regions. Since the choice of grave-goods is so dissimilar, it is likely that the individuals buried in the graves of group 6, 2, and 7 were regarded as occupying significantly different positions in society. It is difficult to ascertain the relative social relationship between the deceased found in the graves of the three clusters, but it

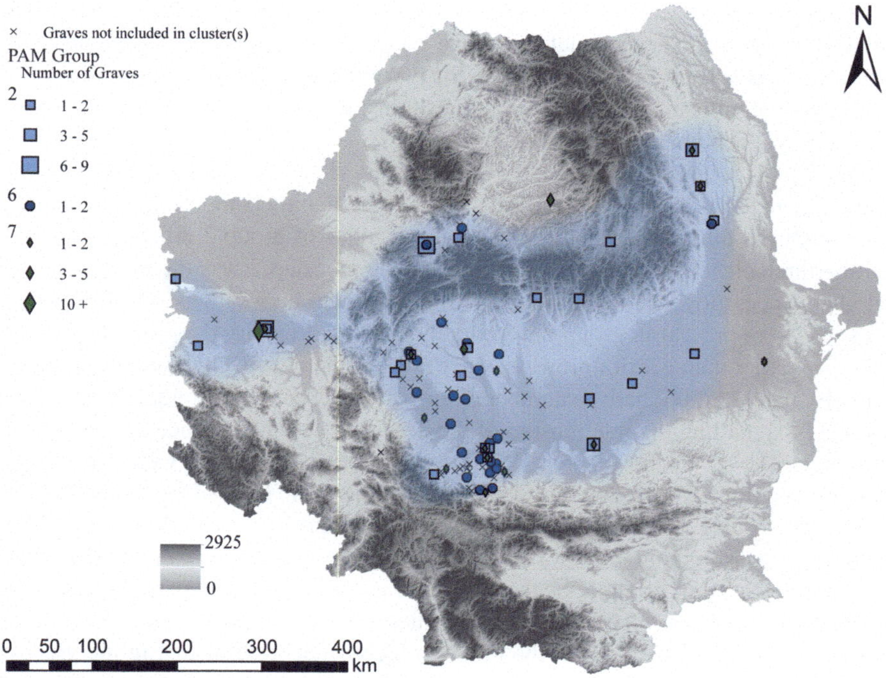

Fig. 5.12 Geographical distribution of PAM groups 2, 6, and 7 with contour of group 2

seems improbable that the individuals of group 6 occupied a very high-status position.

When compared with clusters 1 and 3, group 6 shows the same difference as the other two weapon groups. There is a marked difference in terms of funerary ritual elements, grave-goods, as well as geographical distribution, all of which further reinforce the functioning of different regional identities.

5.1.7 Group 2

Group 2 is the cluster with the widest spatial distribution. It is most similar to group 1, although the two differ considerably in terms of funerary ritual. As for the grave-goods, both group 2 and 1 contained mainly adornments or clothing accessories, but the former included many more such items and a significantly larger variety of other objects, including vessels, tools, as well as a small number of weapons. Since group 2 extended basically over the entire geographical area where graves were encountered, group 1 is included spatially within group 2 (Fig. 5.3). As argued earlier, group 2 and 1 refer to different social status identities, with the individuals of group 2 probably having a relatively higher social standing.

Group 2 has basically no elements of similarity with group 3, since they differ both in terms of funerary ritual and grave-goods. Spatially, group 3 is included in the area where group 2 is found. Hence, the two clusters are representative of people occupying significantly different social positions; the group 2 individuals undoubtedly enjoyed a higher social status.

Groups 4, 5, and 6 shared much of the funerary ritual elements but differed considerably in terms of grave-goods. All clusters were mainly composed of single, flat, or sometimes tumulus, cremations. The grave-goods of group 2 differed from that of the three clusters primarily because the focus in group 2 was on adornments or clothing accessories, while in groups 4, 5, and 6 it was on weapons. The few weapons that were present in group 2 were likely part of a funerary dress that expressed prestige rather than warrior prowess, since most of them were chain-mails, helmets, or belt-chains. Additionally, a number of arrowheads were also found, but they were probably signalling the relationship of the deceased to hunting since they were not accompanied by other weapons.[11] The only offensive weapons were two battle knives, one from Altimir (Nikolov 1965) and another from Konopishte (Theodossiev 2000, pp. 106, 128), although these very likely represent clustering errors. The adornments or clothing accessories found in the group 2 graves can only be compared to those from group 5, as the other two weapon clusters mostly lacked such objects. However, as discussed earlier, although some common elements exist, there are considerable differences in the precise objects that were placed in the graves, suggesting distinct funerary costumes. As for the geographical expansion, group 2 extended over all the regions where the three weapon-dominated clusters were found. Consequently, the people of group 2 were regarded as having a significantly different position in society than the deceased of groups 4, 5, and 6, although they can also be seen as complementary. Given the type of items found in the group 2 graves, and especially their quantity, it seems likely that these were people that enjoyed a high, elite-like social status, probably comparable to the group 5 individuals, although the models they employed to define their social position were not linked to military activities, but to other undeterminable practices. In light of these observations, a possible scenario is that the contrast between clusters 4, 5, and 6, on the one hand, and group 2, on the other, corresponds to a gender difference, with the latter cluster composed of very influential women. Of course, this interpretation is highly speculative given the lack of any other evidence in this respect and anthropological data.

Group 7 is the only other group that occupied a geographical area comparable to group 2 (Fig. 5.13), even though there are some differences in terms of their distribution. One of them is that group 2 extended also in South-West Transylvania, while group 7 did not. Furthermore, the large majority of the group 7 graves came from regions situated in the Western half of the research area, Central Serbia, Oltenia, and

[11] It should be mentioned that for other chronological periods it was noted that arrowheads frequently appeared in the graves of women or children, for which reason they have been interpreted as being highly symbolical, without any reference to martial aspects (Knaut 1993, p. 209).

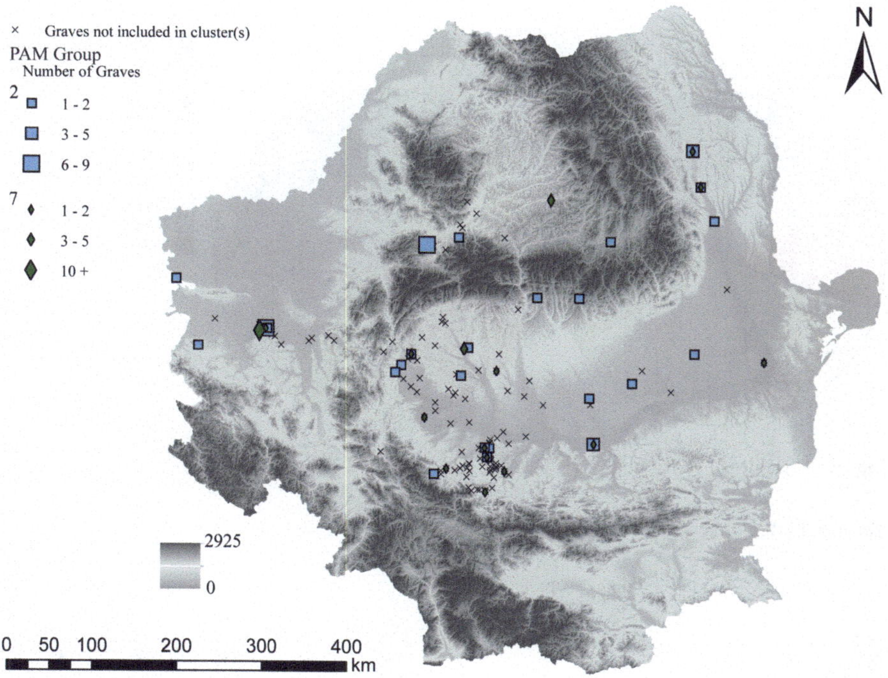

Fig. 5.13 Geographical distribution of PAM groups 2 and 7

North-West Thrace, while those of group 2 were much more evenly distributed (Fig. 5.14, Table 5.4). The two clusters were very close in terms of funerary ritual elements but presented grave-good differences. No adornments or clothing accessories were found in the graves of group 7. Vessels appeared in both clusters, although they were always present in the graves of group 7 and only in two third of those of group 2. Weapons did not play a significant role in any of the clusters. Many of the group 2 grave-goods were part of the funerary dress; they were most likely placed in direct contact with the body and represented personal objects of the deceased. In contrast, the grave-goods of group 7 were much more detached from the dead person. They were probably deposited by the mourners as part of the funerary ritual and did not necessarily represent personal belongings of the deceased. Nonetheless, such items were often placed in the cluster 2 graves as well. Therefore, it appears as if group 7 is missing the personal dimension of group 2, either because the deceased did not own such items, which seems rather unlikely, or because there were a series of regulations in effect, linked to specific religious beliefs or to social status, which limited their use in mortuary contexts. This could suggest the existence of two distinct group identities shared by individuals that were often part of the same communities, especially in Oltenia, North-West Thrace, or Central Serbia. These people occupied different positions in society and had a different social status, with the deceased of group 2 likely enjoying a higher recognition.

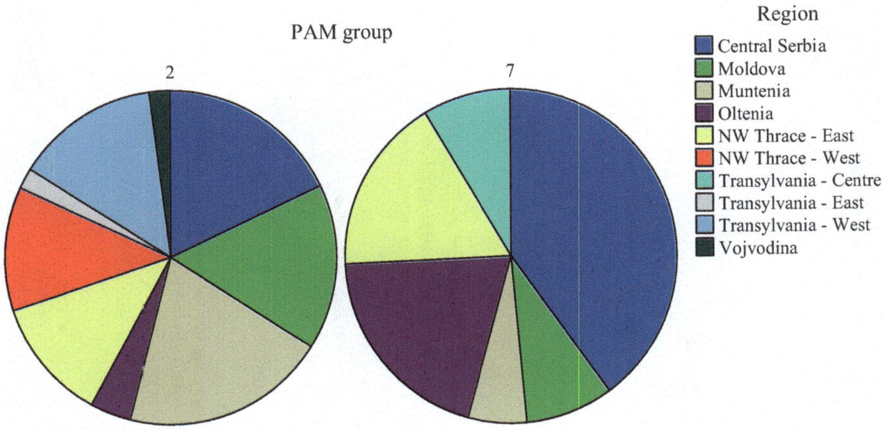

Fig. 5.14 Regional distribution pie charts of PAM groups 2 and 7

Table 5.4 Regional distribution of graves according to the seven PAM groups

		PAM group						
		1	2	3	4	5	6	7
		Count	Count	Count	Count	Count	Count	Count
Region	Central Serbia	0	9	0	9	16	0	14
	Moldova	12	8	4	0	1	1	3
	Muntenia	5	10	11	3	4	0	2
	Oltenia	8	2	22	15	9	12	7
	NW Thrace—East	1	6	0	18	38	13	6
	NW Thrace—West	0	6	0	4	4	0	0
	Transylvania—Centre	2	0	3	0	0	0	3
	Transylvania—East	0	1	0	0	0	0	0
	Transylvania—West	20	7	26	4	6	3	0
	Vojvodina	3	1	0	0	2	0	0

5.1.8 Group 7

As described above, group 7 shows the strongest similarity to group 2. In addition, group 7 also shares the funerary ritual with the three weapon clusters, 4, 5, and 6, although they present significant differences in terms of grave-goods. The latter three groups had a large number of weapons which were entirely absent in group 7. Vessels represented the main type of grave-good for group 7, as they appeared in all graves. They were also found in the three weapon clusters, although only 30–50% of the graves included such items (Fig. 5.15, Table 5.5). However, when looking at the frequency of each functional type, it becomes clear that the group 2 and 5 graves were the only ones that contained a comparable number of vessels to those of group 7 (Table 5.3). The same observation stands true when looking at the specific vessel shapes, though it should be remarked that all vessel types appeared more often in

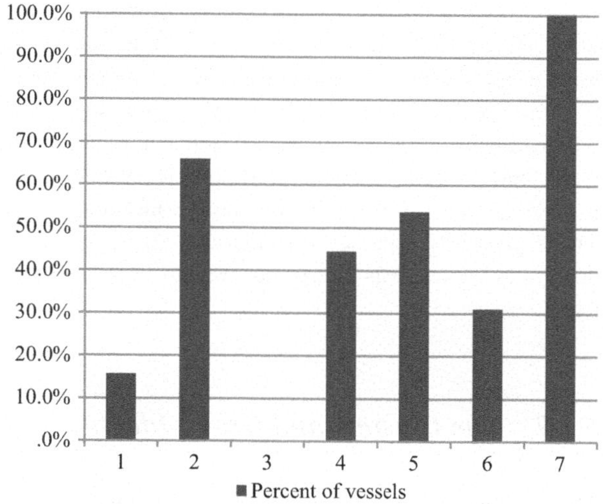

Fig. 5.15 Percentage of graves with vessels per PAM group

Table 5.5 Count and percentage of graves with vessels per PAM group

		Object category 1	
		Vessels and vessel implement	
		Count	Percent
PAM group	1	8	15.6
	2	33	66.0
	3	0	0.0
	4	24	44.4
	5	43	53.7
	6	9	31.0
	7	35	100.0

the graves of group 7, with one exception: fruit bowls. These were more numerous in the case of group 5. On the other hand, group 7 is the only one which contained small pots. All these observations may be influenced by a recording bias linked to vessels. Spatially, group 7 extended into the same region where clusters 4, 5, and 6 were found, with the exception of South-West Transylvania. These observations suggests that the burial practices associated with group 7, on the one hand, and clusters 4, 5, and 6, on the other, may be referring to particular group identities shared by individuals who could coexist in the same communities, but were not necessarily directly linked to one another. These were people that occupied significantly different positions in society and were likely involved in distinct activities.

Clusters 1 and 3 compare to group 7 in the same manner as they did to group 2. The funerary ritual was almost entirely separate. In addition, there are barely any similarities in terms of funerary assemblage, since the group 3 graves had practically no grave-goods and those of grave 1 contained mainly adornments or clothing accessories and, only on very rare occasions (eight graves), vessels. Spatially, group 7 incorporated all the regions where clusters 1 and 3 were found, with the same exception of South-West Transylvania. However, it should be noted that while there were graves in the Eastern regions (i.e., Oltenia, Muntenia, Eastern Transylvania), most group 7 graves came from the Western ones (i.e., Oltenia, North-West Thrace, Central Serbia). Therefore, the group is not particularly characteristic of the areas where clusters 1 and 3 dominated. Hence, it could be argued that group 7, on the one hand, and groups 1 and 3, on the other, were based on burial practices that were usually not encountered in the same communities, but could nevertheless occur. These practices reflected considerably different ideas about the treatment of the dead, since there was nearly no overlap in terms of grave-good items or funerary ritual.

5.1.9 The Clusters and Group Identity

The comparison of the group between one another has revealed that the seven clusters are probably linked to some loose concepts of group identity. This means that the clusters refer to identities that are hard to pinpoint exactly as they could involve a large spectrum of particular identity types.

In some instances, based on the grave-goods, it is possible to assess the nature of the relationships in which the individuals were involved and implicitly the particular position that the deceased and their group occupied in society. This is the case with clusters 4, 5, and 6, where, given the dominant presence of weapons in their graves, it is possible to assume that the deceased saw themselves and were seen by other people as being defined, at least in death, by their martial activities.[12] The specific place in society is much harder to grasp in the case of the other groups, although a more detailed analysis can give some indications (see Micro Dimensions section). The individuals of groups 1 and 3 are especially problematic, since the treatment of the body in that case can be a response to different bodily concepts or may indicate the presence of slaves and/or human sacrifices as has already been suggested. Despite the difficulties in asserting the position of these individuals in society, the identification of the groups and their comparison is enlightening since it sketches the nature of social relations in the Late Iron Age communities of the Eastern Carpathian basin and the Lower Danube.

Some of the detected funerary practice patterns may be related to gender distinctions, which, in certain cases, may have represented a notable factor of differentiation. The few data that are available about the sex of the deceased, mainly only for groups 1 and 3, reveal a relatively balanced ratio of males to females (Fig. 5.16) and do not indicate any difference in treatment. The only conclusions that can be drawn,

[12] The presence of weapons in graves does not necessarily imply that those individuals were full-time warriors during their lifetimes. Such an assumption would have to be backed up by anthropological analyses to confirm the presence of battle injuries (cf. Hausmair 2015). Nonetheless, in this study I refer to the deceased of groups 4, 5 and 6 as having a martial identity, even though they may well not have been (all) warriors.

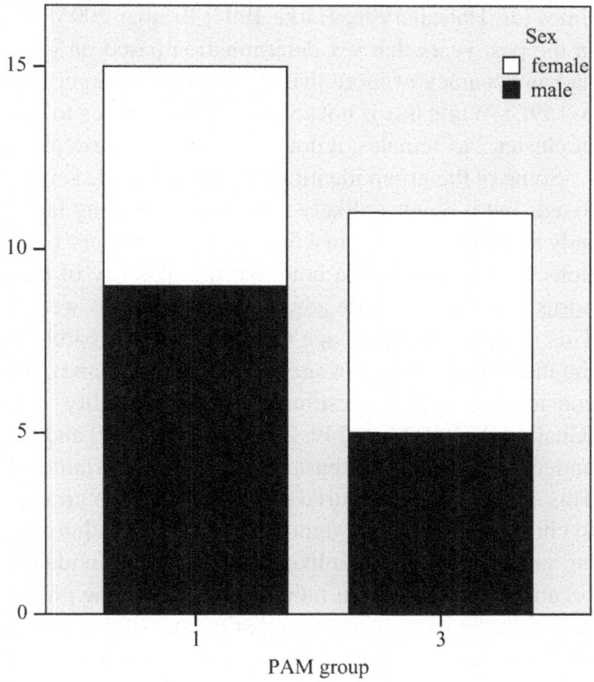

Fig. 5.16 Count of males and females for PAM groups 1 and 3

which are by no means certain given the small figures involved, suggest that tools and weapons were only discovered in the male graves, while adornments and clothing accessories as well as vessels were found with both males and females. Yet, some adornments, such as earrings, were uncovered solely next to females, while others, for instance belts, only appeared with males. It is dangerous to generalize these observations since they are based on less than 10% of the total sample. In addition, many of the graves with sex information come from a single site, Hunedoara-Grădina Castelului. Hypothetically, it may also be asserted that the graves of groups 4, 5, and 6 belonged primarily to males, which would mean that martial-related items, the main grave-goods for these clusters, were an important element of male identity in areas such as Central Serbia, Oltenia, North-West Thrace, and Transylvania. However, this model of male identity could not have been the only possibility, since there were also male graves that did not contain such items. In contrast, the graves of group 2 may have belonged to important women, local leaders, or family members of local ruling dynasties. This interpretation is somewhat supported by the grave-goods, and the partially complementary nature of the graves of cluster 2, with those of groups 4, 5 and 6. Therefore, in this case, gender may have indeed been a significant factor for differentiation, although the social status of these women was undoubtedly one of their main identity-defining features. Although the discussion along these lines cannot be corroborated with osteological data, the importance of gender distinctions in the case of funerary rituals is not surprising when compared with data coming from other periods, such as Early Medieval times (cf. Halsall 1996; Härke 1997; Brather 2005). In addition, it has been shown in the past years that sex determination based on grave-goods alone has generally had an accuracy of more than 95% (Gerstenberger 2002, p. 81f.; Kokkotidis 1999, p. 159f.). While this is not solid enough evidence to identify positively the deceased of cluster 2 as females, it does make this scenario plausible.

Some of the group identities connected to the seven groups may partly be related to age, but it seems unlikely that it was a defining factor. Age-related information is only available, apart from a few cases, for clusters 1 and 3, basically for the inhumations. It is interesting to note that the majority of the skeletons belonged to newborns or children, while adults and adolescents were fewer in number (Fig. 5.17). This gives an abnormal age ratio, since adults barely accounted for a quarter of all the individuals that were aged. Such a result stands out as extremely unusual when considering that the estimated child mortality rate for prehistory was 50% (Chamberlain 1997, p. 249, 2000, pp. 208–209) and that children are nearly always underrepresented in the burial record (Chamberlain 2000; Lucy 1994; Röder 2002). This suggests that the burial practice specific to groups 1 and 3 was usually granted to children. Yet, since a significant number of adults were also laid to rest in a similar manner, it seems unlikely that these individuals received such a treatment because of their age, but rather because of some property that they shared. As suggested in the section above, a distinct possibility is that the specific burial practice was reserved for people who were not considered to be full members of society: children because of their age and the adults because of physical or social impedi-

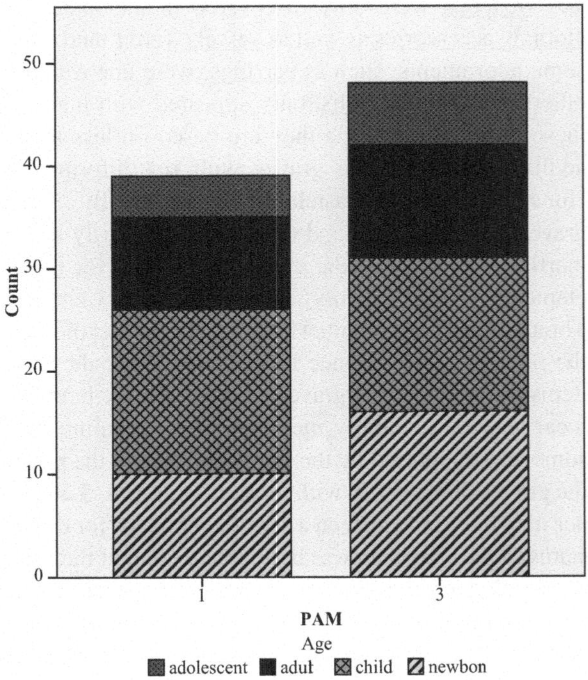

Fig. 5.17 Count of *age* values for PAM groups 1 and 3

ments. Therefore, one cannot speak in this case of a real age identity, but of an identity that was dependent on elements that were often, but not exclusively, shared by individuals of a certain age group, namely children.

The comparison between the seven clusters reveals that social status was one of the principal identity components that found its way into the mortuary practices of the Eastern Carpathian basin and the Lower Danube during the Late Iron Age.[13] This affirmation is based on the observations that graves belonging to different clusters were found in the same area or even on the same site. Since individuals who were catalogued by communities as having significantly different identities, referring to different groups solidarities, appeared in the same area, it can be inferred that the groups with these particular identities were both part of the same societies and, thus, in a way, symbiotic; they were complementary rather than exclusionary to one another. Age and gender could correspond to such a relationship between identity groups, but it has already been stated that data support for either of these two possibilities is severely lacking, although gender differentiation may be speculated in the case of clusters 2, 4, 5, and 6. Status, however, best explains the discrepancies observed in the way the body was treated and the amount and type of objects placed in the graves. While an exact measure of the social status enjoyed by the individuals of each group is hard to determine, it is possible to assess the relative social position of one group to another (e.g., individuals of group 5 enjoyed a higher status than those of groups 4 or 6) since through their comparison principles of social differentiation are put into balance (Babić 2005). In this line of reasoning, it can be postulated that the individuals of certain groups had a comparable higher standing in society than those of other groups, especially in the cases where graves from different clusters were discovered in the same geographical area.

The importance of social status as a main element for segmenting society and community solidarities is also supported by settlement evidence and ancient written sources. Several large settlement sites, such as Brad or Popeşti, were clearly demarcated physically into what could be considered to be quarters, with one occupying a central position, while two or three others were secondary (Figs. 5.18 and 5.19). The central quarter, referred by some as an acropolis (Ursachi 1995; Vulpe 2004), contained a series of large buildings, some of which can be interpreted as temples or palaces, and an open place that may have functioned as a square. There were also dwellings that were on average considerably more elaborate, both in terms of their plan and the construction technique and material, than those from the secondary quarters. As a result, it has been proposed that the central area was reserved for individuals that belonged to the higher strata of the population, as well as for buildings of a ritual and public nature. The other areas were lived in by people who were not regarded as highly since they contained considerably more modest dwellings and pits. In South-West Transylvania, many settlements do not retain this divisional structure so clearly, although even in the case of this region a spatial separation may

[13] Brather (2004) reaches a similar conclusion in his work on Early Medieval graves. However, his idea that social status is the only element involved in the preparation of the mortuary ritual and the choice of grave-goods is exaggerated, as some have recently argued (Hausmair 2015).

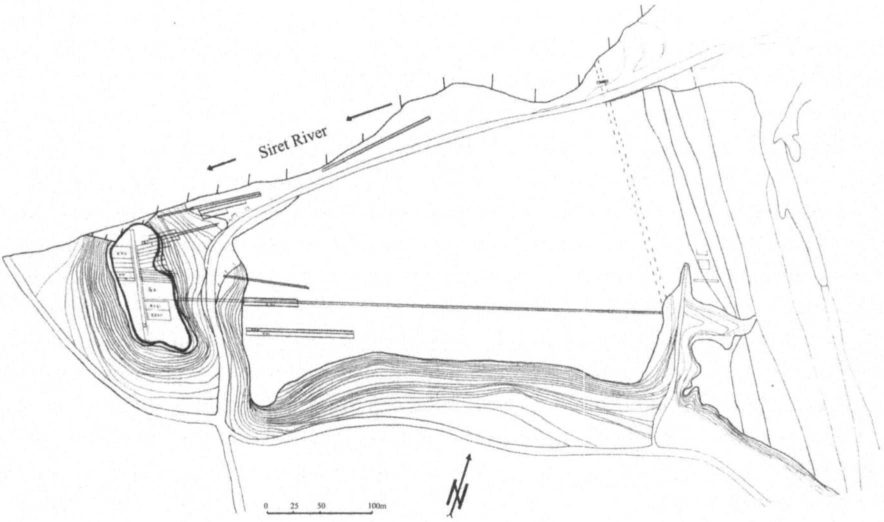

Fig. 5.18 Plan of Brad settlement (after Ursachi 1995, p. 10, Fig. 1)

be traced through the way the fortifications were placed in the landscape, probably reflecting similar status differences (Florea 2011, pp. 89–94). There are also a number of so-called tower-dwellings, which clearly stand out from all other buildings, through their dimensions, construction technique, and positioning. These have been widely interpreted as residences of the high elite (Florea 2011, pp. 107–168; Oltean 2007, pp. 115–116). The written sources also describe a two-tiered society. Authors writing about the communities living in the Eastern Carpathian basin mention the existence of an aristocratic class, *pileati* or *tarabostes*, which visually signalled their position through tall hats and hereditary-passed tattoos (see Pliny the Elder, *Nat. Hist.* VII.11 (10) 50; XXII.1.2) and a class of free men, *comati*. There may also have been slaves, but the extent of the phenomenon is not mentioned and cannot be guessed (Bodor 1981; Florea 2006; Gostar and Lica 1984).[14] Although texts from that period cannot be taken *ad litteram*[15] and it is difficult to generalize their information for the entire study area, it still constitutes evidence that deserves consideration, supporting the importance of status-centred divisions in the Late Iron Age communities of the Eastern Carpathian basin and the Lower Danube.

In light of the settlement data and the information left by ancient written sources, it has been proposed that the individuals of group 5 enjoyed a high status in society, one that was comparably higher than that of the deceased of groups 4 and 6, and which relied heavily on ideas of martial prowess. They probably represented the high elite of their communities, although the individuals of clusters 4 and 6 may also have enjoyed a relatively high status. An elite recognition may have been

[14] An excellent analysis of the written sources is offered by Petre (2004).

[15] Accepting uncritically the information coming from the ancient texts could also place present interpretations in terms of the world picture of their authors.

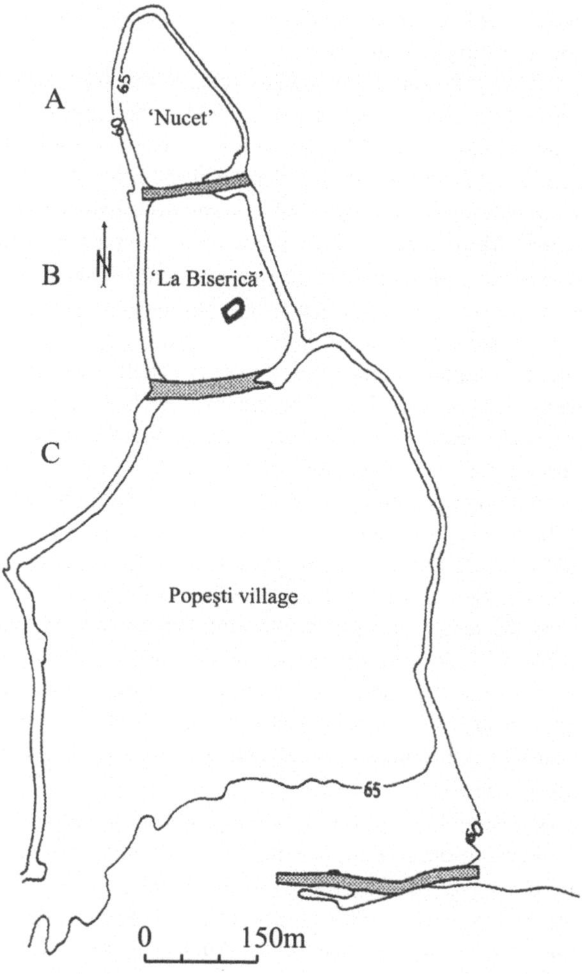

Fig. 5.19 Plan of Popeşti settlement (after Vulpe 2004, p. 21, Fig. 2)

enjoyed by the individuals of group 2 as well, yet their source of status, or at least its expression in death, was different from that of group 5, since no weapons were present in the graves of cluster 2. On the opposite side of the spectrum, lay the individuals of groups 1 and 3, who were probably not highly regarded in society.

5.2 The Macro Dimension. The Supra-Groups

Initial empirical observations suggested that there may be two larger, supra-group formations. These observations were confirmed through the intra-group comparison since significant divisions were remarked between some of the clusters. One supra-group was located in the Eastern part of the analysed area and one in the Western part.[16] The Eastern one incorporated clusters 1 and 3, while the Western one contained groups 4, 5, and 6.

Contrasting the supra-groups reveals much clearer patterns than in the case of many of the cluster comparisons. The Eastern supra-group consisted almost entirely of flat inhumations, 61% of which came from multiple burials. Nearly a third of them were found within the perceivable limits of a settlement. The Western supra-group was made of graves that were predominantly flat, although nearly a third were tumuli. More than 90% of them were cremations and came from single burials located near, rather than inside a settlement (Table 5.6). As for the grave-goods, with the exception of adornments or clothing accessories, all other items were found almost exclusively in the Western supra-group graves. The two supra-groups contained an equal number (49) of graves with adornments, but their proportion was overall higher in the East. The graves from both supra-groups mostly contained only one such item, although in the case of the Western two or more were sometimes found together. Further important differences can be noted about the actual types of adornments or clothing accessories. Bead and pendant necklaces represented some of the most common type of adornments found in the Eastern supra-group, but they only appeared in one or two instances in the Western. On the other hand, belts and bracelets were far more numerous in the Western one. Fibulae were more common in the Western supra-group, although they were found on 13 occasions in the Eastern (Table 5.7). Despite this apparent similarity, a closer analysis of the exact brooch types reveals that there was, with one exception,[17] no actual overlap between the two supra-groups (Table 5.1). Summing up, there are virtually no common features in regard to both funeral ritual and grave-goods between the Eastern and Western supra-groups.

As pointed out in the previous section, and also suggested by their names, the two supra-groups occupied mostly different spaces. Yet there was an area of overlap, described by South-West Transylvania, Eastern Oltenia, and partly Muntenia. Graves from both supra-group appeared, at first glance, in seven places: Corlate, Hunedoara-Grădina Castelului, Poiana, Popeşti, Răcătău, Spahii, and Vârţ.[18] A closer look at the graves from these sites reveals, however, that in some cases the overlap did not actually occur, while in others a mixing of ritual and/or grave-goods items appeared (Fig. 5.20).

At Corlate, four cremation graves were found together, two containing mainly weapons and two that included objects which were melted together with the bones,

---

[16] To be fair it is more Centre-West, but to allow for easier language and contrast West will be used.

[17] The only type that appeared in both instances was the type 17 fibula as defined by Rustoiu, also known as the Jezerine fibula. However, the brooch from the Western supra-group, coming from Piatra Craivii, was signaled as being a local variation since it was made of iron, rather than bronze, and it was considerably larger than all other Jezerine fibulae. Hence, it has been argued that the brooch from Piatra Craivii was in fact not part of the regular dress in which such fibula types were normally included (Rustoiu and Gheorghiu 2009, 2010).

[18] It should be noted that the graves of Poiana and Răcătău, both found in Moldova, were situated outside of the regular distribution area for the Western supra-group, which already signals their unusual character. Only one grave appeared in each instance.

Table 5.6 Eastern and Western supra-group counts for *grave type, ritual type, multiple burials, river proximity,* and *settlement proximity* variables

		Supra-group			
		Eastern		Western	
		Count	Percent	Count	Percent
Grave type	Construction	2	1.7	0	0.0
	Flat	108	92.3	114	70.4
	Tumular	7	6.0	48	29.6
Ritual type	Cenotaph	1	0.9	4	2.5
	Cremation	11	9.4	152	93.8
	Inhumation	105	89.7	6	3.7
Multiple burials	No	45	38.5	157	96.9
	Yes	72	61.5	5	3.1
River proximity	NA	1	0.9	2	1.2
	Banks	36	30.8	54	33.3
	Near	80	68.4	96	59.3
	Far	0	0.0	10	6.2
Settlement proximity	NA	3	2.6	41	25.3
	Inside	37	31.6	1	0.6
	Near	76	65.0	105	64.8
	Far	1	0.9	15	9.3

Table 5.7 Eastern and Western supra-group counts for *object category 3* costume adornments or clothing accessories

		Supra-group			
		Eastern		Western	
		Count	Percent	Count	Percent
Object Category 3	NA	4	3.4	4	2.4
	Bead necklace	17	14.5	2	1.2
	Belt	2	1.7	12	7.4
	Bracelet	5	4.2	12	7.4
	Earring	1	0.8	0	0.0
	Fibula	13	11.1	27	16.6
	Lunar necklace	0	0.0	1 0	0.6
	Pendant necklace	7	5.9	1	0.6
	Torque	0	0.0	2	1.2

because of the high burning temperature, and were thus not identifiable (Nicolăescu-Plopşor 1945, pp. 20–23). The two graves with weapons were placed by the clustering procedure into groups 5 and 6, respectively, but the remaining two were included wrongly in group 3. This mistake appeared because the similarity algorithm could not compare any of the unidentifiable grave-goods with any other object, producing a situation similar to the lack of any grave-goods. Therefore, Corlate actually contained just graves from the Western supra-group.

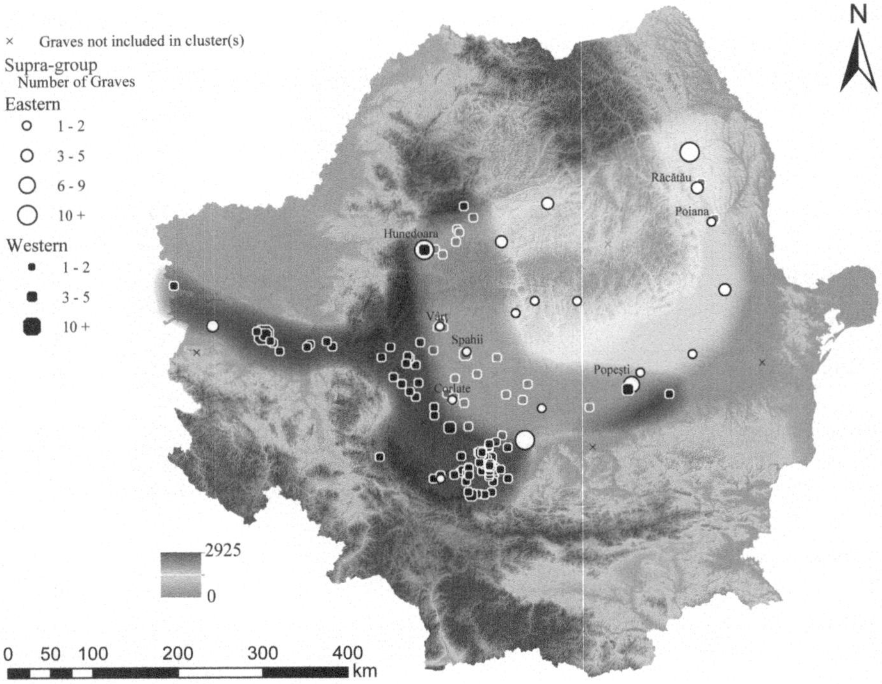

Fig. 5.20 Geographical distribution of Eastern and Western supra-groups with their contours

The graves from Spahii were part of a large cremation necropolis, which supposedly consisted of 29 graves. It was not possible in most cases to determine the full range of the grave-goods in the graves because of intense ploughing. Only a small number of the funerary finds were published to an acceptable standard and were used in this study (Gherghe 1978, 1983, 2008). Of the graves from Spahii that were included in the analysis, one was placed by the clustering procedure in group 1, while the rest were put in groups 4, 5, and 6, but also groups 2 and 7.[19] The group 1 grave, identified by Gherghe as burial M6, was a flat cremation that included as grave-goods sherds from one or more vessels as well as a yellow, simple, spherical bead, which may have been part of a bead necklace or a similar adornment. The grave-goods do indeed fit well with the types of objects that were regularly found in the group 1 graves, especially given the presence of the bead. Yet the funerary ritual is not comparable, as group 1 was characterized by the use of inhumation, not cremation. Grave M6 thus shows an interesting mix of grave-goods typical of group 1 and ritual elements characteristic of the Western supra-group, as well as groups 2 and 7. Through these features, this grave could be placed either in cluster 1 or in cluster 2, occupying an in-between position.[20] Therefore, Spahii may represent a case of fusion, of adaptation and entanglement, where elements of the two supra-groups combined as a response to contact.

[19] The graves usually contained a combination of weapons and vessels or just simply vessels.

[20] Such a situation is not surprising since it should be remembered that clusters 1 and 2 were statistically similar.

The situation at Vârţ is very similar to the one in Spahii, although only three flat cremations were uncovered in this case (Gherghe 1983, pp. 54–59).[21] Two of them were placed in group 6 by the clustering procedure, while the last was included in group 1 since it had a similar range of grave-goods to grave M6 from Spahii. Hence, just like at the previous site, this grave can be considered as part of either group 1 or 2 and can be the result of a combination of elements from both supra-groups.

The site of Poiana refers to a large Late Iron Age settlement on the banks of the Siret River, next to which a tumulus necropolis was uncovered. Of the 20 odd graves that were identified, only five were investigated and published in a manner that allowed for their use in the analysis of this study (Sîrbu 1994, pp. 125–126; Vulpe 1976, pp. 206–207; Vulpe and Teodor 2003). All of them were either cremations or cenotaphs. Two graves were placed by the clustering algorithm in group 1, another two were put in group 2, while the fifth was included in group 6. The funerary assemblages generally consisted of a mix of adornments or clothing accessories and vessels, in smaller or larger quantities. The group 6 grave, identified in other studies as tumulus 2, also contained vessels but additionally included arrowheads. Given that no other weapon types were found in the grave, it is safe to assume that the reference was to hunting rather than war-like activities. Yet, the clustering algorithm wrongly placed the grave in group 6, when in fact it is a better match for group 2 or 7. As for the two group 1 graves, tumuli 3 and 4, they may have also been wrongly clustered since neither of them used inhumation and they were not flat. Each of them contained only a fibula, but many of their grave-goods may have disappeared through grave robbing or erosion, since the nearby tumuli 1 and 5, placed in group 2, had a wide range of adornments or clothing accessories and vessels.[22] Therefore, it seems likely that Poiana was in fact not a site where the Eastern and Western supra-group came in contact, but one where all the graves were part of one single group, namely group 2.

The situation in Răcătău was somewhat similar to Poiana, which corresponds to their relative spatial proximity and placement next to the same river. At this site, a large Late Iron Age settlement was uncovered. Inside it, three flat inhumation graves were found, containing adornments or clothing accessories as grave-goods (Sîrbu 1993, p. 92). They were included in group 1. Next to the settlement, a small cremation, tumulus cemetery was discovered, of which only three graves were excavated (Căpitanu 1986, pp. 119–120; Sîrbu 1994, p. 128). One of these, tumulus 1, was placed by the clustering procedure in group 5, while the rest were put in groups 2 and 7 because of the presence of several adornments or clothing accessories and vessels. Tumulus 1 had in all respects a very similar range of grave-goods to the other two, but included additionally two pieces of chain-mail, probably belonging to one item. This chain-mail may have been an import from the Roman Empire, although it also resembles objects found among the steppe populations to the North of the Black Sea (A. Rustoiu personal comment). The appearance of an isolated defensive weapon in a grave, especially a chain-mail, was rather unusual. Given that

[21] It should be noted that one of the graves is an uncertain discovery.

[22] Some of the adornments were quite lavish and unique in character, such as a gilded mask and other golden objects.

this item was accompanied by numerous vessels, including amphorae, and by several unidentified objects which were likely adornments, the chain-mail was probably not placed to refer to war-like activities. Instead, the entire ensemble may refer to the wide commercial relations of the individual and to his or her wealth. As such, tumulus 1 fits much better in cluster 2 rather than 5. Therefore, Răcătău, just like Poiana, was not a place where the two supra-groups interacted. Nonetheless, it is interesting to note that the tumulus cremations, of group 2, were clearly spatially delimited from the three flat inhumations of group 1. This overt separation of people that were certainly part of the same community suggests that those graves belonged to people that occupied very different positions in society, which may also have involved distinct beliefs about death and the afterlife. A parsimonious explanation is that the tumulus necropolis belonged to a part of the population that enjoyed a high social status, maybe some kinds of elites, while the flat inhumations were of individuals of a lower social standing.[23]

At Popeşti, another large Late Iron Age settlement was identified. Next to it, just like in the two cases above, a series of cremation, tumulus graves were placed, four of which were excavated. The clustering algorithm put two of them in group 5, one in group 4 and another in group 2. The group 4 and 5 graves contained weapons as well as a considerable number of vessels and/or adornments or clothing accessories, which suggests that they were correctly clustered.[24] Inside the settlement, seven skeletons were uncovered: two placed together in one pit and another three in a different pit; the last two were isolated discoveries (Sîrbu 1993, p. 92; Vulpe and Gheorghiţă 1979, p. 96). The skeletons were usually in partly anatomically correct positions and some of them had a heavily crouched posture, most likely because of the restricted size of the pits, indicating that the bodies may have been thrown in rather than laid out carefully. The only skeleton found in a position that was less unusual was also the one that had a bracelet, and possibly some vessels, as grave-goods (Fig. 5.21). However, another body was placed on top of it without signs of a similarly careful attention. Additionally, the scattered remains from another individual were found in the same pit. On the whole, at Popeşti, the two supra-groups unequivocally appeared together, though at the site level a clear separation between the two was obvious. This dissociation suggests that there were clearly different ideas behind the interment of the two groups, although they were both enacted by members of the same community. There is little doubt that the cremations belonged to people that occupied a high social standing, possibly elites, whereas the inhumations were of individuals occupying a comparatively much lower position in society.[25]

The last of the six sites is the cemetery of Hunedoara-Grădina Castelului. This necropolis was made up of a large number of, generally multiple, inhumation graves

---

[23] A nearly identical situation was encountered at the site of Brad, which was another Late Iron Age settlement placed on the same Siret River and situated several kilometres to the North of Răcătău.

[24] However, tumulus 1, which was placed in cluster 4, actually fits better in group 5. Still, that would not change its inclusion in the larger Western supra-group.

[25] In this respect it is worth mentioning again the relatively higher investment required for cremations when compared with inhumations (cf. Williams 2004).

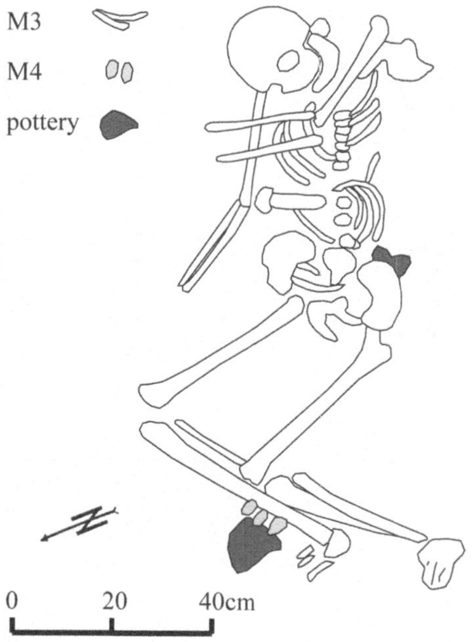

Fig. 5.21 Drawing of inhumation 4 from Popeşti (after Vulpe and Gheorghiţă 1979, p. 99, pl. I/2)

(Sîrbu et al. 2007a, b). Many of them had no grave-goods or just one adornment or clothing accessory item and were thus included in groups 1 and 3. Six of them were put by the clustering procedure in group 2 since they had several adornments or clothing accessories and/or vessels. However, given that they lacked the generally larger assemblages of the group 2 graves, at least some would fit better in group 1. There were also five graves from the Western supra-group, one in group 4, two in group 5, and another two in group 6. The group 4 and 5 graves were all cremations, which immediately makes them stand out from the rest of the necropolis. Additionally, unlike any of the other graves, they included weapons among the grave-goods, together with several adornments or clothing accessories and vessels. Hence, the assignment made by the clustering algorithm appears to be correct in their case. The two graves put in group 6 were inhumations that only received arrowheads as grave-goods. These items most likely referred to hunting rather than war-like activities. Therefore, the two graves were wrongfully clustered and most likely belonged to group 1. Since no particular separation could be distinguished between the inhumations and cremations, Hunedoara-Grădina Castelului was a site where graves from the two supra-groups appeared together without any observable barriers or significant shifts in terms of funerary ritual or grave-goods.[26] This is indicative of a community where genuine coexistence occurred, although social differences were likely still operating, with the weapon bearers probably still enjoying a higher social status.

[26] Nevertheless, it should be noted that the inhumations pertaining to the Eastern supra-group were found in this case outside a settlement, in a place that was specifically reserved for the dead, which did not happen at most other sites where such graves were uncovered.

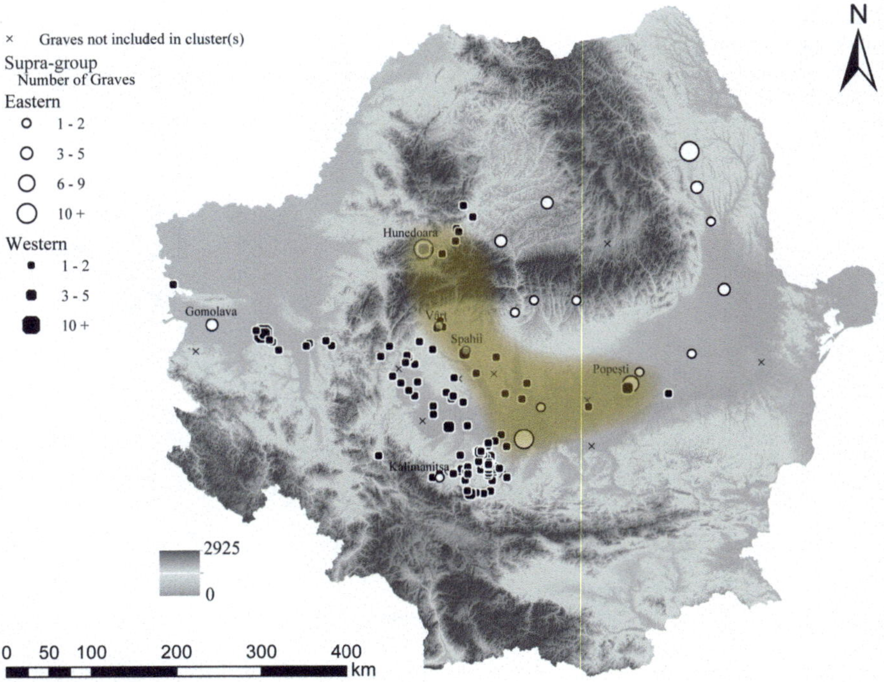

Fig. 5.22 Geographical distribution of Eastern and Western supra-groups with contour of buffer area. Point corrections have been implemented based on the supra-groups interaction site analysis

The conclusion that can be drawn from the short analysis of these six sites is that, in general, the two supra-groups did not mix, although it sometimes occurred. This happened particularly in South-West Transylvania, but partially also in Eastern Oltenia and Western Muntenia, in a space that can be seen as a buffer zone between the two supra-groups. On two occasions, at Gomolava and Kalimanitsa, graves from the Eastern supra-group even appeared in territories West of this area, but these were isolated cases representing exceptions.[27] Even within the buffer zone, the boundary between the two supra-groups could still be encountered, as was the case at the site of Popeşti, where there was a clear spatial separation of the placing of the dead. On the other hand, the intensity of the boundary was reduced at Hunedoara-Grădina Castelului and maybe at Spahii and Vârţ, possibly allowing for harmonious interaction (Fig. 5.22).

[27]The three graves from Gomolava are clearly isolated finds for the area of Vojvodina and may be indicative of contracts with the main area of the Eastern supra-group (see discussion for Central Serbia and Vojvodina in the following subsection of this chapter). As for Kalimanitsa, the grave may have been erroneously placed in cluster 1 and could be e better fit for cluster 4, which would put it in the Western supra-group (see discussion for North-West Thrace in the following subsection of this chapter).

The two grave supra-groups thus bear witness to the existence of two distinct regional identities. These identities were not (only) embraced by the individuals that were laid to rest in the graves, but also by the communities of which the deceased were part. As it has been pointed out, the graves of groups 1 and 3, which form the Eastern supra-group, when compared to those of groups 4, 5, and 6, which make up the Western supra-group, reveal a marked difference in the social status of the deceased and implicitly distinct group identities. On the other hand, the specific funerary practices involved in laying those individuals to rest, practices which were of course carried out by surviving members of the community, show that there was a specific body of beliefs which was shared by the deceased's communities. These distinct types of funerary practices represented an element that set these entire communities apart, not only the deceased themselves. Although the majority of the population employed a mortuary ritual that left no archaeological trace, the graves that were found are the outcome of practices carried out by other community members, most of whom were likely buried in a non-traceable manner. The presence or lack of such practices, and the differences observed between them, is what makes communities as a whole similar or different. This does not imply that Late Iron Age people were defining themselves actively through these specific mortuary practices. Many other elements, such as religion, language, physical appearance, etc., may have been considerably more significant. However, archaeologically, the mortuary practices leave much more evidence and it is through them that the existence of some sort of large regional liaison can be postulated for the two geographical areas. These people were not different because of these particular funerary practices, but rather the funerary practices differed because of the people.

5.3 The Micro Dimension. The Regions

Despite the identification of the seven clusters through the use of the statistical analysis, further localized dimensions may be grasped by focussing on each particular geographical region from the study area. This gives the possibility to determine whether the variations, which can be remarked in most of the groups, were linked to the existence of more localized identities.

5.3.1 Moldova

The graves from Moldova are linked to the three large settlements situated on the banks of the Siret River: Brad, Răcătău, and Poiana. The three settlements are thought to have functioned in close connection to one another, given their close positioning and the similarity in material culture. Additionally, the development of the settlements and even their spatial organization shows a close resemblance (Florea 2011, pp. 75–87). It is thus no surprise that the burials associated with them followed the same pattern. A small group of cremation tumulus graves was uncovered next to each settlement. Additionally, in Brad and Răcătău, a series of inhumations were found inside the settlement.[28]

The most striking feature of the graves of Moldova is that no offensive weapons were found in any of the graves, which is in stark contrast to all other regions. The few items of weaponry that appeared were either hunting arrows, in a tumulus grave from Poiana (Vulpe 1976, pp. 206–207) and another from Brad (Ursachi 1995, pp. 106–110), or a chain-mail, found in a tumulus at Răcătău (Sîrbu 1994, p. 128). The placement of these objects was not related to war-like attributes as has already been argued.

Given the absence of offensive weapons in the tumulus cremation graves, they were included by the clustering procedure in groups 2 and 7, although some of the above weapon graves were wrongly put into groups 5 and 6. Moldova can thus be identified as the region with the highest number of tumulus graves that did not have any reference to warrior-activities, giving the largest concentration of cluster 2 tumulus graves. The graves contained larger or smaller quantities of adornments or clothing accessories and/or vessels, some of which were Greek or Roman imports.

It is worth noting that, apart from these specific grave-goods, the use of cremation, the construction of a tumulus, and the placement of the graves in a small group just outside the limits of a large settlement made these graves similar to those found at Popeşti, Radovanu or Piscu Crăsani in Muntenia, or Cugir in South-West Transylvania. However, the similarities stop there. Unlike the tumuli further West, those from Moldova show traces of a wooden funerary chamber (A. Rustoiu personal comment) and one of them even contained secondary inhumation graves, which resembles the mortuary finds from North of the Black Sea (cf. Symonenko 1995).[29] In addition, the grave-goods, some of which, such as the chain-mail from Răcătău, show a similar North Pontic influence, also point to the particular character of these funerary finds and their separation from those further West. This indicates that, while the Moldavia tumuli may have been part of a wider phenomenon, the mortuary ritual underwent a strong local adaptation. A similar conclusion can be reached when comparing the tumuli to the graves of groups 2 and 7. While they had broadly the same grave-goods, they differed because of the construction of a tumulus, since the large majority of the group 2 and 7 graves were flat. Hence, regardless of what methodological approach is taken, the tumulus cremations from Brad, Răcătău, and Poiana undoubtedly indicated the existence of a localized burial practice.

Besides the cremations, two of the settlements also contained a series of inhumations. These were placed mostly in pits, although two of those from Brad were found in the mantle of one of the cremation tumuli. The grave-goods found in these

[28] Inhumation graves were not found within the settlement of Poiana. This may be because much of the site has eroded into the Siret River (Vulpe and Teodor 2003).

[29] The area North of the Black Sea, also known as the North Pontic region, was inhabited by steppe populations often denominated in ancient texts and modern studies as Sarmatians. Recently however, this term, together with the cultural and ethnical unity of the region, has come under heavy criticism (Mordvintseva 2013).

inhumations were either minimal or nonexistent, and it is for this reason that most of them have been included in groups 1 and 3. Generally, it can be said that they received considerably less attention compared with the tumulus cremations. The only exception might be four inhumations found at Brad, where the skeletons, along with one or two grave-goods, were carefully laid out, in pits, on specially prepared earthen platforms (Ursachi 1995, pp. 259–261).The inhumation graves were clearly meant for a different layer of society than the cremations. Therefore, overall, the inhumations fit well within the general pattern of the Eastern supra-groups graves (clusters 1 and 3), indicating no particular further variation.

The different treatment and placement of the cremations and inhumations clearly indicates that there was a marked difference between the inhumed and cremated individuals. Since more effort was put into the construction of the tumuli, as well as into the actual act of cremation, and many more grave-good objects were placed in the graves, it is safe to assume that the cremated deceased held a much more important position in their communities. They were probably local elites. By comparison, the inhumations belonged to individuals that had a much lower social background.

The graves of Moldova show this region to be well-integrated into the Eastern supra-group area in terms of the inhumations, while also revealing the presence of a local fingerprint in the case of the cremations. Whatever the beliefs behind the inhumations, the community members of Brad, Răcătău, and Poiana likely shared the same ideas as the people from Muntenia and South-West Transylvania where similar practices were encountered. However, the three communities had a slightly different way of burying important members of their societies, possibly as a result of influence from the North Pontic region, and only broadly resembled some of the practices found further West. It may thus be concluded that the Late Iron Age people of Moldova embraced the larger regional identity inherent of the Eastern supra-group. They also shared the broader identity linked to groups 2 and 7, but in this case an important variation of the mortuary practices was obvious.[30] This shows the existence of a locally rooted tradition, which suggests that the three communities had a strongly localized identity that set them apart from the inhabitants of other regions.

5.3.2 *Muntenia*

In Muntenia, mortuary finds were identified at 13 sites, with each producing a relatively small number of graves. The only exceptions were the sites of Popeşti and Zimnicea, though in the latter case only six of the graves were dated to the period of interest. The funerary finds of Muntenia had considerable differences in terms of their characteristics, which indicate the existence of significantly more variation than in Moldova. The clustering procedure placed most of the graves of Muntenia in the Eastern supra-group, clusters 1 and 3, as well as in group 2. There were nonetheless

[30] The same observation can be made if one considers the tumuli of Moldova to be similar to those from Muntenia or South-West Transylvania, which were included in the Western supra-group.

also seven graves which were included in groups 4 and 5. The three cluster 4 graves from Muntenia are, however, problematic. One of them, identified as tumulus 1 from Popeşti (Vulpe 1976, pp. 193–194), has features which resemble more the group 5 graves, since it included a considerable array of vessels. In addition, the grave was not flat, which is very unusual for any group 4 grave from North of the Danube. The tumulus was thus included in cluster 4 simply because it contained a single item of weaponry. However, during excavation, a large hole, probably from robbers, was uncovered in the middle of the mound where the funerary pyre would have been, which would explain the lack of any other items of weaponry or of adornments.[31] The two other group 4 graves, discovered close to one another, at Slatina and Teiuşi (Butoi 1974) were undoubtedly placed in the right group, but they were positioned practically on the banks of the Olt River, which separates the region of Muntenia and Oltenia.[32] Therefore, their inclusion in the analysis of Muntenia may not be revealing for the region as a whole, but only for its Western border.

The mortuary finds of Muntenia do not reveal the existence of a particularly localized identity, but some barriers may have been in effect. Most graves were part of the large Eastern supra-group, signalling that many of the communities of Muntenia were engaged in similar funerary practices to the people of Moldova and Transylvania and thus shared some broad level of identity. The cluster 2 graves, together with the two cluster 7 ones, may be indicative of larger identity connections, since this was a funerary tradition common to most other regions. However, these graves did not present the local variation from Moldova, since most of them were flat in Muntenia rather than tumulus, which suggests some level of separation between the two regions. The remaining graves contained weapons and were part of cluster 5, which connects the region to its Western neighbour, Oltenia. However, it is worth noting that all but one of the graves of Oltenia were flat, while in Muntenia the weapon graves were all placed under tumuli, with the exception of the two from Slatina and Teiuşi, situated in the fringe zone between the two regions. Hence, one could speculate that some kind of barrier was in effect between Oltenia and Muntenia and that the group 5 graves from the latter region incorporated a local variation.[33]

5.3.3 Oltenia

The mortuary finds from Oltenia came from a large number of sites, many of which contained only one grave. The only notable exceptions are Orlea and Spahii, where several burials were uncovered, although only a small sample of the graves of Spahii were employed as it was already pointed out in the previous section.

[31] It should also be noted that the grave was placed in group 5 rather than 4 by the Diana clustering method.

[32] It is worth mentioning that with the exception of these two finds, all the other group 4 graves were located geographically West of the river Olt.

[33] The same conclusion was reached in earlier studies (Popa 2012, 2014).

At first glance, it would appear that the graves from Oltenia were split, relatively equally between the Eastern and Western supra-groups, plus a small number of graves that were placed in clusters 2 and 7. Yet, when the location of the graves is considered, it can be observed that, of the 28 Eastern supra-group graves, 23 were uncovered at the site of Orlea (Comşa 1991, 1972), while the rest came from four other sites: Onciţa (Berciu 1983), Spahii, Vârţ and Sprâncenata (Preda 1986, p. 51). The graves from Spahii and Vârţ may, however, be considered as being part of cluster 2 rather than 1, as has already been noted, reducing the number of sites to three. In contrast, nearly 30 different sites had graves that were included in clusters 4, 5, or 6. These were spread out relatively equally throughout the entire region, although the group 5 graves are concentrated much more in the Western part, close to the Iron Gates.

Oltenia appears thus to be quite different from Muntenia and especially Moldova, but similar to areas further West and South. Weapon graves were very common, while the inhumations typical of groups 1 and 3 were concentrated basically in one site. The preponderance of cluster 4, 5, and 6 graves makes this area well-integrated into the larger Western supra-group, signalling the connection of the local population with other regions where a similar situation was encountered. The closest connections seem to be with Central Serbia and the Western part of North-West Thrace, since these are the only other areas where all, or nearly all, cremation graves were flat, rather than tumulus (Table 5.8). However, the object shapes point towards connections with the Eastern part of North-West Thrace and South-West Transylvania.

5.3.4 Central Serbia and Vojvodina

The funerary finds from Central Serbia and Vojvodina were dominated by the necropolis of Karaburma and Rospi Ćuprija which produced together 42 graves for this study. A much smaller number of graves were uncovered at seven other locations. All of these finds represented flat cremations, with the exception of three individuals from Gomolava.

The inhumations of Gomolava are very similar to the graves common to clusters 1 and 3 of which they are actually part. The deceased, two adults and an approximately 4 year old child, were found together, in partially anatomically correct positions, in a pit located inside a large settlement. In the pit, together with the skeletons, several intact or broken vessels were discovered as well as a bronze fibula. The Gomolava inhumation graves are the only finds of this type in the West of the Iron Gates, which may suggest that there was some kind of connection between some of the inhabitants of this site and those living around the Carpathian Mountains. This connection is partly sustained by the nature of the material culture finds from the settlement, as it has been pointed out that at least some of the vessel shapes were similar to those found in Transylvania, Moldova, or Muntenia (Jovanović 1971, 1988).

All the other graves of Central Serbia and Vojvodina were single, flat cremations, similar to those of Oltenia, half of them containing weapons. It should, however, be

Table 5.8 Grave count crosstabulation of *grave type*, *ritual type*, and *region*

Region			Ritual type			Total
			Cenotaph	Cremation	Inhumation	
Central Serbia	Grave type	Flat	0	48	0	48
	Total		0	48	0	48
Moldova	Grave type	Flat	0	1	16	17
		Tumular	2	8	2	12
	Total		2	9	18	29
Muntenia	Grave type	Construction	0	2	0	2
		Flat	0	11	14	25
		Tumular	2	6	0	8
	Total		2	19	14	35
Oltenia	Grave type	Construction	0	0	1	1
		Flat	0	46	25	71
		Tumular	0	1	2	3
	Total		0	47	28	75
NW Thrace—East	Grave type	Flat	0	40	0	40
		Tumular	1	36	5	42
	Total		1	76	5	82
NW Thrace—West	Grave type	Flat	0	12	1	13
		Tumular	0	0	1	1
	Total		0	12	2	14
Transylvania—Centre	Grave type	Flat	0	0	8	8
	Total		0	0	8	8
Transylvania—East	Grave Type	Flat	0	1	0	1
	Total		0	1	0	1
Transylvania—West	Grave type	Flat	0	10	51	61
		Tumular	1	4	0	5
	Total		1	14	51	66
Vojvodina	Grave type	Flat	0	3	3	6
	Total		0	3	3	6
Total	Grave type	Construction	0	2	1	3
		Flat	0	172	118	290
		Tumular	6	55	10	71
	Total		6	229	129	364

noted that all the weapon graves were included in clusters 4 or 5; cluster 6 graves, which represent the weapon graves with the simplest possible grave-goods and were common of Oltenia, North-West Thrace, and South-West Transylvania, were not encountered here. The rest of the cremation graves from Central Serbia and Vojvodina are part of clusters 2 and especially 7. It is worth mentioning that this area contained 14 of the 35 group 7 graves (Table 4.32), which indicates that the beliefs behind the cluster 7 mortuary practice were especially prevalent in this region.

Overall, it appears that the communities West of the Danube Gorges shared most elements of funerary practice with Oltenia and partly with North-West Thrace and South-West Transylvania, although there were also elements which set them apart. The grave-good combinations were similar enough for the statistical analysis to cluster the graves together with those further East, but a detailed look at the exact item shapes reveals differences. For instance, the battle knives of Central Serbia and Vojvodina were, with one exception, of types 2, 3, and 4, which only rarely appeared in other areas, where instead type 1 was dominant (Fig. 5.23). A similar observation can be made about type 2, 3, and 4 *kantharos*-like vessels, type 1, 2, and 3 porringers, type 6 and 7 bracelets, as well as storage pots and small pots. Therefore, even though the practices in which people engaged may have been similar, the communities of Central Serbia and Vojvodina utilized slightly different object forms. This may indicate that while these people probably shared some sort of a broader identity, there was also a more local dimension to it, making the communities of this region feel more alike, particularly when compared to those further East.[34] These localized elements may be what Egri and Rustoiu (2008) identify as specific practices of conviviality, developed in a competitive society that revolved around the acquisition of prestige, and which was dominated by a warrior elite.

5.3.5 North-West Thrace

North-West Thrace is the region with the largest number of funerary finds from the entire area employed for this study. The 96 graves were generally isolated finds, which explains the very high number of find spots (64).[35] More than 90% of the mortuary finds of this region were single cremations, either flat or tumulus. Since many of those contained weapons, the majority of graves were included in the Western supra-group, clusters 4, 5 and 6, although there were also some that were put in cluster 2 and rarely 7.

There were seven inhumations found in North-West Thrace. Of these, only a single one was included in the Eastern supra-group, namely cluster 1, the funerary find from Kalimanitsa (Theodossiev 2000, p. 118). The grave was originally part of a group of three tumuli, of which only two were excavated and only one had adequate information recorded. The reason for its inclusion in cluster 1, besides the use of inhumation, was the discovery of glass beads, probably from a bead necklace, in the grave. Besides this item, sherds from unidentified vessels as well as a belt chain,

[34] The only area that seems to have shared the material culture forms of Central Serbia and Vojvodina is the Western part of North-West Thrace.

[35] In spite of most of the graves being isolated finds, many of them were actually part of small groups of burials, usually three to five. However, it rarely happened that more than one of the graves was excavated (cf. Theodossiev 2000).

which may have been used for fixing the sword, were deposited as grave-goods. This last item was the only find of this type from cluster 1, which raises questions regarding its inclusion in this group. The presence of the belt chain may be indicative that weapons were initially included among the grave-goods, which is a distinct possibility given that the grave was recorded as being disturbed by later intervention, probably treasure hunters.[36] Given these elements, the grave of Kalimnitsa probably fits better into one of the Western supra-group clusters, with the particular characteristic of inhumation being used instead of cremation and the presence of a bead necklace as a grave-good. This variation may have occurred as a result of the mixture of funerary elements typical of North-West Thrace with those from regions such as Muntenia or Moldova, although the relatively large geographical distance between Kalimnitsa and the latter two regions does not support such a scenario.

Four of the other six inhumation graves, those from Kostolac (Kossorić 1960), Leskovets (Agre 1987), Rogozen (Theodossiev 2000, p. 135), and Vratsa (Theodossiev 2000, p. 143), were put in clusters 4 and 5 due to the presence of weapons, offensive or defensive, as well as the inclusion of horse gear elements in two cases, which indicates that they were rightly clustered. The remaining two, one also from Leskovets and another from Milosevac (Theodossiev 2000, p. 129), were included in group 2 due to the presence of numerous adornments. In addition, the graves from Leskovets also contained a chain-mail, which was probably just part of the funerary dress and did not relate to martial attributes given the lack of other weapons. The inclusion of the two mortuary finds in cluster 2 thus seems reasonable given the funerary items, although this may represent one of the cases where it is problematic to make a clear distinction between group 1 and 2 graves.

The large majority of the funerary finds of North-West Thrace consisted of cremations included in the Western supra-group, suggesting that the communities of this region shared a broad identity with many of those from Oltenia and Central Serbia. However, there may have been also a more localized dimension of these peoples' identity. This is indicated, for instance, by the widespread employment of tumulus graves, producing by far the highest occurrence of tumuli of all the regions included in the Western supra-group. Another element which can be considered a local feature is the frequent inclusion of horse gear elements as grave-goods. Of a total of 73 graves which had such items, 52 came from North-West Thrace, notably from its Eastern part, while the rest came mainly from Oltenia and South-West Transylvania. This indicates that many of the deceased from North-West Thrace were identified as being horsemen and that the horse may have occupied a special position in the habitus of the communities of that region. Such an idea has already been suggested by other authors (Kuzmanov 2005), pointing out that this practice may be rooted in local traditions that go further back in time.

[36] The region of Thrace, and North-West Thrace in particular, is an area where mortuary finds are badly affected by treasure hunters. This is due to the landscape being dotted with a multitude of tumulus graves, dated to the Early or Late Iron Age, some of which contain items made of precious metal (see Dyer 2005; also press articles such as http://btvnews.bg/vsichko-ot-dnes/imanyari-rushat-na-poraziya-kulturnoto-nasledstvo-na-blgariya.html).

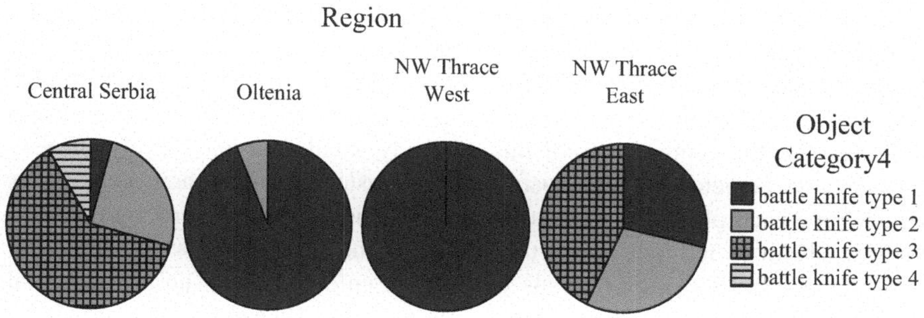

Fig. 5.23 Count of battle knife types for Central Serbia, Oltenia, NW Thrace—East and NW Thrace—West. NA values were omitted

The region of North-West Thrace contained a division between its Eastern and Western part, separated by the Timok river valley, already signalled by Theodossiev (2000). With this in mind, the ideas introduced in the paragraph above are mainly characteristic of the Eastern part of North-West Thrace, which contained the large majority of the mortuary finds, since in the Western part only one of the 14 graves was found under a tumulus and none of them contained horse gear elements. Some of the material culture forms from the Western side suggest connections with Central Serbia and Vojvodina, such as the presence in graves of type 2 and 3 battle knives or the deposition of belts, of types 1 or 2. On the other hand, on the Eastern side of the Timok, the type 1 battle knife dominated, typical also of Oltenia, and only one belt, of type 5, was discovered (Fig. 5.23). Taking account of these differences, it may be postulated that the communities from the Western and Eastern part of North-West Thrace saw themselves as sharing slightly different traditions and thus group identities. It may be that the people from the Western side of the Timok River saw themselves more like those from Central Serbia.[37] On the other hand, the communities from the Eastern side of the river probably constructed their group identity on elements that can be traced further back in time, such as the significant role of horses, and shared a closer connection with the people of Oltenia.

5.3.6 *Transylvania*

The funerary finds from Transylvania are dominated by the cemetery of Hunedoara-Grădina Castelului, since 54 of a total of 75 graves came from that location. Apart from that, the site of Sighişoara-Wietenberg (Rustoiu et al. 1993) gave eight graves and those of Cugir (Crişan 1980; Teleagă et al. 2014) and Şura Mică (Sîrbu 1986, pp. 101–102) had three each. The rest of the graves were single occurrences.

[37] It is interested to remark that according to Strabo (*Geography*, VII.4.12) the Western side of North-West Thrace and Central Serbia were inhabited by closely related people.

Transylvania is undoubtedly dominated by graves from the Eastern supra-group, since it includes 70% of all the funerary finds. Yet, one needs to remark that in its South-Western part alone, graves from six of the seven clusters can be found, although the cremation graves were few. Such a great variety in funerary practices indicates that the communities of this relatively small area may have been very mixed. In the cemetery of Hunedoara–Grădina Castelului alone, there were graves which have been placed by the clustering procedures in five different groups. As mentioned earlier, this was one of the few, if not the only site, in which one could find graves from both supra-groups without the enforcement of an actual spatial barrier between the two, as was the case at Popeşti, for instance.

Unlike all of the other regions, there does not seem to be any particular element characteristic of this area alone. Graves were flat, single or multiple, inhumations, as well as flat or tumulus cremations. They were located inside, near, or far from any settlement. Both cremations and inhumations contained varying quantities of adornments or clothing accessories, tools, vessels, and weapons. The cremations could also include horse gear elements. The object types showed a comparable variation[38]; only in few instances did just one particular type appear. Such is the case of battle knives, all of which were of type 1, typical of Oltenia and North-West Thrace. Types 2, 3, and 4, mostly found in Central Serbia, were not encountered. In general, most object shapes were shared with the regions of Moldova, Muntenia, Oltenia, and North-West Thrace, but far less with Central Serbia.[39] Therefore, no particular regional burial pattern can be said to exist in Transylvania, which suggests that there is little to be seen in terms of a local identity. Rather, the communities of this area shared elements with people from several other regions, giving the impression that Transylvania, and specifically its South-Western side, functioned as a melting pot, where traditions combined and coexisted, although some may have been more common than other.[40]

Overall, the regional, group and supra-group interpretation corresponds with the existence of relatively large identity groups, with the addition of strongly localized elements in some areas such as Moldova. Generally there is a large degree of overlap and entanglement between the different groups, although the two large supra-groups that were uncovered appear to have had very little in common. Some of the group solidarities probably corresponded to particular social status identities, while the supra-groups were likely linked to regional, territorial-based identities. More particular characteristics of these larger identities can be grasped by correlating the results with other archaeological and textual information about the Late La Tène of the Eastern Carpathian basin and the Lower Danube. This represents the focus of the final chapter of this volume.

[38] For example, there were 13 graves in South-West Transylvania that contained fibulae and these represented 8 different fibula types (Table 5.1).

[39] Some examples include bead necklaces, pendant necklaces, fruit-bowls, jugs etc. (Fig. 5.24, 5.25, 5.26, and 5.27).

[40] This can be said due to the preponderance of graves from the Eastern supra-group, characteristic of Moldova, Muntenia and parts of Oltenia.

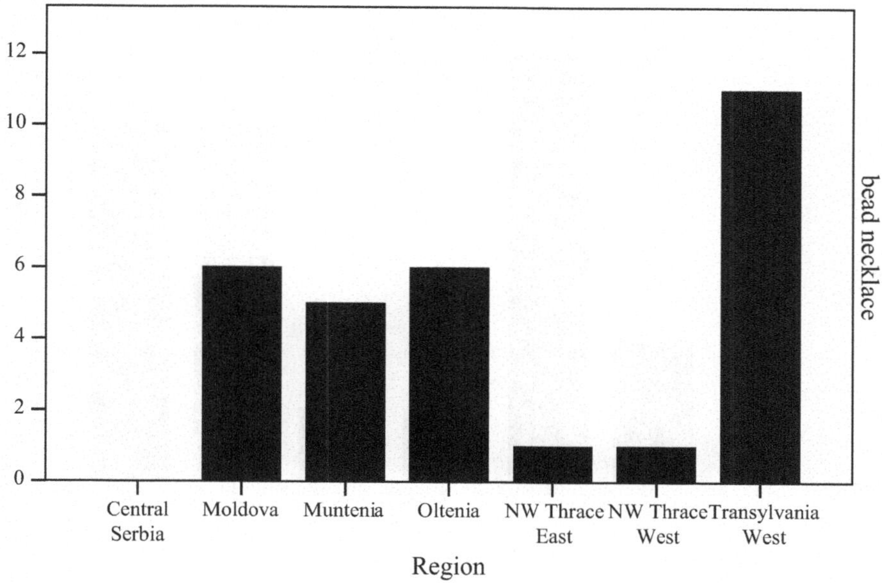

Fig. 5.24 Count of *object category 3* bead necklace per region

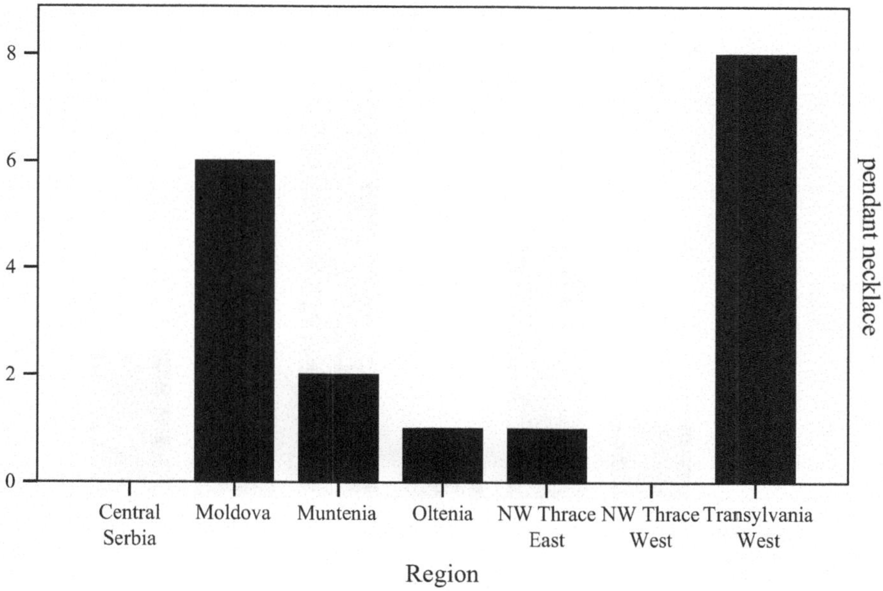

Fig. 5.25 Count of *object category 3* pendant necklace per region

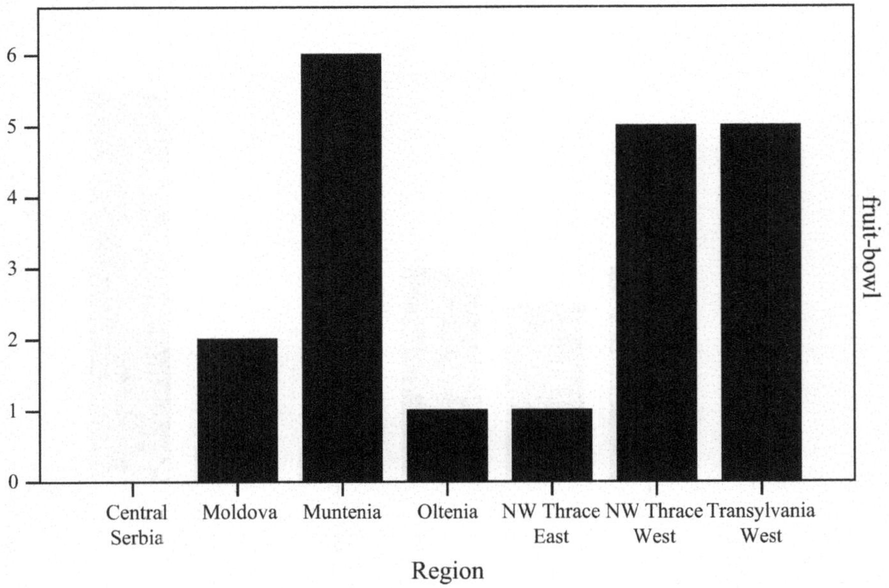

Fig. 5.26 Count of *object category 3* fruit bowls per region

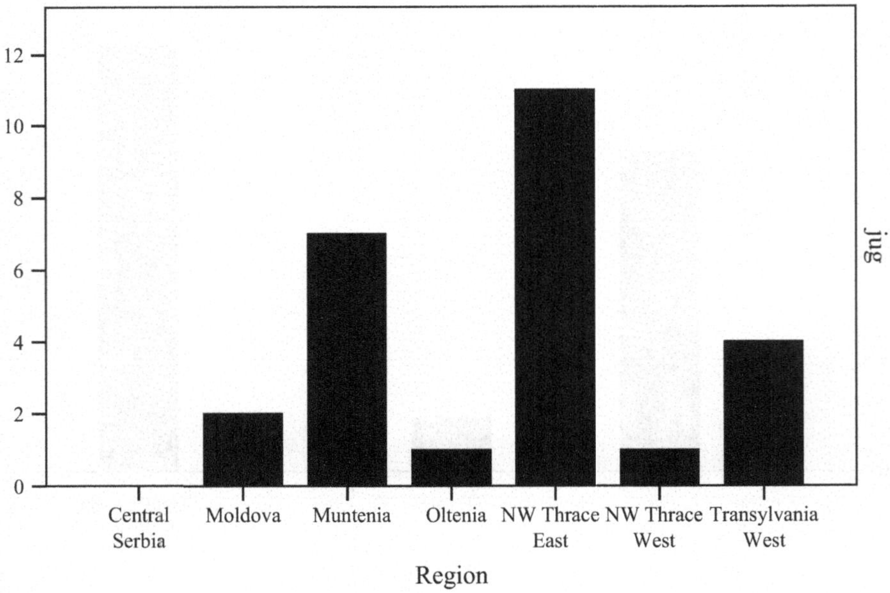

Fig. 5.27 Count of *object category 3* jugs per region

References

Agre, D. (1987). Leskovskoto gradishte i nekropolat kray nego, Mihaylovgradski okrug. In *Arheologicheski Otkritiya i Razkopki prez 1986* (pp. 91–93). Razgrad.

Armit, I. (2012). *Headhunting and the body in Iron Age Europe*. Cambridge: Cambridge University Press.

Babić, S. (2005). Status identity and archaeology. In M. Díaz-Andreu, S. Lucy, S. Babić, & D. Edwards (Eds.), *The archaeology of identity: Approaches to gender, age, status, ethnicity and religion* (pp. 67–85). London: Routledge.

Berciu, D. (1983). Mormintele de înhumaţie de la Ocniţa-Buridava. *Thraco-Dacica, 4*(1–2), 32–38.

Bodor, A. (1981). Structura societăţii dacice. In H. Daicoviciu (Ed.), *Studii dacice* (pp. 7–22). Cluj-Napoca.

Botezatu, D., & Miu, C. (1989). Studiul scheletelor in mormintele de la Brad aparţinând perioadei dacice. *Carpica, 20*, 297–304.

Brather, S. (2004). *Ethnische Interpretationen in der frühgeschichtlichen Archäologie. Geschichte, Grundlagen und Alternativen*. Berlin: W. de Gruyte.

Brather, S. (2005). Soziale Strukturen und frühmittelalterliche Reihengräberfelder. In J. Müller (Ed.), *Alter und Geschlecht in ur- und frühgeschichtlichen Gesellschaften : Tagung Bamberg, 20.-21. Februar 2004* (pp. 157–178). Bonn: R. Habelt.

Butoi, M. (1974). Mormânt de incineraţie din epoca fierului descoperit la Slatina. *Oltenia. Studii şi comunicări, 1*, 29–32.

Căpitanu, V. (1986). Cercetările arheologice de la Răcătău, jud. *Bacău. Materiale şi Cercetări Arheologice, 16*, 109–120.

Carr, G., & Knüsel, C. J. (1997). The ritual framework of excarnation by exposure as the morutary practice of the early and middle Iron Ages of central southern Britain. In A. Gwilt & C. Haselgrove (Eds.), *Reconstructing Iron Age societies: New approaches to the British Iron Age* (pp. 167–173). Oxford: Oxbow Books.

Chamberlain, A. (1997). Commentary: Missing stages of life – towards the perception of children in archaeology. In J. Moore & E. Scott (Eds.), *Invisible people and processes: Writing gender and childhood into European archaeology* (pp. 248–250). London: Leicester University Press.

Chamberlain, A. (2000). Minor concerns: A demographic perspective on children in past societies. In J. S. Derevenski (Ed.), *Children and material culture* (pp. 206–212). London: Routledge.

Comşa, E. (1972). Contribuţie la riturile funerare din secolele II-I îen., din sud-estul Olteniei (mormintele de la Orlea). *Apulum, 10.*

Comşa, A. (1991). Date cu privire la structura antropologică şi la unele ritualuri funerare la getodaci (secolele VI îen. – I en.) *Thraco-Dacica, 12*(1–2), 153–166.

Crişan, I. H. (1980). Necropola dacică de la Cugir. *Apulum, 18*, 81–87.

Dyer, J. (2005). Bulgarian archaeologists race looters for ancient Thracian prize. *AP Worldstream*. Retrieved April 22. 2013, from http://www.highbeam.com/doc/1P1-116008280.html.

Egri, M., & Rustoiu, A. (2008). The social significance of conviviality in the Scordiscian environment. In V. Sîrbu & D. L. Vaida (Eds.), *Funerary practices of the Bronze and Iron Ages in Central and South-Eastern Europe. Proceedings of the 9th international colloquium of funerary archaeology* (pp. 83–93). Mega: Cluj-Napoca.

Florea, G. (2006). The 'public image' of the Dacian aristocracy. Studia Universitatis "Babeş-Bolyai". *Historia, 51*(1), 1–11.

Florea, G. (2011). *Dava et oppidum. Débuts de la genèse urbaine en Europe au deuxième âge du Fer*. Cluj-Napoca: Acadèmie Roumaine. Centre d'Études Transylvaines.

Fowler, C. (2004). *The archaeology of personhood: An anthropological approach*. London: Routledge.

Gerstenberger, J. (2002). *Analyse alter DNA zur Ermittlung von Heiratsmustern in einer frühmittelalterlichen Bevölkerung (PhD)*. Göttingen: Georg-August-Universität zu Göttingen.

Gherghe, P. (1978). Cercetările arheologice de salvare efectuate în necropola şi aşezarea getodacică de la Turburea-Spahii. *Litua. Studii şi Cercetări, 1*, 15–31.

Gherghe, P. (1983). Cercetări şi descoperiri arheologice cu privire la civilizaţia geto-dacică pe teritoriul judeţului Gorj. *Arhivele Olteniei, 2*, 49–73.
Gherghe, P. (2008). The necropolis and the Geto-Dacian settlement of the Turburea locality, Spahii village, Gorj county. In V. Sîrbu & I. Stângă (Eds.), *The Iron Gates region during the Second Iron Age. Settlements, necropolises, treasures* (pp. 140–149). Drobeta Turnu-Severin; Craiova: Editura Universitaria.
Gostar, N., & Lica, V. (1984). *Societatea geto-dacică de la Burebista la Decebal*. Bucureşti: Junimea.
Hakenbeck, S. (2007). Situational ethnicity and nested identities: New approaches to an old problem. *Anglo-Saxon Studies in Archaeology and History, 14*, 19–27.
Halsall, G. (1996). Female status and power in early Merovingian central Austrasia. The burial evidence. *Early Medieval Europe, 5*, 1–24.
Härke, H. (1997). Early Anglo-Saxon social structure. In J. Hines (Ed.), *The Anglo-Saxons from the migration period to the eighth century: An ethnographic perspective* (pp. 125–160). Woodbridge: Boydell Press.
Hausmair, B. (2015). *Am Rande des Grabs. Todeskonzepte und Bestattungsritual in der frühmittelalterlichen Alamannia*. Leiden: Sidestone Press.
Jovanović, B. (1971). The settlement of Scordisci on Gomolava – excavation from 1967-1971. *Rad Vojvodine Muzeja. Novi Sad, 20*, 123–146.
Jovanović, B. (1988). *Gomolava: Naselje Mlađeg Gvozdenog Doba. Late La Tène settlement*. Novi Sad: Vojvođanski muzej.
Knaut, M. (1993). *Die alamannischen Gräberfelder von Neresheim und Kösingen, Ostalbkreis*. Stuttgart: Kommissionsverlag K. Theiss.
Kokkotidis, K. G. (1999). *Untersuchungen zur Paläodemographie der Alamannen des Frühmittelalters (PhD)*. Köln: Universität Köln.
Kossorić, M. (1960). Tumulus de Kostolac. *The Star, 11*, 197–198.
Kuzmanov, M. (2005). The horse in the Thracian burial rites. *Helis, 4*, 98–107.
Lucy, S. (1994). Children on early medieval cemeteries. *Archaeological Review from Cambridge, 13*, 21–34.
Malinowski, B. (2004). Magic, science and religion. In A. C. G. M. Robben (Ed.), *Death, mourning, and burial: A cross-cultural reader* (pp. 19–22). Malden, MA: Blackwell.
Mordvintseva, V. (2013). The Sarmatians: The creation of archaeological evidence. *Oxford Journal of Archaeology, 32*(2), 203–219.
Nicolăescu-Plopşor, C. S. (1945). Antiquités celtiques en Olténie. *Dacia, 11–12*, 17–33.
Nicolăescu-Plopşor, D., & Ricuşiţa, C. (1969). Caracterizarea antrolologică şi morfobiologică a scheletelor din complexul funerar de la Orlea (sec. II-I î.e.n). *Revista Muzeelor, 1*, 69–73.
Nikolov, B. (1965). Thrakische Denkmäler in Bezirk Vraca. *Bulletin of the Institute of Archaeology, 28*, 163–202.
Oltean, I. A. (2007). *Dacia: Landscape, colonisation and romanisation*. London: Routledge.
Parker Pearson, M. (1999). *The archaeology of death and burial*. Stroud: Sutton.
Petre, Z. (2004). *Practica nemuririi: O lectură critică a izvoarelor greceşti referitoare la geţi*. Iaşi: Polirom. http://www.scribd.com/doc/129112274/Zoe-Petre-Practica-Nemuririi.
Popa, C. N. (2012). Till death do us part. A statistical approach to identifying burial similarity and grouping. The case of the Late La Tène graves from the Eastern Carpathian basin. In S. Berecki (Ed.), *Iron Age rites and rituals in the Carpathian basin* (pp. 401–412). Târgu Mureş: Mega.
Popa, C. N. (2014). The quest for group identity in Late Iron Age Romania. Statistical reconstruction of groups based on funerary evidence. In C. N. Popa & S. Stoddart (Eds.), *Fingerprinting the Iron Age* (pp. 108–122). Oxford: Oxbow.
Popescu, E., & Vulpe, A. (1982). Nouvelles découvertes du type Ferigile. *Dacia, 26*, 77–114.
Preda, C. (1986). *Geto-dacii din bazinul Oltului inferior: Dava de la Sprincenata*. Bucuresti.
Röder, B. (2002). Statisten in der Welt der Erwachsenen: Kinder auf archäologischen Lebensbildern. In K. W. Alt & A. Kemkes-Grottenthaler (Eds.), *Kinderwelten: Anthropologie, Geschichte, Kulturvergleich* (pp. 95–105). Köln: Böhlau.

Rustoiu, A., & Gheorghiu, G. (2009). An iron variant of the Jezerine-type brooches from Pre-Roman Dacia. *Instrumentum, 30*, 30–31.

Rustoiu, A., & Gheorghiu, G. (2010). 'General' and 'particular' in the dressing fashion and metal-work of Pre-Roman Dacia (an iron variant of the Jezerine-type brooches from Piatra-Craivii – Alba County). In I. Cândea (Ed.), *The Thracians and their neighbours in antiquity. Studia in honorem Valerii Sîrbu* (pp. 447–457). Brăila.

Rustoiu, A., Comşa, A., & Lisovschi-Cheleşanu, C. (1993). Practici funerare în aşezarea dacică de la Sighişoara-Wietenberg (observaţii preliminare). *Ephemeris Napocensis, 3*, 81–95.

Sîrbu, V. (1986). Rituels et pratiques funéraires des gèto-daces IIe siècle av. n.è - Ier siècle de n.è. *Dacia N.S., 30*(1–2), 91–108.

Sîrbu, V. (1993). *Credinţe şi practici funerare, religioase şi magice în lumea geto-dacilor (pornind de la descoperirile arheologice din Câmpia Brăilei)*. Galaţi: Porto-Franco.

Sîrbu, V. (1994). Morminte tumulare din zona Carpato-Dunăreană (sec. I î. d. Chr. – I d. Chr.) *Istros, 7*, 123–160.

Sîrbu, V. (1997). Sacrifices humains et pratiques funéraires insolites dans l'areal thrace du Hallstatt et du La Tène. In *Prima epocă a fierului la gurile Dunării şi în zonele Circumpontice. Lucrările colocviului internaţional, septembrie* 1993, Tulcea (pp. 193–221). Tulcea: Institutul de Cercetări Eco-Muzeale.

Sîrbu, V., Luca, S. A., & Roman, C. (2007a). Tombs of Dacian warriors (2nd – 1st C. BC) found in Hunedoara–Grădina Castelului (Hunedoara county). *Acta Terrae Septemcastrensis, 7*(1), 155–177.

Sîrbu, V., Luca, S. A., Roman, C., Purece, S., Diaconescu, D., & Cerişor, N. (2007b). *Vestigiile dacice de la Hunedoara/The Dacian vestiges in Hunedoara*. Sibiu: Muzeul Naţional Brukenthal.

Strathern, M. (1999). *Property, substance and effect: Anthropological essays on persons and things*. London: Athlone.

Symonenko, O. (1995). Catacomb graves of the Sarmatians of the North Pontic region. *MFMÉ—Studia Archáeologica, 1*, 345–374.

Teleagă, E., Bălăşescu, A., Soficaru, A., & Schoch, W. (2014). Die Scheiterhaufen aus Cugir und Tarinci. Ein Beitrag zu den Bestattungssitten der Balkanhalbinsel und des vorrömischen Dakiens in der Spätlatènezeit. *Praehistorische Zeitschrift, 89*(2), 305–336.

Theodossiev, N. (2000). *North-Western Thrace from the fifth to first centuries BC*. Oxford: Archaeopress.

Tonkova, M. (2010). On human sacrifice in Thrace (on archaeological evidence). In I. Cândea (Ed.), *The Thracians and their neighbours in antiquity. Studia in honorem Valerii Sîrbu* (pp. 503–522). Brăila.

Ursachi, V. (1995). *Zargidava: Cetatea dacică de la Brad*. Bucureşti: Caro Trading.

Vulpe, A. (1976). La nécroplole tumulaire gète de Popeşti. *Thraco-Dacica, 1*, 193–215.

Vulpe, A. (2004). 50 years of systematic excavations at the pre- and protohistoric site at Popeşti. *Dacia N.S., 48–49*.

Vulpe, A., & Gheorghiţă, M. (1979). Şantierul arheologic Popeşti. com. Mihăileşti, jud. Ilfov. Raport preliminar asupra rezultatelor din campania anilor 1976-1977. *Cercetări arheologice Muz. Istorie România, 3*, 95–105.

Vulpe, R., & Teodor, S. (2003). *Piroboridava aşezarea geto-dacică de la Poiana*. Bucureşti: Vavila Edinf.

Walker, L. (1984). The deposition of human remains. In B. Cunliffe (Ed.), *Danebury: An Iron Age hillfort in Hampshire* (Vol. 2, pp. 442–463). London: CBA.

Williams, H. (2004). Death warmed up: The agency of bodies and bones in Early Anglo-Saxon cremation rites. *Journal of Material Culture, 9*, 263–291.

Chapter 6
The Overall Picture. Concluding Interpretations

6.1 Correspondence to Earlier Statistical Study

The results of this volume correspond well with a preliminary analysis carried out using the same method, but on a smaller sample of mortuary finds gathered from Moldova, Muntenia, Oltenia, and Transylvania only, basically much of today's Romania (Popa 2012, 2014).[1] In the two papers, it was argued that the graves can be split in two large, nearly completely overlapping groups: one characterized by flat, single or multiple inhumations and the other by flat or tumulus cremations. Furthermore, each of these groups was divided into further subgroups. Group 1 was split in two subgroups: one which presented no grave-goods and generally less attention to the laying out of the body, and one which had some grave-goods, usually personal items, such as adornments or clothing accessories, and there was comparatively more attention to the setting out of the body and the preparation of the funerary ritual, although it was not overwhelming. Group 2 was also found to contain two further subgroups, each having several variants. The first subgroup was made of relatively simple flat cremations, some of which contained usually just one or two weapons, giving the first variant, and the other having a small number of vessels and/or adornments, forming the second variant. This subgroup was mainly centred on Oltenia, partly spreading into Muntenia and South-West Transylvania. The second subgroup was made of flat and tumulus cremations, generally with a considerable amount of grave-goods, and was spread throughout all the regions. It contained three further variations. The first was of tumulus graves that included weapons and several other items, present in Muntenia and South-West Transylvania. The second variant comprised flat cremations with weapons or other items and existed

[1] The study was carried out after gathering the data from Romania and developing the statistical method. It was aimed initially to test whether the statistical procedures developed for this study can produce usable results.

C. N. Popa, *Modelling Identities*, Quantitative Archaeology and Archaeological Modelling, https://doi.org/10.1007/978-3-319-63267-4_6

in Oltenia and South-West Transylvania. The third variant represented tumulus graves that lacked weapons and had only adornments or clothing accessories and was placed in Moldova.

Based on these observed divisions, it was concluded that the two large groups can be interpreted as representing different parts of society, people that had a different social position and status. Group 1 was thought as belonging to individuals that did not enjoy a very high stats, although the funerary practices defining this group may also be related to particular afterlife beliefs and to a different perception of the body. The cremations, on the other hand, likely belonged to individuals that occupied a comparatively higher position in society. Group 2, with its subgroups and variants, referred to particular local practices and possibly related to different group identities. This led to distinct elements being integrated into mortuary practices, although many of those individuals probably occupied homologous position in society and recognized each other in that manner. In some regions, only one pattern dominated, as was the case of Moldova, signalling the existence of a strong local identity. In Muntenia and Oltenia, two different funerary practice patterns were encountered, although a porous barrier seems to have been in force between the two regions. Finally, South-West Transylvania appeared as an area of profound entanglement and mixture, since several different mortuary practices were definitely in use there without any particular separation, suggesting a melting pot of identities (Figs. 6.1, 6.2, 6.3, and 6.4).

The study summarized above basically represents a micro analysis of some of the main areas looked at in this volume. The groups, subgroups, and variants introduced above correspond closely with the supra-groups, groups, and regional patterns established in this study and described in the two previous chapters. The interpretations proposed are also very similar, as in both cases the link to social status and social position-related identities was suggested. Moreover, the same conclusions were reached about the existence of distinct local identity constructions for some regions, as well as the presence of identity barriers in certain areas. The analysis from this volume adds considerable further perspectives to the previous smaller study by showing that some of the groups actually extend far beyond what was initially thought, indicating the presence of larger-scale regional identities not initially captured. For instance, group 2 of the study above corresponds to a large degree with the Western supra-group and partially with groups 2 and 7 of the current analysis. The Western supra-group refers to a broad warrior elite identity which was shared not only by the communities of Oltenia, parts of Muntenia, and South-West Transylvania, but also by those of North-West Thrace and Central Serbia. Yet, group 1 of the above study, which corresponds exactly with the Eastern supra-group, was not found to incorporate any further areas. The two large-scale group identities, associated with the two supra-groups, were not noted in the micro study, since the broader dimension was missing, but were only uncovered in the analysis of this volume.

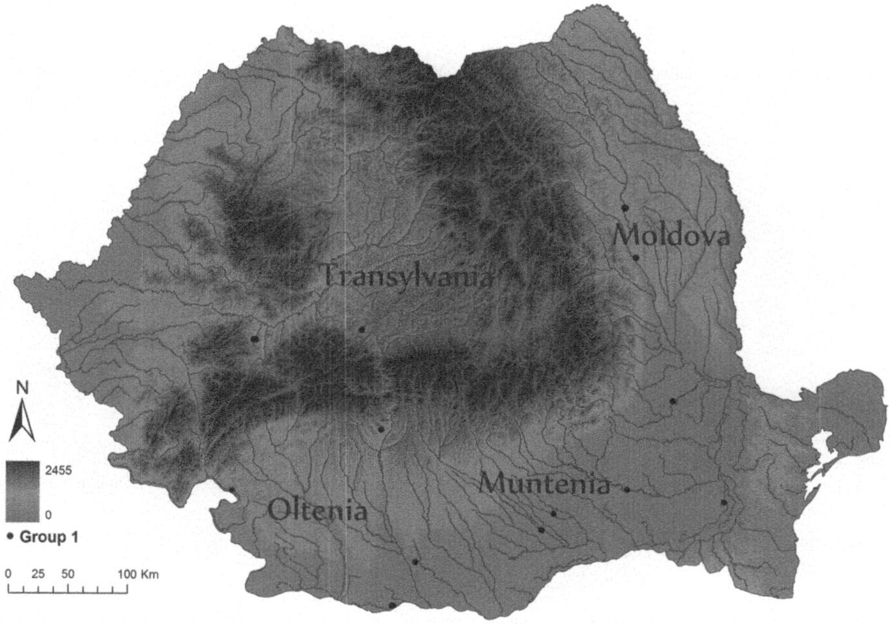

Fig. 6.1 Geographical distribution of preliminary study group 1 (Popa 2012, p. 410, Fig. 7.1)

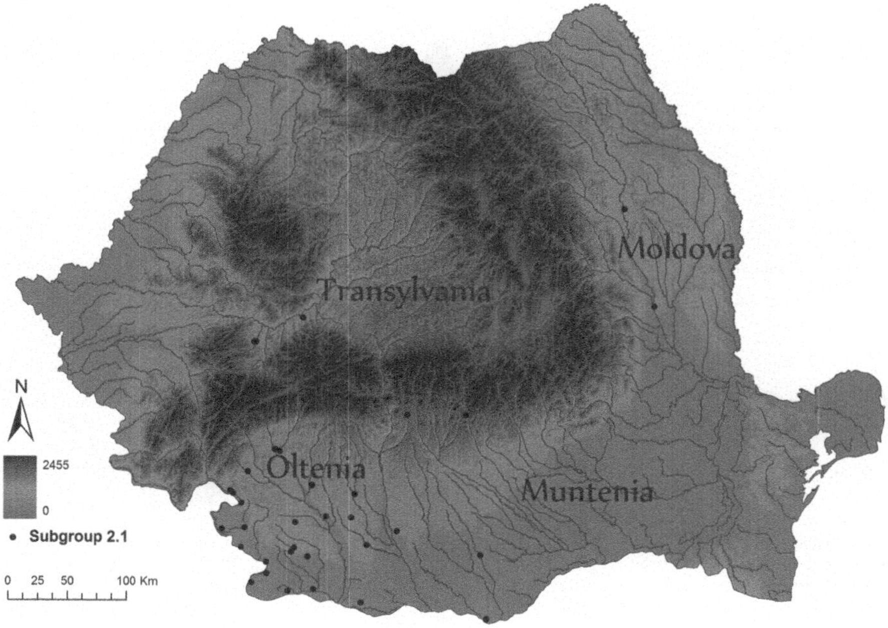

Fig. 6.2 Geographical distribution of preliminary study subgroup 2.1 (Popa 2012, p. 410, Fig. 7.2)

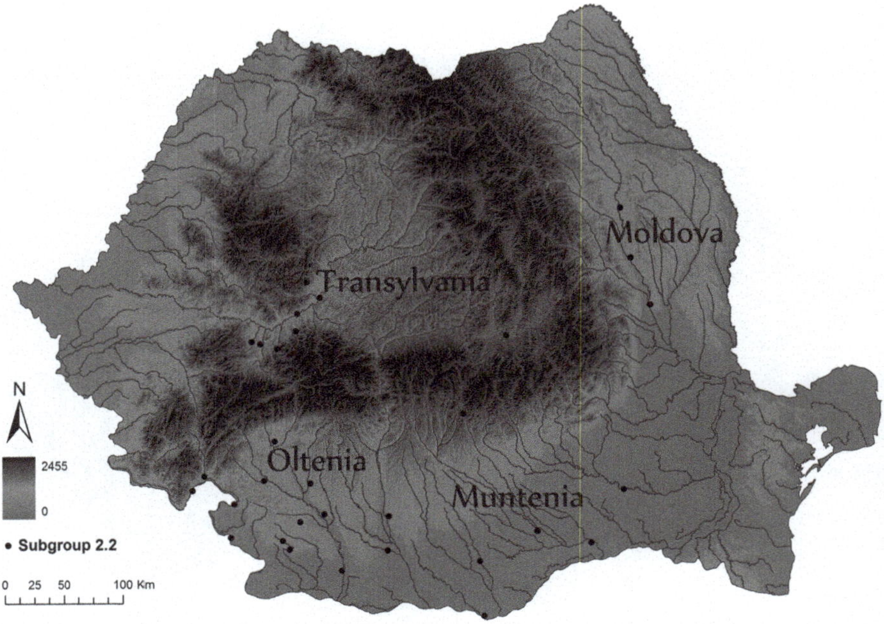

Fig. 6.3 Geographical distribution of preliminary study subgroup 2.2 (Popa 2012, p. 410, Fig. 7.3)

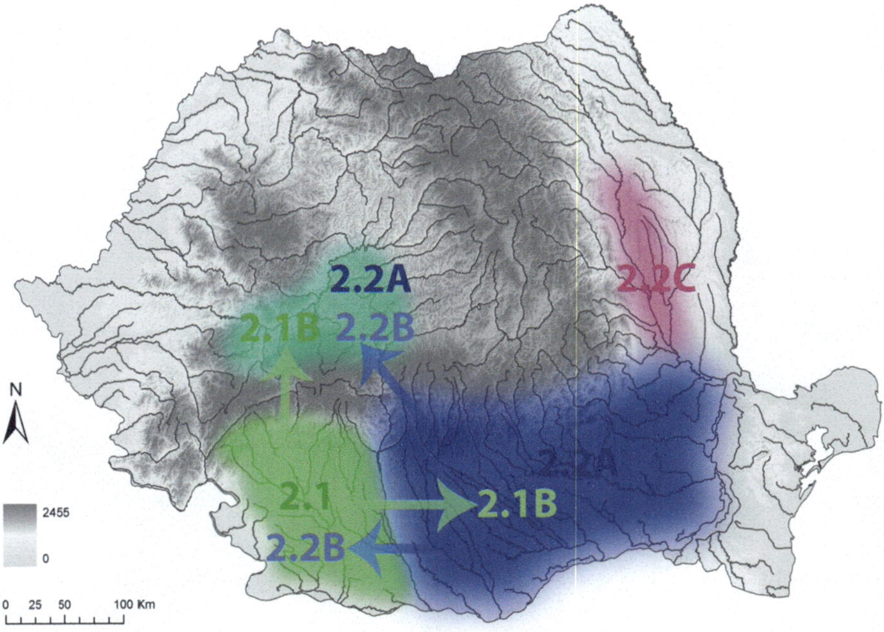

Fig. 6.4 Subgroup and subgroup variants interactions within preliminary study group 2 (Popa 2014, p. 119, Fig. 11.4)

6.2 Identity and Political Development in the Late Iron Age of the Eastern Carpathian Basin and the Lower Danube

Most archaeologists today agree that during the period covering the first century BC and first century AD, there were a series of smaller or larger political formations that coagulated in the Eastern Carpathian basin and the Lower Danube for a shorter or longer duration of time. The largest and most powerful of these is thought to have had its capital in South-West Transylvania, in the Orăştie Mountains, at the site of Grădiştea de Munte—Sarmizegetusa Regia.[2] The leaders from Sarmizegetusa controlled a territory that probably included parts of Transylvania, Moldova, Muntenia, Oltenia, and at times even areas further East and West. Even though much of the literature relating to this topic was undoubtedly touched by more overt or covert nationalist ideas about the Dacians (Popa 2013, 2015), the existence of some kind of political entity or entities cannot be denied given the overwhelming evidence that has been presented in favour of this idea (see for instance Daicoviciu 1981; Lockyear 2004; Oltean 2007; Florea 2011).[3]

It is hard not to remark that the area of the Eastern supra-group corresponds quite closely with the presumed territory of the largest of these Late Iron Age political entities. Even though it is not possible to affirm that all the sites containing finds of groups 1 and 3 were for certain part of the same state, the spatial overlap is too great for this to be a simple coincidence. It seems likely that there was a direct relationship between the existence of a large regional identity in this area, as suggested by the Eastern supra-group, and the emergence of a state. Determining which one acted as a catalyst for the other is not easy to establish based on this observation alone. It could be that the establishment of a large political entity in that territory was facilitated by the already existing close identity ties between the people inhabiting it. On the other hand, it is also possible that people became more alike and started to think of themselves as being part of a larger whole because the entire territory was brought together under the same political administration, which led to more contact and interaction between the different local communities.

The chronological information helps to clarify this dilemma, pushing the balance towards the first scenario. The time interval for most cluster 1 and 3 graves is rather wide and relative. Just over half have a possible starting date before the first century BC, although the end date is practically always well after the beginning of that century. However, it should be noted that graves which resemble, at least at first glance, those of groups 1 and 3 can be found across much of the same territory, although mainly in Moldova and Muntenia, as far back as the end of the fifth century BC (see

[2] It is uncertain whether the centre was at Sarmizegetusa Regia from the very beginning. It is conceivable that the first capital was actually at Costeşti, located only a few kilometres from Sarmizegetusa.

[3] In the following pages, for reasons of fluency, the words state and kingdom will be employed as perfect synonyms for political entity, although the two latter terms involve a level of organization that may not have actually been achieved, at least during the first century BC (for a condensed discussion on this topic see Lockyear 2004).

Sîrbu 1993). Therefore, it is possible that the funerary practices identified through the two clusters go back in time several hundred years and thus the group identity referred to by the Eastern supra-group existed well before the first century BC. Yet, one must also consider that fragile political entities may have preceded the large state from the final part of the La Tène. Although there is little archaeological evidence for this, written sources mention the names of leaders that probably ruled territories North of the Danube, such as Dromichete (Petre 2004, pp. 185–192). Based on this, one can assume that there were other similar leaders, whose names were not passed to us by the Greek or Latin writers. The small states they ruled may well have contributed to ever-growing regional solidarities. Nevertheless, it is improbable that at any point before the first century BC, there was a political entity even remotely close in size to the Eastern supra-group. Consequently, it is more likely that at the time of the establishment of a kingdom that included Moldova, Muntenia, Oltenia, and Transylvania, the communities of these regions already shared a broad regional identity which favoured their living together under one large political administration.

Besides the presence of a large political entity, some researchers have proposed for the Late La Tène of the Eastern Carpathian basin and the Lower Danube the existence of a large military alliance, the so-called Padea-Panagjurski Kolonii group.[4] This term was first put together by Woźniak (1974, 1975, 1976, 1971) after observing that there are a large number of graves, mainly coming from Oltenia and North-West Thrace, characterized by the use of cremation and the presence of swords, spearheads, shields, curved battle knives, and horse bits. Later, it was proposed that funerary finds coming from the Iron Gates region, parts of Muntenia, and South-West Transylvania also fulfil the above criteria (Sîrbu and Rustoiu 1999). All these graves are thought to have belonged to a warrior elite class that engaged in actions of pillaging to the South, especially after the Roman province of Macedonia was established in 146 BC. Their incursions may have been quite frequent and extensive, given that the Romans thought it necessary to take military actions against them during the second and first centuries BC, as recorded also by Strabo (Rustoiu 2008, p. 149). While many of the grave-goods were generally the same across this group, it was observed that there were still differences from one region to another in terms of some funerary ritual elements and other grave-goods items. These differences were interpreted as evidence of diverse ethnic origins, incorporating Dacians, Moesians, Tribalians, and Scordisci, so as to correspond with the pre-conceived ethnic distribution of South-East Europe in the Late La Tène. Hence, the Padea group was defined as being an ethnically diverse group of martial elites which engaged in common military action. Their specialization in fast pillaging incursions led to the development of a unitary military equipment optimized for such actions (Rustoiu 2002, pp. 11–23).

While some ideas about the Padea-Panagjurski Kolonii group appear simplistic, one cannot but remark on its large overlap with the Western supra-group (Figs. 5.2 and 6.5). This comes as no surprise, since some the grave-goods which were used to define the Padea group are also the ones that characterize, at least partially, groups 4,

[4] For reasons of fluidity the name will be shortened from this point onwards to the Padea group.

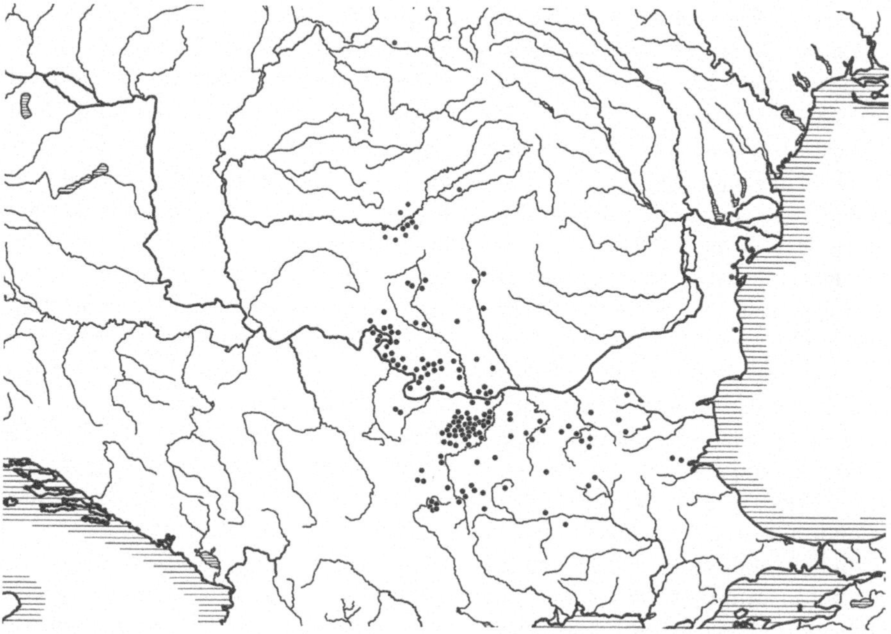

Fig. 6.5 Map of Padea-Panagjurski Kolonii group burials (Rustoiu 2015, p. 27, Fig. 27; after Rustoiu 2005, p. 270, Fig. 1)

5, and 6. The only significant difference is that clusters 4 and 5 also extended into Central Serbia, which the Padea group did not, mainly because of the lack of horse riding equipment and curved battle knives.[5] Regional differences, interpreted as ethnic variety in the case of the Padea group, were also identified in the Western supra-group. Yet, these differences were generally minor, referring to the use of flat or tumulus burials, the presence of some items, or their substitution with other ones which fulfilled a similar function. Saying that these elements account for ethnic differences seems rather forced; it is more likely that they were the result of some localized variation of a more widely spread practice. However, overall, the identification of the Padea graves as belonging to a martial elite corresponds with the observations made in regard to the Western supra-group in this study. The communities from which they originated had close ideas about how warriors should look like in death and thus shared a broad understanding of social differentiation and death concepts. Therefore, while the Padea group may be considered to be some sort of military alliance of the elite, its establishment was only possible because the communities of the area were already engaged in a series of similar practices and had a comparable structure of society. The variation observed within the Western supra-group, as determined by the three clusters that comprise it, probably accounts for social differentiation within the ranks of the martial elite. Such differences were also identified in the

[5] Or battle knives type 1 according to the typology of this study. In Central Serbia, as already mentioned, types 2, 3 and 4 dominated.

case of the Padea group, for which Rustoiu postulated the existence of an internal hierarchy, although not precisely among the same lines (Rustoiu 2008, p. 162).

Associated with the Padea group is also the idea of a North-South migration that occurred during the middle of the second century BC, from Oltenia and North-West Thrace to Transylvania. Such a movement of population, which probably only involved a group of military elites, has been theorized based on the break in material culture forms and settlement occupation that can be seen in the latter region around that time, followed by an apparent demographic explosion. Before the middle of the second century BC, many objects resembled the material culture from areas West of the Carpathians, while afterwards the similarities were mainly with the regions from the South and East of the mountains. Given the appearance of the martial Padea graves, it was proposed that a hostile takeover of territory occurred. The newcomers established their centre of power in South-West Transylvania, which later contributed to the establishment of a large political entity (Rustoiu 2008, pp. 149–152). While this migration theory has not been fully confirmed, many of its arguments seem sound. In addition, such a phenomenon connects well with the results of this volume as well as with that of other previous studies (Popa 2012, 2014).

In light of this probable, but unconfirmed, migration, the state established around the power centre of the Orăştie Mountains involved a clash of identities, which defined its characteristics. The Eastern supra-group suggests that the communities of Moldova, Muntenia, Transylvania, and parts of Oltenia were tied together by a broad sense of group identity that their members experienced. It seems likely that these people represented the regular population of the Iron Age state, carrying out all activities which form the economic infrastructure of any political entity. However, the incentive behind the organization of this state did not come from these people, but rather from the war-like elites identified through the Western supra-group. These high-status people, which most likely held much of the political power, clearly separated themselves from the rest of the population, both in life and in death, as it was seen in the case of Brad or Popeşti. This two-stepped social system was also mentioned in ancient writings, as already introduced in the previous chapter.

A vital element of state control, for what was an essentially foreign elite, seems to have been religion. Strabo (*Geography*, VII.3.11) mentions that the formation of the first large political entity, which he attributed to Burebista and high priest Dekaineos, was accompanied by an extensive religious reform, stressing the ideas of obedience, austerity, and temperance. It is thought that religion was one of the main elements that kept together the state, acting as an agent that reinforced political and military authority (Oltean 2007, p. 48). It has been noticed that religious structures were closely associated with elite residences, as the two generally shared the same areas in settlements, as was the case at Popeşti, Brad, Costesti-Cetățuie, and Costesti-Blidaru. In addition, the widespread votive offerings of the first century BC to first century AD, interpreted as the outcome of religious beliefs, involved objects made of precious metal, especially silver,[6] to which only the elite would have had access

[6] One good example of this is the silver hoard of Lupu, which contained bronze and silver vessels, several large silver fibulae and a series of anthropomorphically decorated silver *phalerae* (Glodariu and Moga 1994).

(Florea and Pupeză 2008, pp. 291–292). It has even been suggested recently that many of the silver hoards of this period were female dress elements belonging to a priest class (Egri and Rustoiu 2014). In this regard, it should also be mentioned that after 106 AD, when Transylvania, Oltenia, and parts of Mutenia were conquered by the Roman Empire and transformed into a Roman province, all temples built before this date rapidly fell in disarray, including those from areas where there was never any Roman military presence (Babeş 2000, p. 331). Florea and Pupeză (2008) consider that the destruction of temples occurred because of the fall of the power centre from the Orăştie Mountains following the Roman intervention, which also meant a "beheading" of the Late Iron Age elites. With the fall of the core, the entire power structure disintegrated because it had no support from the mass of the population. It is not surprising then, that some consider the ruling politico-military elite to have also held religious functions (Bodor 1981, p. 7). Overall, the importance and role of religion in the organization of the La Tène state support the idea of a deep identity split between the elite and the inhabitants of the areas surrounding the Carpathian arch, similar to that observed between the Eastern and Western supra-groups.

Since the kingdom established by the martial elite of cluster 4, 5, and 6, around the power centre from South-West Transylvania, eventually controlled vast areas South and East of the mountains, the lack or small number of graves from the Western supra-group in Moldova, Muntenia, and Transylvania becomes problematic. If these high status warriors took control over such a vast spread of land, why is it that their graves do not appear in these regions in comparable numbers to Oltenia, North-West Thrace, or Central Serbia? Why do they become invisible in the funerary record?

The answers to these questions can be grasped by considering the chronological spread of the Western supra-group graves and coupling this with the ideas that archaeologists have put forward about power control in the La Tène state. A simple listing of the proposed dates for the cluster 4, 5, and 6 graves reveals that, with seven exceptions, none of them were dated after the end of the first century BC (Fig. 6.6). Sîbu and Rustoiu even argue that most of them can be placed before 50 BC (Rustoiu 2005, p. 268; Sîrbu and Rustoiu 1999, pp. 84–85). Such an early chronology means that the Western supra-group graves were earlier than or at most contemporary with the first phase of establishment of the large political entity centred around the Orăştie Mountains. This first state, attributed to king Burebista,[7] is thought to have been more of a tribal union, established through military force, which disintegrated after a revolt of the local aristocracy around the middle of the first century BC (Oltean 2007, pp. 41–59). Given the fate of this first attempt at a state, it is conceivable that the following leaders, or even Burebista himself, attempted to centralize the state and limit the power of the elites. The almost complete lack of items made of gold outside of the Orăştie Mountains area supports this interpretation. Objects made of precious metal still appeared in the surrounding territories, particularly in votive depositions, but they were always made of silver. Often, gold items found around

[7] Lica (2000, pp. 62–91) and Jordanov (2009) give a good account of the information there is about Burebista, mostly coming from ancient sources but also the epigraphic record, and based on which the political events from the Eastern Carpathian basin and the Lower Danube were reconstructed. However, Lockyear (2004) doubts many of the achievements associated with Burebista's name.

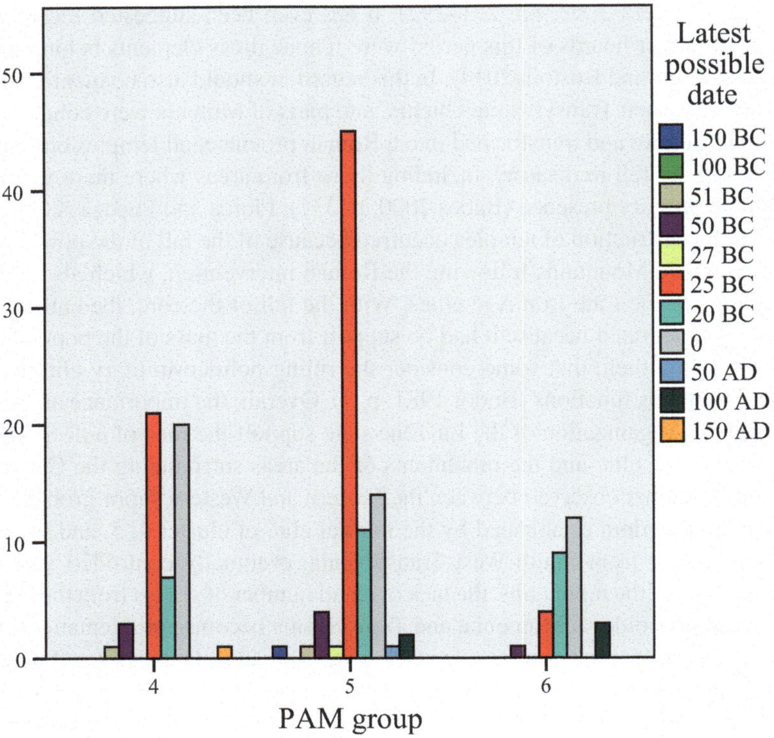

Fig. 6.6 Count of latest possible dates for the graves of PAM groups 4, 5, and 6 (Western supra-group)

the site of Sarmizegetusa Regia had very close parallels to silver objects uncovered in other areas.[8] The lack of golden objects is surprising, given their occasional appearance in the centuries preceding this period and considering the large ore deposits of gold, but not of silver, from the Western Carpathian Mountains, which were definitely being exploited during the Late Iron Age (Spânu 2006). This has led some to consider that, in the La Tène kingdom, gold was reserved for the leader alone, while the other elite were only permitted to employ silver objects as prestige items (Glodariu 2001, p. 772). The increased centralization and control over the high-status individuals, argued for by Avram (1989) and agreed by Florea (2006, pp. 3–5), can be thought of as a process of transformation, from a traditional, tribal warrior elite to a ruling, administrative aristocracy. This development was undoubtedly correlated with the demise of the weapon cremation graves. Through the mortuary rituals, the foreign elites and their successors solidified their personal control over the land as these were occasions where personal power, prestige, and military

[8] One of the most recent example of this is the large gold spiralled bracelets uncovered by treasure hunters at Grădiştea de Munte and which have numerous analogies in silver, such as the ones found in the hoard of Sărăcsău (Constantinescu et al. 2010; Floca 1956; Medeleț 1974).

prowess got overtly expressed. Moreover, through their dimensions and location, just outside but within visible range of the settlement, some of the small tumulus necropoleis were physically marking the landscape and establishing ownership of the land.[9] It is easy to see how such practices enhanced the control of local elites over an area to the detriment of the central power and thus needed to be stopped.

The region of Moldova, more specifically the three settlements from Poiana, Răcătău, and Brad, may represent a case where the newly established elites managed to "entrench" themselves and escape the control of the Orăştie Mountains power centre. The first argument in support of this theory is the settlements' defensive system. Around the middle of the first century BC at Poiana, Răcătău, and Brad, a fortification system was developed that took advantage of the natural shape of the terrain and encircled the central area of each site. However, the newly built fortifications were abandoned shortly after the start of the first century AD, following which the defensive lines were overbuilt by domestic structures (Căpitanu 1986, p. 120; Ursachi 1995, p. 102; Vulpe and Teodor 2003, pp. 15–21). It is interesting to note that the construction of the fortification system coincides with the fall of Burebista and the disintegration of the first state, which could indicate that the palisades were erected as a defensive measure against subsequent claims of control by the power centre in South-West Transylvania. The elites that were in control in Poiana, Răcătău, and Brad may well have decided to support each other and resist any further intervention from the West. If this was the case, the abandonment of the fortifications barely over half a century later appears at first glance surprising. Yet, one must take into account that, in 15 AD, the Roman province of Moesia was formed and the Roman Empire assumed indirect control of Dobrudja. This region, situated between the Danube and the Black Sea, contained a series of Greek colonies, which were important trading partners of the three Moldavian settlements.[10] Considering the pivotal role of commerce in the economies of Poiana, Răcătău, and Brad (Florea 2011, pp. 75–88), the three settlements surely sought to establish friendly relationships with the newly arrived Romans. In the face of constant threat from South-West Transylvania, it is conceivable that they also asked for Roman military protection. The dismantling of the fortifications could thus be the outcome of a sense of security in light of this situation, or it may have been a condition put forward by the Romans. The second argument for Moldova breaking away from the control of the Orăştie Mountains comes from the tumulus cemeteries associated with the Poiana, Răcătău, and Brad. The small groups of burials, through their positioning, just outside of the three settlements, and funerary ritual elements, such as the use of cremation and the construction of tumuli, were similar in character to those found at Popeşti in Muntenia or Cugir in South-West Transylvania. The difference between

[9] This is especially valid for the tumulus cemeteries from sites such as Cugir, Popeşti, Piscu Crăsani or Radovanu, which undoubtedly belonged to the local ruling dynasties.

[10] The commerce was probably done by water, as the three settlements were situated on the banks of the navigable Siret River, which flows, not far from Poiana, into the Danube and then the Black Sea. The three settlements were just over 40 km apart from each other, which could be approximated to a full day's travel.

them lies in the lack of offensive weapons from the Moldavian graves, for which reason the statistical algorithm has placed them in cluster 2. Yet, these graves undoubtedly show a local adaptation of cluster 2, or otherwise of the tumulus weapon graves from Muntenia and Transylvania, as was suggested in previous studies (Popa 2012, 2014). Their localized character is also sustained by the presence of funerary ritual elements and grave-goods that may have been the result of contact with people from the North Pontic region. As argued earlier, through their presence, this kind of small tumulus cemeteries can be thought as symbolic markers of local power and land ownership for which reason the leaders of the Orăştie Mountains wanted them stopped. Consequently, the construction of such tumulus graves ceased before the end of the first century BC. But Moldova did not follow this pattern since the graves of Poiana, Răcătău, and Brad were dated to the first century BC and, in seven cases, even the first century AD (Figs. 6.7 and 6.8).Therefore, the apparent ban of such practices was not in effect in this region, suggesting that this area was outside the control of the political entity centred around South-West Transylvania. By bringing together the two arguments, one can conclude that the elites of Moldova refused to bow to the power centre of the Orăştie Mountains after the middle of the first century BC, building fortifications around settlements to defend their positions and engaging in funerary practices that expressed their power and prestige and solidified their control over the territory.

The questions still remaining about Moldova are linked to the character of these elites from this region, since the graves show striking resemblance to those from Muntenia or Transylvania, but at the same time include clearly local characteristics. One possible scenario is that these individuals were originally part of the Western supra-group warriors, but, as they took control of the settlements of Moldova, they lost their military features or at least stopped defining themselves through it. This may have happened because martial symbols were not highly regarded among the communities of that region, which seems plausible given that practically no weapons were found in any of the three large settlements despite extensive excavations. Instead, the elites adopted symbols relating to commercial activities, as many of the grave-goods uncovered in the tumuli were Greek or Roman imports, which coincides with the abundance of imported goods found in the settlements of Poiana, Răcătău, and Brad (Căpitanu 1976, 1981, 1986; Ursachi 1995; Vulpe and Teodor 2003). A second possibility is that these were actually local elites that emulated the ones from the Western regions. As the three settlements were integrated in the large La Tène political entity of the first half of the first century BC, the local elites adopted the use of cremation and the construction of burial mounds, but not the martial component as it carried no significance for the people of Moldova. After the disintegration of the first state, the funerary practice continued since it had already become the regular burial custom for high-status individuals. In the end, the difference between these two scenarios is whether the foreign or local element took primacy. Whichever may be the answer, the fact still remains that Moldova was an area where local elements came out much stronger than in any of the other regions surrounding the Carpathian Mountains.

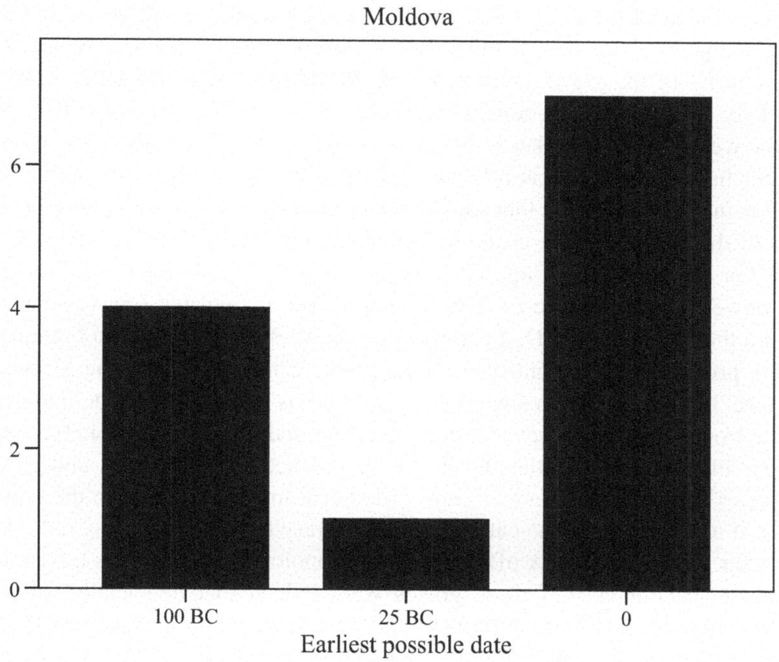

Fig. 6.7 Count of earliest possible dating of the graves of Moldova

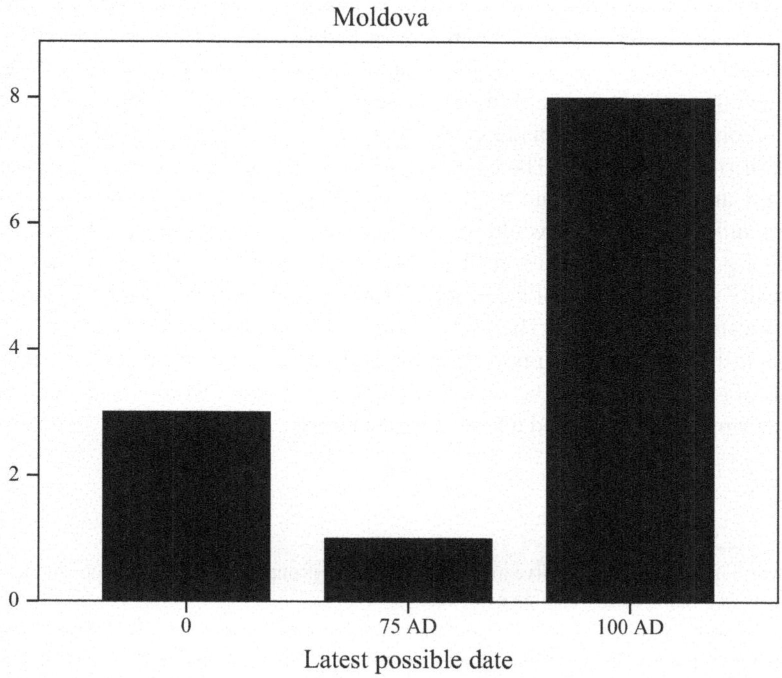

Fig. 6.8 Count of latest possible dating of the graves of Moldova

In the context of these divisions, the graves of clusters 2, and partially of cluster 7, would appear to function as links. In the case of group 7, as already stated, the large majority of the graves came from the Western supra-group areas, making it very likely that the two phenomena were associated. Still, their distinct character from the weapon graves makes it difficult to infer the nature of this association. On the other hand, cluster 2 was relatively evenly spread out across the entire study area. It is interesting to note that such graves were integrated into the tumulus cemeteries of the Western supra-group in Muntenia and South-West Transylvania, like at Cugir or Popeşti, suggesting that some of the group 2 individuals got integrated in the power structure of the La Tène kingdom. Yet, the cluster 2 graves expanded well into the first century AD, a period when the Western supra-group funerals had stopped, probably due to control from the power centre in the Orăştie Mountains. Therefore, the group 2 graves were not perceived as threatening to the integrity of the Late Iron Age kingdom, even though the deceased probably occupied important positions in their communities. Given the abundance of adornments and clothing accessories and the analogies with Early Medieval finds mentioned in the previous chapter, it may be possible to catalogue the funerary finds as belonging to high status women, although the lack of extensive anthropological data makes this assumption rather speculative.[11] If these graves were indeed that of socially important women, it may be that their continuation into the first century AD can be explained by them no longer being part of the actual administrative elite of the Late Iron Age state, which may have comprised an exclusively male quality. If this scenario is correct, the graves of cluster 2 could have been that of women who were somehow related to this ruling male elite. Continuing along the same line, the large area of occurrence of cluster 2 indicates that female identity, at least the one shared by the individuals of this group, was widely shared across the study area, which may be explained through a process of bridal exchange between local elites. An alternative explanation, proposed by Mândescu (2006, p. 29) for Cetăţeni, is that these were the graves of ritual specialists. The existence of such people in the communities of the Eastern Carpathian basin and the Lower Danube was indeed mentioned by some ancient authors,[12] and this would explain the wide geographical distribution of the cluster 2 graves through a level of shared religious beliefs. However, there were practically no items in any of the group 2 graves to indicate clearly that the deceased were priests or priestesses. Therefore, while such an explanation seems tempting, there is little evidence to support it. In the end, the exact identification of the individuals of group 2 proves to be very challenging, although I would be inclined to see them as women who enjoyed a high social standing.

[11] It is worth mentioning that the five individuals from this group that were sexed were all identified as women, but that is hardly enough evidence.

[12] The most important piece of writing mentioning a priest class was left to us by Jordanes, quoting Dio Cassius (Jordanes, *Getica*, V.40). Other indications can also be found in the writings of Strabo (*Geography*, VII.3.3) and Flavius Josephus (*Antiquities of the Jews*, XVIII.1.5)

6.3 Ethnicity in the Late Iron Age

A final thing that needs to be discussed is whether the results of this volume agree with the existence of a Getic, Dacian, or Geto-Dacian ethnicity, an idea which is widely accepted today. However, before embarking on such an endeavour, it is necessary to introduce the intricate relationship that Iron Age research in general has had with ethnicity. Much of the work done on the Iron Age, and the Late Iron Age in particular, has been aimed at identifying archaeologically pre-conceived ethnic entities. This was not the purpose of this volume. Nevertheless, because of the prominent nature of the ethnicity issue, the final part of this section seeks to determine to what degree the names Getae and Dacians, left to us by the ancient writers, correspond with the results of this study and whether the statistical groups sustain their use as ethnic names.

6.3.1 The Issue of Ethnicity in the Iron Age

Iron Age research on identity is not only about studying ethnicity, as some volumes accurately illustrate (cf. Popa and Stoddart 2014). However, a large number of Iron Age scholars seem to be mainly focused on characterizing past identities in terms of ethnicity, for which reason there are numerous publications concerned with Celts, Thracians, Dacians, Germans, Scythians, etc. This statement is largely untrue for studies dealing with other periods of European prehistory (i.e., Mesolithic, Neolithic, Bronze Age). In those cases, a large array of identities is discussed and their interplay in different contexts is often highlighted. Yet, in the case of the Iron Age, and especially the Late Iron Age, this happens much less. Why is this so? Did Europe change so radically in the Iron Age? Probably not! Rather than being based on a real change in terms of people's identities, it seems far more likely that the reason for focusing on ethnicity has to do with the literary sources derived from Mediterranean authors, who provided (often cryptic) names of some presupposed populations. These names fuelled the idea that Europe had suddenly become divided into ethnic groups, all of which appeared miraculously nearly at the same time. There are numerous studies which have successfully deconstructed the picture illustrated through the literary sources, showing that it is a biased vision, full of gross overgeneralizations, and thus cannot be employed for drawing up an ethnic map of the continent (e.g., Edward and van der Vliet 2003). It is an account from the outside, put together according to the world view of the authors and their readers, mainly people from Greece and Italy. Despite such facts being acknowledged by a large majority of today's scholars, there are still numerous volumes focusing on Iron Age ethnic groups which were defined mostly through ancient texts (e.g., Derks and Roymans 2009; Cunliffe and Koch 2010).

The Iron Age is not the only period that has to deal with this kind of problems. The issue of ethnicity also occupies Early Medieval researchers. Early Medieval Europe is pictured in numerous archaeological studies as a place inhabited by well-defined groups such as Franks, Bavarians, Alamani, Ostrogoths, Vizigoths, Lombards, etc., an image constructed with the help of a large number of writings that employ specific names for different populations. This approach has come under heavy criticism, arguing that such names refer to constructions of the Late Antique authors or to specific identity types that only have meaning in the context of interaction with the Roman Empire administration (Brather 2000, 2004; Geary 2002) or later with large political structures like the Frankish state (Fehr 2010).

The reasons behind the categorization of past populations using ethnic terms are undoubtedly much more complex than just believing blindingly the antique writings. While, indeed, the Iron Age is, with some exceptions,[13] the only period of European prehistory whose people were divided in ethnic groups by scholars, archaeologists imposed a compartmentalization on the Neolithic and Bronze Age as well through the use of archaeological cultures. Even though arguments have been given for the existence of such cultures and attempts were made to ground them in the archaeological record, a principal element that stands behind such categorizations, including Iron Age ethnicities, is the practical need to organize data. Just like researchers from other disciplines, archaeologists need to organize their data in order to allow for easier comprehension. Categorization can even be claimed to be a fundamental feature of humanity. This, nevertheless, leads to simplifications, generalizations, and thus the loss of a large amount of details, but it also has the effect of allowing for easier judgments and interpretations, resulting ultimately in more rather than less information (Latour 1999). Cognitive psychologists explain this categorization of our world, and this includes archaeological data and the past, as a process that is inherent to human brain mechanics; humans understand reality by segmenting it into categories each of which is characterized according to a specific set of properties (Boyer and Ramble 2001; Kurzban et al. 2001). Therefore, it comes as no surprise that archaeologists divided the past, and implicitly past people, into units that lend themselves useful to research.

Although the mechanisms behind dividing the Iron Age people and material evidence ethnically are grounded in logical processes, the categories that have been enforced onto the past are not driving research forward. Following Latour, people simplify and categorize data so as to gain more information in the end. However, the use of ethnic constructs for the Iron Age falls outside of this logic since it does not result in more information. The categories that have been imposed on the Iron Age do not contribute to the creation of knowledge, but rather inhibit it, as they discourage from asking a wide variety of identity-related questions to the archaeological record. Hence, despite the sound logical and cognitive arguments behind a division of the past in ethnic terms, the process fails its purpose.[14]

The issue with using ethnicity is one of methodology not of concept, as it was already well-pointed out more than 60 years ago by Eggers (1950, 1959). The prob-

[13] The main exception is found in the work of Kossinna, who attempted to map German ethnicity in the Bronze Age (Kossinna 1911, 1926).

[14] This observation is only valid of course if it is assumed that the purpose of archaeological research is to produce knowledge about how past people lived and not a narrative of the past that only mirrors today's society.

lem lies not with the concept of ethnicity itself or with the ancient texts available for the Iron Age, but with the methodology deployed in the study of this period and with the questions that are posed to the archaeological record. If the scope of archaeological research is to obtain an insight into the identity constructions of Iron Age people as suggested by the material evidence, then we need not to be fixed on one particular type of identity, which may or may not be actually present in the archaeological record, but rather allow for all possible scenarios to unfold and pick the one(s) that seem(s) most plausible. This implies a 180° turn in the relationship between identity concepts and the material record. One should not categorize the material record based on some large (ethnic) identities that we assume people shared, but rather reconstruct past identities based on the material record patterns.

Approaching Iron Age identity in this manner has the advantage of making redundant a problem that archaeologists have struggled with for quite some time: the direct link between material culture forms and ethnicity. This is an issue that was mainly constructed in the process of explaining material culture patterns using *a priori* defined ethnic groups, strongly exemplified in the work of Kossinna who desperately tried to trace back the Germans into prehistory (Kossinna 1911, 1926). The problem of ethnically labelling specific material forms disappears if past identity is inferred starting from the archaeological record instead of simply searching for Germans, Celts, or Scythians in the variations of pots. The challenge then becomes to reconstruct identity using the evidence that has been uncovered.

6.3.2 The Getae and Dacian Correspondence

According to the ancient written sources, much of the Eastern Carpathian basin and the Lower Danube were inhabited by the Getae and the Dacians, raising thus the question of whether the two names can be linked to any of the clusters identified in this study. The best candidates for such a correspondence are undoubtedly the Eastern and the Western supra-groups since these covered relatively large areas. Based on the data used for this analysis alone, it is hard, if not impossible, to deduce whether the Late Iron Age people surrounding the Carpathian arch shared an identity that could be denoted ethnic. The single possible approach is to attempt to connect the results with information coming from ancient authors and with ideas put forward by other scholars.

An immediate point for this endeavour is the apparent similarity between the East-West separation of the two supra-groups and the East-West separation between the Getae and Dacians recorded by Strabo. In his *Geography*, Strabo writes:

> But there is also another division of the country which has endured from early times, for some of the people are called Daci, whereas others are called Getae—Getae, those who incline towards the Pontus [Black Sea] and the East, and Daci, those who incline in the opposite direction towards Germany and the sources of the Ister [Danube]. (Strabo, *Geography*, VII.3.12)

The geographical references given by Strabo are vague and should not be given much trust. In the period that he was writing, the geographical knowledge of the area was most likely extremely limited. Nemeti (2011) convincingly argued that until the conquest of the land by the Roman Empire, at the beginning of the second century AD, there was little understanding for the size and geography of the area North of the Danube River. In addition, it has been well pointed out that, for ancient writers, terms such as Dacians, Getae, Celts, or Scythians referred primarily to geographical units rather than ethnic realities (Brather 2002, p. 150). Therefore, Strabo's reference cannot be taken as evidence for the existence of the two ethnic groups.[15] Despite this critique, one cannot overlook the fundamental East-West division that he proposes, which refers to relative rather than exact localization and may be more trustworthy, and how well this division corresponds to the separation of the two supra-groups. While this observation cannot in any manner lead to immediate identification, it is by far the best ancient reference that describes the positioning of the two supra-groups.

The geographical positioning of the Eastern supra-group suggests that the large-scale group identity embraced by the communities living in Moldova, Muntenia, Oltenia, and Transylvania corresponds well with the area described as Getic in antiquity, but cannot be backed up with other arguments. The main reason for this situation is the almost complete lack of any elements that can be linked to the communities that shared this group identity, since the Eastern supra-group was identified through a proxy, the cluster 1 and 3 graves. Basically, the existence of this large group identity was determined based on the practice of burying certain individuals in a particular manner, individuals who were not characteristic of the main mass of the population. Apart from this distinct mortuary ritual, it is difficult to say what other practices or ideas linked the members of these communities together, although a large similarity in terms of material culture forms is evident in this area during the Late Iron Age. In addition, looking at items of jewellery coming from all possible contexts, Rustoiu (2002, pp. 97–116) defines an Eastern group during the first century BC and first century AD, which corresponds closely geographically with the supra-group from this volume. Therefore, the identification of the Eastern supra-group with the Getae may be possible, although more evidence would be needed to support it. Inferring the nature of this group identity, specifically whether it can be characterized as ethnic, would be unrealistic based on the current results alone.

For the Western supra-group, there is an extra element of comparison giving more grounds for a possible identification with the name Dacians. First of all, like in the case of the Getae, there is a relatively good correlation between the geographical regions occupied by the supra-group and the area designated as Dacian in antiquity. Secondly, given the martial nature of the Western supra-group graves, other associations can be proposed. If the identification of this supra-group with the Padea-Panagjurski Kolonii warriors is correct, it may be that the name Dacians was instigated through the contact brought about by the pillaging campaigns carried out in the Southern Balkan regions, then already under Roman administration. This name may have actually been employed by some of the raiders themselves, either to signal their affiliation to a particular tribe or to refer to their warrior status. The

[15] For a discussion on the way Strabo populated his *Geography* with ethnic names see the article by Edward and van der Vliet (2003).

hypothesis that the label Dacian was initially associated with a limited group of warriors was already proposed by Eliade (1959), although he also suggested that it derived from the term used for wolf. Eliade's theory enjoys considerable recognition, as numerous scholars embraced his idea (e.g., Crişan 1986: 36–43, 413–414; Franga 1993: 16–17; Sanie 1999: 106–112). Yet, Dana (2000) has argued against the correlation between Dacian and wolf, considering it based on incorrect linguistic assumptions. Whichever position is taken, what emerges is that the name Dacian could have originally referred to a group of warriors who may or may not have thought of themselves metaphorically as wolves. From this point, it is relatively easy to understand how the name got associated with the entire area surrounding the Carpathian arch and its population. Through the contact established during the pillaging campaigns of the Padea warriors, the name got transmitted to the Roman administration and literary sources. As the group expanded into Transylvania and contributed to the establishment of a La Tène state in the area, the name became associated with the entire land and was propagated given the intense interaction with the large Mediterranean empire (cf. Egri 2014). Furthermore, with the Roman Empire constantly expanding into the Middle and Lower Danube regions, the local population that lived within its borders had to accept this ethnic label in its dealings with the Roman military and administration. This explains the existence of Roman military diplomas containing the ethnonym *Dacus* for people recruited as far back as the middle of the first century AD from North-West Thrace (Dana and Matei-Popescu 2009). Similar scenarios, where a name given initially to a small group of elite individuals ended up being used to refer to an entire area and eventually an ethnic group, can be encountered in Early Medieval times (cf. Fehr 2010). Therefore, the identification of the Western supra-group with the Dacians may be accurate, but only with two observations: that Dacian was not employed to refer to an ethnic group; that the name, in its broad understanding, only made sense from the perspective of an external observer from the Roman Empire.

The results of this volume may be thus correlated with the names Getae and Dacians, but not with their ethnic meaning, and function as an argument against the synonymity of the two terms. The large group identities that were uncovered correspond broadly in terms of geography with the information provided by antique writers, but this alone cannot act as an argument for their ethnic identification. The large Iron Age political entity, centred around Sarmizegetusa Regia, benefited from a broad sense of identity that the inhabitants of much of the Eastern Carpathian basin and the Lower Danube shared, but there is not enough evidence for giving the ethnic appellative Getae to those people. Furthermore, based on geographical correspondence and previous theories, the term Dacian originally designated a small group of warriors, which was later extended to designate the high elite of the Iron Age state, without any kind of ethnic reference. Yet, what comes out most clearly is the deep division between the two identity groups, which was transposed in the social organization of the Iron Age kingdom. It is for this reason that the term Geto-Dacian can at most describe a symbiotic coexistence under one political umbrella of two distinct groups of people during the first century BC and first century AD.

References

Avram, A. (1989). Gedanken über den thrakisch-geto-dakischen Adel. *Studii Clasice, 26*, 11–25.

Babeş, M. (2000). La conquête Trajane vue par l'archéologie. In A. Avram & M. Babeş (Eds.), *Civilisation Grecque et cultures antiques périphériques: Hommage à Petre Alexandrescu à son 70e anniversaire*. Editura Enciclopedică: Bucarest.

Bodor, A. (1981). Structura societății dacice. In H. Daicoviciu (Ed.), *Studii dacice* (pp. 7–22). Cluj-Napoca: Editura Dacia.

Boyer, P., & Ramble, C. (2001). Cognitive templates for religious concepts: Cross-cultural evidence for recall of counter-intuitive representations. *Cognitive Science, 25*, 535–564.

Brather, S. (2000). Ethnische Identitäten als Konstrukte der frühgeschichtlichen Archäologie. *Germania, 78*, 139–177.

Brather, S. (2002). Ethnic identities as constructions of archaeology: The case of the Alamanni. In A. Gillett (Ed.), *On barbarian identity: Critical approaches to ethnicity in the Early Middle Ages* (pp. 149–176). Turnhout: Brepols.

Brather, S. (2004). *Ethnische Interpretationen in der frühgeschichtlichen Archäologie. Geschichte, Grundlagen und Alternativen*. Berlin: W. de Gruyte.

Căpitanu, V. (1976). Principalele rezultate ale săpăturilor arheologice în aşezarea geto-dacică de la Răcătău (judeţul Bacău). *Carpica, 8*, 48–120.

Căpitanu, V. (1981). Raport privind cercetările arheologice de la Răcătău, jud. Bacău. *Materiale şi Cercetări Arheologice, 15*, 201–210.

Căpitanu, V. (1986). Cercetările arheologice de la Răcătău, jud. Bacău. *Materiale şi Cercetări Arheologice, 16*, 109–120.

Constantinescu, B., Oberländer-Târnoveanu, E., Bugoi, R., Cojocaru, V., & Radtke, M. (2010). The Sarmizegetusa bracelets. *Antiquity, 84*, 1024–1042.

Crişan, I. H. (1986). *Spiritualitatea geto-dacilor: Repere istorice*. Bucureşti: Albatros.

Cunliffe, B., & Koch, J. T. (Eds.). (2010). *Celtic from the West: Alternative perspectives from archaeology, genetics, language, and literature*. Oxford: Oxbow.

Daicoviciu, H. (Ed.). (1981). Studii dacice. Cluj-Napoca Editura Dacia.

Dana, D. (2000). Dacii şi lupii. Pe marginea teoriei lui Mircea Eliade. *Studii şi Cercetări de Istorie Veche şi Arheologie, 51*(3–4), 153–174.

Dana, D., & Matei-Popescu, F. (2009). Soldats d'origine dace dans les diplomes militaires. *Chiron, 39*, 209–256.

Derks, T., & Roymans, N. (Eds.). (2009). *Ethnic constructs in antiquity: The role of power and tradition*. Amsterdam: Amsterdam University Press.

Edward, C., & van der Vliet, L. (2003). The Romans and us: Strabo's 'Geography' and the construction of ethnicity. *Mnemosyne, 56*(3), 257–272.

Eggers, H. J. (1950). Das Problem der ethnischen Deutung in der Frühgeschichte. In H. Kirchner (Ed.), *Ur- und frühgeschichte als historische Wissenschaft: Festschrift zum 60 Geburtstag von Ernest Wahle* (pp. 49–59). Heidelberg: Carl Winter.

Eggers, H. J. (1959). *Einführung in die Vorgeschichte*. München: R. Piper.

Egri, M. (2014). Enemy at the gates? The interactions between Dacians and Romans in the 1st century AD. In M. A. Janković, V. D. Mihajlović, & S. Babić (Eds.), *The edges of the Roman world* (pp. 172–193). New Castle: Cambridge Scholars.

Egri, M., & Rustoiu, A. (2014). Sacred conviviality in the Lower Danube region. The case of the Sâncrăieni hoard. *Studia Universitatis "Babeş-Bolyai". Historia, 59*(1), 153–188.

Eliade, M. (1959). Les Daces et les loups. *Numen, 6*, 15–31.

Fehr, H. (2010). Am Anfang war das Volk? Die Entstehung der bajuwarischen Identität als archäologisches und interdisziplinäres Problem. In W. Pohl & M. Mehofer (Eds.), *Archaeology of identity – Archäologie der Identität* (pp. 211–223). Wien: Verlag der Österreichsichen Akademie der Wissenschaften.

Floca, O. (1956). *Contributii la cunoasterea tezaurelor de argint dacice, tezaurul de la Sărăcsău şi Şeica Mică*. Bucureşti.

Florea, G. (2006). The 'public image' of the Dacian aristocracy. *Studia Universitatis "Babeş-Bolyai". Historia, 51*(1), 1–11.

Florea, G. (2011). *Dava et oppidum. Débuts de la genèse urbaine en Europe au deuxième âge du Fer*. Cluj-Napoca: Acadèmie Roumaine. Centre d'Études Transylvaines.

Florea, G., & Pupeză, P. (2008). Les diuex tués. La destruction du chef-lieu du royaume dace. In I. Piso (Ed.), *Die Römischen Provinzen. Begriff und Gründung* (pp. 281–296). Mega: Cluj-Napoca.

Franga, L. (1993). Les daces et le mort 'simbolique'. Considérations sur la mort chez les daces et les thraces. *Thraco-Dacica, 14*, 13–23.

Geary, P. J. (2002). *The myth of nations: The medieval origins of Europe*. Princeton: Princeton University Press.

Glodariu, I. (2001). Civilizaţia geto-dacă din a doua jumătate a secolului al II-lea a. Chr. până la începutul secoului al II-lea p. Chr. In M. Petrescu-Dîmboviţa & A. Vulpe (Eds.), *Istoria Românilor. Moştenirea timpurilor îndepărtate* (Vol. 1, pp. 725–797). Bucureşti: Enciclopedică.

Glodariu, I., & Moga, V. (1994). Tezaurul dacic de la Lupu. *Ephemeris Napocensis, 4*, 33–48.

Jordanov, K. (2009). Histoire politique des gètes à l'époque de Burebista et de ses successeurs. In *Studia Archaeologiae et Historiae Antiquae* (pp. 277–284). Chişinău.

Kossinna, G. (1911). *Die Herkunft der Germanen: zur Methode der Siedlungsarchäologie*. Würzburg: C. Kabitzsch.

Kossinna, G. (1926). *Ursprung Und Verbreitung Der Germanen in Vor- Und Fruhgeschichtlicher Zeit*. Berlin: Germanen Verlag.

Kurzban, R., Tooby, J., & Cosmides, L. (2001). Can race be erased? Coalitional computation and social categorization. *Proceedings of the National Academy of Sciences of the United States of America, 98*(26), 15,387–15,392. doi:10.1073/pnas.251541498.

Latour, B. (1999). *Pandora's hope: Essays on the reality of science studies*. Cambridge, MA: Harvard University Press.

Lica, V. (2000). *The coming of Rome in the Dacian world* (Vol. 44). Konstanz: Universitätsverlag Konstanz.

Lockyear, K. (2004). The Late Iron Age background to Roman Dacia. In W. S. Hanson & I. P. Haynes (Eds.), *Roman Dacia. The making of a provincial society* (pp. 33–74). Rhode Island: Portsmouth.

Măndescu, D. (2006). *Cetăţeni: Staţiunea geto-dacă de pe valea Dâmboviţei superioare*. Brăila: Editura Istros.

Medeleţ, F. (1974). Brăţările spiralice Dacice de argint. In H. Daicoviciu (Ed.), *In memoriam Constantini Daicoviciu* (pp. 229–244). Cluj-Napoca: Dacia.

Nemeti, S. (2011). In circuitu tenuit …Dacia and Roman geographical knowledge. *Ephemeris Napocensis, 21*, 37–50.

Oltean, I. A. (2007). *Dacia: Landscape, colonisation and romanisation*. London: Routledge.

Petre, Z. (2004). *Practica nemuririi: O lectură critică a izvoarelor greceşti referitoare la geţi*. Iaşi: Polirom. Retrieved from http://www.scribd.com/doc/129112274/Zoe-Petre-Practica-Nemuririi.

Popa, C. N. (2012). Till death do us part. A statistical approach to identifying burial similarity and grouping. The case of the Late La Tène graves from the Eastern Carpathian basin. In S. Berecki (Ed.), *Iron Age rites and rituals in the Carpathian basin* (pp. 401–412). Târgu Mureş: Mega.

Popa, C. N. (2013). The trowel as chisel. Shaping modern Romanian identity through the Iron Age. In V. Ginn, R. Enlander, & R. Crozier (Eds.), *Exploring prehistoric identity. Our construct or theirs?* (pp. 164–174). Oxford: Oxbow.

Popa, C. N. (2014). The quest for group identity in Late Iron Age Romania. Statistical reconstruction of groups based on funerary evidence. In C. N. Popa & S. Stoddart (Eds.), *Fingerprinting the Iron Age* (pp. 108–122). Oxford: Oxbow.

Popa, C. N. (2015). Late Iron Age archaeology in Romania and the politics of the past. *Dacia N.S., 59*, 337–361.

Popa, C. N., & Stoddart, S. (Eds.). (2014). *Fingerprinting the Iron Age*. Oxford: Oxbow.

Rustoiu, A. (2002). *Războinici şi artizani de prestigiu în Dacia preromană*. Cluj-Napoca: Nereamia Napocae.

Rustoiu, A. (2005). The Padea-Panagjurski Kolonii group in South-Western Transylvania (Romania). In H. Dobrzańska, J. V. S. Megaw, P. Poleska, & Z. Woźniak (Eds.), *Celts on the margin: Studies in European cultural interaction 7th Century BC - 1st Century AD. Dedicated to Zenon Woźniak* (pp. 109–120). Institute of Archaeology and Ethnology of the Polish Academy of Sciences: Kraków.

Rustoiu, A. (2008). *Războinici şi societate în aria celtică transilvăneană. Stuidii pe marginea mormântului cu coif de la Ciumeşti.* Cluj-Napoca: Mega.

Rustoiu, A. (2015). The Celtic horizon in Transylvania. Archaeological and historical evidence. In S. Berecki (Ed.), *Iron Age settlement patterns and funerary landscape in Transylvania (4th-2nd centuries BC)* (pp. 9–29). Târgu Mureş: Mega Publishing House.

Sanie, S. (1999). *Din istoria culturii şi religiei geto-dacice* (Ediţia a 2-a, revăzută şi adăugită.). Iaşi: Editura Universităţii 'Al. I. Cuza'.

Sîrbu, V. (1993). *Credinţe şi practici funerare, religioase şi magice în lumea geto-dacilor (pornind de la descoperirile arheologice din Câmpia Brăilei).* Galaţi: Porto-Franco.

Sîrbu, V., & Rustoiu, A. (1999). Découvertes funéraires Géto-Daces du Sud-Ouest de la Roumanie (150-50av.J.C.) In M. Vasić (Ed.), *Le Djerdap - les Portes de Fer a la deuxiéme moitie du premier millenaire av. J. Ch. jusqu aux guerres daciques. Kolloquim in Kladovo-Drobeta-Tr. Severin* (pp. 77–91). Arheološki institut: Beograd.

Spânu, D. (2006). *Piesele de orfevrerie din Dacia din secolele II a.Chr. - I p. Chr.* PhD Thesis, Universitatea Bucureşti, Bucureşti.

Ursachi, V. (1995). *Zargidava: Cetatea dacică de la Brad.* Bucureşti: Caro Trading.

Vulpe, R., & Teodor, S. (2003). *Piroboridava aşezarea geto-dacică de la Poiana.* Bucureşti: Vavila Edinf.

Woźniak, Z. (1971). Die Gräberfelder des Latènetypus aus dem Niederdonaugebiet und ihre Beziehungen zu Mitteleuropa. In M. Garašanin, A. Benac, N. Tasić, & G. Novak (Eds.), *Actes du VIIIe congrès international des sciences préhistoriques et protohistoriques: Beograd, 9-15 Septembre 1971* (pp. 250–256). Beograd: Union internationale des sciences préhistoriques et protohistoriques.

Woźniak, Z. (1974). *Wschodnie pogranicze kultury Lateńskiej.* Zakład Narodowy im. Ossolińskich.

Woźniak, Z. (1975). Die Kelten und die Latènekultur auf den Trakischen Gebieten. *Alba Regia, 14*, 177–184.

Woźniak, Z. (1976). Die östliche Randzone der Latène Kultur. *Germania, 54*(2), 382–402.

Annex

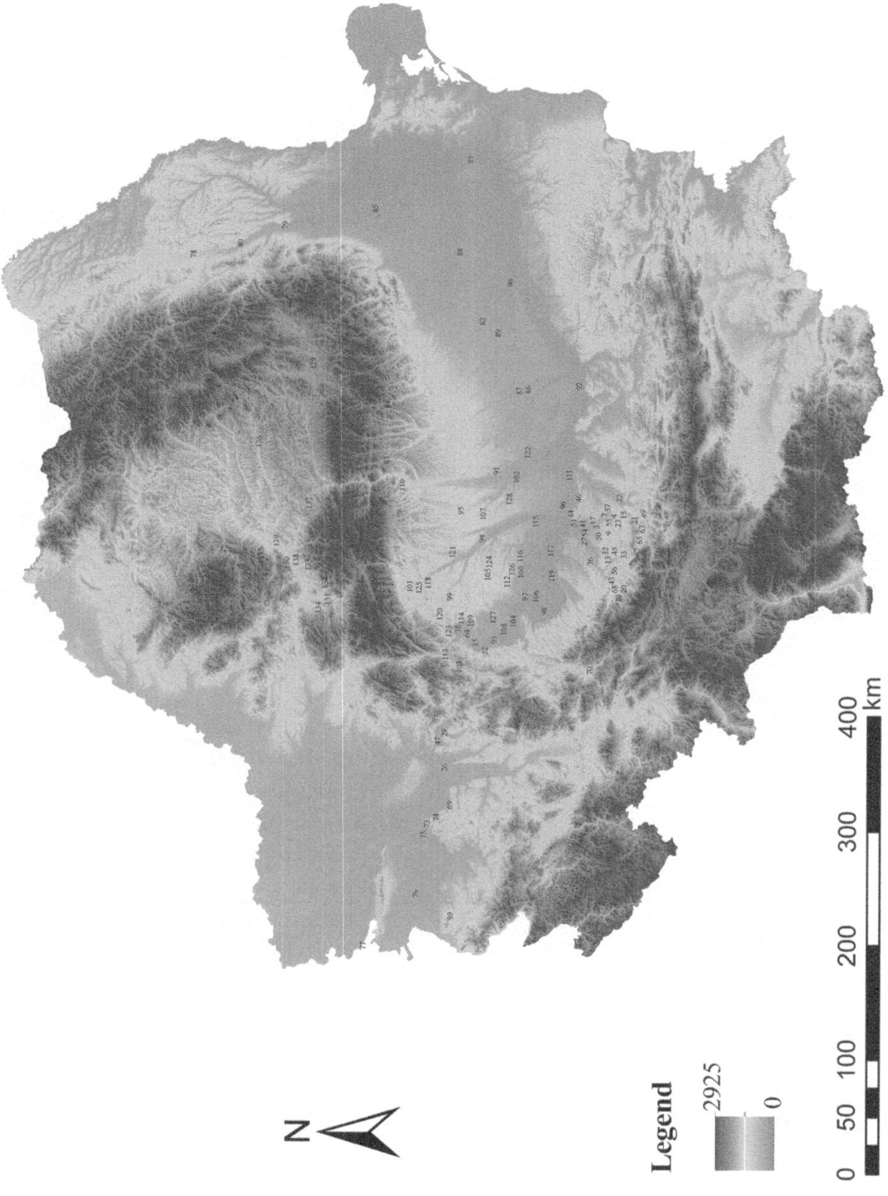

C. N. Popa, *Modelling Identities*, Quantitative Archaeology and Archaeological
Modelling, https://doi.org/10.1007/978-3-319-63267-4

Annex A.1 List of all sites per region. The geographical location of each site is marked on the associated map through the number corresponding to the Map no. column. Several sites are represented on the map by the same number due to their high proximity. Some locations were moved by a small distance to avoid overlapping with other sites

Region	Map no.	Site no.	Location
North-West Thrace	3	1	Altimir
	3	2	Altimir (Bresta)
	3	3	Altimir (Ulovitsa)
	4	4	Barkachevo
	7	5	Biala Slatina
	7	6	Biala Slatina (Liubomir)
	7	7	Biala Slatina (Varha)
	9	8	Borovan
	9	9	Borovan (Ezeroto)
	9	10	Borovan (Tihov Lag)
	50	11	Dobrolevo (Ulovitsa)
	13	12	Dobrusha
	13	13	Dobrusha (Izvoro)
	14	14	Enitsa (Bekrievets)
	15	15	Gabare
	45	16	Galatin (Massurkovoto)
	17	17	Galiche
	17	18	Galiche (Prapora)
	65	19	Gorna Kremena (Pcheshko Hraste)
	20	20	Kalimanitsa
	21	21	Kameno Pole (Ossen)
	22	22	Koinare (Gruia)
	23	23	Komarevo (Kirkov Vrah)
	23	24	Komarevo (Vrachanka)
	26	25	Kostolac
	26	26	Kostolac (Dunavac)
	27	27	Kriva Bara (Manafska Padina)
	41	28	Krushovitsa
	29	29	Kumano (Kusice)
	30	30	Leskovets
	32	31	Lessura
	32	32	Lessura (Varnitsite)
	33	33	Lili(y)ache (Kuklite)
	54	34	Lipnitsa (Starchi Krak)
	35	35	Liubichevats (Bilievina)
	36	36	Madan (Mogilata)
	38	37	Mala Vrabitsa (Aymana)
	38	38	Mala Vrabitsa (Konopishte)
	39	39	Milosevac
	41	40	Mizia
	41	41	Mizia (Rupite)

(continued)

Annex A.1 (continued)

Region	Map no.	Site no.	Location
	41	42	Mizia (Tatarlaka)
	43	43	Montana
	44	44	Ori(y)ahovo (Markov Bair)
	45	45	Ossen
	46	46	Ostrov
	47	47	Ostrovo
	7	48	Popitsa
	49	49	Radovene (Maniovets)
	50	50	Rogozen
	51	51	Saraevo
	52	52	Slatina
	54	53	Sofronievo
	54	54	Sofronievo (Balevi Livadi)
	55	55	Sokolare (Ilievski Geran)
	56	56	Stubel (Pliochata)
	57	57	Tarnak (Selishteto)
	3	58	Tarnava (Devette Mogili)
	3	59	Tarnava (Mitkov Vrah
	3	60	Tarnava (Mitkov Vrah)
	3	61	Tarnava (Pette Mogili)
	63	62	Tsarevets (Kraina Mogila)
	63	63	Tsarevets (Liaskov Dol)
	64	64	Vajuga
	65	65	Varbeshnitsa
	67	66	Vratsa
	67	67	Vratsa (Bistrets quarter)
Central Serbia	69	69	Brestovik
	70	70	Debelice (near Knjazevac)
	73	71	Karaburma
	74	72	Ritopek
	73	73	Rospi Ćuprija
	74	74	Vinča
	75	75	Zemun – Gardoš
Vojvodina	76	76	Gomolava
	77	77	Sotin (Zmajevac)
Moldova	78	78	Brad
	79	79	Poiana
	80	80	Răcătău
Muntenia	81	81	Borduşani
	82	82	Bucureşti (Căţelu-Nou)
	83	83	Cepari
	84	84	Cetăţeni
	85	85	Grădiştea

(continued)

Annex A.1 (continued)

Region	Map no.	Site no.	Location
	86	86	Lăceni
	87	87	Orbeasca de Sus
	88	88	Piscu Crăsani
	89	89	Popeşti
	90	90	Radovanu
	91	91	Teiuşi
	92	92	Zimnicea
Oltenia	93	93	Balta Verde
	94	94	Beharca
	95	95	Blăbeni-Olteţu
	96	96	Călăraşi
	97	97	Cetate
	98	98	Ciupercenii Vechi
	99	99	Corcova
	100	100	Corlate
	101	101	Corneşti (Bălava)
	102	102	Dobrosloveni
	103	103	Dubova
	104	104	Gârla Mică
	105	105	Gogoşiţa
	106	106	Golenţi
	107	107	Gropşani
	108	108	Gruia
	109	109	Hinova
	110	110	Ocniţa
	111	111	Orlea
	112	112	Orodel
	113	113	Orşova
	114	114	Ostrovul Şimian
	115	115	Padea
	116	116	Perişor
	117	117	Plosca
	118	118	Poiana (Gorj)
	119	119	Rastu
	120	120	Siseştii de Jos
	121	121	Spahii
	122	122	Sprâncenata
	123	123	Turnu Severin
	124	124	Urdiniţa
	125	125	Vârţ
	126	126	Vârtopu
	127	127	Viaşu
	128	128	Viişoara Mică

(continued)

Annex A.1 (continued)

Region	Map no.	Site no.	Location
Transylvania	129	129	Ariuşd
	130	130	Blandiana
	131	131	Călan
	132	132	Costeşti - Cetăţuie
	133	133	Cugir
	134	134	Hunedoara – Grădina Castelului
	135	135	Piatra Craivii
	136	136	Sighişoara - Wietenberg
	137	137	Şura Mică
	138	138	Tărtăria
	139	139	Teleac

Annex A.2 Full list of category 1, 2, 3, and 4 values

Category 1	Category 2	Category 3	Category 4
Adornment or clothing accessory	Costume	Bead necklace	Ribbed
Adornment or clothing accessory	Costume	Bead necklace	Simple spherical
Adornment or clothing accessory	Costume	Bead necklace	Tubular
Adornment or clothing accessory	Costume	Bead necklace	With eyes
Adornment or clothing accessory	Costume	Belt	Belt type 1
Adornment or clothing accessory	Costume	Belt	Belt type 2
Adornment or clothing accessory	Costume	Belt	Belt type 3
Adornment or clothing accessory	Costume	Belt	Belt type 4
Adornment or clothing accessory	Costume	Belt	Belt type 5
Adornment or clothing accessory	Costume	Bracelet	Bracelet type 1
Adornment or clothing accessory	Costume	Bracelet	Bracelet type 2
Adornment or clothing accessory	Costume	Bracelet	Bracelet type 3
Adornment or clothing accessory	Costume	Bracelet	Bracelet type 4
Adornment or clothing accessory	Costume	Bracelet	Bracelet type 5
Adornment or clothing accessory	Costume	Bracelet	Bracelet type 6
Adornment or clothing accessory	Costume	Bracelet	Bracelet type 7
Adornment or clothing accessory	Costume	Bracelet	Bracelet type 8
Adornment or clothing accessory	Costume	Earring	Earring type 1
Adornment or clothing accessory	Costume	Earring	Earring type 2
Adornment or clothing accessory	Costume	Fibula	Fibula type 1
Adornment or clothing accessory	Costume	Fibula	Fibula type 2
Adornment or clothing accessory	Costume	Fibula	Fibula type 3
Adornment or clothing accessory	Costume	Fibula	Fibula type 4
Adornment or clothing accessory	Costume	Fibula	Fibula type 6
Adornment or clothing accessory	Costume	Fibula	Fibula type 7

(continued)

Annex A.2 (continued)

Category 1	Category 2	Category 3	Category 4
Adornment or clothing accessory	Costume	Fibula	Fibula type 8
Adornment or clothing accessory	Costume	Fibula	Fibula type 10
Adornment or clothing accessory	Costume	Fibula	Fibula type 11
Adornment or clothing accessory	Costume	Fibula	Fibula type 13
Adornment or clothing accessory	Costume	Fibula	Fibula type 16
Adornment or clothing accessory	Costume	Fibula	Fibula type 17
Adornment or clothing accessory	Costume	Fibula	Fibula type 19
Adornment or clothing accessory	Costume	Fibula	Fibula type 20
Adornment or clothing accessory	Costume	Fibula	Fibula type 28
Adornment or clothing accessory	Costume	Fibula	Fibula type 30
Adornment or clothing accessory	Costume	Fibula	Fibula type Gomolava
Adornment or clothing accessory	Costume	Fibula	Fibula type Vinkovci
Adornment or clothing accessory	Costume	Lunar necklace	Lunar necklace
Adornment or clothing accessory	Costume	Pendant necklace	Axe pendant
Adornment or clothing accessory	Costume	Pendant necklace	Bucket pendant
Adornment or clothing accessory	Costume	Pendant necklace	Effigy pendant
Adornment or clothing accessory	Costume	Pendant necklace	Profiled bar pendant
Adornment or clothing accessory	Costume	Pendant necklace	Rings pendant
Adornment or clothing accessory	Costume	Ring	Ring
Adornment or clothing accessory	Costume	Torque	Simple
Adornment or clothing accessory	Costume	Torque	Spiralled
Adornment or clothing accessory	Costume	Torque	Twisted
Adornment or clothing accessory	Toiletry	Mirror	Mirror
Adornment or clothing accessory	Toiletry	Razor	Razor
Coin	Coin	Coin	Dinar
Coin	Coin	Coin	Histrian
Coin	Coin	Coin	Local emission
Horse gear	Parade	Harness	Zoomorphic
Horse gear	Parade	Wagon	Wagon
Horse gear	Parade	Phalera	Phalera type 1
Horse gear	Parade	Phalera	Phalera type 2
Horse gear	Riding	Buckle (hg)	Rectangular
Horse gear	Riding	Horse bit	Horse bit type 4
Horse gear	Riding	Horse bit	Horse bit type 5
Horse gear	Riding	Horse bit	Horse bit type 8
Horse gear	Riding	Horse bit	Horse bit type 13
Horse gear	Riding	Horse bit	Horse bit type 14
Horse gear	Riding	Horse bit	Horse bit type 15
Horse gear	Riding	Horse bit	Horse bit type 16
Horse gear	Riding	Horse bit	Horse bit type 17
Horse gear	Riding	Spur	Spur type 1
Horse gear	Riding	Spur	Spur type 2

(continued)

Annex A.2 (continued)

Category 1	Category 2	Category 3	Category 4
Other	Figurine	Anthropomorphic	Anthropomorphic
Tool	Agriculture	Grinding stone	Grinding stone
Tool	Agriculture	Sickle	Sickle
Tool	Cutting	Axe	Axe
Tool	Cutting	Knife	Knife
Tool	Cutting	Scissors	Scissors type 1
Tool	Cutting	Scissors	Scissors type 2
Tool	Metalworking	Crucible	Crucible
Tool	Perforating	Awl	Awl
Tool	Perforating	Nail	Nail
Tool	Perforating	Needle	Needle
Tool	Perforating	Skewer	Skewer
Tool	Sharpening	Sharpening stone	Sharpening stone
Tool	Weaving	Spindle whorl	Spindle whorl
Unidentified object			
Vessels and vessel implements	Drinking	Cups and tumblers	Cup type 1
Vessels and vessel implements	Drinking	Cups and tumblers	Cup type 2
Vessels and vessel implements	Drinking	Cups and tumblers	Cup type 3
Vessels and vessel implements	Drinking	Cups and tumblers	Pedestalled cup
Vessels and vessel implements	Drinking	Cups and tumblers	Tumbler
Vessels and vessel implements	Drinking	Drinking implements	Simpulum
Vessels and vessel implements	Drinking	Jugs	Round belly jugs
Vessels and vessel implements	Drinking	Jugs	Rhombic belly short-necked jugs
Vessels and vessel implements	Drinking	Jugs	Rhombic belly straight-necked jugs
Vessels and vessel implements	Drinking	Kantharos-like vessels	Kantharos type 1
Vessels and vessel implements	Drinking	Kantharos-like vessels	Kantharos type 2
Vessels and vessel implements	Drinking	Kantharos-like vessels	Kantharos type 3
Vessels and vessel implements	Drinking	Kantharos-like vessels	Kantharos type 4
Vessels and vessel implements	Drinking	Pitchers	Pitcher type 1
Vessels and vessel implements	Drinking	Pitchers	Pitcher type 2
Vessels and vessel implements	Drinking	Situlae and cauldrons	Situla

(continued)

Annex A.2 (continued)

Category 1	Category 2	Category 3	Category 4
Vessels and vessel implements	Drinking	Situlae and cauldrons	Small cauldron
Vessels and vessel implements	Eating and cooking	Bowls and porringers	Bowl
Vessels and vessel implements	Eating and cooking	Bowls and porringers	Porringer type 1
Vessels and vessel implements	Eating and cooking	Bowls and porringers	Porringer type 2
Vessels and vessel implements	Eating and cooking	Bowls and porringers	Porringer type 3
Vessels and vessel implements	Eating and cooking	Bowls and porringers	Porringer type 4
Vessels and vessel implements	Eating and cooking	EC implements	Fork
Vessels and vessel implements	Eating and cooking	EC implements	Patera
Vessels and vessel implements	Eating and cooking	Fruit-bowls	Fruit-bowl type 1
Vessels and vessel implements	Eating and cooking	Fruit-bowls	Fruit-bowl type 2
Vessels and vessel implements	Eating and cooking	Fruit-bowls	Fruit-bowl type 3
Vessels and vessel implements	Eating and cooking	Fruit-bowls	Fruit-bowl type 4
Vessels and vessel implements	Eating and cooking	Plates and trays	Plate
Vessels and vessel implements	Eating and cooking	Plates and trays	Tray
Vessels and vessel implements	Lighting	Small lighting vessels	Cup (VL)
Vessels and vessel implements	Lighting	Small lighting vessels	Tumbler (VL)
Vessels and vessel implements	Storage	Amphorae	Amphora
Vessels and vessel implements	Storage	Jars	Jar type 1
Vessels and vessel implements	Storage	Jars	Jar type 2
Vessels and vessel implements	Storage	Pots	Pot type 1
Vessels and vessel implements	Storage	Pots	Pot type 2
Vessels and vessel implements	Storage	Pots	Pot type 3
Vessels and vessel implements	Storage	Small pots	Small pot type 1
Vessels and vessel implements	Storage	Small pots	Small pot type 2
Vessels and vessel implements	Storage	Small pots	Small pot type 3
Weapons	Costume (W)	Belt chain	Belt chain
Weapons	Defensive	Chainmail	Chainmail
Weapons	Defensive	Helmet	Helmet type 1
Weapons	Defensive	Helmet	Helmet type 2

(continued)

Annex A.2 (continued)

Category 1	Category 2	Category 3	Category 4
Weapons	Defensive	Shield	Shield type 1
Weapons	Defensive	Shield	Shield type 2
Weapons	Defensive	Shield	Shield type 3
Weapons	Hunting	Arrowhead (WH)	Arrowhead (WH)
Weapons	Offensive	Arrowhead	Arrowhead
Weapons	Offensive	Battle knife	Battle knife type 1
Weapons	Offensive	Battle knife	Battle knife type 2
Weapons	Offensive	Battle knife	Battle knife type 3
Weapons	Offensive	Battle knife	Battle knife type 4
Weapons	Offensive	Sauroter	Sauroter
Weapons	Offensive	Spear	Spear type 1
Weapons	Offensive	Spear	Spear type 2
Weapons	Offensive	Spear	Spear type 3
Weapons	Offensive	Spear	Spear type 4
Weapons	Offensive	Spear	Spear type 5
Weapons	Offensive	Sword	Sword type 1
Weapons	Offensive	Sword	Sword type 2

Annex A.3 List of values and their labels taken by the variables used to describe the burials

Variable	Value	Label
Supra-group	1	Eastern
	2	Western
Country	1	Bulgaria
	2	Romania
	3	Serbia
Region	1	Central Serbia
	2	Moldova
	3	Muntenia
	4	North-West Thrace
	5	Oltenia
	6	Transylvania
	7	Vojvodina
Grave type	1	Construction
	2	Flat
	3	Tumulus
Ritual type	1	Cenotaph
	2	Cremation
	3	Inhumation
Multiple burials	0	No
	1	Yes
River proximity	1	Banks

(continued)

Annex A.3 (continued)

Variable	Value	Label
	2	Far
	3	Near
	4	unknown
Settlement proximity	1	Far
	2	Inside
	3	Near
	4	Unknown
Age	1	Adolescent
	2	Adult
	3	Child
	4	Elder
	5	Newborn
	6	Unknown
Sex	1	Female
	2	Male
	3	Unknown
Object category 1	2	Adornment or clothing accessory
	3	Coin
	4	Horse gear
	5	Tool
	6	Vessel or vessel implement
	7	Weapon
Object category 2	2	Agriculture
	3	Coin
	4	Costume
	5	Costume (W)
	6	Cutting
	7	Defensive
	8	Drinking
	9	Eating and cooking
	10	Hunting
	11	Lighting
	12	Metalworking
	13	Offensive
	14	Parade
	15	Perforating
	16	Riding
	17	Sharpening
	18	Storage
	19	Toiletry
	20	Weaving

(continued)

Annex A.3 (continued)

Variable	Value	Label
Object category 3	2	Amphora
	3	Arrowhead
	4	Arrowhead (WH)
	5	Awl
	6	Axe
	7	Battle knife
	8	Bead necklace
	9	Belt
	10	Belt chain
	11	Bowls and porringers
	12	Bracelet
	13	Buckle (HG)
	14	Chainmail
	15	Coin
	16	Crucible
	17	Cups and tumblers
	18	Drinking implements
	19	Earring
	20	EC implements
	21	Fibula
	22	Fruit-bowls
	23	Grinding stone
	24	Harness
	25	Helmet
	26	Horse bit
	27	Jars
	28	Jugs
	29	Kantharos-like vessels
	30	Knife
	31	Lunar necklace
	32	Mirror
	33	Nail
	34	Needle
	35	Pendant necklace
	36	Phalera
	37	Pitchers
	38	Plates and trays
	39	Pots
	40	Razor
	41	Ring
	42	Sauroter
	43	Scissors

(continued)

Annex A.3 (continued)

Variable	Value	Label
	44	Sharpening stone
	45	Shield
	46	Sickle
	47	Situlae and cauldrons
	48	Skewer
	49	Small lighting vessels
	50	Small pots
	51	Spear
	52	Spindle whorl
	53	Spur
	54	Sword
	55	Torque
	56	Wagon
Object category 4	2	Amphora
	3	Arrowhead
	4	Arrowhead (WH)
	5	Awl
	6	Axe
	7	Axe pendant
	8	Battle knife type 1
	9	Battle knife type 2
	10	Battle knife type 3
	11	Battle knife type 4
	12	Belt chain
	13	Belt type 1
	14	Belt type 2
	15	Belt type 3
	16	Belt type 4
	17	Belt type 5
	18	Bowl
	19	Bracelet type 1
	20	Bracelet type 2
	21	Bracelet type 3
	22	Bracelet type 4
	23	Bracelet type 5
	24	Bracelet type 6
	25	Bracelet type 7
	26	Bracelet type 8
	27	Bucket pendant
	28	Chainmail
	29	Crucible
	30	Cup (VL)

(continued)

Annex A.3 (continued)

Variable	Value	Label
	31	Cup type 1
	32	Cup type 2
	33	Cup type 3
	34	Dinar
	35	Earring type 1
	36	Earring type 2
	37	Effigy pendant
	38	Fibula type 1
	39	Fibula type 10
	40	Fibula type 11
	41	Fibula type 16
	42	Fibula type 17
	43	Fibula type 19
	44	Fibula type 2
	45	Fibula type 20
	46	Fibula type 28
	47	Fibula type 3
	48	Fibula type 30
	49	Fibula type 4
	50	Fibula type 6
	51	Fibula type 7
	52	Fibula type Gomolava
	53	Fibula type Vinkovci
	54	Fork
	55	Fruit-bowl type 1
	56	Fruit-bowl type 2
	57	Fruit-bowl type 3
	58	Fruit-bowl type 4
	59	Grinding stone
	60	Helmet type 1
	61	Helmet type 2
	62	Histrian
	63	Horse bit type 13
	64	Horse bit type 14
	65	Horse bit type 15
	66	Horse bit type 16
	67	Horse bit type 17
	68	Horse bit type 4
	69	Horse bit type 5
	70	Horse bit type 8
	71	Jar type 1
	72	Jar type 2

(continued)

Annex A.3 (continued)

Variable	Value	Label
	73	Kantharos type 1
	74	Kantharos type 2
	75	Kantharos type 3
	76	Kantharos type 4
	77	Knife
	78	Local emission
	79	Lunar necklace
	80	Mirror
	81	Nail
	82	Needle
	83	Patera
	84	Pedestalled cup
	85	Phalera type 1
	86	Phalera type 2
	87	Pitcher type 1
	88	Pitcher type 2
	89	Plate
	90	Porringer type 1
	91	Porringer type 2
	92	Porringer type 3
	93	Porringer type 4
	94	Pot type 1
	95	Pot type 2
	96	Pot type 3
	97	Profiled bar pendant
	98	Razor
	99	Rectangular
	100	Rhombic belly short-necked jugs
	101	Rhombic belly straight-necked jugs
	102	Ribbed
	103	Ring
	104	Rings pendant
	105	Round belly jugs
	106	Sauroter
	107	Scissors type 1
	108	Scissors type 2
	109	Sharpening stone
	110	Shield type 1
	111	Shield type 2
	112	Shield type 3
	113	Sickle
	114	Simple

(continued)

Annex A.3 (continued)

Variable	Value	Label
	115	Simple spherical
	116	Simpulum
	117	Situla
	118	Skewer
	119	Small cauldron
	120	Small pot type 1
	121	Small pot type 2
	122	Small pot type 3
	123	Spear type 1
	124	Spear type 2
	125	Spear type 3
	126	Spear type 4
	127	spear type 5
	128	Spindle whorl
	129	Spiralled
	130	Spur type 1
	131	Spur type 2
	132	Sword type 1
	133	Sword type 2
	134	Tray
	135	Tubular
	136	Tumbler
	137	Tumbler (VL)
	138	Twisted
	139	Wagon
	140	With eyes
	141	Zoomorphic
Material	2	Bone
	3	Bronze
	4	Bronze and amber
	5	Bronze and glass
	6	Bronze and iron
	7	Clay
	8	Glass
	9	Glass and amber
	10	Gold
	11	Iron
	12	Not stated
	13	Other
	14	Silver
	15	Stone

Annex A.4 Table displays all employed burial data and contains the variables utilized in the clustering procedure with additional variables used in the interpretation, as well as the PAM group and supra-group membership. Each row corresponds to a grave-good entry. Since many graves included multiple objects, the variables which do not refer to grave-goods contain the same information for each entry of the same grave, for which reason their values are not repeated. In order to allow for all variables values to be displayed in printed form, they were numerically encoded. For *Chronology Start* and *Chronology End* negative values correspond to BC dates, while positive values represent AD dates

Grave number	Supra-group	PAM group	Country	Region	Location	Grave type	Ritual type	Multiple burials	River proximity	Settlement proximity	Latitude	Longitude	Age	Sex	Chronology start	Chronology end	Object category 1	Object category 2	Object category 3	Object category 4	Material
167	NA	2	1	4	Altimir	3	2	0	3	3	43.533	23.817	6	3	−150	−25	2	4	12	19	3
																	4	16	26	66	11
																	7	13	7	8	11
170	2	5	1	4	Altimir	3	2	0	3	3	43.533	23.817	6	3	−150	−25	7	13	54	133	11
																	7	13	51	NA	11
																	7	13	7	NA	11
																	4	16	26	66	11
																	6	NA	NA	NA	7
																	7	7	45	NA	11
172	NA	2	1	4	Altimir	2	2	0	3	3	43.533	23.817	6	3	−150	−25	2	4	21	NA	3
																	6	NA	NA	NA	7
																	7	5	10	12	3
350	2	4	1	4	Altimir	3	2	0	3	3	43.533	23.817	6	3	−270	−20	7	13	7	NA	11
																	7	13	54	NA	11
																	4	16	26	NA	11
171	2	4	1	4	Altimir (Bresta)	3	2	0	3	3	43.533	23.817	6	3	−150	−25	4	16	13	99	11
																	4	16	26	66	11
																	7	13	51	127	11
																	7	13	7	8	11
																	6	8	37	88	7
351	NA	7	1	4	Altimir (Bresta)	3	2	0	3	3	43.533	23.817	6	3	−270	−20	6	8	17	33	7

																	6	8	17	33	7
																	6	8	28	101	7
																	6	9	11	93	7
168	2	4	1	4	Altimir (Ulovitsa)	3	2	0	3	3	43:533	23.817	6	3	−150	−25	2	4	21	44	11
																	6	NA	NA	NA	7
																	7	13	54	133	11
169	2	4	1	4	Altimir (Ulovitsa)	3	2	0	3	3	43.533	23.817	6	3	−150	−25	7	13	54	132	11
																	7	13	7	8	11
																	2	4	21	44	3
																	6	NA	NA	NA	7
238	NA	2	2	6	Ariuşd	2	2	0	3	3	45.788	25.666	6	3	0	100	2	4	21	43	3
																	5	6	30	77	11
																	6	8	17	NA	7
																	7	10	4	4	11
243	2	4	2	5	Balta Verde	2	2	0	3	4	44.34	22.573	6	3	−150	0	7	13	54	132	11
																	7	13	51	124	11
																	7	NA	NA	NA	11
173	2	4	1	4	Barkachevo	3	2	0	3	3	43.400	23.933	6	3	−155	−25	7	13	54	NA	11
																	7	13	7	NA	11
																	4	16	26	NA	11
262	2	4	2	5	Beharca	2	2	0	3	4	44.447	23.682	6	3	−120	−50	4	16	13	99	11
																	4	16	26	69	11
																	7	13	54	132	11
																	7	13	51	124	11
263	2	6	2	5	Beharca	2	2	0	3	4	44.447	23.682	6	3	−150	0	7	13	54	NA	11
176	2	6	1	4	Biala Slatina	2	2	0	3	3	43.469	23.945	6	3	−270	−20	4	16	26	NA	11

(continued)

Annex A.4 (continued)

Grave number	Supra-group	PAM group	Country	Region	Location	Grave type	Ritual type	Multiple burials	River proximity	Settlement proximity	Latitude	Longitude	Age	Sex	Chronology start	Chronology end	Object category 1	Object category 2	Object category 3	Object category 4	Material
																	6	NA	NA	NA	7
																	7	13	54	NA	11
174	NA	NA	1	4	Biala Slatina (Liubomir)	3	2	0	3	3	43.469	23.945	6	3	−155	−25	4	16	26	64	11
																	4	16	26	NA	11
																	4	14	36	85	3
																	4	14	36	86	3
175	NA	NA	1	4	Biala Slatina (Varha)	3	2	0	3	1	43.469	23.945	6	3	−155	−25	4	NA	NA	NA	11
																	4	14	36	NA	3
240	2	6	2	5	Blăbeni–Olteţu	2	2	0	3	4	44.616	23.983	6	3	−150	0	6	NA	NA	NA	7
																	7	13	54	132	11
129	2	4	2	6	Blandiana	2	2	0	1	1	45.967	23.383	6	3	−175	−50	4	16	13	99	11
																	4	16	26	66	11
																	7	13	7	8	11
																	7	13	51	123	11
																	6	NA	NA	NA	7
																	6	8	28	NA	7
																	6	18	NA	NA	7
100	NA	7	2	3	Borduşani	2	3	0	1	2	44.483	27.905	1	3	−100	0	6	9	22	NA	7
353	2	5	1	4	Borovan	2	2	0	3	3	43.433	23.75	6	3	−155	−25	7	13	51	NA	11
																	7	13	51	NA	11
																	7	13	54	NA	11
																	7	7	45	NA	11
177	2	5	1	4	Borovan (Ezeroto)	3	2	0	3	3	43.433	23.75	6	3	−155	−25	2	4	55	138	14

																	4	16	26	66	11
																	7	7	45	110	11
																	7	13	54	133	11
352	2	4	1	4	Borovan (Tihov Lag)	2	2	0	3	3	43.433	23.75	6	3	−270	−20	7	13	51	NA	11
																	7	13	54	NA	11
																	4	16	26	NA	11
1	1	1	2	2	Brad	3	3	1	3	3	46.726	26.965	6	3	0	100	2	4	8	115	8
2	1	1	2	2	Brad	3	3	1	3	3	46.726	26.965	6	3	0	100	2	4	8	115	8
15	1	1	2	2	Brad	2	3	1	3	2	46.726	26.952	2	1	0	100	2	4	8	115	8
16	1	3	2	2	Brad	2	3	1	3	2	46.726	26.952	3	3	0	100	NA	NA	NA	NA	NA
17	NA	2	2	2	Brad	2	3	1	3	2	46.726	26.952	3	3	0	100	2	4	35	97	3
																	2	4	35	27	11
18	1	1	2	2	Brad	2	3	1	3	2	46.726	26.952	3	3	0	100	2	4	35	27	11
19	NA	2	2	2	Brad	2	3	1	3	2	46.726	26.952	3	3	0	100	2	4	35	27	11
																	2	4	21	45	11
20	1	3	2	2	Brad	2	3	1	3	2	46.726	26.952	3	3	0	100	NA	NA	NA	NA	NA
21	1	3	2	2	Brad	2	3	0	3	2	46.726	26.952	3	3	0	100	NA	NA	NA	NA	NA
22	1	1	2	2	Brad	2	3	1	3	2	46.726	26.952	3	3	0	100	5	12	16	29	13
																	5	12	16	29	13
																	2	4	35	27	11
23	NA	2	2	2	Brad	2	3	1	3	2	46.726	26.952	3	3	0	100	2	4	21	45	3
																	2	4	35	97	3
24	NA	2	2	2	Brad	2	3	0	3	2	46.726	26.952	3	3	0	100	2	4	35	27	11
																	2	4	8	115	8
25	1	3	2	2	Brad	2	3	0	3	2	46.726	26.952	6	3	0	100	NA	NA	NA	NA	NA
26	1	1	2	2	Brad	2	3	0	3	2	46.726	26.952	2	3	0	100	5	15	33	81	11
																	5	15	33	81	11

(continued)

Annex A.4 (continued)

Grave number	Supra-group	PAM group	Country	Region	Location	Grave type	Ritual type	Multiple burials	River proximity	Settlement proximity	Latitude	Longitude	Age	Sex	Chronology start	Chronology end	Object category 1	Object category 2	Object category 3	Object category 4	Material
																	6	18	27	71	7
																	6	18	27	71	7
																	2	4	12	21	3
																	5	NA	NA	NA	13
27	1	1	2	2	Brad	2	3	0	3	2	46.726	26.952	2	3	0	100	2	4	19	36	3
																	5	2	23	59	15
130	NA	7	2	2	Brad	3	2	0	3	3	46.726	26.965	6	3	0	100	5	17	44	109	15
																	6	NA	NA	NA	7
																	6	8	28	105	7
131	NA	2	2	2	Brad	3	2	1	3	3	46.726	26.965	6	3	0	100	2	4	NA	NA	3
																	2	4	9	16	3
																	6	NA	NA	NA	3
																	6	NA	NA	NA	3
																	7	10	4	4	11
132	NA	7	2	2	Brad	2	2	0	3	3	46.726	26.965	6	3	0	100	6	8	29	73	7
																	6	8	17	84	7
																	6	8	17	136	8
																	6	8	28	105	7
																	5	17	44	109	15
																	6	9	38	89	7
341	NA	NA	2	2	Brad	3	1	0	3	3	46.726	26.965	6	3	0	100	NA	NA	NA	NA	NA
293	2	5	3	1	Brestovik	2	2	0	1	4	44.653	20.754	6	3	−100	−25	7	13	7	10	11
																	7	13	51	125	11
																	7	13	51	125	11
																	5	17	44	109	15

101	1	3	2	3	București (Cățelu-Nou)	2	3	0	4	2	44.433	26.1	5	3	−200	0	NA	NA	NA	NA	NA
165	2	5	2	6	Călan	3	2	0	3	4	45.733	22.983	6	3	−100	0	4	16	26	66	11
																	4	16	26	66	11
																	4	16	26	66	11
																	7	13	7	8	11
																	7	13	54	NA	11
																	7	13	51	123	11
241	2	4	2	5	Călărași	2	2	0	3	4	43.800	24.050	6	3	−150	0	7	13	7	8	11
																	7	13	51	123	11
																	7	13	51	123	11
133	NA	2	2	3	Cepari	2	2	0	3	4	45.208	24.551	6	3	−100	−50	2	4	8	NA	8
																	2	4	21	49	3
																	4	NA	NA	NA	11
																	5	6	30	77	11
134	1	1	2	3	Cepari	2	2	0	3	4	45.208	24.551	6	3	−150	−50	2	4	12	NA	8
																	4	NA	NA	NA	11
																	5	6	30	77	11
135	1	3	2	3	Cepari	2	2	0	3	4	45.208	24.551	6	3	−150	−50	NA	NA	NA	NA	NA
242	2	4	2	5	Cetate	2	2	1	3	4	44.100	23.050	6	3	−150	0	7	13	54	NA	11
																	7	13	7	8	11
																	7	13	51	123	11
136	NA	2	2	3	Cetățeni	1	2	0	1	3	45.200	25.183	6	3	−150	−100	2	4	8	NA	8
																	2	4	12	NA	2
																	2	4	8	NA	8
																	6	NA	NA	NA	7
																	6	NA	NA	NA	7

(continued)

Annex A.4 (continued)

Grave number	Supra-group	PAM group	Country	Region	Location	Grave type	Ritual type	Multiple burials	River proximity	Settlement proximity	Latitude	Longitude	Age	Sex	Chronology start	Chronology end	Object category 1	Object category 2	Object category 3	Object category 4	Material
																	2	NA	NA	NA	10
																	6	18	2	2	7
																	7	7	14	28	11
137	1	1	2	3	Cetăţeni	1	2	0	1	3	45.200	25.183	6	3	0	100	2	4	21	43	3
244	NA	7	2	5	Ciupercenii Vechi	2	2	0	3	4	43.942	22.897	6	3	−200	0	6	8	29	74	7
245	2	5	2	5	Corcova	2	2	0	3	4	44.697	23.037	6	3	−150	0	7	13	7	8	11
																	7	13	54	NA	11
																	7	13	51	NA	11
																	2	4	21	NA	3
																	6	NA	NA	NA	7
246	2	5	2	5	Corlate	2	2	0	3	4	44.177	23.316	6	3	−150	−50	2	4	21	44	11
																	7	5	10	12	11
																	7	7	45	111	11
																	7	13	54	132	11
247	1	3	2	5	Corlate	2	2	0	3	4	44.177	23.316	6	3	−150	0	NA	NA	NA	NA	NA
248	2	6	2	5	Corlate	2	2	0	3	3	44.177	23.316	6	3	−150	0	6	NA	NA	NA	7
																	7	13	51	123	11
249	1	3	2	5	Corlate	2	2	0	3	3	44.177	23.316	6	3	−150	0	NA	NA	NA	NA	NA
250	2	5	2	5	Corneşti (Bălava)	2	2	0	1	4	44.995	23.145	6	3	−150	0	7	13	54	132	11
																	7	13	7	8	11
																	7	13	51	123	11
																	7	7	45	NA	11

347	2	5	2	6	Costeşti Cetăţuie	3	1	0	2	3	45.700	23.167	6	3	50	100	6	8	17	NA	7
																	6	8	28	NA	7
																	7	13	7	NA	11
																	7	13	7	NA	11
																	7	13	51	NA	11
																	2	4	9	NA	11
																	3	3	15	62	3
																	4	14	56	139	11
																	6	NA	NA	NA	3
																	6	9	22	NA	7
138	NA	2	2	6	Cugir	3	2	0	3	3	45.833	23.367	6	3	−100	0	2	4	8	NA	3
																	2	4	21	NA	11
																	6	NA	NA	NA	7
																	6	9	22	NA	7
139	2	5	2	6	Cugir	3	2	0	3	3	45.833	23.367	6	3	−100	−50	2	4	NA	NA	14
																	2	4	21	44	14
																	4	14	24	141	10
																	4	14	56	139	13
																	4	16	26	66	11
																	4	16	26	66	11
																	4	16	26	66	11
																	7	7	14	28	11
																	7	7	45	110	11
																	7	7	25	60	11
																	7	13	54	NA	11
																	7	13	51	NA	11

(continued)

Annex A.4 (continued)

Grave number	Supra-group	PAM group	Country	Region	Location	Grave type	Ritual type	Multiple burials	River proximity	Settlement proximity	Latitude	Longitude	Age	Sex	Chronology start	Chronology end	Object category 1	Object category 2	Object category 3	Object category 4	Material
																	7	13	7	NA	11
																	6	NA	NA	NA	7
																	6	8	47	117	3
																	6	9	22	NA	7
140	2	4	2	6	Cugir	3	2	0	3	3	45.833	23.367	6	3	−100	0	7	13	51	NA	11
																	7	13	7	NA	11
																	6	NA	NA	NA	7
																	6	9	22	NA	7
292	2	4	3	1	Debelice (near Knjazevac)	2	2	0	4	4	43.571	22.265	6	3	−100	−25	7	13	54	132	11
																	7	13	51	123	11
																	2	4	21	44	3
354	2	4	1	4	Dobrolevo (Ulovitsa)	2	2	0	3	3	43.5	23.783	6	3	−155	−25	7	13	51	NA	11
																	7	13	54	133	11
251	2	5	2	5	Dobrosloveni	2	2	0	3	4	44.173	24.356	6	3	−150	0	7	13	51	NA	11
																	7	13	54	133	11
																	7	13	51	NA	11
																	4	16	26	69	11
																	7	7	45	NA	11
178	2	5	1	4	Dobrusha	2	2	0	3	1	43.414	23.426	6	3	−155	−25	7	13	54	NA	11
																	7	13	7	NA	11
																	4	16	26	NA	11
																	7	7	45	NA	11
355	2	5	1	4	Dobrusha (Izvoro)	3	2	0	3	3	43.440	23.464	6	3	−155	−25	4	16	53	130	11

																	4	16	26	66	11
																	7	13	51	127	11
																	7	13	51	125	11
																	7	13	7	8	11
																	7	13	54	133	11
																	7	13	7	8	11
																	7	5	10	12	11
																	7	7	45	NA	11
239	2	5	2	5	Dubova	2	2	0	3	4	44.615	22.27	6	3	−150	0	4	16	26	66	11
																	4	16	53	130	11
																	7	13	51	123	11
																	7	13	7	9	11
																	7	13	7	8	11
																	2	4	12	22	14
																	7	7	45	110	11
179	NA	7	1	4	Enitsa (Bekrievets)	3	2	0	3	3	43.383	24.067	6	3	−270	−20	6	8	28	105	7
																	6	8	17	31	7
																	6	8	17	31	7
																	6	18	39	95	7
356	2	5	1	4	Gabare	2	2	0	3	3	43.317	23.917	6	3	−270	−20	7	13	54	NA	11
																	7	13	51	NA	11
																	6	NA	NA	NA	7
																	7	7	45	NA	11
180	2	5	1	4	Galatin	3	2	0	3	3	43.417	23.533	6	3	−270	−20	7	13	51	123	11
																	7	13	54	133	11
																	7	13	7	8	11

(continued)

Annex A.4 (continued)

Grave number	Supra-group	PAM group	Country	Region	Location	Grave type	Ritual type	Multiple burials	River proximity	Settlement proximity	Latitude	Longitude	Age	Sex	Chronology start	Chronology end	Object category 1	Object category 2	Object category 3	Object category 4	Material
																	2	4	NA	NA	3
																	4	16	26	66	11
181	2	4	1	4	Galiche	2	2	0	3	3	43.561	23.880	6	3	−270	−20	7	13	7	NA	11
																	7	13	51	NA	11
																	6	NA	NA	NA	7
182	2	4	1	4	Galiche	2	2	0	3	3	43.564	23.842	6	3	−270	−20	7	13	51	NA	11
																	7	13	54	NA	11
																	4	16	26	NA	11
																	6	18	2	2	7
339	2	5	1	4	Galiche	3	2	0	3	3	43.559	23.867	6	3	−155	−25	4	16	13	NA	11
																	4	16	53	NA	11
																	4	16	26	NA	11
																	7	13	51	127	11
																	7	13	7	NA	11
																	7	13	54	133	11
																	2	4	21	NA	12
																	7	7	45	NA	11
183	2	5	1	4	Galiche (Prapora)	2	2	0	3	3	43.560	23.831	6	3	−150	−27	7	13	51	NA	11
																	7	13	54	133	11
																	4	16	26	NA	11
																	6	18	39	96	7
																	7	7	45	NA	11
252	2	6	2	5	Gârla Mică	2	2	0	3	4	44.206	22.780	6	3	−150	0	7	13	54	132	11
253	2	4	2	5	Gogoşiţa	2	2	0	3	4	44.400	23.356	6	3	−150	0	7	13	54	133	11

																	7	13	54	132	11
																	7	13	51	NA	11
254	2	4	2	5	Golenţi	2	2	0	3	4	44.013	23.055	6	3	−150	0	7	13	7	8	11
																	7	13	51	125	11
126	1	1	3	7	Gomolava	2	3	1	1	2	44.887	19.747	2	2	−25	0	6	8	29	75	7
																	6	8	29	74	7
																	6	8	17	31	7
																	6	18	27	72	7
																	6	18	27	72	7
																	6	18	39	94	7
																	6	18	50	122	7
																	6	18	27	72	7
																	2	4	21	52	3
127	1	1	3	7	Gomolava	2	3	1	1	2	44.887	19.747	2	1	−25	0	6	8	17	31	7
																	6	8	29	74	7
																	6	8	29	75	7
																	6	18	27	72	7
																	6	18	27	72	7
																	6	18	27	72	7
																	6	18	39	94	7
																	6	18	50	122	7
																	2	4	21	52	3
128	1	1	3	7	Gomolava	2	3	1	1	2	44.887	19.747	3	3	−25	0	6	8	29	74	7
																	6	8	17	31	7
																	6	8	29	75	7
																	6	18	50	122	7
																	6	18	39	94	7

(continued)

Annex A.4 (continued)

Grave number	Supra-group	PAM group	Country	Region	Location	Grave type	Ritual type	Multiple burials	River proximity	Settlement proximity	Latitude	Longitude	Age	Sex	Chronology start	Chronology end	Object category 1	Object category 2	Object category 3	Object category 4	Material
																	6	18	27	72	7
																	6	18	27	72	7
																	6	18	27	72	7
																	2	4	21	52	3
184	2	6	1	4	Gorna Kremena	3	2	0	3	3	43.186	23.712	6	3	−270	−20	5	17	44	109	15
																	6	NA	NA	NA	7
																	7	13	7	NA	11
96	1	3	2	3	Grădiştea	2	3	0	1	2	45.262	27.4	1	3	−50	0	NA	NA	NA	NA	NA
97	1	1	2	3	Grădiştea	2	3	0	1	2	45.262	27.4	3	3	−25	25	2	4	21	42	3
98	1	1	2	3	Grădiştea	2	3	0	1	2	45.262	27.4	1	3	−100	−50	2	4	8	NA	8
																	5	6	30	77	11
99	1	3	2	3	Grădiştea	2	3	0	1	2	45.262	27.4	3	3	−100	−50	NA	NA	NA	NA	NA
141	NA	7	2	5	Gropşani	2	2	0	2	4	44.439	23.948	6	3	−200	−75	6	9	22	NA	7
																	6	18	27	NA	7
255	2	5	2	5	Gruia	2	2	0	1	4	44.263	22.691	6	3	−150	0	7	13	51	124	11
																	7	13	54	132	11
																	7	13	54	133	11
																	7	13	51	124	11
																	7	13	51	NA	11
																	7	13	51	127	3
																	7	13	51	127	11
																	7	13	51	124	11
256	2	6	2	5	Hinova	2	2	0	1	4	44.540	22.776	6	3	−150	0	7	13	51	126	11
3	1	1	2	6	Hunedoara Grădina Castelului	2	3	1	3	3	45.749	22.888	5	3	50	106	2	4	21	45	3

4	1	1	2	6	Hunedoara Grădina Castelului	2	3	1	3	3	45.749	22.888	5	3	−100	100	2	4	35	27	3
5	1	1	2	6	Hunedoara Grădina Castelului	2	3	0	3	3	45.749	22.888	1	1	−125	−51	2	4	12	20	11
6	NA	2	2	6	Hunedoara Grădina Castelului	2	3	0	3	3	45.749	22.888	2	1	−100	100	2	4	19	35	3
																	2	4	35	104	3
																	2	4	35	27	11
28	1	1	2	6	Hunedoara Grădina Castelului	2	3	1	3	3	45.749	22.888	3	1	−100	100	2	4	35	27	11
29	1	3	2	6	Hunedoara Grădina Castelului	2	3	1	3	3	45.749	22.888	3	3	−100	100	NA	NA	NA	NA	NA
30	NA	2	2	6	Hunedoara Grădina Castelului	2	3	1	3	3	45.749	22.888	3	1	−100	100	2	4	8	115	8
																	2	4	35	27	11
31	1	1	2	6	Hunedoara Grădina Castelului	2	3	1	3	3	45.749	22.888	5	2	−100	100	2	4	8	140	8
32	1	3	2	6	Hunedoara Grădina Castelului	2	3	1	3	3	45.749	22.888	5	3	−100	100	NA	NA	NA	NA	NA
33	1	3	2	6	Hunedoara Grădina Castelului	2	3	1	3	3	45.749	22.888	1	3	−100	100	NA	NA	NA	NA	NA
34	2	6	2	6	Hunedoara Grădina Castelului	2	3	1	3	3	45.749	22.888	6	3	−100	100	7	10	4	4	3
35	1	3	2	6	Hunedoara Grădina Castelului	2	3	1	3	3	45.749	22.888	3	3	−100	100	NA	NA	NA	NA	NA

(continued)

Annex A.4 (continued)

Grave number	Supra-group	PAM group	Country	Region	Location	Grave type	Ritual type	Multiple burials	River proximity	Settlement proximity	Latitude	Longitude	Age	Sex	Chronology start	Chronology end	Object category 1	Object category 2	Object category 3	Object category 4	Material
36	1	3	2	6	Hunedoara Grădina Castelului	2	3	1	3	3	45.749	22.888	5	2	−100	100	NA	NA	NA	NA	NA
37	2	6	2	6	Hunedoara Grădina Castelului	2	3	1	3	3	45.749	22.888	6	3	−100	100	7	10	4	4	3
38	1	1	2	6	Hunedoara Grădina Castelului	2	3	0	3	3	45.749	22.888	5	2	−100	100	2	4	8	140	2
39	1	1	2	6	Hunedoara Grădina Castelului	2	3	1	3	3	45.749	22.888	5	3	−100	100	2	4	35	7	13
40	1	3	2	6	Hunedoara Grădina Castelului	2	3	1	3	3	45.749	22.888	3	3	−100	100	NA	NA	NA	NA	NA
41	1	3	2	6	Hunedoara Grădina Castelului	2	3	1	3	3	45.749	22.888	5	2	−100	100	NA	NA	NA	NA	NA
42	1	3	2	6	Hunedoara Grădina Castelului	2	3	1	3	3	45.749	22.888	3	3	−100	100	NA	NA	NA	NA	NA
43	NA	2	2	6	Hunedoara Grădina Castelului	2	3	0	3	3	45.749	22.888	5	3	35	106	2	4	8	115	8
																	2	4	21	45	3
																	2	4	35	37	14
																	2	4	35	27	11
																	2	4	8	135	8
44	1	3	2	6	Hunedoara Grădina Castelului	2	3	1	3	3	45.749	22.888	5	2	−100	100	NA	NA	NA	NA	NA
45	1	3	2	6	Hunedoara Grădina Castelului	2	3	1	3	3	45.749	22.888	3	3	−100	100	NA	NA	NA	NA	NA

46	1	1	2	6	Hunedoara Grădina Castelului	2	3	0	3	3	45.749	22.888	6	3	−100	100	NA	NA	NA	NA	3
47	1	1	2	6	Hunedoara Grădina Castelului	2	3	1	3	3	45.749	22.888	3	2	35	106	2	4	21	45	3
																	5	15	34	82	11
48	1	3	2	6	Hunedoara Grădina Castelului	2	3	1	3	3	45.749	22.888	2	3	−100	100	NA	NA	NA	NA	NA
49	1	1	2	6	Hunedoara Grădina Castelului	2	3	1	3	3	45.749	22.888	5	2	35	106	2	4	21	45	3
50	1	3	2	6	Hunedoara Grădina Castelului	2	3	1	3	3	45.749	22.888	5	3	−100	100	NA	NA	NA	NA	NA
51	1	3	2	6	Hunedoara Grădina Castelului	2	3	1	3	3	45.749	22.888	5	3	−100	100	NA	NA	NA	NA	NA
52	1	3	2	6	Hunedoara Grădina Castelului	2	3	1	3	3	45.749	22.888	5	3	−100	100	NA	NA	NA	NA	NA
53	1	1	2	6	Hunedoara Grădina Castelului	2	3	0	3	3	45.749	22.888	3	3	50	106	2	4	21	43	3
54	1	1	2	6	Hunedoara Grădina Castelului	2	3	1	3	3	45.749	22.888	3	3	50	106	2	4	21	45	3
55	1	3	2	6	Hunedoara Grădina Castelului	2	3	1	3	3	45.749	22.888	5	3	−100	100	NA	NA	NA	NA	NA
56	1	1	2	6	Hunedoara Grădina Castelului	2	3	1	3	3	45.749	22.888	2	3	−100	0	2	4	21	38	14
57	1	3	2	6	Hunedoara Grădina Castelului	2	3	0	3	3	45.749	22.888	5	3	−100	100	NA	NA	NA	NA	NA

(continued)

Annex A.4 (continued)

Grave number	Supra-group	PAM group	Country	Region	Location	Grave type	Ritual type	Multiple burials	River proximity	Settlement proximity	Latitude	Longitude	Age	Sex	Chronology start	Chronology end	Object category 1	Object category 2	Object category 3	Object category 4	Material
58	1	3	2	6	Hunedoara Grădina Castelului	2	3	0	3	3	45.749	22.888	3	3	−100	100	NA	NA	NA	NA	NA
59	1	1	2	6	Hunedoara Grădina Castelului	2	3	1	3	3	45.749	22.888	5	1	−100	100	2	4	8	115	8
60	1	3	2	6	Hunedoara Grădina Castelului	2	3	1	3	3	45.749	22.888	2	1	−100	100	NA	NA	NA	NA	NA
61	1	1	2	6	Hunedoara Grădina Castelului	2	3	0	3	3	45.749	22.888	5	2	−100	100	2	4	8	115	8
62	1	1	2	6	Hunedoara Grădina Castelului	2	3	0	3	3	45.749	22.888	3	3	−100	100	2	4	35	7	2
63	1	1	2	6	Hunedoara Grădina Castelului	2	3	0	3	3	45.749	22.888	3	2	−100	100	2	4	8	102	8
64	NA	2	2	6	Hunedoara Grădina Castelului	2	3	1	3	3	45.749	22.888	3	1	50	106	2	4	21	45	3
																	2	4	21	48	3
																	2	4	19	35	3
																	2	4	8	140	8
65	1	3	2	6	Hunedoara Grădina Castelului	2	3	1	3	3	45.749	22.888	3	3	−100	100	NA	NA	NA	NA	NA
66	NA	2	2	6	Hunedoara Grădina Castelului	2	3	1	3	3	45.749	22.888	5	1	−100	100	2	4	35	27	11
																	2	4	19	35	14
67	1	3	2	6	Hunedoara Grădina Castelului	2	3	1	3	3	45.749	22.888	3	3	−100	100	NA	NA	NA	NA	NA

68	NA	2	2	6	Hunedoara Grădina Castelului	2	3	1	3	3	45.749	22.888	5	1	50	106	2	4	21	39	3
																	2	4	19	35	14
69	1	3	2	6	Hunedoara Grădina Castelului	2	3	1	3	3	45.749	22.888	2	3	−100	100	NA	NA	NA	NA	NA
70	1	3	2	6	Hunedoara Grădina Castelului	2	3	0	3	3	45.749	22.888	3	3	−100	100	NA	NA	NA	NA	NA
142	2	5	2	6	Hunedoara Grădina Castelului	2	2	0	3	3	45.749	22.888	2	2	−125	−25	2	4	9	NA	11
																	2	4	9	NA	11
																	2	4	8	102	8
																	6	9	22	56	7
																	6	9	22	55	7
																	7	13	51	123	11
																	7	13	7	8	11
143	1	1	2	6	Hunedoara Grădina Castelului	2	2	1	3	3	45.749	22.888	2	2	−125	−51	2	4	12	20	11
144	1	3	2	6	Hunedoara Grădina Castelului	2	2	1	3	3	45.749	22.888	6	3	−125	−51	NA	NA	NA	NA	NA
145	1	1	2	6	Hunedoara Grădina Castelului	2	2	0	3	3	45.749	22.888	2	3	−125	−51	2	4	8	NA	8
167	NA	2	1	4	Hunedoara Grădina Castelului	3	2	0	3	3	43.533	23.817	6	3	−150	−25	2	4	35	NA	3
236	2	4	2	6	Hunedoara Grădina Castelului	2	2	0	3	3	45.749	22.888	2	2	−150	−51	2	4	9	15	11

(continued)

Annex A.4 (continued)

Grave number	Supra-group	PAM group	Country	Region	Location	Grave type	Ritual type	Multiple burials	River proximity	Settlement proximity	Latitude	Longitude	Age	Sex	Chronology start	Chronology end	Object category 1	Object category 2	Object category 3	Object category 4	Material
																	2	4	9	13	6
																	7	13	51	124	11
																	7	13	7	8	11
																	6	8	28	105	7
237	2	5	2	6	Hunedoara Grădina Castelului	2	2	0	3	3	45.749	22.888	6	3	−150	−51	7	7	14	28	11
																	7	7	45	NA	11
																	7	7	25	NA	11
																	4	16	26	NA	11
369	1	3	2	6	Hunedoara Grădina Castelului	2	3	0	3	3	45.749	22.888	6	3	−100	0	NA	NA	NA	NA	NA
8	1	1	1	4	Kalimanitsa	3	3	0	3	1	43.349	23.152	6	3	−270	−20	2	4	8	NA	8
																	6	NA	NA	NA	7
																	7	5	10	12	11
185	2	6	1	4	Kameno Pole (Ossen)	2	2	0	2	3	43.207	23.893	6	3	−270	−20	4	16	26	66	11
																	7	13	54	132	11
305	NA	7	3	1	Karaburma	2	2	0	1	3	44.815	20.512	6	3	−125	−25	6	18	50	120	7
																	6	18	39	96	7
																	6	8	29	75	7
																	6	9	11	90	7
306	NA	2	3	1	Karaburma	2	2	0	1	3	44.815	20.512	6	3	−125	−25	2	4	21	47	3
																	2	4	12	24	11
																	5	6	43	108	11
																	6	8	29	75	7

307	2	5	3	1	Karaburma	2	2	0	1	3	44.815	20.512	6	3	−125	−25	6	8	18	116	3
																	6	8	37	88	7
																	6	8	37	88	7
																	6	8	29	75	7
																	7	13	7	10	11
																	7	13	51	126	11
																	7	7	45	NA	11
308	2	4	3	1	Karaburma	2	2	0	1	3	44.815	20.512	6	3	−125	−25	6	8	29	75	7
																	6	8	18	116	3
																	6	9	11	91	7
																	6	9	38	134	3
																	7	13	7	10	11
																	7	13	51	124	11
																	5	17	44	109	15
309	2	5	3	1	Karaburma	2	2	0	1	3	44.815	20.512	6	3	−125	−25	7	13	51	123	11
																	7	13	7	NA	11
																	7	13	51	123	11
																	7	13	51	124	11
																	7	13	54	133	11
310	NA	2	3	1	Karaburma	2	2	0	1	3	44.815	20.512	6	3	−125	−25	2	4	12	24	11
																	2	4	12	NA	3
																	2	4	9	13	6
																	5	6	30	77	11
																	6	9	11	91	7
311	NA	2	3	1	Karaburma	2	2	0	1	3	44.815	20.512	6	3	−125	−25	2	4	9	14	6
																	2	4	21	NA	3
																	5	6	30	77	11

(continued)

Annex A.4 (continued)

Grave number	Supra-group	PAM group	Country	Region	Location	Grave type	Ritual type	Multiple burials	River proximity	Settlement proximity	Latitude	Longitude	Age	Sex	Chronology start	Chronology end	Object category 1	Object category 2	Object category 3	Object category 4	Material
																	6	8	17	31	7
312	NA	2	3	1	Karaburma	2	2	0	1	3	44.815	20.512	6	3	−125	−25	2	4	12	24	11
																	2	4	12	24	11
																	5	6	30	77	11
																	6	9	11	90	7
313	NA	2	3	1	Karaburma	2	2	0	1	3	44.815	20.512	6	3	−125	−25	2	4	12	21	3
																	5	20	52	128	7
																	6	9	11	90	7
314	2	4	3	1	Karaburma	2	2	0	1	3	44.815	20.512	6	3	−125	−25	6	9	11	90	7
																	6	9	11	90	7
																	2	4	21	NA	3
																	7	13	7	10	11
315	NA	7	3	1	Karaburma	2	2	0	1	3	44.815	20.512	6	3	−125	−25	6	NA	NA	NA	3
																	6	18	NA	NA	7
316	NA	7	3	1	Karaburma	2	2	0	1	3	44.815	20.512	6	3	−125	−25	6	8	17	84	7
																	6	9	11	90	7
317	2	5	3	1	Karaburma	2	2	0	1	3	44.815	20.512	6	3	−125	−25	7	13	51	126	11
																	7	13	7	9	11
																	7	13	51	126	11
																	7	13	51	123	11
																	6	8	37	88	7
318	2	4	3	1	Karaburma	2	2	0	1	3	44.815	20.512	6	3	−125	−25	7	13	51	124	11
																	7	13	7	9	11
																	6	NA	NA	NA	7
319	NA	7	3	1	Karaburma	2	2	0	1	3	44.815	20.512	6	3	−125	−25	6	8	18	116	3

																	6	9	11	90	7
320	NA	7	3	1	Karaburma	2	2	0	1	3	44.815	20.512	6	3	−125	−25	5	6	43	107	11
																	6	8	37	88	7
																	6	18	50	121	7
321	NA	2	3	1	Karaburma	2	2	0	1	3	44.815	20.512	6	3	−125	−25	2	4	9	NA	11
																	2	4	21	44	3
																	6	9	11	90	7
																	6	9	11	90	7
																	6	8	17	32	7
																	6	18	27	72	7
322	NA	7	3	1	Karaburma	2	2	0	1	3	44.815	20.512	6	3	−125	−25	6	9	11	90	7
																	6	9	11	90	7
																	6	8	17	32	7
323	2	4	3	1	Karaburma	2	2	0	1	3	44.815	20.512	6	3	−125	−25	7	13	51	125	11
																	7	13	7	10	11
324	NA	7	3	1	Karaburma	2	2	0	1	3	44.815	20.512	6	3	−125	−25	6	8	17	31	7
																	6	9	11	90	7
325	2	5	3	1	Karaburma	2	2	0	1	3	44.815	20.512	6	3	−125	−25	6	8	47	117	11
																	6	8	18	116	3
																	7	7	45	NA	3
																	7	7	45	110	3
																	7	13	7	10	11
																	7	13	51	125	11
																	7	13	54	133	11
																	7	13	51	125	11
																	7	13	51	124	11
																	2	4	9	15	11

(continued)

Annex A.4 (continued)

Grave number	Supra-group	PAM group	Country	Region	Location	Grave type	Ritual type	Multiple burials	River proximity	Settlement proximity	Latitude	Longitude	Age	Sex	Chronology start	Chronology end	Object category 1	Object category 2	Object category 3	Object category 4	Material
																	5	6	43	107	11
																	5	17	44	109	15
																	6	9	20	83	3
																	6	18	39	96	7
																	7	5	10	12	11
326	2	4	3	1	Karaburma	2	2	0	1	3	44.815	20.512	6	3	−125	−25	7	13	51	123	11
																	7	13	7	9	11
327	2	5	3	1	Karaburma	2	2	0	1	3	44.815	20.512	6	3	−125	−25	5	6	43	108	11
																	5	6	30	77	3
																	7	13	7	9	11
																	7	13	51	127	11
																	7	13	51	124	11
																	7	13	51	126	11
																	7	13	51	124	11
																	7	13	54	133	11
																	2	4	9	NA	11
																	5	17	44	109	15
																	6	8	18	116	3
																	7	5	10	12	11
328	NA	7	3	1	Karaburma	2	2	0	1	3	44.815	20.512	6	3	−125	−25	6	9	11	90	7
																	6	9	11	90	7
																	6	8	29	75	7
329	2	4	3	1	Karaburma	2	2	0	1	3	44.815	20.512	6	3	−125	−25	7	13	51	125	11
																	7	13	7	9	11
																	2	4	12	21	11

330	NA	2	3	1	Karaburma	2	2	0	1	3	44.815	20.512	6	3	−125	−25	2	4	12	24	NA
																	2	4	9	13	6
																	2	4	21	44	3
																	6	8	18	116	3
																	6	8	17	32	7
																	6	8	37	88	7
																	5	6	30	77	11
331	2	5	3	1	Karaburma	2	2	0	1	3	44.815	20.512	6	3	−125	−25	6	8	37	88	7
																	6	8	29	75	7
																	7	13	51	123	11
																	7	13	51	123	11
																	7	13	7	8	11
																	5	6	43	108	11
																	7	7	45	110	11
332	NA	7	3	1	Karaburma	2	2	0	1	3	44.815	20.512	6	3	−125	−25	6	8	37	88	7
																	6	8	29	75	7
																	5	6	30	77	11
																	6	9	11	92	7
333	NA	7	3	1	Karaburma	2	2	0	1	3	44.815	20.512	6	3	−125	−25	6	8	29	75	7
																	6	9	11	92	7
334	2	5	3	1	Karaburma	2	2	0	1	3	44.815	20.512	6	3	−125	−25	6	8	29	76	7
																	6	8	18	116	4
																	6	8	17	32	7
																	6	8	37	88	7
																	7	13	51	126	11
																	7	13	51	126	11
																	2	4	12	25	11

(continued)

Annex A.4 (continued)

Grave number	Supra-group	PAM group	Country	Region	Location	Grave type	Ritual type	Multiple burials	River proximity	Settlement proximity	Latitude	Longitude	Age	Sex	Chronology start	Chronology end	Object category 1	Object category 2	Object category 3	Object category 4	Material
																	5	6	43	108	11
335	2	4	3	1	Karaburma	2	2	0	1	3	44.815	20.512	6	3	−125	−25	6	8	29	75	7
																	6	8	17	31	7
																	6	9	11	92	7
																	6	9	11	90	7
																	7	13	7	10	11
																	7	13	51	NA	11
																	5	6	43	107	11
																	6	18	39	95	7
336	NA	7	3	1	Karaburma	2	2	0	1	3	44.815	20.512	6	3	−125	−25	6	8	18	116	3
																	6	8	29	75	7
																	6	8	37	88	7
																	6	18	39	95	7
337	2	5	3	1	Karaburma	2	2	0	1	3	44.815	20.512	6	3	−125	−25	6	8	17	31	7
																	6	8	29	75	7
																	6	9	11	90	7
																	6	9	11	90	7
																	6	9	11	90	7
																	7	13	54	133	11
																	7	13	51	123	11
																	7	13	7	10	11
																	2	4	12	24	11
																	5	6	43	108	11
																	7	7	45	NA	11
338	NA	7	3	1	Karaburma	2	2	0	1	3	44.815	20.512	6	3	−125	−25	6	18	39	95	7

																	6	18	50	121	7
																	5	6	43	NA	11
186	2	5	1	4	Koinare (Gruia)	2	2	0	3	3	43.350	24.133	6	3	−150	−25	7	13	51	123	11
																	7	13	42	106	11
																	7	13	7	8	11
																	7	13	51	123	11
																	7	13	42	106	11
																	7	13	54	132	11
																	4	16	26	66	11
																	7	7	45	110	11
189	2	6	1	4	Komarevo (Kirkov Vrah)	2	2	0	3	3	43.373	23.858	6	3	−150	−25	4	16	53	131	11
																	4	16	26	66	11
																	7	13	7	8	11
187	2	5	1	4	Komarevo (Vrachanka)	3	2	0	3	3	43.397	23.867	6	3	−150	−25	7	13	54	NA	11
																	7	13	7	8	11
																	7	13	51	124	11
																	4	16	26	66	11
																	7	5	10	12	11
188	2	5	1	4	Komarevo (Vrachanka)	3	2	0	3	3	43.397	23.867	6	3	−270	−20	7	13	7	8	11
																	7	13	51	NA	11
																	7	13	51	127	11
																	2	4	55	114	3
																	4	16	26	NA	11
																	6	NA	NA	NA	7

(continued)

Annex A.4 (continued)

Grave number	Supra-group	PAM group	Country	Region	Location	Grave type	Ritual type	Multiple burials	River proximity	Settlement proximity	Latitude	Longitude	Age	Sex	Chronology start	Chronology end	Object category 1	Object category 2	Object category 3	Object category 4	Material
9	2	4	3	4	Kostolac	3	3	0	1	3	44.733	21.200	6	3	−150	−25	7	13	7	10	11
																	7	13	51	124	11
																	2	4	9	14	3
																	5	6	43	108	11
202	2	4	3	4	Kostolac (Dunavac)	2	2	0	1	3	44.705	21.157	6	3	−100	0	6	9	11	90	7
																	6	8	47	119	3
																	6	8	17	31	7
																	6	9	11	90	7
																	6	9	11	90	7
																	7	13	54	133	11
190	2	5	1	4	Kriva Bara (Manafska Padina)	2	2	0	3	1	43.629	23.697	6	3	−150	−25	7	13	51	124	11
																	7	13	7	NA	11
																	7	13	54	NA	11
																	4	16	26	66	11
																	6	NA	NA	NA	7
																	7	7	45	NA	11
340	NA	2	1	4	Krushovitsa	2	2	0	3	3	43.628	23.849	6	3	−270	−20	2	4	12	26	3
																	2	4	12	26	3
																	6	18	39	96	7
357	NA	2	1	4	Krushovitsa	3	2	0	3	3	43.625	23.813	6	3	−270	−20	2	NA	NA	NA	3
																	2	4	55	NA	3
191	2	5	3	4	Kumano (Kusice)	2	2	0	3	4	44.717	21.533	6	3	−150	−25	6	9	11	90	7
																	6	9	11	90	7

																	7	13	51	125	11
																	7	13	7	10	11
																	7	13	51	123	11
																	2	4	NA	NA	10
																	6	18	39	95	7
146	2	5	2	3	Lăceni	3	2	0	3	3	44.083	25.333	2	3	−100	0	6	9	22	55	7
																	6	9	22	NA	7
																	2	4	21	NA	3
																	6	8	28	NA	7
																	7	7	45	110	11
																	7	13	3	3	11
10	NA	2	1	4	Leskovets	3	3	0	2	3	43.350	23.048	6	3	−150	−25	2	4	55	NA	3
																	2	4	21	NA	3
																	2	NA	NA	NA	3
																	6	NA	NA	NA	14
																	7	7	14	28	11
11	2	5	1	4	Leskovets	3	3	0	2	3	43.350	23.048	6	3	−150	−25	2	4	21	NA	3
																	2	4	12	NA	3
																	4	16	53	NA	11
																	4	16	53	NA	11
																	6	8	28	NA	7
																	6	8	28	NA	7
																	7	13	7	NA	11
																	7	13	51	NA	11
																	7	13	51	NA	11
																	5	6	30	77	11
																	5	15	34	82	11

(continued)

Annex A.4 (continued)

Grave number	Supra-group	PAM group	Country	Region	Location	Grave type	Ritual type	Multiple burials	River proximity	Settlement proximity	Latitude	Longitude	Age	Sex	Chronology start	Chronology end	Object category 1	Object category 2	Object category 3	Object category 4	Material
																	6	9	11	NA	7
																	7	7	45	NA	11
192	2	5	1	4	Leskovets	3	2	0	2	3	43.350	23.048	6	3	−275	−150	6	NA	NA	NA	7
																	6	NA	NA	NA	7
																	7	13	51	NA	11
																	7	13	42	106	11
																	5	6	30	77	11
																	7	7	45	NA	11
194	2	5	1	4	Lessura	2	2	0	3	3	43.465	23.557	6	3	−150	−20	7	13	51	NA	11
																	7	13	54	NA	11
																	4	16	26	NA	11
																	7	7	45	NA	11
193	2	5	1	4	Lessura (Varnitsite)	3	2	0	3	3	43.459	23.559	6	3	−150	−20	7	13	51	NA	11
																	7	13	7	NA	11
																	7	13	54	NA	11
																	4	16	26	NA	11
																	6	NA	NA	NA	7
348	2	6	1	4	Lili(y)ache (Kuklite)	3	1	0	3	3	43.322	23.522	6	3	−150	−25	4	16	26	66	11
																	6	8	28	105	7
																	6	9	11	90	7
																	7	13	51	125	11
195	2	6	1	4	Lipnitsa (Starchi Krak)	2	2	0	3	3	43.587	23.793	6	3	−270	−20	4	16	26	66	11
																	7	13	51	123	11

196	NA	2	3	4	Liubichevats (Bilievina)	2	2	0	1	3	44.487	22.538	6	3	−150	−20	2	4	NA	NA	3
																	6	NA	NA	NA	7
																	7	NA	NA	NA	12
358	2	6	1	4	Madan (Mogilata)	3	2	0	2	1	43.583	23.450	6	3	−150	−20	4	16	26	NA	11
																	4	16	53	NA	11
																	7	13	51	NA	11
199	2	5	3	4	Mala Vrabitsa (Aymana)	2	2	0	3	4	44.601	22.686	6	3	−100	−50	2	4	21	50	11
																	2	4	21	44	3
																	6	8	18	116	3
																	6	8	17	136	7
																	6	8	29	74	7
																	6	9	38	134	3
																	6	9	11	18	7
																	6	9	22	58	7
																	6	18	39	94	7
																	6	18	39	95	7
																	7	13	51	NA	11
																	7	13	7	9	11
																	7	13	7	10	7
																	7	13	51	126	11
																	7	13	51	126	11
																	7	13	7	8	11
200	NA	2	3	4	Mala Vrabitsa (Aymana)	2	2	0	3	4	44.601	22.686	6	3	−100	0	6	9	22	58	7

(continued)

Annex A.4 (continued)

Grave number	Supra-group	PAM group	Country	Region	Location	Grave type	Ritual type	Multiple burials	River proximity	Settlement proximity	Latitude	Longitude	Age	Sex	Chronology start	Chronology end	Object category 1	Object category 2	Object category 3	Object category 4	Material
																	6	9	11	90	7
																	2	4	9	13	6
																	6	8	28	100	3
																	6	18	27	72	7
201	NA	2	3	4	Mala Vrabitsa (Aymana)	2	2	0	3	4	44.601	22.686	6	3	−150	0	2	4	9	NA	6
																	2	4	12	NA	12
																	6	9	22	NA	7
198	NA	2	3	4	Mala Vrabitsa (Konopishte)	2	2	0	1	3	44.601	22.686	6	3	−150	−25	2	4	21	NA	11
																	2	4	21	NA	14
																	6	NA	NA	NA	7
																	6	8	18	116	3
																	7	13	7	NA	11
12	NA	2	3	4	Milosevac	2	3	0	3	4	44.601	19.524	6	3	−270	−20	2	4	NA	NA	14
																	2	4	NA	NA	14
																	2	4	8	NA	8
361	2	6	1	4	Mizia	2	2	0	3	3	43.683	23.853	6	3	−150	−20	4	16	26	NA	11
																	7	13	54	NA	11
197	2	5	1	4	Mizia (Rupite)	2	2	0	3	3	43.677	23.854	6	3	−150	−20	4	16	26	NA	11
																	7	7	45	NA	11
																	7	13	54	NA	11
359	2	5	1	4	Mizia (Tatarlaka)	2	2	0	1	3	43.683	23.848	6	3	−150	−20	7	13	51	NA	11

																7	13	7	NA	11
																7	13	54	NA	11
																4	16	26	NA	11
																7	7	45	NA	11
360	2	6	1	4	Mizia (Tatarlaka)	2	2	0	1	3	43.683	23.848	6	3	−150	−20	6	NA	NA	NA	7
																7	13	51	NA	11
203	NA	7	1	4	Montana	3	2	0	3	3	43.408	23.225	6	3	−270	−20	6	NA	NA	NA	7
																6	NA	NA	NA	7
103	1	3	2	5	Ocnița	3	3	1	3	3	45.083	24.266	2	1	−150	−100	NA	NA	NA	NA	NA
104	1	1	2	5	Ocnița	3	3	1	3	3	45.083	24.266	3	3	−150	−100	2	4	35	27	6
147	NA	2	2	3	Orbeasca de Sus	3	2	0	3	4	44.150	25.317	2	3	−100	0	2	4	9	NA	11
																6	9	11	18	7
362	2	6	1	4	Ori(y)ahovo (Markov Bair)	2	2	0	1	3	43.734	23.961	6	3	−150	−20	4	16	26	64	11
																4	16	53	130	11
																4	16	53	130	11
363	2	5	1	4	Ori(y)ahovo (Markov Bair)	2	2	0	1	3	43.734	23.961	6	3	−150	−20	7	13	54	133	11
																7	13	51	123	11
																7	13	7	8	11
																4	16	26	66	11
73	1	1	2	5	Orlea	2	3	1	1	3	43.75	24.383	5	3	−200	0	2	4	8	NA	9
74	1	3	2	5	Orlea	2	3	1	1	3	43.75	24.383	5	3	−200	0	NA	NA	NA	NA	NA
75	1	3	2	5	Orlea	2	3	1	1	3	43.75	24.383	2	1	−200	0	NA	NA	NA	NA	NA
76	1	3	2	5	Orlea	2	3	1	1	3	43.75	24.383	2	2	−200	0	NA	NA	NA	NA	NA

(continued)

Annex A.4 (continued)

Grave number	Supra-group	PAM group	Country	Region	Location	Grave type	Ritual type	Multiple burials	River proximity	Settlement proximity	Latitude	Longitude	Age	Sex	Chronology start	Chronology end	Object category 1	Object category 2	Object category 3	Object category 4	Material
77	1	3	2	5	Orlea	2	3	1	1	3	43.75	24.383	1	1	−200	0	NA	NA	NA	NA	NA
78	1	1	2	5	Orlea	2	3	1	1	3	43.75	24.383	1	1	−200	0	2	4	8	NA	8
79	1	3	2	5	Orlea	2	3	1	1	3	43.75	24.383	2	2	−200	0	NA	NA	NA	NA	NA
80	1	3	2	5	Orlea	2	3	1	1	3	43.75	24.383	1	1	−200	0	NA	NA	NA	NA	NA
81	1	1	2	5	Orlea	2	3	1	1	3	43.75	24.383	5	3	−200	0	2	4	8	NA	4
82	1	3	2	5	Orlea	2	3	1	1	3	43.75	24.383	5	3	−200	0	NA	NA	NA	NA	NA
83	1	3	2	5	Orlea	2	3	1	1	3	43.75	24.383	2	1	−200	0	NA	NA	NA	NA	NA
84	1	1	2	5	Orlea	2	3	1	1	3	43.75	24.383	2	2	−200	0	2	4	9	13	6
85	1	3	2	5	Orlea	2	3	1	1	3	43.75	24.383	6	3	−200	0	NA	NA	NA	NA	NA
86	1	3	2	5	Orlea	2	3	1	1	3	43.75	24.383	6	3	−200	0	NA	NA	NA	NA	NA
87	1	3	2	5	Orlea	2	3	1	1	3	43.75	24.383	6	3	−200	0	NA	NA	NA	NA	NA
88	1	3	2	5	Orlea	2	3	1	1	3	43.75	24.383	6	3	−200	0	NA	NA	NA	NA	NA
89	1	3	2	5	Orlea	2	3	1	1	3	43.75	24.383	6	3	−200	0	NA	NA	NA	NA	NA
90	1	3	2	5	Orlea	2	3	1	1	3	43.75	24.383	2	3	−200	0	NA	NA	NA	NA	NA
91	1	1	2	5	Orlea	2	3	1	1	3	43.75	24.383	3	3	−200	0	2	4	8	NA	5
92	1	3	2	5	Orlea	2	3	1	1	3	43.75	24.383	2	3	−200	0	NA	NA	NA	NA	NA
93	1	3	2	5	Orlea	2	3	0	1	3	43.75	24.383	2	3	−125	0	NA	NA	NA	NA	NA
94	1	3	2	5	Orlea	2	3	0	1	3	43.75	24.383	5	3	−125	0	NA	NA	NA	NA	NA
95	1	3	2	5	Orlea	2	3	0	1	3	43.75	24.383	5	3	−125	0	NA	NA	NA	NA	NA
257	2	5	2	5	Orodel	2	2	0	3	4	44.245	23.242	6	3	−150	0	7	13	51	125	11
																	7	13	7	8	11
																	7	13	54	133	11
																	4	16	26	67	11
370	2	4	2	5	Orşova	2	2	0	3	4	44.725	22.396	6	3	−150	0	5	6	30	77	11
																	5	6	43	NA	11

																7	13	3	3	11
																7	13	54	NA	11
																5	2	46	113	11
204	2	5	1	4	Ossen	2	2	0	2	1	43.387	23.561	6	3	−155	−25	7	13	7	8	11
																7	13	51	126	11
																7	13	54	133	11
																4	16	26	66	11
																6	NA	NA	NA	7
205	2	5	1	4	Ossen	2	2	0	2	1	43.387	23.561	6	3	−155	−25	7	13	54	132	11
																7	13	51	123	11
																7	13	7	8	11
																4	16	26	66	11
																6	NA	NA	NA	7
206	2	5	1	4	Ostrov	3	2	0	3	3	43.675	24.130	6	3	−150	−20	7	13	7	NA	11
																7	13	51	NA	11
																7	13	54	NA	11
																2	4	NA	NA	3
																4	16	26	NA	11
207	2	4	3	4	Ostrovo	2	2	0	1	3	44.766	21.446	6	3	−150	−25	7	13	54	NA	11
																7	13	51	NA	12
																5	6	30	77	11
71	NA	7	2	5	Ostrovul Şimian	2	3	0	1	2	44.613	22.684	3	3	−100	0	6	NA	NA	NA	7
72	NA	7	2	5	Ostrovul Şimian	2	3	0	1	2	44.613	22.684	3	3	−100	0	6	NA	NA	NA	7
258	2	6	2	5	Ostrovul Şimian	2	2	0	1	3	44.613	22.684	6	3	−150	0	4	16	26	66	11
																7	13	54	133	11

(continued)

Annex A.4 (continued)

Grave number	Supra-group	PAM group	Country	Region	Location	Grave type	Ritual type	Multiple burials	River proximity	Settlement proximity	Latitude	Longitude	Age	Sex	Chronology start	Chronology end	Object category 1	Object category 2	Object category 3	Object category 4	Material
261	NA	NA	2	5	Padea	2	2	0	1	4	44.02	23.868	6	3	−150	0	3	3	15	34	14
																	4	16	26	66	11
																	2	4	21	50	11
																	2	4	21	NA	11
																	7	13	7	11	11
																	7	13	7	11	11
																	7	13	7	9	11
																	7	13	7	8	11
																	7	13	51	NA	11
																	7	13	51	127	11
																	7	13	51	127	11
																	7	13	51	124	11
																	7	13	51	123	11
																	7	13	51	124	11
																	6	NA	NA	NA	7
																	7	13	54	133	11
																	7	13	54	133	11
																	7	13	51	124	11
																	7	13	51	123	11
																	7	13	51	123	11
																	7	13	51	123	11
																	7	13	51	123	11
																	7	13	51	124	11
																	7	13	51	127	11
																	7	13	51	124	11

																	7	13	51	124	11
																	7	13	51	124	11
																	6	NA	NA	NA	7
																	6	18	27	NA	7
																	6	NA	NA	NA	7
																	6	8	28	NA	7
																	6	NA	NA	NA	7
																	6	NA	NA	NA	7
																	6	NA	NA	NA	7
																	6	NA	NA	NA	7
																	6	NA	NA	NA	7
																	6	9	38	89	7
																	6	NA	NA	NA	7
																	6	NA	NA	NA	7
																	6	8	28	105	7
																	6	NA	NA	NA	7
																	2	NA	NA	NA	14
																	6	NA	NA	NA	7
259	2	6	2	5	Perişor	2	2	0	3	4	44.143	23.49	6	3	−150	0	7	13	54	NA	11
283	2	5	2	6	Piatra Craivii	2	2	0	2	3	46.209	23.485	6	3	−25	50	2	4	21	53	12
																	2	4	21	42	11
																	7	13	54	NA	11
																	7	13	7	NA	11
																	7	13	51	NA	12
102	1	3	2	3	Piscu Crăsani	2	3	0	1	2	44.606	26.880	3	3	−200	0	NA	NA	NA	NA	NA
342	NA	2	2	3	Piscu Crăsani	3	1	0	1	3	44.595	26.885	6	3	−150	0	2	4	35	NA	12
																	2	4	21	NA	12

(continued)

Annex A.4 (continued)

Grave number	Supra-group	PAM group	Country	Region	Location	Grave type	Ritual type	Multiple burials	River proximity	Settlement proximity	Latitude	Longitude	Age	Sex	Chronology start	Chronology end	Object category 1	Object category 2	Object category 3	Object category 4	Material
																	7	7	25	61	3
260	2	5	2	5	Plosca	2	2	0	1	4	43.896	23.553	6	3	−150	0	7	13	51	123	11
																	7	13	54	133	11
																	7	7	45	111	11
148	NA	2	2	2	Poiana	3	2	0	3	3	45.983	27.25	6	3	−25	75	2	4	8	NA	8
																	2	4	21	41	3
																	2	4	21	NA	3
																	6	NA	NA	NA	7
																	6	NA	NA	NA	8
																	2	NA	NA	NA	14
																	2	19	32	80	3
																	5	6	30	77	11
																	6	9	22	NA	7
																	6	18	2	2	7
149	1	1	2	2	Poiana	3	2	0	3	3	45.983	27.25	6	3	−100	0	2	4	21	NA	11
150	NA	2	2	2	Poiana	3	2	0	3	3	45.983	27.25	6	3	−100	0	2	4	NA	NA	13
																	2	4	21	NA	12
																	2	4	8	NA	8
																	2	4	19	NA	12
																	2	4	12	NA	12
																	4	16	53	NA	11
																	6	18	2	2	7
343	2	6	2	2	Poiana	3	1	0	3	3	45.983	27.25	6	3	−100	100	6	NA	NA	NA	7
																	6	18	2	2	7
																	7	10	4	4	11

344	1	1	2	2	Poiana	3	1	0	3	3	45.983	27.25	6	3	−100	0	2	4	21	NA	11
151	2	4	2	5	Poiana (Gorj)	3	2	0	4	4	44.933	23.183	6	3	−100	0	7	7	25	61	3
																	7	7	14	28	11
111	1	3	2	3	Popeşti	2	3	1	3	2	44.311	25.965	6	3	−150	−25	NA	NA	NA	NA	NA
112	1	3	2	3	Popeşti	2	3	1	3	2	44.311	25.965	6	3	−150	−25	NA	NA	NA	NA	NA
113	1	3	2	3	Popeşti	2	3	1	3	2	44.311	25.965	1	3	−150	−25	NA	NA	NA	NA	NA
114	1	1	2	3	Popeşti	2	3	1	3	2	44.311	25.965	1	3	−150	−25	2	4	12	NA	11
																	6	NA	NA	NA	7
																	6	9	22	NA	7
115	1	3	2	3	Popeşti	2	3	1	3	2	44.311	25.965	6	3	−150	−25	NA	NA	NA	NA	NA
116	1	3	2	3	Popeşti	2	3	0	3	2	44.311	25.965	3	3	−150	−25	NA	NA	NA	NA	NA
117	1	3	2	3	Popeşti	2	3	0	3	2	44.311	25.965	6	3	−150	−100	NA	NA	NA	NA	NA
152	2	5	2	3	Popeşti	3	2	0	3	3	44.300	25.950	6	3	−50	0	2	4	35	27	11
																	2	4	12	NA	3
																	2	4	8	115	8
																	2	4	9	NA	12
																	2	4	35	27	11
																	2	4	21	40	11
																	2	4	8	NA	3
																	2	4	8	115	8
																	2	4	35	27	11
																	2	4	12	NA	3
																	6	NA	NA	NA	7
																	6	NA	NA	NA	7
																	6	NA	NA	NA	7
																	6	8	29	73	7
																	6	8	29	NA	7

(continued)

Annex A.4 (continued)

Grave number	Supra-group	PAM group	Country	Region	Location	Grave type	Ritual type	Multiple burials	River proximity	Settlement proximity	Latitude	Longitude	Age	Sex	Chronology start	Chronology end	Object category 1	Object category 2	Object category 3	Object category 4	Material
																	6	8	28	NA	7
																	6	9	11	NA	7
																	6	9	22	NA	7
																	6	9	11	18	7
																	6	9	22	56	7
																	6	9	11	NA	7
																	6	9	22	57	7
																	6	9	11	18	7
																	6	18	NA	NA	7
																	6	18	2	2	7
																	6	18	2	2	7
																	7	7	45	NA	11
																	7	7	14	28	11
																	7	13	51	123	11
																	7	13	54	133	11
																	2	19	32	80	3
																	5	6	30	77	11
153	NA	2	2	3	Popeşti	3	2	0	3	3	44.300	25.950	6	3	−35	25	6	9	22	NA	7
																	6	9	22	55	7
																	2	4	21	46	3
																	6	NA	NA	NA	7
																	6	18	2	2	7
																	7	7	14	28	11
154	2	5	2	3	Popeşti	3	2	0	3	3	44.300	25.950	6	3	−150	−50	4	16	26	70	11
																	4	16	26	70	11

																	4	16	13	99	11
																	6	9	11	NA	7
																	6	9	11	NA	7
																	6	18	2	2	7
																	6	18	2	2	7
																	6	18	2	2	7
																	7	7	25	61	3
																	7	7	14	28	11
																	7	7	45	NA	11
																	7	13	3	3	11
																	7	13	54	132	11
																	7	13	7	8	11
																	7	13	51	123	11
																	3	3	15	78	14
																	5	2	46	113	11
																	5	6	30	77	11
																	6	NA	NA	NA	7
																	6	8	28	NA	7
345	2	4	2	3	Popeşti	3	1	0	3	3	44.300	25.950	6	3	−100	0	6	8	28	NA	7
																	6	8	28	NA	7
																	6	9	11	18	7
																	6	9	22	NA	7
																	6	9	22	NA	7
																	6	9	11	18	7
																	6	9	11	NA	7
																	6	18	2	2	7
																	7	13	51	NA	11

(continued)

Annex A.4 (continued)

Grave number	Supra-group	PAM group	Country	Region	Location	Grave type	Ritual type	Multiple burials	River proximity	Settlement proximity	Latitude	Longitude	Age	Sex	Chronology start	Chronology end	Object category 1	Object category 2	Object category 3	Object category 4	Material
208	2	5	1	4	Popitsa	3	2	0	3	3	43.433	23.950	6	3	−150	−20	7	13	54	NA	11
																	7	13	51	NA	11
																	4	16	26	NA	11
																	7	7	45	NA	11
364	2	6	1	4	Popitsa	2	2	0	3	3	43.414	23.951	6	3	−150	−20	4	16	53	130	11
																	4	16	53	130	11
																	4	16	26	NA	11
																	7	13	54	133	11
105	1	1	2	2	Răcătău	2	3	0	1	2	46.347	27.058	3	3	−100	100	2	4	NA	NA	12
106	1	1	2	2	Răcătău	2	3	0	1	2	46.347	27.058	3	3	−100	100	2	4	NA	NA	12
107	1	1	2	2	Răcătău	2	3	0	1	2	46.347	27.058	3	3	−100	100	2	4	NA	NA	12
156	2	5	2	2	Răcătău	3	2	0	3	3	46.347	27.058	6	3	0	100	6	8	17	84	7
																	6	8	17	NA	7
																	7	7	14	28	11
																	7	7	14	28	11
																	6	9	22	NA	7
																	6	11	49	NA	7
																	6	18	2	2	7
157	NA	2	2	2	Răcătău	3	2	0	3	3	46.347	27.058	6	3	0	100	2	4	21	NA	3
																	2	4	21	NA	3
																	6	8	17	NA	7
																	6	8	17	NA	7
																	6	18	27	NA	7
																	6	18	2	2	7
																	6	18	2	2	7

																6	9	38	NA	7
																6	11	49	NA	7
158	NA	7	2	2	Răcătău	3	2	0	3	3	46.347	27.058	6	3	0	100	6	NA	NA	NA	7
																6	NA	NA	NA	7
																5	6	30	77	11
																6	18	2	2	7
346	NA	NA	2	2	Răcătău	3	1	0	3	3	46.347	27.058	6	3	0	100	NA	NA	NA	NA	NA
155	2	5	2	3	Radovanu	3	2	0	3	3	44.200	26.517	6	3	−100	0	7	13	7	8	11
																7	13	51	123	11
																7	13	51	123	11
																4	16	26	70	11
																7	7	14	28	11
349	NA	NA	1	4	Radovene (Maniovets)	3	1	0	3	3	43.157	23.961	6	3	−270	−20	4	16	26	NA	11
264	2	4	2	5	Rastu	2	2	0	1	4	43.883	23.283	6	3	−150	0	7	13	51	125	11
																7	13	7	8	11
265	2	6	2	5	Rastu	2	2	0	1	4	43.883	23.283	6	3	−150	0	7	13	7	8	11
266	2	4	2	5	Rastu	2	2	0	1	4	43.883	23.283	6	3	−150	0	7	13	51	123	11
																7	13	7	8	11
294	2	5	3	1	Ritopek	2	2	0	1	4	44.737	20.655	6	3	−125	−25	7	13	51	124	11
																7	13	7	10	11
																7	13	54	132	11
																2	4	9	NA	11
																7	7	45	112	11
295	2	5	3	1	Ritopek	2	2	0	1	4	44.737	20.655	6	3	−125	−25	7	13	51	124	11
																7	13	54	132	11
																2	4	9	NA	11

(continued)

Annex A.4 (continued)

Grave number	Supra-group	PAM group	Country	Region	Location	Grave type	Ritual type	Multiple burials	River proximity	Settlement proximity	Latitude	Longitude	Age	Sex	Chronology start	Chronology end	Object category 1	Object category 2	Object category 3	Object category 4	Material
																	7	7	45	112	11
13	2	4	1	4	Rogozen	3	3	0	3	3	43.517	23.717	6	3	−270	−20	7	13	54	NA	11
																	7	13	51	NA	11
																	4	16	26	NA	11
365	2	6	1	4	Rogozen	2	2	0	3	3	43.517	23.717	6	3	−150	−25	4	16	53	NA	11
																	4	16	26	65	11
																	7	13	7	8	11
296	NA	2	3	1	Rospi Ćuprija	2	2	0	1	3	44.818	20.534	6	3	−125	−25	2	4	21	NA	3
																	2	4	21	NA	3
																	2	4	NA	NA	3
																	2	4	9	14	3
																	6	8	17	31	7
																	6	8	17	31	7
																	6	8	29	74	7
																	6	9	11	90	7
																	6	9	11	90	7
																	5	6	30	77	11
																	6	NA	NA	NA	3
297	2	5	3	1	Rospi Ćuprija	2	2	0	1	3	44.818	20.534	6	3	−125	−25	7	13	7	10	11
																	7	13	51	123	11
																	7	13	7	10	11
																	5	6	43	108	11
																	6	8	29	74	7
298	2	5	3	1	Rospi Ćuprija	2	2	0	1	3	44.818	20.534	6	3	−125	−25	7	13	7	11	11
																	7	13	7	10	11

																	7	13	7	10	11
																	7	13	7	NA	11
																	7	13	51	126	11
																	7	13	51	126	11
																	2	4	12	24	11
																	4	16	53	130	11
																	5	15	5	5	11
299	2	5	3	1	Rospi Ćuprija	2	2	0	1	3	44.818	20.534	6	3	−125	−25	7	13	7	10	11
																	7	13	51	123	11
																	7	13	51	123	11
																	2	4	12	24	3
																	5	6	43	107	11
300	2	5	3	1	Rospi Ćuprija	2	2	0	1	3	44.818	20.534	6	3	−125	−25	2	4	21	44	3
																	2	4	12	NA	11
																	2	4	21	44	3
																	2	4	12	NA	3
																	2	4	9	13	6
																	2	4	12	NA	11
																	7	13	7	10	11
																	7	13	51	123	11
301	NA	2	3	1	Rospi Ćuprija	2	2	0	1	3	44.818	20.534	6	3	−125	−25	2	4	21	44	3
																	2	4	21	44	3
																	2	4	21	NA	3
																	6	9	11	90	7
302	NA	7	3	1	Rospi Ćuprija	2	2	0	1	3	44.818	20.534	6	3	−125	−25	6	8	17	84	7
																	6	9	11	91	7
304	NA	7	3	1	Rospi Ćuprija	2	2	0	1	3	44.818	20.534	6	3	−125	−25	6	8	NA	NA	7

(continued)

Annex A.4 (continued)

Grave number	Supra-group	PAM group	Country	Region	Location	Grave type	Ritual type	Multiple burials	River proximity	Settlement proximity	Latitude	Longitude	Age	Sex	Chronology start	Chronology end	Object category 1	Object category 2	Object category 3	Object category 4	Material
																	6	8	29	NA	7
																	6	8	37	88	7
209	2	5	1	4	Saraevo	2	2	0	3	1	43.714	23.862	6	3	−150	−25	4	16	13	NA	11
																	4	16	26	66	11
																	6	NA	NA	NA	7
																	6	NA	NA	NA	7
																	7	13	51	124	11
																	7	13	7	8	11
																	7	13	51	123	11
																	7	13	51	123	11
																	5	6	30	77	11
																	7	7	45	NA	11
118	NA	7	2	6	Sighişoara Wietenberg	2	3	0	3	3	46.23	24.768	5	3	−100	100	6	18	27	NA	7
																	6	18	27	72	7
																	6	11	49	137	7
119	NA	7	2	6	Sighişoara Wietenberg	2	3	1	3	2	46.229	24.767	3	3	−100	100	6	NA	NA	NA	7
																	6	NA	NA	NA	7
120	1	3	2	6	Sighişoara Wietenberg	2	3	1	3	2	46.229	24.767	5	3	−100	100	NA	NA	NA	NA	NA
121	1	3	2	6	Sighişoara Wietenberg	2	3	1	3	2	46.229	24.767	5	3	−100	100	NA	NA	NA	NA	NA
122	NA	7	2	6	Sighişoara Wietenberg	2	3	0	3	2	46.229	24.767	4	2	−100	100	5	2	46	113	11
																	5	2	46	113	11
																	5	20	52	128	7

																5	20	52	128	7
																6	11	49	30	7
123	1	3	2	6	Sighişoara Wietenberg	2	3	0	3	2	46.229	24.767	6	3	−100	100	NA	NA	NA	NA	NA
124	1	1	2	6	Sighişoara Wietenberg	2	3	0	3	2	46.229	24.767	6	3	−100	100	5	6	30	77	11
125	1	1	2	6	Sighişoara Wietenberg	2	3	0	3	2	46.229	24.767	6	3	−100	100	2	4	NA	NA	14
267	2	4	2	5	Siseştii de Jos	2	2	0	3	4	44.777	22.839	6	3	−150	0	7	13	51	124	11
																7	13	51	124	11
																7	13	7	8	11
210	2	4	3	4	Slatina	2	2	0	3	3	44.411	22.450	6	3	−125	−50	7	13	7	8	11
																7	13	51	123	11
																2	4	21	44	14
																6	9	11	92	7
																6	18	27	72	7
211	NA	2	3	4	Slatina	2	2	0	3	3	44.411	22.450	6	3	−150	−25	2	4	12	NA	11
																2	4	21	NA	3
																2	4	9	13	6
																2	4	41	103	12
																2	4	19	35	3
																6	NA	NA	NA	7
																6	9	22	57	7
285	2	4	2	3	Slatina	2	2	0	3	2	44.433	24.370	6	3	−200	0	7	13	51	NA	11
																7	13	7	8	11
																5	6	30	77	11
																6	NA	NA	NA	7

(continued)

Annex A.4 (continued)

Grave number	Supra-group	PAM group	Country	Region	Location	Grave type	Ritual type	Multiple burials	River proximity	Settlement proximity	Latitude	Longitude	Age	Sex	Chronology start	Chronology end	Object category 1	Object category 2	Object category 3	Object category 4	Material
212	NA	2	1	4	Sofronievo	2	2	0	2	3	43.633	23.783	6	3	−150	−25	2	4	12	NA	3
																	2	4	12	NA	3
																	6	8	28	101	7
																	6	8	28	101	7
																	6	NA	NA	NA	7
213	NA	7	1	4	Sofronievo	2	2	0	3	3	43.631	23.776	6	3	−270	−20	6	NA	NA	NA	7
																	6	8	28	100	7
214	NA	7	1	4	Sofronievo	2	2	0	3	3	43.633	23.783	6	3	−270	−20	6	NA	NA	NA	7
217	2	5	1	4	Sofronievo	2	2	0	3	3	43.618	23.737	6	3	−150	−25	7	13	51	NA	11
																	7	13	54	133	11
																	7	13	7	8	11
																	7	13	51	125	11
																	2	4	21	44	11
																	4	16	26	66	11
																	6	8	28	105	7
218	2	5	1	4	Sofronievo	2	2	0	3	3	43.618	23.737	6	3	−150	−25	7	13	51	123	11
																	7	13	7	8	11
																	7	13	54	133	11
																	2	4	21	44	11
																	4	16	26	66	11
																	6	NA	NA	NA	7
219	2	5	1	4	Sofronievo	2	2	0	3	3	43.618	23.737	6	3	−150	−25	4	16	26	66	11
																	4	16	13	99	11
																	7	13	7	8	11
																	7	13	51	123	11

																	2	4	21	44	11
																	6	8	28	100	7
																	7	7	45	NA	11
215	2	5	1	4	Sofronievo (Balevi Livadi)	2	2	0	3	3	43.625	23.753	6	3	−150	−25	7	13	54	NA	11
																	7	13	7	NA	11
																	7	13	51	NA	11
																	4	16	26	NA	11
																	6	NA	NA	NA	7
																	7	7	45	NA	11
216	2	4	1	4	Sofronievo (Balevi Livadi)	2	2	0	3	3	43.625	23.753	6	3	−150	−25	7	13	51	NA	11
																	7	13	7	NA	11
																	4	16	26	NA	11
																	6	NA	NA	NA	7
366	2	4	1	4	Sokolare (Ilievski Geran)	2	2	0	3	3	43.433	23.867	6	3	−150	−25	7	13	54	133	11
																	7	13	7	8	11
289	NA	2	3	7	Sotin (Zmajevac)	2	2	0	1	4	45.286	19.138	6	3	−25	25	2	4	9	13	6
																	2	4	12	23	3
																	2	4	21	51	3
																	2	4	21	NA	11
																	6	8	18	116	3
																	6	8	47	119	6
																	4	16	53	130	11

(continued)

Annex A.4 (continued)

Grave number	Supra-group	PAM group	Country	Region	Location	Grave type	Ritual type	Multiple burials	River proximity	Settlement proximity	Latitude	Longitude	Age	Sex	Chronology start	Chronology end	Object category 1	Object category 2	Object category 3	Object category 4	Material
																	5	6	30	77	11
																	5	15	48	118	11
																	6	9	20	83	3
290	2	5	3	7	Sotin (Zmajevac)	2	2	0	1	4	45.286	19.138	6	3	−125	−25	6	8	47	119	6
																	6	8	47	119	6
																	2	4	12	24	11
																	7	7	45	110	3
																	7	13	51	NA	11
291	2	5	3	7	Sotin (Zmajevac)	2	2	0	1	4	45.286	19.138	6	3	−125	−25	2	4	9	NA	3
																	2	4	12	24	3
																	7	13	7	8	11
																	7	13	51	123	11
																	7	13	51	123	11
																	7	13	51	124	11
																	7	13	7	10	11
																	7	13	7	9	11
																	5	15	48	118	11
																	6	9	20	54	11
																	7	7	45	110	11
268	NA	2	2	5	Spahii	2	2	0	3	3	44.682	23.528	6	3	−200	0	2	4	55	129	11
																	6	8	28	100	7
269	1	1	2	5	Spahii	2	2	0	3	3	44.682	23.528	6	3	−200	0	2	4	8	115	8
																	6	NA	NA	NA	7
270	2	4	2	5	Spahii	2	2	0	3	3	44.682	23.528	6	3	−200	0	6	NA	NA	NA	7

																6	NA	NA	NA	7
																7	13	54	NA	11
																7	13	51	NA	11
271	NA	7	2	5	Spahii	2	2	0	3	3	44.682	23.528	6	3	−200	0	6	NA	NA	NA	7
																6	NA	NA	NA	3
272	NA	7	2	5	Spahii	2	2	0	3	3	44.682	23.528	6	3	−200	0	6	NA	NA	NA	7
																6	9	11	NA	7
273	2	6	2	5	Spahii	2	2	0	3	3	44.682	23.528	6	3	−200	0	6	NA	NA	NA	7
																6	9	NA	NA	7
																7	13	51	123	11
274	2	5	2	5	Spahii	2	2	0	3	3	44.682	23.528	6	3	−200	0	7	13	51	123	11
																7	13	51	NA	11
																7	13	7	8	11
																7	13	51	NA	11
																6	NA	NA	NA	7
275	NA	7	2	5	Spahii	2	2	0	3	3	44.682	23.528	6	3	−200	0	6	NA	NA	NA	7
7	1	3	2	5	Sprâncenata	1	3	0	3	2	44.083	24.633	1	3	0	50	NA	NA	NA	NA	NA
367	2	5	1	4	Stubel (Pliochata)	2	2	0	2	1	43.390	23.35	6	3	−150	−25	4	16	13	NA	11
																4	16	26	66	11
																7	13	51	NA	11
																7	13	54	133	11
																7	13	7	8	11
																7	7	45	110	11
108	1	1	2	6	Şura Mică	2	3	0	3	2	45.832	24.058	6	3	−100	25	2	4	9	NA	6
109	1	3	2	6	Şura Mică	2	3	1	3	2	45.832	24.058	6	3	25	75	NA	NA	NA	NA	NA
110	1	3	2	6	Şura Mică	2	3	1	3	2	45.832	24.058	6	3	25	75	NA	NA	NA	NA	NA

(continued)

Annex A.4 (continued)

Grave number	Supra-group	PAM group	Country	Region	Location	Grave type	Ritual type	Multiple burials	River proximity	Settlement proximity	Latitude	Longitude	Age	Sex	Chronology start	Chronology end	Object category 1	Object category 2	Object category 3	Object category 4	Material
220	2	4	1	4	Tarnak (Selishteto)	3	2	0	3	3	43.444	24.023	6	3	−150	−25	7	13	51	124	11
																	7	13	54	133	11
223	2	5	1	4	Tarnava (Devette Mogili)	3	2	0	1	3	43.487	23.869	6	3	−150	−25	2	4	21	44	3
																	2	4	12	20	11
																	4	16	13	NA	11
																	4	16	26	66	11
																	7	7	14	28	11
																	7	7	25	NA	3
																	7	7	45	NA	11
																	7	13	7	8	11
																	7	13	51	NA	11
																	7	13	54	NA	11
																	6	8	28	NA	7
224	2	6	1	4	Tarnava (Devette Mogili)	3	2	0	1	3	43.487	23.869	6	3	−150	−25	7	13	7	NA	11
225	2	5	1	4	Tarnava (Devette Mogili)	3	2	1	1	3	43.487	23.869	6	3	−150	−25	4	16	26	66	11
																	4	16	53	131	11
																	7	13	7	8	11
																	7	13	3	3	11
																	7	13	51	123	11
																	7	13	54	NA	11
																	2	4	21	NA	11

																6	NA	NA	NA	7
																6	9	22	57	7
																7	7	45	NA	11
226	2	5	1	4	Tarnava (Devette Mogili)	3	2	1	1	3	43.487	23.869	6	3	−150	−25	2	4	21	NA	3
																2	4	21	NA	3
																4	16	13	NA	11
																4	16	26	NA	11
																7	13	7	8	11
																7	13	51	123	11
																7	13	54	NA	11
																6	NA	NA	NA	7
																6	9	11	90	7
																7	7	45	NA	11
222	2	5	1	4	Tarnava (Mitkov Vrah)	3	2	0	3	1	43.506	23.873	6	3	−150	−25	7	13	51	125	11
																7	13	51	125	11
																7	13	54	133	11
																7	13	7	8	11
221	2	5	1	4	Tarnava (Mitkov Vrah)	3	2	0	3	1	43.506	23.873	6	3	−150	−25	7	13	54	NA	11
																7	13	51	126	11
																7	13	51	127	11
																2	4	21	NA	14
227	2	5	1	4	Tarnava (Pette Mogili)	3	2	0	1	3	43.486	23.866	6	3	−150	−25	2	4	31	79	3

(continued)

Annex A.4 (continued)

Grave number	Supra-group	PAM group	Country	Region	Location	Grave type	Ritual type	Multiple burials	River proximity	Settlement proximity	Latitude	Longitude	Age	Sex	Chronology start	Chronology end	Object category 1	Object category 2	Object category 3	Object category 4	Material
																	2	4	21	NA	11
																	2	4	9	17	3
																	6	NA	NA	NA	3
																	6	NA	NA	NA	7
																	6	NA	NA	NA	3
																	7	13	51	NA	11
																	7	13	7	NA	11
																	7	13	54	NA	11
																	4	16	26	NA	11
																	7	7	45	NA	11
166	2	6	2	6	Tărtăria	2	2	0	3	1	45.933	23.417	1	3	−150	−50	4	16	26	66	11
																	7	13	7	8	11
286	2	4	2	3	Teiuşi	2	2	0	3	4	44.337	24.433	6	3	−200	0	7	13	51	NA	11
																	7	13	7	NA	11
159	2	4	2	6	Teleac	2	2	0	3	4	46.088	23.628	6	3	−175	0	6	8	28	100	7
																	6	8	28	100	7
																	7	13	7	8	11
																	7	13	51	NA	11
228	2	4	1	4	Tsarevets (Kraina Mogila)	3	2	0	2	3	43.18	23.793	6	3	−150	−25	7	13	54	NA	11
																	7	13	51	NA	11
																	2	4	21	NA	3
																	6	8	28	100	7
																	6	9	11	NA	7

229	NA	7	1	4	Tsarevets (Liaskov Dol)	2	2	0	2	3	43.167	23.800	6	3	−270	−20	6	8	28	NA	7
																	6	8	28	NA	7
																	6	NA	NA	NA	7
276	2	6	2	5	Turnu Severin	2	2	0	1	4	44.631	22.656	6	3	−150	0	7	13	54	133	11
287	NA	2	2	5	Urdinița	2	2	0	2	4	44.388	23.426	6	3	−150	0	5	6	30	77	11
																	5	6	30	77	11
																	5	6	43	107	11
																	5	6	30	77	11
																	7	10	4	4	12
																	7	10	4	4	12
																	2	4	9	17	12
																	4	16	53	NA	11
230	2	5	3	4	Vajuga	2	2	0	1	1	44.556	22.635	6	3	−150	−25	7	13	7	NA	11
																	7	13	7	NA	11
																	2	4	21	NA	3
																	6	NA	NA	NA	7
																	7	7	45	NA	11
231	2	5	3	4	Vajuga	2	2	0	1	1	44.556	22.635	6	3	−100	0	6	8	17	136	7
																	6	8	17	136	3
																	6	9	11	90	7
																	6	9	22	58	7
																	7	13	51	127	11
																	7	13	7	9	11
																	7	13	54	132	11
368	2	5	1	4	Varbeshnitsa	3	2	0	3	3	43.189	23.681	6	3	−150	−25	4	16	26	NA	11

(continued)

Annex A.4 (continued)

Grave number	Supra-group	PAM group	Country	Region	Location	Grave type	Ritual type	Multiple burials	River proximity	Settlement proximity	Latitude	Longitude	Age	Sex	Chronology start	Chronology end	Object category 1	Object category 2	Object category 3	Object category 4	Material
																	4	16	53	130	11
																	4	16	26	NA	11
																	4	16	26	NA	11
																	7	7	14	28	11
																	7	7	45	NA	11
																	7	13	7	8	11
																	7	13	54	NA	11
278	1	1	2	5	Vârţ	2	2	0	1	3	44.946	23.130	6	3	−200	0	2	4	8	NA	12
																	6	NA	NA	NA	7
279	2	6	2	5	Vârţ	2	2	0	1	3	44.946	23.130	6	3	−200	0	6	NA	NA	NA	7
																	7	13	51	123	11
280	2	6	2	5	Vârţ	2	2	0	1	3	44.946	23.130	6	3	−200	0	7	13	7	8	11
277	2	4	2	5	Vârtopu	2	2	0	3	4	44.208	23.345	6	3	−200	0	7	13	51	123	11
																	7	13	51	124	11
281	2	4	2	5	Viaşu	2	2	0	3	4	44.353	22.817	6	3	−150	0	7	13	7	8	11
																	7	13	51	125	11
																	4	16	26	68	11
282	2	4	2	5	Viişoara Mică	2	2	0	3	4	44.231	24.113	6	3	−200	0	7	13	7	8	11
																	7	13	51	NA	11
303	2	4	3	1	Vinča	2	2	0	1	3	44.755	20.612	6	3	−125	−25	7	13	51	124	11
																	7	13	7	9	11
																	5	6	6	6	15
232	2	4	1	4	Vratsa	3	2	0	1	3	43.177	23.593	6	3	−275	150	7	13	54	132	11
																	7	13	7	8	11
																	2	4	21	NA	14

																	4	16	26	NA	11
																	6	NA	NA	NA	7
233	2	4	1	4	Vratsa	3	2	0	1	3	43.177	23.593	6	3	−150	−25	7	13	51	124	11
																	7	13	54	133	11
																	2	4	21	NA	3
																	4	16	26	NA	11
																	6	NA	NA	NA	7
234	2	4	1	4	Vratsa	2	2	0	3	3	43.194	23.589	6	3	−270	−20	7	13	51	NA	11
																	7	13	7	NA	11
																	6	NA	NA	NA	7
14	2	4	1	4	Vratsa (Bistrets quarter)	3	3	0	3	1	43.209	23.552	6	3	−270	−20	7	13	3	3	11
																	7	13	51	NA	11
																	7	13	51	NA	11
																	6	NA	NA	NA	7
288	2	5	3	1	Zemun Gardoš	2	2	0	1	4	44.848	20.407	6	3	−100	0	4	16	53	130	11
																	4	16	26	63	11
																	7	13	54	132	11
																	7	13	7	11	11
																	7	13	51	126	11
																	2	19	40	98	11
																	6	8	47	119	3
																	6	18	39	94	7
																	7	7	45	110	11
235	2	5	1	4	Zhivovtsi	3	2	0	3	1	43.383	23.15	6	3	−270	−20	7	13	51	NA	11
																	7	13	54	NA	11

(continued)

Annex A.4 (continued)

Grave number	Supra-group	PAM group	Country	Region	Location	Grave type	Ritual type	Multiple burials	River proximity	Settlement proximity	Latitude	Longitude	Age	Sex	Chronology start	Chronology end	Object category 1	Object category 2	Object category 3	Object category 4	Material
																	7	7	45	NA	11
160	NA	2	2	3	Zimnicea	2	2	0	3	3	43.667	25.367	6	3	−150	−100	2	4	21	44	3
																	2	4	NA	NA	11
																	6	8	37	87	11
161	NA	7	2	3	Zimnicea	2	2	0	3	3	43.667	25.367	6	3	−150	−100	6	8	28	101	7
162	NA	2	2	3	Zimnicea	2	2	0	3	3	43.667	25.367	6	3	−150	−100	2	4	8	140	8
																	2	4	NA	NA	13
																	6	8	28	100	7
																	6	8	28	101	7
																	6	11	49	30	7
163	NA	2	2	3	Zimnicea	2	2	0	3	3	43.667	25.367	6	3	−150	−100	2	4	21	NA	11
																	6	8	17	84	7
																	6	18	2	2	7
164	NA	2	2	3	Zimnicea	2	2	0	3	3	43.667	25.367	3	3	−150	−100	6	8	17	31	7
																	6	8	28	100	7
																	2	4	21	47	3
																	6	11	49	30	7
284	NA	2	2	3	Zimnicea	2	2	0	3	3	43.667	25.367	2	3	−25	75	2	4	21	41	3
																	2	19	32	80	12
																	7	7	25	61	3

Index

A
Anthropological analysis, 100
ArcGIS, spatial analysis, 72, 73
ASTER Global Digital Elevation Model (Aster GDEM2), 72

B
Battle knife types, 43
Brad settlement, 150
Burial number, 28
Burials, site locations, 15–19

C
Carpathian Mountains, 124
Carpathian Mountains arch, 100
Central and Northern Serbia, 1
Chronological information, 179
Chronological limits, 21–22
Cluster analysis, 123
Clustering algorithms
  description, 67
  dissimilarity matrix, 67
  Divisive Analysing Clustering, 68
  Dunn coefficient, 70
  Fuzzy clustering, 69
  groupings, 74
  hierarchical clustering, 68
  hierarchical procedures, 67
  limiting factor, 67
  multidimensional scaling, 70
  nonmetric multidimensional scaling, 70
  PAM, 68
Comparative contextual modelling, 1
Complex data, 2
Contextual statistical analysis, 1
Continuous data, 59
Count of object category, 97, 169
Cremations, 175, 176, 180, 184–186
CutreeDynamic, 68

D
Dacians, 179, 180, 189, 191–193
Danube gorges, 105
Danube River, 124
Data issues, 24–25
Data limits
  burials in void, 23–24
  chronological limits, 21–22
  spatial limits, 20–21
  void of burials, 23
Data organization, 28–31
  data issues, 24–25
  data structure, 25–27
  queries and reports, 32
  variable, burials table
    burial number, 28, 30
    chronology variable, 30
    country, region, and location, 28
    cremation number variable, 30
    grave dimension, 30
    inhumation/cremation/cenotaph/unknown grave number, 31
    intact variable, 29, 31
    inventory number, 31
    latitude, longitude, and height, 29
    location of object, 31
    multiple burials, 28

C. N. Popa, *Modelling Identities*, Quantitative Archaeology and Archaeological Modelling, https://doi.org/10.1007/978-3-319-63267-4

Data organization (*cont.*)
object description, object dimensions, and observations, 31
object image variable, 31
observation, 29, 30
ritual type, 28, 29, 31
river proximity, 29
settlement proximity, 29
tumulus diameter and height, 28
Data structure, 25–27
Death and burial, 16–18
practical arguments, 19
site locations, 15–19
theoretical concepts
community off balance, 16
funerary feasts, 18
funerary practices, 16
funerary ritual, 16, 17
grave-goods, 18
simplistic interpretations, 18
social relationships and afterlife beliefs, 17
well-controlled social context, 16
Diana algorithm, 99
Diana clustering, 101
Diana group 7, 117
Divisive Analysing Clustering, 68
Dunn coefficient, 70, 71
Dunn index, 87
Dynamic Tree Cut package, 68

E

Eastern and Western supra-group counts, 153
Employed burial data, 6, 7, 15–20, 24–32, 38
Ethnicity
description, 52
Getae and Dacian correspondence, 191, 192
group identity, 52
identification of, 52
in Iron Age, 189–191
and material culture, 53
Western supra-group, 192

F

Fruit-bowl types, 42
Funerary finds
Transylvania, 167
Funerary ritual elements, 142
Fuzzy clustering, 69

G

Geographical distribution of preliminary study group 1, 177
Geographical distribution of preliminary study subgroup 2.1, 177
Geographical distribution of preliminary study subgroup 2.2, 178
Geographical spread of group 2, 99
Geographical spread of group 3, 102
Geographical spread of group 4, 107
Geographical spread of group 5, 112
Geographical spread of group 6, 116
Geographical spread of group 7, 118
Getae, 189, 191–193
Grave count crosstabulation, 164
Grave M6, 154
Grave-goods, 8, 34, 175, 180, 186
Graves of Moldova, 161, 187
Greek or Roman imports, 160
Group 1 PAM, 92
Group 2 PAM and Diana counts, 96
Group 3 PAM counts, 101
Group 4 PAM and Diana counts, 103
Group identity, 55–58, 73
large-scale, 192
subgroups and variants, 176

H

Hierarchical Cluster Analysis or Agglomerative Nesting (Agnes), 67
Hierarchical Clustering, 67, 68, 76, 80
Horse gear elements, 108
Hungarian method, 62
Hybrid dynamic tree cut method, 118

I

Identity theory
description, 52
and ethnicity, 52
group identity, 55, 56
to habitus, 54
implementation, 55, 56
individual/group, 52
inter-human interaction and human-object relationships, 54
use of, 53
vertical hierarchy, 55
Imagined community, 53
Initial empirical observations, 151
Instrumentalist approach, 53

Interpretation, 9
Iron Age Europe, 132

J
Jaccard's coefficients, 60
Jug types, 41

L
Late Iron age, 149
  identity and political development, 179, 180, 182
Late Iron Age communities, 146
Late Iron Age settlement, 155, 156
Late Iron Age society, 146

M
Macro dimension, 151–159
Mortuary finds
  Central Serbia and Vojvodina, 163
  Muntenia, 161, 162
  Oltenia, 162
Mortuary finds tumulus, 162
Multidimensional scaling, 70, 72, 73

N
Non-clustered graves, 119–120
North-West Thrace, 165
North-Western Bulgaria, 1

O
Object categorization, 35–43
  construction, 34–35
  list of, 32–44
  theoretical principles, 33–34
  variables
    functional categories, 36–37
    information, 35–36
    typological categories, 37–43
Overdetermination, 56

P
Padea-Panagjurski Kolonii group, 180
PAM group counts, 129
Partitioning Around Medoids (PAM), 68, 70, 76–82, 87
Personhood theory, 132
Popeşti settlement, 151
Practical tools
  data characteristics, 51
  spatial analysis, ArcGIS, use of, 72, 73
  statistical analysis, 57, 58
  types, tools, 51

R
Regional distribution, 119, 144
Regional identity, 133, 136, 161
Research justification, 6
Results description
  adornments or clothing accessories, 103
  anthropological analysis, 100
  bowls and porringers, 110
  clothing accessories, 96
  clustering algorithm, 88
  contemporary settlement, 116
  Dunn index, 87
  flat cremations, 95
  funerary assemblages, 103
  geographical distribution, 112, 115
  geographical spread, 93
  grave assemblage, 116
  grave-goods, 105
  graves of group 2, 99
  group identities, 89
  hunting weapons, 113
  hybrid dynamic cut, 87
  inhumations, 91
  PAM, 87
  sex, 107
  sober and militaristic appearance, 105
  tumulus cenotaphs, 120
  tumulus graves, 91
  validation procedures, 119
  vessel implements, 92
  vessel shapes, 98
  weapons, 102
River proximity, 29

S
Settlement proximity, 29
Similarity algorithm
  algorithm function, 66
  basic functioning principle, 61
  continuous data, 59
  empirical observations, 59
  grave comparisons, 61
  Hungarian method, 62
  into dissimilarity index, 64
  mathematical calculation, 63

Similarity algorithm (*cont.*)
operations and phases, 60
parameter (α), 66
properties, 65
simple arithmetical mean, 65
variables, 60
weighing system, 61, 62
Simple matching, 60
Single Linkage Hierarchical Algorithm, 67
Social status, 149
Spatial limits, 20–21
Spear types, 44
State of research
archaeological investigation, 2, 3
burial practices, 3
funerary behaviour, 4
grave-goods, 4, 5
Iron Age graves, 4
late Iron Age archaeological discoveries, 4
late Iron Age funerary behaviour, 5
military campaigns, 2
non-funerary contexts, 4
radical political shifts, 3
Roman administration, 3
settlements and coin hoards, 4
settlements and military fortification, 3
Statistical algorithm, 1
Statistical analysis, 59, 66
algorithm, 57
clustering algorithms
(*see* Clustering algorithms)
data recording, 57
exploratory methods, 57
for modelling techniques, 57
pattern, 57
similarity algorithm (*see* Similarity algorithm)
SPSS, use of, 71, 72
subjectivity, 57
use of R, 58, 59
Statistical programme (SPSS), 57, 59, 71, 72, 75, 80
Statistical results, 8
age and gender, 149
archaeological traces, 159
assignment, 157
average separation matrix, 134
behaviour, 132
burial practice, 140
characteristics, 128
clothing accessories, 129
clustering algorithm, 155, 156
clustering errors, 142
clusters, 123, 138
cremation tumulus graves, 160
cremations, 124, 160
excarnation practices, 132
flat inhumation, 155
funerary assemblages, 155
funerary practice, 129, 159, 165
funerary ritual, 126, 131
funerary ritual elements, 135
funerary ritual features, 134
gender distinctions, 146
geographical expansion, 142
geographical spread, 137
grave-good items, 146
grave-goods, 125, 138
group identities, 148
human sacrifice, 131
individuals, 132
interpretation, 123
material culture, 134
mortuary finds, 161
people's identity, 130
quasi complete separation, 130
regional identities, 159
ritual features, 132
social death, 131
social status, 128, 149
social understanding, 124
spatial distribution, 127, 133
supra-groups, 152
tower-dwellings, 150
treatment, 131, 146
Supra-groups, 9
Eastern, 176, 179, 180, 182, 192
Western, 176, 180–184, 186, 188, 191
Symbiotic relationship, 52

T
Tower-dwellings, 150
Tumulus cremation graves, 160

V
Variables and values labels, 8, 27–31, 34, 35, 37–43, 60–64, 72–76, 80, 81, 83
Void of burials, 23

W
Weapon groups, 141
Weapons-dominated clusters, 139
Weight calibration functions
PAM, use, 76
ritual weights, 76
steps, 76, 77, 79–83
Western supra-group clusters, 166

The manufacturer's authorised representative in the EU is Springer Nature Customer Service Centre GmbH, Europaplatz 3, 69115 Heidelberg, Germany. If you have any concerns regarding our products, please contact ProductSafety@springernature.com

Printed and bound by CPI Group (UK) Ltd, Croydon, CR0 4YY
05/10/2026
02228139-0007